PATERNOSTER BIBLICAL MONOC

Eve: Accused or Acquitted?

An Analysis of Feminist Readings of the Creation Narrative Texts
in Genesis 1–3

PATERNOSTER BIBLICAL MONOGRAPHS

Full listings of all titles in both Paternoster Biblical and
Theological Monographs appear at the close of this book

Eve: Accused or Acquitted?

An Analysis of Feminist Readings of the Creation Narrative Texts in Genesis 1–3

Joseph Abraham

Foreword
by
Gordon McConville

Paternoster:
thinking faith

First Published 2002 by Paternoster

Paternoster is an imprint of Authentic Media,
9 Holdom Avenue, Bletchley, Milton Keynes, MK1 1QR, U.K.
and
P.O.Box 1047, Waynesboro, GA 30830-2047, U.S.A.

08 07 06 05 04 03 02   7 6 5 4 3 2 1

British Library Cataloguing in Publication Data
A catalogue record for this book is available from the British Library

ISBN-10 0–85364–971–5
ISBN-13 978–0–85364–971–7

Typeset in Luther W. New Theological College by Prem Kumar.T, India
and printed and bound in Great Britain by
Nottingham AlphaGraphics

Series Preface

One of the major objectives of Paternoster is to serve biblical scholarship by providing a channel for the publication of theses and other monographs of high quality at affordable prices. Paternoster stands within the broad evangelical tradition of Christianity. Our authors would describe themselves as Christians who recognise the authority of the Bible, maintain the centrality of the gospel message and assent to the classical credal statements of Christian belief. There is diversity within this constituency; advances in scholarship are possible only if there is freedom for frank debate on controversial issues and for the publication of new and sometimes provocative proposals. What is offered in this series is the best of writing by committed Christians who are concerned to develop well-founded biblical scholarship in a spirit of loyalty to the historic faith.

Series Editors

Dedicated to the memory of my beloved mother,
Aleyamma Abraham

Contents

Foreword   XIII
Preface   XV
Abbreviations   XVII
Introduction   XXI

Part One: Methods in Reading the Bible

Chapter 1
The Question of Method in Reading the Bible   3
1.0   Preliminary Remarks   3
1.1   The Nature of the Text and Textuality in Relation to Reading 3
1.2   Theories of Reading the Text   4
1.2.1 *Philosophical theories and the hermeneutics of understanding* 4
1.2.2 *Literary theories and the aesthetic reading of the text*   7
1.2.3 *Reader–oriented theories and the production of 'meaning'* 10
1.2.4 *Linguistic theories of meaning and 'indeterminate meaning'* 13
1.3   Observation, Discussion and Evaluation   16
1.4   The Reader in Relation to the Text   17
1.4.1 *Does the reader determine the meaning of the text?*   17
1.5   Is the Biblical Text in the Same Category as Literature?   18
1.6   Can there be a Correct Model?   20
1.7   A Methodological Proposal   24
       Conclusion   26

Chapter 2
Feminist Readings of the Old Testament: A Brief Survey
of History and Hermeneutical Approaches   29
2.1   Brief Survey of History   29
2.1.1 *Judith Sargent Murray (1751–1820)*   29
2.1.2 *Sarah (1792–1873) and Angelina Grimké (1805–1879)*   30
2.1.3 *Frances Willard (1839–1898)*   31
2.1.4 *Elizabeth Cady Stanton (1815–1902)*   32
2.1.5 *Margaret Brackenbury Crook*   33
2.1.6 *Simone de Beauvoir and Kate Millet*   34
2.2   Hermeneutical Approaches   35
2.2.1 *Hermeneutics of recuperation*   36
2.2.2 *Hermeneutics of suspicion*   38
2.2.3 *Hermeneutics of resistance*   39
2.2.4 *Other feminist writers*   40
2.2.5 *Womanist writers*   41
       Conclusion   42

Part Two: Feminist Readings of Genesis 1–3

Chapter 3
Feminist Literary–Readings of the Creation Narratives
(Gen. 1–3)   **45**
        Introduction   45
3.0   Preliminary Remarks   46
3.1   Rhetorical Criticism and the Old Testament   46
3.1.1   *Definition of rhetorical criticism*   46
3.1.2   *Method of rhetorical criticism*   47
3.1.3   *Strength and weakness of this method*   50
3.2   Trible's Reading   51
3.2.1   *Life and work*   51
3.2.2   *Hermeneutical presupposition*   52
3.2.3   *Methodology*   53
3.3   Trible's Reading of the Creation Narrative (Gen. 2–3)   56
3.4   Eros Created   57
3.4.1   האדם*: an earth creature*   58
3.4.2   *Woman a corresponding companion*   59
3.4.3   *Woman as culmination of creation*   62
3.4.4   *Naming of the woman*   63
3.4.5   *Woman not a derivative*   63
3.5   Eros contaminated   64
3.5.1   *Woman a spokesperson*   64
3.5.2   *Man as passive*   64
3.6   Eros Condemned (Gen. 3:8–24)   65
3.6.1   *The judgement for the disobedience*   65
3.6.2   *Man's ruling—the consequence of disobedience*   65
3.6.3   *The disintegration of eros*   66
3.7   Genesis 1:27 and Feminine Imagery in the Old Testament   67
3.8   Genesis 1–3 and Feminist Old Testament Theology   68
3.9   Observation, Discussion and Evaluation   69
3.9.1   *Strength of Trible's reading*   69
3.9.2   *Problems of Trible's reading*   70
        Conclusion   109
        Other Writers   112
3.10   Joy Elasky Fleming: Rhetorical–Theological Reading   112
3.11   Alice Laffey: Literary Reading   114
3.12   Ellen Van Wolde: Semantic Reading   116
3.13   Mary Phil Korsak: Philological Reading   119
3.14   Ilana Pardes: Heteroglossia   121
3.15   Ilona N. Rashkow: Psycho–analytic Reading   126
3.16   Athalya Brenner: Socio–Literary Reading   129
3.17   D. N. Fewell and D. M. Gunn: Narrative Reading   130

3.18   Mieke Bal: Semiotic Psycho–analytic Reading   133
3.19   Pamela J. Milne: Structuralist Reading   137

Chapter 4
Feminist Social–Scientific Readings of the Creation
Narrative (Genesis 2–3)   **139**
4.0   Preliminary Remarks   139
4.1   Sociology and Old Testament Interpretation   139
4.1.1   *The Definition of Method*   140
4.1.2   *The Contributions and Limitations of the Social–*
        Scientific Approach   142
4.2   Carol Meyers' Reading of the Creation Narratives   144
4.2.1   *Life and Work*   144
4.2.2   *Methodological Presuppositions*   145
4.3   The Creation Narrative in Feminist Perspective   150
4.3.1   *Preliminary Considerations*   150
4.3.2   *The Social Setting of the Eden Narrative*   150
4.4   Genesis in a Highland Setting   153
4.4.1   *Preliminary remarks*   153
4.4.2   *Genesis 3 as a setting of Israel's formative period* 154
4.4.3   *Eating and sustenance as the main theme*   155
4.4.4   *Genesis 3 as part of a wisdom tale*   155
4.5   Genesis Paradigms for Female Roles   155
4.5.1   *Meyers' exegesis of Genesis 3:16*   155
4.5.2   *Genesis 3:16—A close reading*   156
4.6   The Eden Oracle in Context   160
4.7   The Gender Roles of Women in the Rest of the Old
        Testament   161
4.8   Observation, Discussion and Evaluation   162
4.8.1   *The Strength of Meyers' Reading*   162
4.8.2   *The Problems of Meyers' Reading*   163
        Conclusion   183
        Other writers
4.9   Tikva Frymer–Kensky   186

Chapter 5
Feminist Historical–Critical Readings of the
Creation Narratives (Genesis 1–3)   **189**
5.0   Preliminary Remarks   189
5.1.   Phyllis Bird's Reading   190
5.1.1   *Life and Work*   190
5.1.2   *Bird's Methodology*   190
5.1.3   *Hermeneutical Assumptions*   191
5.2   Bird's Readings of Genesis 1:26–28   192

5.2.1   *Image of God and Dominion*   194
5.2.2   *Sexual Distinction and Blessing*   196
5.2.3   *Fertility and Dominion*   197
5.2.4   *The Implications of Bird's Reading*   198
5.2.5   *P and Theology of Sexuality*   198
5.3   Bird's Reading of Genesis 2–3   199
5.3.1   *The אדם and the Woman in the Narrative*   199
5.3.2   *The Prohibition and Sin*   200
5.3.3   *The Consequence of Sin*   202
5.3.4   *The Woman's Subordination as Descriptive*   203
5.4   Development of Bird's Theology of Sexuality   204
5.5   Observation, Discussion and Evaluation   207
5.5.1   *The Strength of Bird's Reading*   207
5.5.2   *The Problem of Bird's Reading*   208
         Conclusion   224
         Other Writers
5.6   Helen Schüngel–Straumann   226
5.7   Luise Schottroff   229
5.8   Mary Hayter   230
         Conclusion   230

         Conclusion   **233**
6.1   Is the Old Testament Irredeemably Patriarchal?   233
6.2   The Communicative Intention of the Text   235
6.3   Further Implications   239
6.4   Are Feminist Readings Open to Critique?   243

         Bibliography   **247**

         Subject Index   **267**

         Author Index   **269**

FOREWORD

Joseph Abraham's careful scholarship in the present volume testifies to the huge importance of feminist interpretation in modern biblical studies and theology. It is clear that feminist interpretation offers profound challenges to traditional theological attitudes. However, the nature of that challenge must be understood, and needs an informed response that may show welcome as well as caution..

While some feminist theologians have bidden Christianity farewell because of where their critique has led them, it is clear that the feminist challenge need not be an absolute showdown with Christian theology. Indeed in biblical studies it most often is not. Feminist interpretation is not cast in a single mould, as Abraham's thesis shows well, with its sensitivity to the nuances in the different authors' work that he reviews (Christian and Jewish). A number of leading feminist authors, though they may seem radical, are aiming in their work to do Christian biblical theology.

Furthermore, it is in the nature of theology both to challenge and be challenged, as it seeks to interpret a changing world. A dialogue with feminist scholarship from the basic perspective of traditional Christian theology is possible, therefore, and should be fruitful for both traditionalists and those who wish to explore 'emancipatory' hermeneutical approaches like feminism. Abraham is well aware that feminist criticism has often been justified in its exposure of male-dominated interpretation. His evaluation is consequently sympathetic, and his concern for orthodox Chistian theology has been educated by the encounter.

Abraham's book is a major attempt to re-examine a foundational biblical text in dialogue with serious feminist reinterpretations. The choice of Genesis 1-3 as the primary biblical text hardly needs justifying, since it has been central in feminist re-readings, and because of its place in Christian theology. The belief that past misuse of it has contributed to a negative view of women in the Church is a powerful impetus to the feminist challenge, and to theological rethinking generally, not least because vital theological interests are at stake.

However, the focus on Genesis 1-3, and on three prominent feminist scholars, is also a means by which to unpack wider issues. In India, the author's home country, where he still lives and works, the issues aired here look different from the way in which they are perceived in the west. By drawing that situation into the discussion, he shows that the western feminist scholarship that he primarily investigates is part of larger questions of justice in the world. A key premise of his work is that there is a connection not only between hermeneutics and theology, but also between hermeneutics and justice. Interpretation has a vital moral component. It involves humility, repentance, and the willingness to be weak.

I have been privileged to be associated with Joseph Abraham's work since he began it as a doctoral project in Oxford in 1992. And I am delighted that it is being offered to a wider readership in the Paternoster Dissertations series.

Gordon McConville
Cheltenham,
September 2001

PREFACE

The genesis of this work is to be found in a doctoral thesis submitted to Coventry University in 1996, in collaboration with Wycliffe Hall, Oxford, England.

So many people have helped me over the course of the production of this work. I am deeply indebted to Dr. J. Gordon McConville, my *Doktorvater,* for his meticulous guidance, and invaluable suggestions at every stage in the writing of the thesis. He read through many drafts of the work and has made many incisive and erudite comments that stimulated my thinking and helped me formulate my ideas clearly.

I have much pleasure in acknowledging my gratitude to Dr. Grace Emmerson, my external supervisor, whose thoughtful reading of every chapter and many insightful comments and questions have been immensely helpful in keeping me on the right track.

George Taylor has been kind enough to read through a draft of this work and made language corrections and many literary and stylistic improvements.

In the course of my research, I had the opportunity of meeting and discussing personally with the three major feminist biblical scholars whose work I analyse in this work: Prof. Phyllis Trible of Union Theological Seminary, New York, Prof. Carol Meyers of Duke University, Durham, North Carolina, and Prof. Phyllis A. Bird of Garret–Evangelical Theological Seminary, Evanston, Chicago. They gave great assistance during my research visit to the United States of America.

None of my work on the thesis would have been possible without adequate finance to study in Oxford. For the financial support, I am greatly indebted to the Langham Research Scholarship fund in liaison with Tear Fund, Interserve and the Daily Prayer Union Trust which supported me and my family. I do acknowledge the sincere efforts of the Revd. Dr. Idicheria Ninan who had been instrumental in making all the preparations for my study in England. My life and worship in the Wycliff Community was an enriching experience. I record my sense of gratitude to every member of the college for their friendship and fellowship. Our association with the Oxford Community Church has been a refreshing spiritual experience. I would like to thank the Rev. Steve Thomas, the Senior Pastor, my Pastor Mike Beaumont and rest of the pastoral team and all the members of the Church for their contributions.

I owe a great debt of gratitude to many people in New Theological College, Dehra Dun, India where I have been teaching since 1996. The Revd. George Chavanikamannil, the founder, and my long-term colleague, the Revd. Dr. P. B. Thomas and all others in the college, both the staff and students have been a great source of encouragement and support to me.

It would be impossible to express adequately my personal debt to my wife Jessy, and our three children, Oswin, Osmint and Anugraha for their love, support and prayers during the writing of this work, which has detached me from them for too many hours over many years. The German saying 'ein Mensch ist kein Mensch' (one human is no human) has become more meaningful to me during this period. My heart–felt appreciation goes to them for their indefatigable support.

I am grateful to my student, Prem Kumar, who has helped in typesetting and re–formatting. Finally to Paternoster Press for accepting the manuscript into the *Paternoster Biblical and Theological Monographs*, with so many valuable suggestions.

ABBREVIATIONS

AB	The Anchor Bible
ABD	*The Anchor Bible Dictionary*
AM	*The Atlantic Monthly*
ANET	*Ancient Near Eastern Texts* (J. B. Pritchard ed.).
ATJ	*The Asbury Theological Journal*
BA	*Biblical Archaeology*
BALS	Bible and Literature Series
BARev	*Biblical Archaeology Review*
BBR	*Bulletin of Biblical Research*
BDB	F. Brown, S.R. Driver, and C.A. Briggs, *Hebrew and English Lexicon of the Old Testament*
BHS	*Biblia Hebraica Stuttgartensia*
Bib	*Biblica*
BibInt	*Biblical Interpretation*
BibRev	*Bible Review*
BibToday	*The Bible Today*
BIS	Biblical Interpretation Series
BJRL	*Bulletin of the John Rylands University Library of Manchester*
BJS	Brown Judaic Studies
BLS	Bible and Literature Series
BN	*Biblische Notizen*
BST	The Bible Speaks Today
CBQ	*Catholic Biblical Quarterly*
CD	*Church Dogmatics*
CMBC	*Canadian Mennonite Bible College*
CUP	Cambridge University Press
DM	*Duke Magazine*
EcR	*Ecumenical Review*
EgT	*Église et Théologie*
Ex Audi	*Ex Auditu*
ExpTim	*Expository Times*
ET	English Translation
FCB	[A] Feminist Companion to the Bible
GCT	Gender, Culture, Theory
GTS	Gettysburg Theological Studies
HAR	*Hebrew Annual Review*
HTR	*Harvard Theological Review*
HUP	Harvard University Press
ICC	International Critical Commentary
IDBS	*Interpreter's Dictionary of the Bible Supplement Volume*
Int	*Interpretation*

ITC	International Theological Commentary
IVP	Inter–Varsity Press
JAAR	*Journal of American Academy of Religion*
JBC	*Jerome Biblical Commentary*
JBL	*Journal of Biblical Literature*
JBTh	*Jahrbuch für Biblische Theologie*
Jeev	*Jeevdhara*
JFSR	*Journal of Feminist Studies in Religion*
JLT	*Journal of Literature and Theology*
JPT	*Journal of Pentecostal Theology*
JSOT	*Journal for the Study of the Old Testament*
JSOTS	*Journal for the Study of the Old Testament Supplement Series*
JSNT	*Journal for the Study of the New Testament*
JTS	*Journal of Theological Studies*
KB	L. Koehler and W. Baumgartner, *Lexicon in Veteris Testamenti Libros*
KJV	King James Version
NIV	New International Version
LXX	Septuagint
NCBC	The New Century Bible Commentary
NEB	New English Bible
NIB	*The New Interpreter's Bible* (12 vols.)
NICOT	The New International Commentary on the Old Testament
NJBC	*The New Jerome Biblical Commentary*
NRSV	New Revised Standard Version
OBS	The Oxford Bible Series
OBT	Overtures to Biblical Theology
OUP	Oxford University Press
OT	Old Testament
OTG	Old Testament Guides
OTL	Old Testament Library
PSB	*The Princeton Seminary Bulletin*
REB	Revised English Bible
RelS	*Religious Studies*
RelSRev	*Religious Studies Review*
RSV	Revised Standard Version
SBL	Society of Biblical Literature
SBLSP	SBL Seminar Paper
SBTS	Sources for Biblical and Theological Study, Winona Lake
SCM	Students Christian Movement
SJT	*Scottish Journal of Theology*
SPCK	The Society for the Promotion of Christian Knowledge
SSN	Studia Semitica Neerlandica

SWBA	The Social World of Biblical Antiquity Series
TynB	*Tyndale Bulletin*
Them	*Themelios*
TOTC	Tyndale Old Testament Commentary
TS	*Theological Studies*
TToday	*Theology Today*
Theology	*Theology*, London
USQR	*Union Seminary Quarterly Review*
VT	*Vetus Testamentum*
VTS	Vetus Testamentum Supplement
WBC	Word Biblical Commentary
W/JKP	Westminster/John Knox Press
WTJ	*Westminster Theological Journal*
ZAW	*Zeitschrift für die alttestamentliche Wissenschaft*

INTRODUCTION

1. Feminist Readings of the Old Testament

The proliferation of methods in biblical interpretation has become a notable trend in contemporary biblical scholarship. These trends have produced a climate that has been favourable to modern feminist readings of the Old Testament. It is widely held that those who are in power have often exploited the weak, and manipulated the biblical text in order to safeguard their vested interests. In her 1987 presidential address to the Society of Biblical Literature, Elisabeth Schüssler Fiorenza, a feminist biblical scholar, affirmed: 'If scriptural texts have served not only noble causes but also to legitimate war, to nurture anti–Judaism and misogynism, to justify the exploitation of slavery, to promote colonial dehumanization, then biblical scholarship must take the responsibility not only to interpret biblical texts in their historical contexts but also to evaluate the construction of their historical worlds and symbolic universes in terms of a religious scale of values.'[1] The Women's Liberation Movement began in the United States first in the context of the fight against slavery and then in the later struggles for racial equality. Women began to question their role and function in the church and society, which had been assigned to them by men. The result has been a re–examination of many biblical passages and a dynamic process of interpreting the scriptures from a feminist perspective, which has questioned and challenged many of the traditional male interpretations of the text.

Until the 1970s feminist criticism was not reckoned to be a distinct academic discipline among biblical scholars. The proliferation of multi–faceted feminist readings given by prominent feminist biblical scholars during the last decades has attracted the attention of the academy. The growing influence of feminist scholarship may be quickly illustrated. For instance, in 1970 the female membership in the Society of Biblical Literature was only three percent of the total. It has risen to more than sixteen percent in the 1990s. Feminist influence does not end there. Elisabeth Schüssler Fiorenza, a well-known feminist biblical scholar at Harvard Divinity School, was selected as the first woman president of SBL in 1987, followed by Phyllis Trible, the second woman president in 1995.

In 1992, *The Women's Bible Commentary* was published by forty one American scholars, among them thirty eight of whom are on the faculties of prominent Universities and Colleges and hold doctoral degrees in biblical and related fields. The other three were already Ph.D. candidates in Harvard, Yale, and Princeton Universities. Another 10 volume work, *The Feminist Companion to the Bible* (Sheffield Academic Press, 1993–97)

---

[1] E. Schüssler Fiorenza, 'The Ethics of Biblical Interpretation: De–Centering Biblical Scholarship', *JBL* 107 (1988), p. 15.

provides a work of an international flavour (mainly American & European) in feminist hermeneutics which aims to be used as a 'companion' (complementary and supplementary) to traditional studies. A second series to the feminist companion to the Bible are already on print (Sheffield Academic Press, 1998–). The present influx of feminist materials itself shows how this topic has become important in biblical research. Therefore, it is important to evaluate the feminist contributions to Old Testament Study. J. W. Rogerson rightly points out that 'the future existence of Old Testament study depends upon how it reacts to the questions that are being put to it by liberation hermeneutics and the enterprise culture'.[2] One cannot deny that feminist hermeneutics shares the major characteristics of liberation hermeneutics. David J. A. Clines also points out that feminist criticism holds 'great promise (or challenge) for biblical interpretation, as well as also for the other theological disciplines'.[3]

2. The Basis of Modern Feminist Readings

The feminist readings challenge traditional readings, finding male bias in much previous scholarship. Feminist readers ask how far the patriarchal texts (Bible) can be authoritative and normative in articulating the theology and practices of the church. So feminists are involved in offering alternative readings: either a non–sexist, egalitarian reading with an aim to de–patriarchalize the text, or a 'resistance' reading, that is, one which reads 'against the grain' of the text. So feminist readings challenge the authority, canonicity, veracity, and the normativity of the biblical texts because of their perceived patriarchal–androcentric orientation. They are, therefore, radical. But we need to establish their hermeneutical foundations carefully. Feminist readings are part of the modern and post–modern hermeneutical movement. Clines aptly summarises these hermeneutical developments: '"ideology" is going to be the catchword of the 1990s in biblical criticism, just as "the reader" was of the 1980s, "the text" was of the 1970s, and "the author" was of previous decades of critical scholarship.'[4] Like other post–modern approaches, feminist readings are very diverse, as we shall see and therefore, we need to consider each writer, and even each writing, individually. A fundamental question is how far feminist Old Testament scholarship remains within the main stream of Old Testament scholarship.

---

[2] J. W. Rogerson, 'What Does it Mean to be Human? The Central Question of Old Testament Theology?', in D. J. A. Clines *et al.*, (eds.), *The Bible in Three Dimensions: Essays in Celebration of Forty Years of Biblical Studies in the University of Sheffield*, (JSOTS 87; Sheffield: JSOT Press, 1990), p. 298.

[3] See D. J. A. Clines, 'Possibilities and Priorities of Biblical Interpretation in an International Perspective', *BibInt* 1 (1993), p. 83.

[4] Ibid., p. 86.

3. Method

I do not approach the feminist readings with any strict methodological pre-suppositions. Nonetheless, I think each methodology has a certain value in its own right in recovering and reconstructing the meaning of any particular text. I shall argue that a synthesis of methods will produce maximum results in comprehending the text more effectively, and I will be critical of the post–modern reader–response claim that only the readers determine the meaning of a text.

The first section of this work will introduce contemporary biblical hermeneutics as a prelude to an examination of the feminist readings in particular. Then a brief history of feminist readings and a survey of feminist hermeneutical approaches will be considered. In the main section, feminist readings will be studied in their own terms. I will identify the general issues which they bring out and will also respond to them both critically and sympathetically in various ways.

This study will analyse feminist readings of the creation narrative texts (Gen. 1–3) and examine their potential implications for biblical interpretation. This metacritical interpretative task involves the description and critical evaluation of the major feminist readings of the creation narratives. Therefore my research material primarily consists of feminist readings of Genesis 1–3, together with secondary materials which deal with those readings. My interaction will be mainly with the feminist biblical scholars and their readings of the text rather than with the theological and philosophical aspects of feminism. So it is not the main purpose of this work to deal with all the theological and philosophical questions in relation to feminist theology.

4. Selection Criteria

My selection is based mainly on three criteria: first of all, I will take into consideration the respective scholars' works and their contribution to my research area and generally their influence and positions in the academy. In other words, I will consider those feminist Old Testament scholars who have been most influential because of their contributions. Secondly, the scholars who have focused mainly on the creation narratives (Gen. 1–3) have been selected for this research purpose. Finally, the scholars chosen have employed the principal methodologies used in Old Testament research to read the texts. It is a fortuitous coincidence that the three major feminist scholars whom I study employ the three most important hermeneutical paradigms of biblical interpretation, literary, social–scientific and historical–critical methods, and all three come from different ecclesiastical and religious backgrounds.

In addition to detailed readings of the above three scholars, I will also examine some other shorter feminist writings of Gen. 1–3. For the sake of convenience, they are grouped with the above major writers according to the methods they use.

Although I attempt to address all the important issues within feminist readings, this work does not claim to be in any way exhaustive. The influx of materials on feminist criticism due to the revived interest in feminist concerns brings in new material to the field every day. It is quite impossible to deal with all the feminist readings of the Old Testament in a study like this because those readings are legion. Moreover there is no single monolithic approach in the feminist readings; rather they employ a variety of interpretative models and methods, which make the evaluation complex and difficult. So the scope of this research is limited to the creation accounts of Genesis 1–3 which are so important for the question of male–female relationship.

5. Results

I will draw conclusions about whether feminist scholarship has universal applications and relevance to situations faced in the modern church and world, whether by males or females.

PART ONE

METHODS IN READING THE BIBLE

CHAPTER 1

The Question of Method in Reading The Bible

1.0 Preliminary Remarks

The purpose of this section is to review the various methods of reading the Bible in the broader context of hermeneutical theories. For more than two centuries, biblical interpretation was mainly based on historical–critical investigation. Hence biblical interpreters tried to understand any text with the help of its historical background, the worldview in which it was produced, and the background and intention of the author. This method has been losing ground with the advent of new literary, structuralist and post–structuralist approaches. David Clines notes this change 'as a shift in focus that has moved from *author* to *text to reader*'.[1] This proliferation of methods in reading the biblical text in the post–modern era necessitates our present enquiry. Since 'hermeneutics' is 'the theory of interpretation' and 'reading' is an 'interpretative activity',[2] one has to have some knowledge of the philosophical, literary and linguistic theories which have shaped contemporary hermeneutical epistemology. Accordingly, one's approach to any reading of the text is shaped by any one of the above metaphysical theories.

1.1 The Nature of the Text and Textuality in Relation to Reading

The fundamental hermeneutical question is where the meaning resides in a literary work. Is it with the mind of the author, or with the particular text, or with the recipients who comprehend the text? Again, one might ask in this post–modern climate, is there any meaning inherent in the text at all? One even could ask, does any text actually exist? The answers to these hermeneutical questions depend on one's understanding of the nature of the text and the theory of textuality. So 'what theorists count as reading or as

---

[1] See D. J. A. Clines, *What Does Eve Do to Help: And Other Readerly Questions to the Old Testament* (JSOTS 94; Sheffield: JSOT Press, 1990), pp. 9–10.

[2] See Werner G. Jeanrond, *Theological Hermeneutics: Development and Significance* (Basingstoke/London: Macmillan), 1991, p. 93.

interpretation serves to condition their view about the nature of texts'.[3] In this context Thiselton aptly notes:

> [D]ifferences between theories of the nature of texts and textuality carry with them fundamentally different conceptions of what it is for a text to convey meaning. In particular, different theories of textuality either link the text's author and context of situation inseparably with its meaning, or view meaning as a more pluralistic range of possibilities generated either by the sign–system of the text itself and its relation to other texts, or by the relation between a text and successive readers or reading communities, or by both.[4]

The very concept of 'meaning' and how it functions in a text also determines one's method of reading the Bible. One thing seems to be clear: the reading of any text is mainly shaped by our conception of the nature of the text and our understanding of the reading process. The following discussion is an attempt to deal with these basic hermeneutical questions in the light of philosophical, literary and linguistic theories.

1.2 Theories of Reading the Text

1.2.1 Philosophical theories and the hermeneutics of understanding

In the process of discovering meanings, literary theorists are greatly influenced by philosophical conceptions of what meaning is and how it can be discerned.[5] Notable contributions were made by Friedrich Schleiermacher, Wilhelm Dilthey, Emilio Betti,[6] Martin Heidegger,[7] Hans–Georg

---

[3] Anthony C. Thiselton, *New Horizons in Hermeneutics: The Theory and Practice of Transforming Biblical Reading* (London: Harper Collins), 1992, p. 19. For a detailed discussion of the nature of text and textuality see W. G. Jeanrond, *Text and Interpretation as Categories of Theological Thinking* (Dublin: Gill & Macmillan, 1988), pp. 73–103; Jeanrond, *Theological Hermeneutics*, pp. 78–92; Thiselton, pp. 19–21, 55–75.

[4] Thiselton, *New Horizons*, p. 55.

[5] M. A. Powell, *The Bible and Modern Literary Criticism: A Critical Assessment and Annotated Bibliography* (New York: Greenwood Press, 1992), pp. 4–5.

[6] Schleiermacher is known as 'the father of modern hermeneutics'. Thiselton classifies these three under the 'Romanticist' model. See Anthony C. Thiselton, 'On Models and Methods: A Conversation with Robert Morgan', in *The Bible in Three Dimensions,* pp. 337–356 [343].

[7] Martin Heidegger, *Being and Time,* trans. by John Macquarrie & Edward Robinson (London: SCM Press, 1962).

Gadamer,[8]Jürgen Habermas, and Paul Ricoeur.[9] They have contributed in various ways to the modern understanding of literature and its interpretation. Although the detailed discussion of their hermeneutical theories falls outside the scope of this work, I will note some aspects of their theories, which are essential to our discussion.[10]

In traditional hermeneutics, *understanding* of any text is the purpose of whole interpretation. This hermeneutic of understanding involves unearthing the thoughts, ideas and expressions of the original author (Schleiermacher). In other words, interpreters seek to locate 'what lies behind the text' (Dilthey, Betti etc.). Thiselton effectively summarises the aim: 'The goal of interpretation according to Dilthey and Betti is to come to understand the mind, life process, and life–world of a text's author. The reader must learn what it is to stand in the shoes of the author.'[11] The author–centred hermeneutical method, as in the historical–critical approach, is deeply rooted in this philosophy, where the aim of the interpretation is to reconstruct the original intention of the author.

According to Gadamer two factors are essential to recover meaning: the horizon of the text and the horizon of the reader. The dialectic of these horizons produces meaning, which Gadamer calls 'the fusion of horizons'. He writes:

> In the process of understanding there takes place a real fusing of horizons, which means that as the historical horizon is projected, it is simultaneously removed. We describe the conscious act of this fusion as the task of the effective–historical consciousness.[12]

Although Gadamer recognises the reality of the 'historical construction of the past world' of the work, he emphasises the fact that 'the work belongs to our world'. Therefore, in Gadamer's approach, reading is not

---

[8] Hans–Georg Gadamer, *Truth and Method* (London: Sheed and Ward, 1981). He represents the 'ontological model'.

[9] Habermas is the proponent of 'socio–critical models', the prominent model employed in liberation, feminist and other similar hermeneutics. Ricoeur contributed 'the hermeneutics of suspicion' which is often used in feminist readings. For details of his hermeneutics, see P. Ricoeur, 'Biblical Hermeneutics', *Semeia* 4 (1975), pp. 27–148. See also Ricoeur, *Essays on Biblical Interpretation* (Philadelphia: Fortress Press, 1981).

[10] For an elaborate discussion of each philosophical hermeneutical model, see Thiselton, *New Horizons;* Josef Bleicher, *Contemporary Hermeneutics: Hermeneutics as Method, Philosophy and Critique* (London: Routledge & Keegan Paul, 1980). For a concise but useful discussion on the subject, see Jeanrond, *Theological Hermeneutics,* pp. 44–77; Randy L. Maddox, 'Contemporary Hermeneutic Philosophy and Theological Studies', *RelS* 21 (1985), pp. 517–529.

[11] Thiselton, *New Horizons*, p. 33.

[12] Gadamer, pp. 273–74.

merely a 'past' historical activity but a present conception of meaning. This is one of the greatest advantages of this approach. So he writes:

> Understanding is not to be thought of so much as an action of one's sub-
> jectivity, but as the placing of oneself within a process of tradition, in
> which *past* and *present* are constantly fused. This is what must be ex-
> pressed in hermeneutical theory, which is far too dominated by the idea
> of process, a method.[13]

In post–Gadamerian hermeneutics, the text is treated as an autonomous entity free from the author, so the sense of the text lies 'in front of' not behind the text. Paul Ricoeur's conception of the text is different from Schleiermacher's and Gadamer's position. Ricoeur argues: 'Writing renders the text autonomous with respect to the intention of the author. What the text signifies no longer coincides with what the author meant.'[14] Ricoeur asserts: 'The reader is absent from the act of writing; the writer is absent from the act of reading. The text thus produces a double eclipse of the reader and the writer. It thereby replaces the relation of dialogue, which directly connects the voice of one to the hearing of the other.'[15] Therefore for Ricoeur, '[t]he sense of a text is not behind the text, but in front of it'.[16] Ricoeur's method allows one to take into consideration the text as it stands, rather than struggling with what lies behind the text.

Mention must be made of the socio–critical theory proposed by Jürgen Habermas as feminist hermeneutics falls generally under socio–critical hermeneutics. Habermas pointed out 'ideological repression' and 'distorted communication' in human communication and called for a 'depth–hermeneutics'.[17] In the words of Thiselton, 'Habermas offers to hermeneutics a vigorous socio–critical conceptual apparatus for metacritical enquiry. He acknowledges the inevitability of metacritical questions, and rightly ex-

---

[13] Ibid., p. 258, emphasis mine. For an elaborate discussion of Gadamerian hermeneutics, see Thiselton, *The Two Horizons: New Testament Hermeneutics and Philosophical Description with Special Reference to Heidegger, Bultmann, Gadamer, and Wittgenstein* (Grand Rapids: Eerdmans/Exeter:Paternoster, 1980), pp. 293–326; Jeanrond, *Text and Interpretation*, pp. 8–37.

[14] Paul Ricoeur, *Hermeneutics and the Human Sciences* (Cambridge/New York: CUP, 1981), p. 139.

[15] Ibid., p. 147.

[16] Ricoeur, *Interpretation Theory: Discourse and the Surplus of Meaning* (Fort Worth: Texas Christian University Press, 1976) as cited by Jeanrond, *Theological Hermeneutics*, p. 73.

[17] See Jeanrond, *Theological Hermenutics*, p. 68. For a detailed discussion of liberation hermeneutics in relation to Habermas' socio–critical theory, see John Rogerson, 'What Does it Mean to be Human? The Central Question of Old Testament Theology?', in *The Bible in Three Dimensions*, pp. 289–298; Thiselton, *New Horizons*, pp. 379–393.

plores the extra–linguistic presuppositons of language in shared worlds of human behaviour.'[18] Thiselton positively views the role of socio–critical aspects in hermeneutics. He gives a clear definition of socio–critical hermeneutics

> as an approach to texts (or to traditions and institutions) which seeks to penetrate beneath their surface–function *to expose their role as instruments of power, domination, or social manipulation. To use Habermas' terms, "critical" hermeneutics (which looks back to Marx) and "depth" hermeneutics (which looks back to Freud) aim to achieve the liberation of those over whom this power or social manipulation is exercized.*[19]

Thus socio–critical hermeneutics aims to offer 'emancipatory critique' from injustice and oppression—in the case of feminist hermeneutics, liberation from patriarchal domination and manipulation. So socio–critical hermeneutics has wider scope in the present context of oppression, exploitation and marginalisation of the poor or the weaker by the 'dominant power structures'.[20]

1.2.2 Literary theories and the aesthetic reading of the text

Modern biblical interpretation has been influenced by literary and linguistic theories more than by any other disciplines and they discover similar possibilities to hermeneutics as philosophical theories. In his classic work, *The Mirror and the Lamp*, M. H. Abrams[21] classifies different schools of literary theory. Though Abrams' work mainly deals with romantic theory in English poetry and literature, biblical interpreters are indebted to him for providing an 'Orientation of Critical Theories' in his introduction.[22] He classifies literary theories mainly into four categories, namely *mimetic*, *pragmatic*, *expressive* and *objective* theories.[23]

Mimetic theory treats literary art 'as essentially an imitation of aspects of the universe'.[24] Therefore, a work is evaluated in terms of truth or accuracy

---

[18] Thiselton, *New Horizons*, p. 393.

[19] Thiselton, *New Horizons*, p. 379, emphasis original.

[20] Rogerson's comment that 'the future existence of Old Testament study depends upon how it reacts to the questions that are being put to it by liberation hermeneutics and the enterprise culture' is very relevant in this regard. See p. XXII in our 'Introduction'.

[21] M. H. Abrams, *The Mirror and the Lamp: Romantic Theory and the Critical Tradition* (New York: OUP, 1953).

[22] Ibid., pp. 3–29. Cf. John Barton, 'Classifying Biblical Criticism', *JSOT* 29 (1984), pp. 19–35. Also Powell, *The Bible and Modern Literary Criticism*, pp. 1–19.

[23] Abrams, pp. 3–29.

[24] Ibid., p. 8.

of its imitation or representation. It is considered to be the oldest aesthetic theory. According to the expressive theory a literary art is essentially the internal expression of a poet or an author and his/her perceptions, thoughts and feelings. It is an author–centred theory. The objective theory 'on principle regards the work of art in isolation from all these external points of reference, analyses it as a self–sufficient entity constituted by its parts in their internal relations, and sets out to judge it solely by criteria intrinsic to its own mode of being'.[25] It is a text–centred approach. Pragmatic theory relates 'the aim of the artist and the character of the work to the nature, the needs, and the springs of pleasure in the audience...'[26] All present methods of biblical interpretation fall into any one of the above categories. In the expressive theory of literary criticism, the role of the author is emphasised whereas in the objective and pragmatic ones the text and the readers respectively are focused on.

Powell deals with this from another angle, focusing on the functions of the literature. According to him literature has two main functions, namely, referential and poetic function.[27] In the referential function, 'the literary work serves as a means to an end—it is valued primarily for its ability to point beyond itself, to tell us something about either the world in which it was produced (mimetic) or about the person who produced it (expressive)'.[28] Whereas in the poetic function 'the literary work serves as an end in itself—it is valued primarily for its own sake (objective) or the effects it achieves on those who receive it (pragmatic)'.[29]

For well over two centuries biblical interpreters focused their attention on the text in finding the referential functions, but modern literary critics are interested in poetic functions rather than referential function. The crucial issue in contemporary hermeneutics is which model could be paradigmatic for interpreting the Scripture more effectively. Scholars have reached no consensus on this, resulting in a plethora of models in hermeneutics.

If the terms of Abrams' theory are borrowed, some contemporary literary readings might be categorised under objective criticism and reader–response under pragmatic criticism. Since 1920, the literary approach has had much prominence resulting in new criticism, european formalism and French structuralism. Due to the influence of new criticism, literary critics have shifted their attention from the historical and authorial backgrounds behind the text, to the text itself as a work of art. Literary criticism holds the view that authorial considerations are 'irrelevant to the literary critic, because meaning and value reside within the text of the finished, free–

---

[25] Ibid., p. 26.
[26] Ibid., pp. 20–21.
[27] Powell, pp. 5–6.
[28] Ibid.
[29] Ibid., p. 6.

standing, and public work of literature itself'.[30] The modern literary critics of the Bible owe much to new criticism in arguing their case. In other words, 'new hermeneutics' 'set the stage for the current interaction of biblical and literary interpretation... it accelerated the awareness that theology and biblical studies need not necessarily be carried out in a confessional framework'.[31] This is a new step in biblical interpretation. Previously the Bible was studied and interpreted within the religious and scriptural framework. Due to the influence of new criticism, the Bible has begun to be studied purely as literature rather than as scripture. All the text–centred methods such as the new literary criticism, rhetorical criticism and narrative criticism are greatly influenced by these theories.

I will take up narrative criticism as a case in point. Narrative criticism is interested in finding the surface meaning of a narrative.[32] It is not interested in locating the historical situation of the actual readers since it interprets 'the text from the perspective of an idealised *implied reader* who is presupposed by and constructed from the text itself'.[33] The *implied reader* and the *implied author* are different from the real author and the real reader.[34] Narrative critics always approach the text from the perspective of the *implied reader*. Generally a narrative consists of a story, which is the content of the narrative and it will have three essential elements, namely character, plot, and style.[35]

---

[30] M. H. Abrams, *A Glossary of Literary Terms,* 4th ed. (New York/Chicago/San Francisco/ Dallas/Montreal/Toronto/London/Sydney: Holt, Rinehart & Winston, 1981), p. 83.

[31] Robert Detweiler & Vernon K. Robbins, 'From New Criticism to Poststructuralism: Twentieth Century Hermeneutics', (ed.) Stephen Prickett, in *Reading the Text: Biblical Criticism and Literary Theory* (Cambridge, MA/ Oxford: Blackwell, 1991), p. 238.

[32] For narrative criticism's relationship with other literary models, see Mark Allen Powell, *What is Narrative Criticism? A New Approach to the Bible* (London: SPCK, 1993), pp. 11–21. It is to be noted that in structuralist method, the focus is not on the surface structure, but on deep structures.

[33] Powell, p. 15. Narrative criticism also makes the distinction between real author and *implied author*, text and *narrative*.

[34] See Robert M. Fowler, 'Who is "the Reader" in Reader Response Criticism?', *Semeia* 31 (1985), pp. 5–23. To him, the real author and real reader are 'the living, flesh–and–blood persons who actually produce the text and read it. But in the act of reading we encounter, not a flesh–and–blood author, but the author's second self adopted for purposes of telling this tale, and similarly we as readers as not wholly ourselves as we read, but the reader the text invites us to be'. p. 10

[35] See David M. Gunn & Danna Nolan Fewell, *Narrative in the Hebrew Bible* (Oxford: OUP, 1993), pp. 1–5; Shimon Bar–Efrat, *Narrative Art in the Bible* (JSOTS 70; Sheffield: Almond Press, 1989); Gordon D. Fee & Douglas Stuart, *How to Read the Bible for all its Worth: A Guide to Understanding the Bible* (London: Scripture Union, 1983), see section on 'The Old Testament Narratives–Their Proper Use', pp. 73–86 (originally published in Grand Rapids: Zondervan Corporation, 1982).

Many biblical scholars believe that narrative criticism will have tremendous potential and far reaching influence on the area of hermeneutics, even into the present century.[36] This method has been influential and it is quite true that it has enabled biblical scholars to approach the text in its final form. Robert Alter's *The Art of Biblical Narrative*[37] is an excellent introduction to literary and narrative reading. One effect of his method is to challenge many conclusions drawn by the historical–critical method regarding the unity of certain narrative texts.[38]

1.2.3 Reader–oriented theories and the production of 'meaning'

According to Abrams' classification reader–oriented hermeneutical approaches may be grouped under Pragmatic theory. Generally speaking, the reader–response approach is one of the offshoots of post–modernism. 'Reader–response theories call attention to the active role of communities of readers in constructing what counts for them as "what the text means"'.[39] In the post–modern understanding, '[t]here is no given object world; concepts can have no unrepresented referent; and there is no knowledge outside of specific forms of discourse'.[40] Moreover, there is no objective certitude and fixed reality or truth or fact in post–modernism as in the case of modernity. This rejection of *logocentrism*[41] promotes an iconoclastic atti-

---

[36] See Detweiler & Robinson, 'From New Criticism to Poststructuralism', p. 259. See also pp. 225–280.

[37] Robert Alter, *The Art of Biblical Narrative* (London/Sydney: George Allen & Unwin, 1981).

[38] See Alter's book and his chapter on 'A Literary Approach to the Bible'. See also *The Literary Guide to the Bible,* (ed.) Robert Alter & Frank Kermode (London: Collins, 1987). For details about the narrative reading of the text, see also Shimon Bar–Efrat, *Narrative Art in the Bible* (Sheffield: Almond Press, 1984); Meir Sternberg, *The Poetics of Biblical Narrative*: *Ideological Literature and the Drama of Reading* (Bloomington: Indiana University Press, 1985); Adele Berlin, *Poetics and Interpretation of Biblical Narrative*, (BALS 9; Winona Lake: Eisenbrauns, 1994/Almond Press, 1983).

[39] Thiselton, *New Horizons*, p. 515. For a detailed discussion of different reader–response theories, see Thiselton, *New Horizons,* pp. 515–555.

[40] See Philip Sampson, 'The Rise of Postmodernity', in *Faith and Modernity*, (eds) P. Sampson *et al.* (Oxford: Regnum Press, 1994), pp. 29–57, [p. 38]. Cf. Stanley J. Grenz's general definition of postmodernism as 'an intellectual mood and an array of cultural expressions that call into question the ideals, principles, and values that lay at the heart of the modern mid–set'. See Grenz, *A Primer* on *Postmodernism* (Grand Rapids: William B. Eerdmans, 1996), p. 12.

[41] Logocentrism is 'an excessive faith in the stability of meanings, or excessive concern with distinctions, or with the validity of inferences, or the careful use of reason, or with other traditional aids to sifting truth from falsity, or indeed an excessive faith in the notions of truth and falsity themselves.' See Simon Blackburn, 'Logocentrism', in *Oxford Dictionary of Philosophy* (Oxford: OUP, 1996), p. 224.

tude in readers, giving the reader much freedom to create a variety of meanings as he or she wishes. T. J. Keegan rightly observes: 'Postmodernism, therefore, accepts indeterminacy, polyvalence and subjectivity as necessary elements in the study of a reality that is incapable of ultimate definition.'[42] This post–modern attitude towards reality has been brought to the reading of biblical texts also, advocating indeterminacy and subjectivity in meaning.

In reader–response hermeneutics the text does not have any determinant meaning at all. The meaning is created and determined exclusively by the reader, resulting in a plurality of meanings. In most reader–oriented approaches the meaning is determined not by the text, but by the reader of the text. Robert Morgan writes: 'Texts, like dead men and women, have no rights, no aims, no interests. They can be used in whatever way readers or interpreters choose.'[43]

In the reader–response model the interpretative communities determine the meaning of the text. To Stanley Fish there is no 'right reading'. According to him meaning is not something which is extracted from a work but it is produced by the readers. He argues that the text is *not* the self–sufficient repository of meaning and he challenges the notion that meaning is embedded in the text.[44] He argues that 'indeed, it is interpretive communities, rather than either the text or the reader, that produce meanings and are responsible for the emergence of formal features'.[45] The interpretative communities consist of 'those who share the interpretive strategies'.[46] The advantage of this model according to Fish is that 'the reader was freed from the tyranny of the text and given the central role in the production of meaning'.[47]

---

[42] Terence J. Keegan, 'Biblical Criticism and the Challenge of Postmodernism', *BibInt* 3 (1995), p. 2. For various post-modern approaches to biblical interpretation, see Regina M. Schwartz *et al.*, *The Postmodern Bible: The Bible and Culture Collective* (New Haven/London: Yale University Press, 1995). This work, as its name indicates, is the latest comprehensive analysis of modern hermeneutical approaches in the light of post-modern ideologies. Another notable feature of this work is its combined authorship which consists of ten men and women scholars from Universities and Colleges in the United States—D. Jobling, Robert M. Fowler and Stephen D. Moore among them. This work asserts the Bible's cultural power. They write: 'No reading, our own included, can escape these intricate matrices of power. For us, there is no innocent reading of the Bible, no reading that is not already ideological' (p. 4).

[43] Robert Morgan (with John Barton), *Biblical Interpretation* (Oxford: OUP, 1989), p. 7.

[44] See Stanley Fish, *Is there a Text in this Class? The Authority of Interpretive Communities* (Cambridge, MA: Harvard University Press, 1980), p. 2.

[45] Ibid., p. 14.

[46] Ibid., p.171.

[47] Ibid., p. 7.

There are many other reader–response theories which dominate the thinking process of biblical interpreters. Norman Holland's psycho–analytical reader–response theory considers 'interpretation as being largely determined by the defenses, expectations, and wish–fulfilling fantasies of the reader... a reader makes sense out of a text by transforming the content in accord with his or her own identity'.[48] Holland's approach emphasises the role of the individual reader against communities of readers as in Fish. 'In process of reading, readers shape their strategies and perceptions in *ways which serve their patterns of desire, and what they construct reflects and serves their own unique identity.*'[49] This theory has been instrumental in developing ideological readings like feminist and other liberation readings, projecting their own self–interest in the work.[50]

Generally speaking, reader–response criticism has been gaining momentum during recent years. Edgar V. McKnight does not think that meanings are deposited in the text but that they are produced and created in conjunction with the text.[51] He asserts that 'readers make sense of the Bible in the light of their world, which includes not only linguistic and literary tools but also world views that influence the sorts of meanings and methods that are satisfying'.[52] Moreover, literature for a reader–response critic is not an object but an experience, so the response of the reader is more important than the contents of the work.[53]

The trend towards recognizing the reader's role in determining the meaning of the text has gained much momentum and acceptance among biblical scholars. Clines at Sheffield University is one of the main proponents of reader–centred hermeneutics in Britain today.[54]   According to

[48] See Powell, W*hat is Narrative Criticism*, p. 17; see also Thiselton, *New Horizons,* pp. 529–550.

[49] Thiselton, *New Horizons,* p. 530.

[50] For an application of reader–oriented feminist hermeneutics, see Mary McClintock Fulkerson, 'Contesting Feminist Canons: Discourse and the Problem of Sexist Texts', *JFSR* 7 (1991), pp. 53–73.

[51] See Edgar V. McKnight, 'A Biblical Criticism for American Biblical scholarship', in SBLSP (ed.) Paul J. Achtemeier (Chico: Scholars Press, 1980), p. 126. See also McKnight, *The Bible and the Reader: An Introduction to Literary Criticism* (Philadelphia: Fortress Press, 1985).

[52] Edgar V. McKnight, *Post–Modern Use of the Bible: The Emergence of Reader–Oriented Criticism* (Nashville: Abingdon Press, 1988), p. 58. The main thesis of this book is that 'Readers make sense'.

[53] See Jane P. Tompkins, *Reader Response Criticism: From Formalism to Post–structuralism* (Baltimore: Johns Hopkins University Press, 1980), p. xvii.

[54] See Clines, *What Does Eve Do to Help?,* pp. 9–24; 'A World Established on Water (Psalm 24): Reader–Response, Deconstruction and Bespoke Interpretation', in *The New Literary Criticism and the Bible* (JSOTS 143), (eds.), J. Cheryl Exum & D. J. A. Clines (Sheffield: JSOT Press, 1993), pp. 79–90; Clines, 'Possibilities and Priorities of Biblical Interpretation in an International Perspective', pp. 67–87.

Clines, texts do not have determinate meanings. 'The text means whatever it means to its various readers... There is no one authentic meaning which we must all try to discover, no matter who we are or where we happen to be standing.'[55] So there is no objective criterion to determine whether one interpretation or another is right. Recently, Clines has been more interested in a 'goal–oriented hermeneutic', that is, he wants to produce 'attractive interpretations'. So he writes: '[a]s a bespoke interpreter responding to the needs of the market, I will be interested, not in "the truth", not in universally acceptable meanings, but in eradicating shoddy interpretations that are badly stitched together and have no durability....'[56] To Clines, 'What the academic community today decides counts as a reasonable interpretation of a text *is* a reasonable interpretation.'[57] His concept of academic community is in line with Fish's concept of interpretive communities. So in the same post–modern hermeneutical fashion, Clines also emphasizes that 'texts do not have determinate meanings' and there is no 'methodological purism' in biblical interpretation. Moreover, in the process of making meaning 'readers have a vital part'.[58]

1.2.4 Linguistic theories of meaning and 'indeterminate meaning'

In recent decades linguistics theories have provided many insights into reading the biblical texts. Ferdinand de Saussure, Roman Jacobson, Jacques Derrida, John Austin, and John Searle are the main proponents of linguistic theories. De Saussure's[59] distinction between the concepts of *langue* and *parole*[60] was especially important in the development of hermeneutical theories. These linguistic theories explain how language works.

Structuralism is derived from the linguistic theories of Ferdinand de Saussure and was developed in France during the 1950s and 1960s. Claude Lévi–Strauss's studies in anthropology also provided some basis for biblical structuralism.[61] Hermeneutically speaking, the structuralists focus on the deep structure in a literary work. In relation to the biblical text, 'the struc-

---

[55] Clines, 'Possibilities and Priorities of Biblical Interpretation...', p. 78.

[56] Clines, 'A World Established on Water...', pp. 87–88.

[57] Clines, 'Possibilities and Priorities...', p. 79, emphasis original.

[58] Clines, *What Does Eve Do to Help?*, p. 11. But see below pp. 28–29 for Clines' recent statement on this topic.

[59] Ferdinand de Saussure, *Course in General Linguistics,* (rev. ed.) by Charles Bally and Albert Sechehave in collaboration with Albert Riedlinger, (trans.) by Wade Baskin (London: Peter Owen, 1974).

[60] *Langue* is the system of language and the *parole* is the expression of language. According to Sassure the semiotic interest lies in the *langue,* see Detweiler & Robbins, 'From New Criticism to Poststructuralism', pp. 253–55.

[61] See Claude Lévi–Strauss, *Anthropology, and Myth: Lectures 1957–1982* (New York: Basil Blackwell, 1987).

turalist is interested in analysing the *art* in the biblical text, rather than investigating the documents that lie behind it or the manner in which the editorial conflation took place'.[62] For the structuralists the structure is not inherent to the text but is applied from outside. There are various structures, such as semantic, linguistic, narrative, and mythical, in deriving meaning.

An example of the application of structuralism is 'binary oppositions'. This is used in Old Testament studies of the structure of the narrative and poetry of Hebrew myth (e.g. light and darkness, good and evil, male and female, rich and poor). It is argued that meaning can be obtained in oppositions and contraries. So the meaning of the text is derived from the language itself. 'The meaning of a text is expressed in the binary opposition of its deep structure. Interest is centred, therefore, entirely on this structure rather than on authorship, history or subject matter'.[63] Furthermore, structuralism being a text–immanent method, assumes that the meaning resides in the text and its linguistic structures. 'The structural exegete attempts to uncover, for instance, the linguistic, narrative, or mythical structures of the text under consideration. Whether or not these structures were intended by the author is not a relevant question.'[64] This shift from the historical background of the text to the text itself has resulted in experimentation with other similar methods in the realm of biblical interpretation. Moreover, this methodology could also check the tendency of traditional criticism to tear apart the text into different layers such as original, later additions and gloss, etc.

Despite its usefulness in biblical interpretation, this method has many disadvantages. The major objection is its approach to the biblical text. Generally it treats the biblical text in the same way as any other literary text. It does not take into account its inspired nature of the biblical text.[65] The structuralists' methods can be used for analysing the text rather than interpreting and locating the meaning that can be derived by using exegetical methods. D. C. Greenwood observes: 'Many of these problems arise from the fact that the principles of structural analysis were never intended by their original devisors to be applied to sacred scripture.'[66] Though his ob-

---

[62] David C. Greenwood, *Structuralism and the Biblical Text* (Berlin/New York/ Amsterdam: Mouton Publishers, 1985), p. 8. For a detailed analysis, see Robert A Spivey, 'Structuralism and Biblical Studies: The Uninvited Guest', *Int* 28 (1974), pp. 133–145; Richard Jacobson, 'The Structuralist and the Bible', *Int* 28 (1974), pp. 146–164. See also Thiselton, 'Structuralism and Biblical studies: Method or Ideology?', *ExpTim* 89 (1978), pp. 329–335.

[63] Margaret Davies, 'Literary Criticism', in *A Dictionary of Biblical Interpretation*, (eds.) R.J. Coggins & J. L. Houlden (London: SCM Press, 1990), p. 403.

[64] Daniel Patte, *What is Structural Exegesis* (Philadelphia: Fortress Press, 1976), p. 14.

[65] See Greenwood, *Structuralism and the Biblical Text*, pp. 118–119. He lists many objections in this direction.

[66] Ibid., p.107.

servation seems to be true we cannot ignore the fact that it can also be applied to most literary and linguistic theories.

The theory of deconstruction was developed as a reaction to the structuralist's claim that meaning lies in the deeper structure of the text. Deconstruction and reader–response criticism are closely related. According to the post–modern linguistic theory of deconstruction, there is no determinate meaning in any text. Deconstruction began in France during the late 1960s and came to America and England later. The proponent of this model is Jacques Derrida.[67] Unlike the structuralists who find meaning within the deep structures of the text, the practitioners of this method argue that 'deconstructive criticism is not the application of philosophical lessons to literary studies but an exploration of textual logic in texts...'[68] It advocates that every text is divided against itself or 'deconstructs' itself, resulting in multiple meanings and so it is not possible to obtain any original meaning from any text. It is worth quoting in length the definition given by Abrams:

> 'Deconstruction' is applied to a mode of reading texts which subverts the implicit claim of a text to possess adequate grounds, in the system of language that it deploys, to establish its own structure, unity, and determinate meanings.[69]

According to the theory of deconstruction, there is not a determinant or inherent meaning found in the text. Rather, such meaning is determined by its difference from other texts. Clarence Walhout explains this as follows:

> Meaning thus is *difference*—an inseparable union of the concepts to *differ* and to *defer*—and hermeneutics is the process through which we attempt to deal with the inevitable ambiguity in the interpretive process. Because this process is never completed, meaning is forever indeterminate and changing. Every reader interprets texts in relation to his own cultural situation and thereby participates in the endless, ever–changing process of exploring and creating meaning.[70]

---

[67] See Jacques Derrida, *Of Grammatology*, (trans.) Gayatri Chakravorty Spivak (Baltimore: Johns Hopkins Univ. Press, 1976).

[68] See Jonathan Culler, *On Deconstruction: Theory and Criticism after Structuralism* (London:Routledge & Kegan Paul, 1983), p. 227.

[69] Abrams, A *Glossary of Literary Terms*, p. 38.

[70] Clarence Walhout, 'Texts and Actions', in *The Responsibility of Hermeneutics*, (eds.) Roger Lundin *et al.* (Grand Rapids/Exeter: Paternoster Press, 1985), p. 38, for details see pp. 34–42.

As a result of this theory many ideological readings such as political, materialistic, psycho–analytic, feminist and various liberationist readings have been applied to biblical texts during the last decade.

A somewhat different philosophical theory of language was developed by J. L. Austin, an Oxford philosopher of language, and was systematized and developed by his student John R. Searle. This theory of language, known as *Speech Act Theory*, offers a functional approach to literature, i.e. 'what literature does' and not 'what it means'.[71] According to Austin, 'the issuing of the utterance is the performing of an action–it is not normally thought of as just saying something'.[72] Therefore, the utterance performs certain perlocutionary acts.[73] H. C. White argues that speech act theory can function as a model to bridge the hermeneutical problem between literary criticism and historical criticism, the literary criticism for its formalist approach and the historical critical model for detaching the past from present concerns.[74] We cannot overlook the contributions of speech act theory, especially its emphasis on treating every 'speech' as being in itself an 'act' and its focus on 'communicative context' in determining meaning.

1.3 Observation, Discussion and Evaluation

When we evaluate the different interpretation models in the light of Abrams' literary theory, it is very clear that all of his four types–mimetic, expressive, objective and pragmatic theories–have been employed in biblical hermeneutics to locate the meaning of a literary work. Accordingly, in the past scholars made considerable effort in locating the 'life world' behind biblical writings which would correspond in some measure with mimetic theory. Then the focus was on the author and his/her intentions. Since then the hermeneutical interest has been on the text itself, resulting in many text–immanent literary methods such new literary criticism, rhetorical criticism and structuralism. Now many scholars experiment with what Abrams calls the pragmatic theory, which is basically a reader–centred one. Since all the theories have already been tried, the alternatives before the interpreters are few. Readers could either return to the old mimetic and expressive models or try to derive principles from *all* the models in the location of the meaning of a text. It seems to me that it is vital to explore the mimetic and expressive dimensions in our hermeneutical process without

---

[71] See Hugh C. White, 'Introduction: Speech Act Theory and Literary Criticism', *Semeia* 41 (1988), pp. 1–24.

[72] J. L. Austin, *How to do Things with Words* (Oxford: OUP, 1973), pp. 6–7.

[73] That is 'what we bring about or achieve by saying something, such as convincing, persuading, deterring, and even, say, surprising or misleading'. p. 108.

[74] See White, 'The Value of Speech Act Theory for Old Testament Hermeneutics', *Semeia* 41 (1988), pp. 41–63.

losing the pragmatic aspect. The problem with many modern biblical scholars is that they confine themselves to one single approach.

1.4 The Reader in Relation to the Text

1.4.1 Does the reader determine the meaning of the text?

Many scholars have pointed out the inadequacy of reader–oriented hermeneutics as a comprehensive hermeneutical model for biblical interpretation. Anthony Thiselton raises five objections against reader–oriented theories of meaning. First, he argues: 'If textual meaning is the *product* of a community of readers...texts cannot reform these readers "from outside".'[75] Secondly, prophetic address becomes either illusory or 'explained in terms of pre–conscious inner conflict'. The remaining three points are theological in nature. Therefore, thirdly, grace or revelation becomes illusory as there are no 'givens'. Fourthly, the message of the cross becomes merely a linguistic construct, and finally '[I]t would be impossible to determine what would *count as a systematic mistake in the development of doctrine'.*[76]

A critique of Fish's reader–oriented hermeneutics for biblical studies has been offered quite recently by Paul R. Noble in an analysis of Fish's epistemology.[77] According to Noble, Fish's reader–oriented hermeneutics is 'a form of anti–foundationalist epistemology' which entails a 'non–realist ontology' and which has led him into 'thoroughgoing solipsism'.[78] Noble explains Fish's principle thus:

> No–one can do my reading for me– if *I* want to understand a text then I must interpret it, which by Fish's theories means that I thereby *produce* it.... It is I myself, then,who constitutes interpretative constraints, manufactures evidence, and brings into being the interpretative community– that is, they are because I make them, and they are *what* I make them. There can be nothing "beyond" me that is capable of constraining my in-

---

[75] Thiselton, *New Horizons*, p. 549.

[76] Ibid. Thiselton considers reader–centred reading as a typical example for socio–pragmatic hermeneutics which 'transposes the meaning of texts into projections which are *potentially idolatrous* as instruments of self–affirmation', in contrast to socio–critical hermeneutics which aims 'to unmask uses of texts which serve self–interests or the interests of dominating power structures'. See p. 550 and p. 6, emphasis original. Cf. Jeanrond, *Text and Interpretation*, pp. 112ff.

[77] P. R. Noble, 'Hermeneutics and Post–Modernism: Can We have a Radical Reader–Response Theory?', Part I & Part II, *RelS* 30 (1994), pp. 419–36; *RelS* 31(1995), pp. 1–22.

[78] Noble, 'Hermeneutics and Post–Modernism Part II', pp. 2–4.

terpretations, because nothing can enter *my* world except through my interpretative activities, that is, except as I shape it.[79]

Again, contrary to Fish's argument Noble asserts, 'The text has an independent existence over against the interpreter, and offers very significant resistance to the readers' interpretative strategies,...'[80] Further he argues that 'Fish's hermeneutics could only be imported into biblical studies if we were first to change our exegetical procedures in ways that the overwhelming majority of biblical scholars would find totally unacceptable'.[81] In the light of the above discussion, Noble concludes that Fish's model is 'a form of postmodernism that biblical studies should most definitely reject'.[82]

Daniel Patte rightly notes that interpreting a text involves two factors, namely exegesis and hermeneutic. In his own words, 'exegesis aims at understanding the text in itself, while hermeneutic attempts to elucidate what the text means for the modern interpreter and the people of his culture'.[83] The reader–response critics have failed in differentiating between these two. For the reader–response critics, hermeneutics is their exegesis. The above discussion suggests that there are problems with reader–centred theories as models for a comprehensive biblical hermeneutic.

The main feminist readers whom we shall study consider the text and its interpretation seriously. Trible, for instance, takes the narrative in its final form seriously and like some post–modern feminist readers she does not read 'against the grain of the text'. Although Carol Meyers approaches the text with a hermeneutics of suspicion, in practice she fully acknowledges the veracity of the text in her literary reading of the key passages. Similarly, Bird also takes the text seriously both in her historical–critical analysis and her narrative reading. However, the post–modern development of 'reading against the grain of the text' is to be seen in Bal, Fewell, Rashkow, Brenner and others.

1.5 Is the Biblical Text in the Same Category as Literature?

Generally, modern interpreters consider the Bible in the same way as they would any other piece of literature. But this is arguably inappropriate. We need to remember that the Bible has served as the scripture for the community of faith for centuries. Robert C. Culley clearly points this out. 'The

---

[79] Ibid., p. 16, emphasis original.

[80] Ibid., p. 1.

[81] Noble, 'Hermeneutics and Post–Modernism Part I' p. 424.

[82] Nobel, 'Hermeneutics and Post–Modernism Part II' p. 22; contra Keegan, 'Biblical Criticism and the Challenge of Postmodernism', pp. 1–14.

[83] Daniel Patte, *What is Structural Exegesis*, p. 3.

Bible needs to be treated as a special case. It is not a text like all other texts, at least not like many other texts...'[84]

Ellen Van Wolde shows that the biblical texts are not merely a literary work meant for aesthetic enjoyment; rather, they are unique in the sense that they are 'intended to be read not only as literary texts but also as religious texts. That is to say that they are intended to function as texts in readers' and hearers' lives, ideas and actions, both in the past and now'.[85] In the same vein, Robert Alter insists on 'a complete interfusion of literary art with theological, moral, or historiosophical vision, the fullest perception of the latter dependent on the fullest grasp of the former'.[86] Employing the principles of speech act theory, Van Wolde asserts that '[t]exts are speech acts and are intended to function in a particular manner'.[87] In that respect the text has a reciprocal 'communicative function' between God and humanity. In other words the biblical text still functions as a given revelation to the reading community.[88] Thiselton aptly observes that 'In most Christian traditions, a self–consistency is noted between the Holy Spirit's inspiration of the biblical texts in their origin and transmission, and the Spirit's actualisation of the message of these texts in the lives of successive generations of readers'.[89] Therefore, I would argue the text is not dead, only the human author of the text is dead. So the text could be still alive by the illumination of the Holy Spirit.[90] Therefore, it could still speak and function in the lives of the present community of readers who actualise and acknowledge this dimension of the text and its potentiality. In this context, it is worth quoting Van Wolde's contention:

---

[84] Robert C. Culley, *Themes and Variations: A Study of Action in Biblical Narrative* (Atlanta: Scholars Press, 1992), p. 7.

[85] E. V. Wolde, *Words Become Worlds: Semantic Studies of Genesis 1–11* (BIS 6; Leiden: E. J. Brill, 1994), p. 161.

[86] Alter, *The Art of Biblical Narrative*, p. 19.

[87] Wolde, *Words Become Worlds,* p. 181. She illustrates this by arguing that a Psalm is intended to be read as a human prayer to God, although it can be used for aesthetic and similar reading purposes. When it is read as a prayer, readers address themselves to God and 'transfer the illocutionary force into perlocution' p. 182.

[88] So J. Rogerson, *Genesis 1–11* (Sheffield: JSOT Press, 1991), p. 48; cf. W. G. Jeanrond, 'After Hermeneutics: The Relationship between Theology and Biblical Studies', in *The Open Text: New Directions for Biblical Studies?* (London: SCM Press, 1993), pp. 85–102 [88]; cf. Gerald Bray, *Biblical Interpretation: Past and Present* (Leicester: Apollos, 1996), pp. 14–34.

[89] Thiselton, *New Horizons,* p. 64.

[90] For the role of Holy Spirit in the hermeneutical process, see Clark H. Pinnock, 'The Work of the Holy Spirit in Hermeneutics', *JPT* 2 (1993), pp. 3–23. Pinnock writes: 'The Spirit is active in the life of the whole Church to interpret the biblical message in languages of today. He actualises the word of God by helping us to restate the message in contemporary terminology and apply it to fresh situations', p.16.

[I]n exegesis and in theology biblical texts cannot just be read as texts produced by a particular text–historical, redaction–historical, and philological development, nor as mere literary, linguistic or aesthetical phenomena. They should also be read as acts of speech, as actions in the form of confessions, testimonies of faith, prayers and invitations to lead a good life.[91]

The special religious nature of the biblical text and the way it communicates makes it distinct from other literary texts. Similarly, for a religious community who take seriously 'what the text means' to them, rather than 'what the readers think it means to them' makes the 'reader–response' approach largely inappropriate or at least question begging. Since the religious community considers the text as authoritative, they want to hear 'what the text means'. Otherwise, as we noted earlier, 'grace' or 'revelation' become merely 'illusory' and *'[t]he message of the cross* remains a *linguistic construct* of a tradition'.[92] We need to note in this context that Trible and some other revisionary feminist readers subscribe to the biblical authority to a certain extent.

1.6 Can there be a Correct Model?

We have seen that every method has advantages and limitations. From this we need to infer that no single method is adequate to fathom all interpretative motives and intentions inherent in a text. On the other hand, the exclusive imperialistic claim of any one method as *the* proper method is also misleading. For instance, both the 'distanciation' of the reader from the 'author' in the traditional method, and the post–modern notion of 'reader' as the one who solely determines the meaning of the text have opened a Pandora's box in the interpretative circle. At the same time the concept of an 'autonomous' text does not resolve all interpretative questions because a text is written with a 'communicative function', which takes place only in the process of 'interaction between text and reader'.[93] In the process of reading, the three factors of author, text and reader are all equally important.

Now there is a tendency among biblical scholars to accept the need for a pluralistic interpretative approach to biblical texts. In this regard, Mark G. Brett puts it thus: 'there [is] a wide range of questions one might bring to a text, and therefore it is appropriate to have a wide range of methods in order

---

[91] Van Wolde, *Words Become Worlds*, p. 208.

[92] Thiselton, *New Horizons*, p. 549.

[93] Van Wolde, *Words Become Worlds*, p. 181.

to answer those questions'.[94] In the same vein, John Barton also argues that all these methods have 'something in them, but none of them is the "correct" method which scholars are seeking'.[95] This approach has been reiterated quite recently by John Goldingay. He writes: 'Scripture has a variety of ways of speaking, and the process of interpretation requires a variety of hermeneutical approaches, corresponding to this variety in types of texts.'[96] Therefore, having taken into account various hermeneutical questions and the interpretative possibilities of the text, we affirm that neither the traditional historical nor the contemporary literary paradigm alone can bring out all the insights inherent in a text. So we challenge the post–modern claim that all previous methods in reading the texts have been invalidated by the advent of reader–oriented hermeneutical approaches.

Pluralism, however, may lead to indeterminacy of meaning. This tendency has recently been advocated by David J. A. Clines and J. Cheryl Exum.[97] Clines writes: 'There are no determinate meanings and there are no universally agreed upon legitimate interpretations.'[98] Again pluralism may hamper our attempt to develop a correct hermeneutical model. Barton says: 'I believe that the quest for a correct method is, not just in practice, but inherently, incapable of succeeding.'[99] So can we advocate pluralism and at the same time hope to do justice to the 'text' and of the hermeneutical process? There is a fine balance here, well expressed by Jeanrond: '[A] pluralistic reading of the Bible and a rigorous examination both of the text and of particular acts of reading offer the best guarantee against renewed efforts to reduce the Bible to a mere collection of proof–texts for one theological argument or another'.[100] This is satisfying, because it is cautious about claims to have found 'the' meaning of a text, recognizing that all reading of a text is conditioned by the reader; yet it is prepared to disqualify readings that, by general consent, do violence to the text.

---

[94] Mark G. Brett, 'The Future of Reader Criticisms?', in *The Open Text: New Directions for Biblical Studies* (London: SCM Press, 1993), pp. 13–31 [14]; cf. Jeanrond, 'After Hermeneutics...', p. 93.

[95] See John Barton, *Reading the Old Testament: Method in Biblical Study* (London: Darton Longman & Todd, 1984), p. 5.

[96] J. Goldingay, *Models for Interpretation of Scripture* (Grand Rapids:Eerdmans, 1995), p. 1; for a detailed discussion of various types of texts, see the companion volume to the above work entitled, *Models for Scripture* (Grand Rapids: Eerdmans, 1994).

[97] Clines and Exum, 'The New Literary Criticism', 11–15.

[98] Clines, 'A World Established on Water', pp. 86–87.

[99] Barton, *Reading the Old Testament,* p. 5., see also pp. 206–207; for the same point of view, see Morgan with Barton, *Biblical Interpretation,* pp. 269–296. For a critique of Barton's position, see Thiselton, *New Horizons,* pp. 499–502.

[100] Jeanrond, 'After Hermeneutics', p. 94.

We can go further and return to the idea of the authorial intention.[101] Thiselton also underscores the importance of the authorial intention by arguing that '*many* (not all) *biblical texts address a direct goal* which may directly be identified as its author's intention, provided that intention is understood only "adverbially"'.[102] According to Rolf Rendtorff 'the last writers, whatever we want to call them, were in any case much closer to the original meaning of the text than we can ever be'.[103] From this we suggest that we can reach the original meaning of the text at a certain level. Grant R. Osborne calls for the trialogue between the author, the text and the reader. He argues that 'the original meaning of a text is not a hopeless goal but a possible and positive and necessary one'.[104] So it is arguable that traditional methods of reading the text are still legitimate and valid. Mark G. Brett, in a very recent work, points out the need for the co–existence of models and he argues that 'the concept of authorial intention...is still perfectly respectable as long as one has a rigorous enough understanding of intentionality...the question of what an author might have intended to communicate to his or her original audience is only one of several questions critics might bring to a text'.[105] So now biblical scholars find both historical–critical and literary methods relevant in practice.[106]

John Goldingay is also concerned to reach a right understanding of the text. He reminds us that '[m]issing right understandings is a more threaten-

---

[101] See Mark G. Brett, 'Motives and Intentions in Genesis', *JTS* 42 (1991), pp. 1–16.

[102] Thiselton, *New Horizons*, p. 560. He explains 'to write with an intention is to write in a way that is directed towards a goal', p. 560.

[103] Rolf Rendtorff, 'The Paradigm is Changing: Hopes and Fears', *BiblInt* 1 (1993) p. 52.

[104] G. R. Osborne, *Hermeneutical Spiral: A Comprehensive Introduction to Biblical Interpretation* (Downers Grove: IVP, 1991), p. 415, see also pp. 397–415.

[105] Brett, 'The Future of Reader Criticisms?', pp. 13–14.

[106] See J. Barton, 'Reading the Bible as Literature: Two Questions for Biblical Critics', *JLT* 1 (1987), pp. 135–153; Morgan with Barton, *Biblical Interpretation,* pp. 178–185; Brett, 'Four or Five Things to do with Texts: A Taxonomy of Interpretative Interests', in *The Bible in Three Dimensions,* pp. 357–377; Rogerson, *Genesis 1–11,* pp. 49–52; J. Barton, 'Historical Criticism and Literary Interpretation: Is there any Common Ground?', in *Crossing the Boundaries: Essays in Honour of Michael D. Goulder* (eds.) S. E. Porter *et al.* (BIS 8; Leiden: E. J. Brill, 1994), pp. 3–15; Paul Joyce, 'First Among Equals?: The Historical–Critical Approach in the Marketplace of Methods', in *Crossing the Boundaries,* pp. 17–27; Carl R. Holladay, 'Contemporary Methods of Reading the Bible', in *NIB* vol. 1 (Nashville: Abingdon Press, 1994), pp. 125–149; Moisés Silva, 'Contemporary Theories of Biblical Interpretation', in *NIB* (same vol.), pp. 107–124. According to Silva 'while in certain cases the task of identifying what the biblical author meant is not the *only* legitimate way of proceeding; such a task is *always* legitimate and indeed must continue to function as an essential goal', p. 121, emphasis original.

ing danger than arriving at wrong ones'.[107] Moreover, Goldingay reminds us that 'the impossibility of total understanding does not negate the worth of attempting whatever degree of understanding will turn out to be possible. The attempt is likely to be more successful if we behave as if total understanding is possible. If you aim at the moon, you may hit the lamppost. The notion of determinate meaning has functional efficacy'.[108] Further he asks: 'if meaning is indeterminate, why is there so much overlap between interpretations?'[109]

The concern for the 'determinate meaning' of a text is clearly different from leaving the text exclusively at the disposal of the reader, and stands against the risk of the reader's manipulating a particular text to meet his or her vested interests. In this regard, Thiselton again takes up the issue of socio–critical and socio–pragmatic readings. He rightly asks:

[I]f interests determine how we read the text, and if any interest represents as good a candidate as another, how can biblical texts do more than instrumentally serve interests rather than shape, determine, and evaluate them? How can they unmask oppressive interests if the status of a socio–critical reading is ranked no higher than a socio–pragmatic reading which serves the interests of the oppressor?[110]

The above discussion shows that the effort to find determinant meaning is still relevant on theological and hermeneutical grounds. One should not abandon the idea of a correct understanding of the text despite the problems involved.

Clines' recent statement on the ideology of the writers of the text suggests that they (writers) write with some purpose or interest.[111] In this context, Clines writes:

Writers do not, on the whole, write their texts just for the fun of it; they have a case to put, an argument to advance, or an opponent to overcome. And since the name for their case, their argument, their position, is their "ideology", I say that their text is a realisation of their ideology, a performance of their investment in their ideology...'[112]

---

[107] Goldingay, *Models for Interpretation of Scripture,* p. 52; cf. 'How Far Do Readers Make Sense?: Interpreting Biblical Narrative', *Them.* 18 (1993), p. 8.
[108] Goldingay, *Models for Interpretation,* p. 50.
[109] Goldingay, 'How Far Do Readers Make Sense', p. 8.
[110] Thiselton, *New Horizons,* pp. 602–3; emphasis original.
[111] See D. J. A. Clines, *Interested Parties: The Ideology of Writers and Readers of the Hebrew Bible* (GCT 1; Sheffield: Sheffield Academic Press, 1995).
[112] Ibid., p. 23.

As the title suggests, the main interest of his book is to expose the ideology of the writers and readers of the Hebrew Bible. In order to resist the 'ideology' of the text, he reads 'against the grain of the text' and thereby to a certain extent he acknowledges that there *is* a grain. He notes: 'Reading against the grain implies that there *is* a grain. It implies that texts have designs on their readers and wish to *persuade* [italics mine] them of something or other. It implies that there are ideologies inscribed in texts and that the readers implied by texts share the texts' ideologies'.[113]

Consequently, Clines admits that writers write with some intention or purpose. My main argument here is to show that texts are written with a certain purpose or communicative intention. One might call it the writers' ideology. Whether one agrees or not with the text's ideology is another question. Without this acknowledgement one cannot read against the grain of the text. If there is not a grain, how can one read against it?[114]

1.7 A Methodological Proposal

As a method, I propose that in order to understand any biblical text we need to take into consideration the following aspects. First of all, we need to look at the final form of the canonical text itself to find out what it tries to communicate. In order to achieve this, one has to be aware as far as possible of the historical, social, cultural, and religious milieu in which the text was shaped. In other words, context is very important. Peter Cotterell and Max Turner emphasise the importance of the communication of language. They argue that 'no string of words can be context–less: that any string is produced by someone, somewhere, somehow'. They further comment 'that language is produced in context by particular people, and both a knowledge of the general context and of the specific individual generating the language

---

[113] Ibid., pp. 206–207.

[114] Sometimes Clines' argument is difficult to follow. After having said the above about the grain of the text, he seems to negate this in his footnote. He writes: 'Strictly, speaking, texts do not have grains any more than they "have" meanings. Authors would like to put grains in their texts, of course, and readers are forever finding grains in texts, even though they are not there... So when I am reading against the grain, I am really reading against the practice of an interpretative community, sometimes even against myself and my own reading. Strictly speaking, the text is not to blame for the thoughts that come into my head when I am reading it, but I am not always speaking strictly; like most people, in everyday speaking and writing I go on ascribing meaning and grain to texts', p. 207, note 38.

is usually involved in the process of discerning meaning'.[115] Secondly, the communicative context of the text is of paramount significance in order to understand the 'motive' behind any writing. Mark G. Brett makes a very clear and useful distinction between 'motives' and 'intention'.[116] He shows that both are separate interpretative goals: *what* an author is trying to convey is communicative intention and *why* it is being said is a motive.[117] Though we can infer the intention of a text from its language and the literary genre in its historical context, we cannot find motives from the text itself since they lie behind the text.[118] In this regard, John Rogerson also notes the importance of setting a text in its wider context of the ancient Near East.[119] At the same time, the interpreter should not let the text be dominated by his or her own agendas too much. The above aspects are effectively summarised by Jeanrond in his methodological proposal for a text–interpretation. Hence, he writes: 'Interpreting a text involves now at least simultaneously a threefold act of interpretation: interpretation of the text, interpretation of the world of the interpreter, and interpretation of the self of the interpreter.'[120] Finally, I think that it is also necessary to understand the particular text from a wider theological perspective. This is important because the Bible has served as scripture and a faith document for the Christian church for centuries. So we need a theological hermeneutic to deal with the text to highlight the religious meaning.

To achieve the above goals we must use various methods which are appropriate to the particular text. In the process of reading, there should be a trialogue between the author, the text and the reader.[121] Moreover, '[t]he interpreter must not only address the text but must allow the text to address him or her'.[122] If one does not allow his or her perspectives to be challenged through the text, that will lead to 'ideological' interpretation.[123] Thiselton aptly observes: 'Without the constraints imposed on meaning by the text's

---

[115] P. Cotterell and M. Turner, *Linguistics and Biblical Interpretation* (London: SPCK, 1989), pp. 41–42; see also Jeanrond, *Text and Interpretation*, p. 76. In similar vein, German feminist Stefan Beyerle calls for a historical–critical feminist exegesis, seeking what did the text mean in its own time. See Beyerle, 'Feministische Theologie und Alttestamentliche Exegese', *BN* 59 (1991), pp. 7–11.

[116] Mark G. Brett, 'Motives and intentions in Genesis 1', *JTS* 42 (1991), pp. 1–16.

[117] Ibid., p. 5.

[118] Ibid., He shows 'lying' to be a typical example for motive.

[119] See Rogerson, *Genesis 1–11*, p. 48.

[120] Jeanrond, *Theological Hermeneutics*, p. 112.

[121] So Osborne, *The Hermeneutical Spiral,* pp. 411–415.

[122] Ibid., p. 413.

[123] Jeanrond, *Theological Hermeneutics*, p. 6.

context or situation and the directedness of the author's utterance, meaning becomes almost infinitely variable and polyvalent.'[124]

Following Umberto Eco, Brett notes two kinds of reader's intentions. The first intention of the reader is to make use of a text for his or her purpose (the *intentio lectoris*), and the other, 'interpretation proper', 'which is the attempt to discover the intentions of a text as a coherent whole (*intentio operis*)'.[125] Accordingly, Brett distinguishes two kinds of readerly 'interests', namely the interpretative interest which involves critical reading of the text (one's interest in sources, genre, intention, material conditions, reception etc.). The other interest is the reader's own particular commitments, purposes, values and ideology.[126] He categorises feminist and other ideological readings under the latter. He argues for instance that feminist criticism is not a method, like any other method in biblical interpretation. 'Strictly, speaking, there is probably no such thing as a distinctive feminist criticism; rather there are a variety of methods and strategies which have been adopted by readers with emancipatory commitments.'[127] Brett's classification is useful. So in our reading we consider feminist criticism not as a method but as an ideology. Being an ideological criticism, its significance is considerably limited. However, it is to be borne in mind that no method in biblical studies is beyond criticism and moreover, each method should be self–critical, if it is to stand the test of time.

Conclusion

Modern thinking has recognized the complex dynamics of reading texts. Both Abrams and Powell have shown this complexity through their literary theories. It is very clear that all discussion on contemporary reading revolves around the question of the location of meaning and the role of the reader in the reading process. This is a pervasive issue: how far do texts bear their own meaning and how far are they free for fresh, 'unintended' meanings? Or how far can one read an interpretation *into* a text rather than deriving an interpretation *from* a text?

We need to ask how 'free' is the reader? Reader–response approaches represent an extreme of freedom. Yet there are constraints of general as well as of theological nature. As Jeanrond pointed out, not only the text but also the 'particular acts of reading' need scrutiny. He asks:

---

[124] Thiselton, *New Horizons*, p. 50.

[125] Brett, 'The Future of Reader Criticisms?', p. 25.

[126] Ibid., pp. 25–26; cf. also Alter and Kermode, *The Literary Guide to the Bible*, pp. 4–5. They exclude methods such as feminist, psycho–analytic, deconstructive and Marxist from their analysis due to their ideological nature and particular commitments.

[127] Ibid., p. 26.

What happens to our pre–understanding in the act of reading? Do we allow our pre–understanding to be challenged in the act of reading or do
we impose it uncritically and violently on the text?... it is essential for
any reader who is keen to proceed to a more adequate understanding of a
text to become aware of the possibility of distortions in the act of reading.[128]

The other constraint imposed upon the reader is of a theological nature.
That is the constraint imposed by the use of the text in and by religious
communities. They consider the biblical text as revelation of God and it
functions as scripture not only in their belief and practice[129] but also it is
the basis for the formulation of doctrine and belief. So as a faith document
it is inevitable to recognize the three factors namely author, text and reader
in the meaning–making process. The 'reader' should include not only the
academic community, but also the ecclesiastical community.

Feminists employ almost every hermeneutical method such as historical
criticism and social–scientific criticism to read the text from a feminist perspective. By and large the three main feminist scholars whom we are dealing with in this work often use ordinary scholarly methods. Yet they are
motivated by their special feminist concerns. In hermeneutical terms some
feminists are socio–critics who critique the patriarchal and androcentric culture (Trible and Bird) whereas others, like Bal, Rashkow and Fewell, are
socio–pragmatists. They use the text to communicate their concerns, adapting postmodern reader–response approaches to read the text.

Our study claims that no paradigm shift in method has taken place in
biblical interpretation as post–modern interpreters have claimed. We have
argued that any single method is inadequate to bring out the full potentiality
of a text. A single method can highlight only certain aspects of meaning.
However,we acknowledge some value in each method. So we propose a
comprehensive method, taking into account the role of the author, the text
and the reader. As a religious text, it is also important to underscore the nature of the biblical text and its textuality. Theologians, moreover, will want
to recognise the role of the Spirit in reading. In the reading process, our aim
should be to understand the determinant meaning of the text rather than to
produce polyvalent readings.

We have seen that like other ideological readings, feminist criticism is
not an interpretative method, but only an ideological commitment brought
to the text. If feminist criticism claims to be beyond criticism then it drives
itself into isolation. Along with traditional readings, feminist–readings too
need self–criticism. Otherwise they will fall into the category of socio–

---

[128] Jeanrond, *Theological Hermeneutics*, p. 6.

[129] Cf. B. S. Childs, *Old Testament Theology in a Canonical Context* (London: SCM
Press, 1985), pp. 20–27.

pragmatic criticism rather than socio–critical hermeneutics. Have feminists themselves been side–tracked from their original goal of critiquing male–dominated culture to establishing an exclusive feminist culture (even excluding black feminists, as we shall see) to cherish and promote their own interests?   Is this not similar in kind to male oppression? If this model of feminist liberation leads to the marginalization and oppression of other groups (whether black women or males), can feminist readings be a part of liberation hermeneutics?

CHAPTER 2

Feminist Readings of the Old Testament: A Brief Survey of History and Hermeneutical Approaches

2.1 Brief Survey of History

The aim of this section is to survey the history of feminist readings of the Bible. Although the feminist interpretation of the Bible has only developed as a distinct discipline in recent years, its history can be traced back to the 18th century. The term 'feminism' or 'feminist' was not used until 1895. It was first used in print in a British Journal named, *The Athenaeum* in April 27[1]. By this time women were generally very much more aware of their place and role in society and in the church than during the centuries before. They had started thinking critically about the status that had been assigned to them by the male world. Moreover, women from different backgrounds started questioning the traditional Scriptural interpretations concerning their societal and ecclesiastical roles.

The following women were the pioneers in raising objections in relation to their role and status in Church and society. These women offered their own interpretation on particular Scriptural passages that seemed to sanction their secondary role in Society.

2.1.1 Judith Sargent Murray (1751–1820)

In a sense feminist history during the 18th and 19th century was by and large a history of the American women's struggle for their rights in Society. A Massachusetts woman named Judith Sargent Murray, penned an article entitled 'On the Equality of the Sexes', in the Massachusetts magazine in 1790.[2] In her work she sought more educational opportunities for women since they too had been given 'minds as sharp as men's' by their Creator despite certain claims of male superiority in intelligence allegedly based on Scriptural evidence.

---

[1] Alice S. Rossi, 'Preface: Feminist Lives and Works', in *The Feminist Papers: From Adams to de Beauvoir,* (ed.) A. S. Rossi (New York: Columbia University Press, 1973), pp. xii–xiii.
[2] *The Feminist Papers,* p. 16.

Murray reinterpreted the most common passages in the creation narratives that were used against women as depicting their 'weak' nature by
male interpreters. She considered the act of woman in eating the fruit, not
as a 'sensual appetite', 'but merely by a desire of adorning her mind; a
laudable ambition fired her soul, and a thirst for knowledge impelled the
predilection so fatal in its consequences'.[3] She interpreted that 'he [Adam]
was influenced by no other motive than a bare pusillanimous attachment to
a woman!'[4] Through her reinterpretation she wanted to establish that
woman is not subordinate; rather she is more intelligent than and superior to
man. Though Murray did not use the term 'feminist', in a way her interpretation sowed the seeds of feminist interpretation of the Bible.

2.1.2 Sarah (1792–1873) and Angelina Grimké (1805–1879)

The Grimké sisters were born in an upper class slave owning family in
South Carolina. They fought against the institution of slavery, delivered
anti–slavery lectures and wrote on the equality of the sexes. Although
Church and clergy tried to stop their teaching and lectures in public because
they were female, in her letter[5] Sarah pointed out that 'men and women
were CREATED EQUAL; they are both moral and accountable beings, and
whatever is *right* for man to do, is *right* for woman'.[6]

Citing biblical characters, Angelina Grimké also spoke on women's
strength, dignity and moral courage to be the leaders of the people. She had
pointed to the valiant women of the Bible such as Miriam the prophetess,
Deborah the Judge, Huldah the prophetess, Esther the Queen and together
with others from the New Testament. Although the state laws prohibited it,
she appealed to Christian women to teach slaves to read. She found biblical
sanction in the book of Exodus chapter 1 for her appeal. It is worth quoting
her remarks at length:

> What was the conduct of Shiphrah and Puah, when the king of Egypt is-
> sued his cruel mandate, with regard to the Hebrew children? *"They
> feared God* and did *not* as the king of Egypt commanded them, but saved

---

[3] J. S. Murray, 'On the Equality of the Sexes', (*The Massachusetts Magazine*, March
1790, pp. 132–135 & April 1790, pp. 223–226) compiled and cited in *Feminist Papers*,
p. 23. Many modern feminist biblical scholars like Trible and others have interpreted
this passage exactly like Murray. See P. Trible, *God and the Rhetoric of Sexuality*
(OBT), hereafter *God and the Rhetoric*; (Fortress Press: 1978/ London: SCM Press,
1992), p. 110.

[4] *The Feminist Papers*, p. 24. Cf. Trible, p. 113.

[5] Sarah Grimké, 'Letters on the Equality of the Sexes and the Condition of Women'
(Boston, 1837, pp. pp. 14–121) as cited in *The Feminist Papers*, pp. 306. ff.

[6] Ibid., p. 308; capitalization original.

the men children alive". Did these *women* do right in disobeying that monarch? *"Therefore* (says the sacred text,) *God dealt well* with them, and made them houses."[7]

Finding positive tradition about women in the biblical texts has become one of the prominent methods of feminist biblical hermeneutics today.[8] So Angelina Grimke's contribution of positive tradition to feminist readings so early in the 19th century is very remarkable. Her work may be regarded as a forerunner to contemporary feminist approaches.

Almost all modern feminist writers point out the pejorative sense in considering woman as a 'help–meet' rather than a companion or an equal. Exactly the same point was brought out by Grimké more than a hundred years ago. She refuted the common interpretation of woman as a 'helpmeet to man' (Gen 2: 18) and she rendered this term as 'companion', 'co–worker' and an 'equal'.[9]

2.1.3 Frances Willard (1839–1898)

Frances Willard was for a long time President of the Women's Christian Temperance Union. She had charged that male interpreters approached the texts with biases, and hence she questioned the scientific objectivity of biblical criticism. She held that male interpreters were responsible for the inferior status of women contrary to the message of the Bible. So she proposed a 'locus of a theology of liberation for women'. She phrased it as 'Bible–precept principles'. She wrote: '[A]s the world becomes more deeply permeated by the principles of Christ's Gospel, methods of exegesis are revised. The old texts stand there just as before, but we interpret them less narrowly'.[10] So for Willard, 'Jesus the Emancipator' was the central norm by which to judge the Scripture.[11]

---

[7] Angelina Grimké, 'Appeal to the Christian Women of the South', *The Anti–Slavery Examiner* 1 (1836), 16–26, as cited in *Feminist Papers,* pp. 299–300, emphasis original.

[8] See Trible, *God and the Rhetoric,* Mary Hayter, *The New Eve in Christ; The Use and Abuse of the Bible in the Debate about Women in the Church* (London: SPCK, 1987).

[9] A. Grimké, 'Letters to Catherine Beecher' (Boston: Isaac Knap, 1836), pp. 103–121) as compiled in *The Feminist Papers,* p. 321. See for the same view point, 'Sarah's letter', p. 308. There she treats woman as a 'companion'. Cf. Trible, p. 90. What the modern feminist biblical scholarship brought out recently, had already been brought to light by those lay women preachers a century before.

[10] Frances E. Willard, *Woman in the Pulpit* (Chicago: Woman's Temperance Publication, 1889), p. 23, as cited by Gifford, 'American Women and the Bible: The Nature of Woman as a Hermeneutical Issue', in *Feminist Perspectives on Biblical Scholarship,* (ed.) Adela Yarbro Collins (Chico/California: Scholars Press, 1985), p. 26.

[11] By and large the same principle is adapted by the contemporary feminist liberation theologians to assess the validity of Scripture. For instance, Rosemary Radford Ruether

2.1.4 Elizabeth Cady Stanton (1815–1902)

As years went by, critical awareness became much more developed among women. This was also due to the emergence of Biblical Criticism in Germany and its spread to the other side of the Atlantic. As a result the concept of the Bible as the Word of God and its supernatural inspiration was questioned. The Bible began to be treated as any other literary work. This assumption has enabled many feminists to pursue their task easily. They began to question the authority of the Bible in relation to the condition of women.[12]

Elizabeth Cady Stanton was the first woman who offered feminist readings using the above presupposition though she was not well versed in higher criticism. She was a leading theorist and champion of the women's movement in the 19th century. With the initiative of Stanton, a 'revising committee' was formed to analyse the major texts of the Bible that deal with women. That committee of twenty woman suffragists wrote commentaries on different sections of the Bible, which were published in 1895 and 1898 with the title *The Woman's Bible*.[13] They offered their interpretation in defending the status of women.

Stanton interpreted the creation narrative in Genesis 1 as a simultaneous creation of both sexes. Moreover, she also treated the plural subject in Gen. 1: 26 as a clear evidence of the presence of feminine elements in creation along with the Father and the Son.[14] Hence she wrote: 'If language has any meaning, we have in these texts a plain declaration of the existence of the feminine element in the God–head, equal in power and glory with the masculine.'[15] For Stanton the priestly account of creation was only acceptable and satisfactory to both sexes because of its egalitarian outlook and the presence of 'the Heavenly Mother and Father'. She considered the creation

---

takes the prophetic trajectories as the biblical basis of liberation. She writes: 'the prophetic principles, more fully understood, imply a rejection of every elevation of one social group against others as image and agent of God, every use of God to justify social domination and subjugation'. See Ruether, *Sexism and God Talk* (London: SCM Press, 1983), p. 23; 'Feminism and Patriarchal Religion: Principles of ideological critique of the Bible', *JSOT* 22 (1982), pp. 54–66. See also Elisabeth Schüssler Fiorenza, *In Memory of Her: A Feminist Theological Reconstruction of Christian Origins* (New York: Cross Road Publishing, 1985), p. 32. For Fiorenza, women's experience is the core of feminist hermeneutics.

[12] See Carolyn De Swarte Gifford, 'American Women and the Bible', pp. 22–23.

[13] See Dorothy C. Bass, 'Women's Studies and Biblical Studies: An Historical Perspective', *JSOT* 22 (1982), pp. 10–11.

[14] Elizabeth Cady Stanton, *The Woman's Bible,* Part I & II (original 1895 and 1898), reprint, Salem, New Hampshire, Ayer Company Publishers Inc, 1988, p. 14. She also thinks that the creation account in chapter 1 is 'in harmony with science, common sense, and the experience of mankind in natural laws,...' (see *Woman's Bible,* p. 20).

[15] Ibid.

account in Gen. chapter 2 as a purposeful later creation for the subordination of women. So she wrote: 'It is evident that some wily writer, seeing the perfect equality of man and woman in the first chapter, felt it important for the dignity and dominion of man to effect women's subordination in some way.'[16]

Because of a lack of theological depth, many of Stanton's observations and interpretations seem to be problematic. For instance, the source critics date the Yahwistic account as the earlier one, contrary to Stanton's argument. Again, her treatment of the first plural subject in Gen. 1:26 as an indication for the inclusion of feminine in the God–head also raises difficulties. Despite these, her attempt to challenge the traditional interpretation inspired many feminists to follow her lead, though only after many decades.

Apart from Stanton other women writers had also interpreted the creation narrative in *the Woman's Bible*. Supporting Stanton, Ellen Battelle Dieltrick also takes the first account of creation as authentic.[17] Hence she wrote: 'My own opinion is that the second story was manipulated by some Jew, in an endeavor to give "heavenly authority" for requiring a woman to obey the man she married.'[18] However, Lillie Devereux Blake finds positive elements in the Yahwistic account.[19]

2.1.5 Margaret Brackenbury Crook

Margaret B. Crook was the first female biblical scholar who wrote on the position of women. After Cady Stanton's *The Woman's Bible,* no significant effort was made by feminists to interpret the Bible for a long time. In 1964 Crook, then professor of Religion and Biblical Literature at Smith College published a book entitled *Women and Religion.*[20] It was the beginning of the second wave of feminist criticism.

Crook surveyed the position of women in Judaism and Christianity as reflected in the biblical account. She employed interdisciplinary approaches such as Church History, Theology, Worship Studies and Comparative Religion to produce feminist readings. In the introduction of her book she notes the masculine monopoly in religion. She writes:

> A masculine monopoly in religion begins when Miriam raises her indignant question: "Does the Lord speak only through Moses?" Since then, in all three of the great religious groups stemming from the land and books of Israel—Judaism, Christianity, and Islam—men have formulated

---

[16] Ibid., p. 21.
[17] *The Woman's Bible,* p. 18; cf. Stanton, p. 18; cf. Stanton above.
[18] Ibid.
[19] Ibid., p. 21.
[20] Gifford, p. 31.

doctrine and established systems of worship offering only meager opportunity for expression of the religious genius of womankind.[21]

Although she claims that the intent of her work is not 'feminist', nevertheless, from the nature of her work it is very clear that it is indeed feminist. However, she envisioned a 'balanced partnership' of women and men in the near future.

2.1.6 Simone de Beauvoir and Kate Millet

Simone de Beauvoir and Kate Millet strongly argued in their books that the Bible is permeated with patriarchy. Although neither was a feminist biblical writer, they have argued their case in referring to the creation accounts. Beauvoir's *The Second Sex*[22] (1949) and Millet's *Sexual Politics* (1969) are two classic feminist writings of the period. Both of them believe that the Bible is irredeemably patriarchal. Millet for instance writes:

> Patriarchy has God on its side. One of its most effective agents of control is the powerfully expeditious character of its doctrines as to the nature and origin of the female and the attribution to her alone of the dangers and evils it imputes to sexuality... Patriarchal religion and ethics tend to lump the female and sex together as if the whole burden of the onus and stigma it attaches to sex were the fault of the female alone.[23]

She considers the classical tale of 'Pandora's Box' and the biblical story of the fall as the two leading myths of western culture. As a result, she interprets the story of the creation of woman in a mythological fashion. To Millet the story of the eating of the fruit is a narrative that symbolises how the first couple invented sexual intercourse.[24]

The above two books established the idea of patriarchy in the minds of the readers more strongly than ever before.

Since 1970, a feminist reawakening has been taking place around the globe. In 1970, the female members of the Society of Biblical Literature have asserted the necessity for a feminist interpretation of the Bible. Since then, an enormous amount of literature has been published in the area. Unlike the previous period, many feminists trained in biblical scholarship and theology have entered the scene.

---

[21] Margaret Brackenbury Crook, *Women and Religion* (Boston: Beacon, 1964), p. 1, as cited by Gifford, p. 31.

[22] S. Beauvoir, *The Second Sex*, (trans.) H. M. Parshley (London: Jonathan Cape, 1953).

[23] Kate Millet, *Sexual Politics* (London: Virago, 1977), p. 51, original 1969.

[24] Ibid., p. 53.

During the centennial of SBL in 1980, there was a panel discussion on 'The Effects of Women's Studies on Biblical Studies'.[25] Katharine Doob Sakenfeld pointed out five effects of women's studies on Biblical studies. They are:

i. A systematic inquiry into the status and role of women in ancient Israelite culture.

ii. The rediscovery of long–overlooked traditions (e.g. the story of the daughters of Zelophehad).

iii. The reassessment of the meaning and message of the famous Old Testament texts, dealing with women (e.g. Genesis 2–3).

iv. An alertness to the variety of imagery for God in the Old Testament.

v. The discussion of language–about God.[26]

In a similar vein, the German feminist scholar Eva Renate Schmidt suggests some possible criteria for feminist exegesis. They are: all biblical texts and their interpretations must be suspected of patriarchal falsification; patriarchal texts may be corrected by non–patriarchal texts; and neglected texts may be highlighted. In addition, feminist exegesis must highlight texts concerning women's suffering and oppression. Feminist exegesis also has the prophetic task of showing how male language is always used for God.[27]

2.2 Hermeneutical Approaches

Feminists have evolved polyvalent approaches to reading the Bible. Although they utilise various hermeneutical methods, their individual hermeneutical strategies differ from one another. Their overall method is essentially that an individual's theological perspective on the biblical traditions determines his or her hermeneutical approach to the text. Some for instance, presuppose that the Bible is permeated with patriarchy and therefore develop a rejectionist stance. On the other hand, some still believe that the Bible itself can offer a critique of patriarchal domination and hence develop a revisionary approach.

---

[25] See P. Trible, (Guest ed.) 'The Effects of Women's Studies on Biblical studies', *JSOT* 22 (1982), pp. 3–71. This whole issue discusses the various aspects of feminist studies, cf. K. Doob Sakenfeld, 'Feminist Uses of Biblical Materials', in *Feminist Interpretation of the Bible*, (ed.) L. M. Russel (Oxford/New York: Basil Blackwell, 1985), pp. 55–64.

[26] K. D. Sakenfeld, 'Old Testament Perspectives: Methodological Issues', *JSOT* 22 (1982), pp. 13–20.

[27] E. R. Schmidt, 'Mögliche Kriterien für eine feministische Bibelauslegung', in *Feministisch gelesen* (ed.) E. R. Schmidt *et al.* (Stuttgart: Kreuz, 1988), pp. 12–16 [14–15].

Since I think Carolyn Osiek's categorisation of feminist hermeneutical alternatives[28] is simplistic and inadequate to explain the complex nature of feminist hermeneutics we will follow some of the present hermeneutical categories as used in the *Postmodern Bible* to bring all the feminist hermeneutical approaches together. Before turning to them, however, it is interesting to note that Jonathan Culler provides still another useful categorization of feminist criticism.[29] He classifies the feminist reading process into three 'levels' or 'moments'. In the first 'level', the criticism is focused on the concern of the woman character and her experiences. The second 'level' of feminist criticism aims 'to make readers—men and women—question the liberating and political assumptions on which their reading has been based'.[30] In the third 'level' women readers explore alternative readings. By and large these levels can align with our three categories.

2.2.1 Hermeneutics of recuperation

The *Postmodern Bible* says of this position: '[T]he hermeneutics of recuperation remains thoroughly invested in the economy of truth and offers no critique of the philosophical grounds of the Bible's truth claims.'[31] In this approach feminist interpreters aim to recover the biblical texts from patriarchal mistranslations and misinterpretations. Through their rereading they attempt to 'reclaim' the texts positive to women. Trible, for instance, finds the 'depatriarchalizing principle' at work in the Scripture itself against the patriarchal culture. She writes: 'I affirm that the intentionality of biblical faith, as distinguished from a general description of biblical religion, is neither to create nor to perpetuate patriarchy but rather to function as salvation for both women and men.'[32] She has adapted the method of rereading to depatriarchalising the text. So Trible and others (Phyllis Bird, Joy Elasky Fleming, Mary Phil Korsak, Helen Schüngel–Straumann, Luise Schottroff, Mary Evans,[33] Mary Hayter, Grace Emmerson) have attempted to reread the famous texts used against women (Gen. 1–3).

---

[28] She classifies feminist hermeneutical approaches under five five categories as rejectionist, loyalist, revisionist, sublimationist and liberationist. See Carolyn Osiek, 'The Feminist and the Bible: Hermeneutical Alternatives' in *Feminist Perspectives on Biblical Scholarship*, pp. 97–105. For a recent different classification, see E. Schüssler Fiorenza, *But She Said: Feminist Practices of Biblical Interpretation* (Boston: Beacon Press, 1992), pp. 20–50.

[29] J. Culler, *On Deconstruction: Theory and Criticism after Structuralism* (London: Routledge & Kegan Paul, 1983), pp. 43–64.

[30] Ibid., p. 51.

[31] *Postmodern Bible*, p. 246.

[32] Trible, 'Depatriarchalizing in Biblical Interpretation', *JAAR* 41 (1973), p. 31.

[33] M. Evans, *Women in the Bible* (Exeter: Paternoster Press, 1983).

As part of the recuperative strategy, Trible and some other feminists try to employ a hermeneutics of retrieval by which they want to bring into focus women role models from the Old Testament. J. Cheryl Exum was Associate Professor of Biblical Studies at Boston College. At present she lectures in the Department of Biblical Studies at Sheffield University. She has adapted literary critical analysis in her feminist exegesis and has done a great deal of research on literary approaches to the Bible. Recognising the prevailing patriarchal nature of the Scriptures, she brings out counter pictures through the process of close reading (e.g. the women of Exodus, Ruth, Esther and Judith). So, recognising the prevailing patriarchal nature of the Scripture, Exum provides 'positive portrayals of women'.[34] She writes: 'Within the admittedly patriarchal context of the biblical literature, we find strong countercurrents of affirmation of women: stories that show women's courage, strength, faith, ingenuity, talents, dignity and worth.'[35] Trible aims to unearth the gynomorphic images to depict God in the Bible as a recuperative strategy. Phyllis A. Bird has also read many biblical texts from a feminist perspective. Though her perspective is feminist, her methodology is traditional historical criticism. In her works she attempts to recover the 'hidden history of women'. She has contributed many articles in the area of women's status in early Israel and their position in the Israelite cult.[36] Furthermore, Trible has also attempted to 'recover a neglected history' of abused women, recounting their 'tales of terror *in memoriam*',[37] thereby offering a hermeneutics of remembrance.

---

[34] See J. Cheryl Exum, 'You Shall Let Every Daughter Live: A Study of Exodus 1: 8–2:10', in *The Bible and Feminist Hermeneutics*, (ed.) M. A. Tolbert (Chico, California: Scholars Press, 1983), pp. 63–82; Exum, '"Mother in Israel": A Familiar Figure Reconsidered', in *Feminist Interpretation of the Bible* (ed.) L. M. Russel (Philadelphia: Westminster Press, 1985), pp. 73–85, cf. Trible, 'Bringing Miriam out of the Shadows', *BibRev* 5 (1989), pp. 14–25, 34.

[35] J. C. Exum, 'The Mothers of Israel: The Patriarchal Narratives from a Feminist Perspective', *BibRev* 2 (1986), p. 60. Note her later position in our following discussion.

[36] See Phyllis A. Bird, 'Images of Women in the Old Testament', in *The Bible and Liberation,* (ed.) Norman K. Gottwald (New York: Orbis, 1983), pp. 252–306, (original 1974 in *Religion and Sexism,* (ed.) Ruether; '"Male and Female He created Them": Gen. 1:27b in the Context of the Priestly Account of Creation' (hereafter 'Male and Female'), *HTR*, 74 (1981), pp. 129–159; 'To play the Harlot': An Inquiry into an Old Testament Metaphor in *Gender and Difference in Ancient Israel,* (ed.) Peggy L. Day (Minneapolis: Fortress Press, 1989), pp. 75–94.; 'The Place of Women in Israelite Cultus', in *Ancient Israelite Religion,* (ed.) Patrick D. Miller Jr *et al.* (Philadelphia: Fortress Press, 1987), pp. 397–419.

[37] Trible, *Texts of Terror: Literary—Feminist Readings of Biblical Narratives* (London: SCM Press, 1992), published first by Fortress Press, 1984; cf. Exum, 'Murder They Wrote: Ideology and the Manipulation of Female Presence in Biblical Narrative', *USQR* 43 (1989), pp. 19–39.

2.2.2 Hermeneutics of suspicion

If the hermeneutics of recuperation is text–affirming, the hermeneutics of suspicion 'does not presuppose the feminist authority and truth of the Bible, but takes as its starting point the assumption that biblical texts and their interpretations are androcentric and serve patriarchal functions'.[38] However, Schüssler Fiorenza does not want to reject the Bible as a whole, since she thinks a 'dualistic hermeneutical strategy' can be developed from the Bible. In other words, she locates two contradictory facts concerning women in the Bible. That is, on the one hand, the Bible has promoted patriarchal and androcentric values. On the other hand, 'the Bible has also served to inspire and authorise women and other nonpersons in their struggles against patriarchal oppression'.[39]

Carol Meyers questions the Bible's authority: 'Like most scholars, I do not believe the texts are the direct word of God, ... I believe it is a record of the religious beliefs developed by a society struggling to understand God and the world.'[40] Yet she reads the text more positively.[41] In similar vein, Alice Laffey writes: 'Since the biblical texts are historically conditioned and were produced by patriarchal society, they are patriarchal in character. They must, therefore, be approached with suspicion'.[42] However, she finds that the Bible has liberation potential towards freedom and equality. Recognising the texts' patriarchal orientation, both Meyers and Laffey offer an

---

[38] Elisabeth Schüssler Fiorenza, *Bread Not Stone: The Challenge of Feminist Biblical Interpretation* (Boston: Beacon Press, 1984), p. 15, cf. Culler, p. 51.

[39] Schüssler Fiorenza, 'Transforming the Legacy of The Woman's Bible', in *Searching the Scriptures: A Feminist Introduction*, vol. 1., (ed.) Schüssler Fiorenza (London: SCM Press, 1994), pp. 1–24 [p. 50], published first by (New York: Crossroad Publishing Company, 1993).

[40] William Sasser, 'All About Eve', *DM* (Sept–Oct 1994), p. 3.

[41] See Meyers, '"To Her Mother's House": Considering a Counterpart to the Israelite *Bêt 'ab*', in *The Bible and the Politics of Exegesis* (Gottwald Festschrift), (eds.) D. Jobling *et al.* (Cleveland: Ohio, 1991), pp. 39–51; 'Of Drums and Damsels: Women's Performance in Ancient Israel', *BA* 54 (1991), pp. 16–27; 'Gender Imagery in the Song of Songs', *HAR* 10 (1986), pp. 209–223; 'Returning Home: Ruth 1: 8 and the Gendering of the Book of Ruth', in *A Feminist Companion to Ruth,* pp. 85–114; 'The Hannah Narrative in Feminist Perspective', in *A Feminist Companion to Samuel and Kings,* pp. 93–104; 'Everyday Life: Women in the Period of the Hebrew Bible', in *The Women's Bible Commentary,* (eds.) C. A. Newsome *et al.,* Westminster: John Knox/ London: SPCK, 1992). pp. 244–251; 'The Creation of Patriarchy in the West: A Consideration of Judeo–Christian Tradition', in *Foundations of Gender Inequality,* (ed.) A. Zagarell (Kalamazoo: New Issues Press, 1994), pp. 1–36; 'Women and the Domestic Economy of Early Israel', in *Women's Earliest Records: From Ancient Egypt and Western Asia,* (ed.) B. S. Lesko (BJS 166; Atlanta: Scholars Press, 1989), pp. 265–281.

[42] Alice Laffey, *Wives, Harlots and Concubines: The Old Testament in Feminist Perspective* (London: SPCK, 1990), original, *An Introduction to the Old Testament: A Feminist Perspective* (Philadelphia: Fortress Press, 1988).

egalitarian reading of the creation accounts using their social–scientific and literary methods respectively. Meyers looks behind the text and unearths the social world to locate the biblical woman. Laffey, however, finds a liberation perspective against patriarchy operating within the scripture itself.

2.2.3 Hermeneutics of resistance

The third approach is an ideological reading, 'a deliberate effort to read against the grain—of texts, of disciplinary norms, of traditions, of cultures'.[43] In other words, '[r]esistance readings demonstrate the fundamental openness of texts and how meaning cannot be determined absolutely (that is, meaning cannot be decontexualised) but is itself resistant to ultimate or final interpretation'.[44] In the context of feminist criticism Judith Fetterly writes: 'The first act of a feminist critic is to become a resisting rather than an assenting reader and, by this refusal to assent, to begin the process of exorcising the male mind that has been implanted in us'.[45] Many, perhaps most postmodern feminist readings may be categorised as a hermeneutics of resistance. In this reading strategy, feminists apply various hermeneutical methods such as Structuralism, literary criticism, semiotics, narratology, intertextuality, psycho–analytic criticism, reader–response criticism, deconstruction, and even in some cases certain eclectic methods combining two or more methods together.

The feminist readings of Mieke Bal, Ilana Pardes, Ilona Rashkow, Danna Nolan Fewell, Pamela J. Milne, Athalya Brenner all project to some degree or other a kind of resistant reading. All these feminists analyse the Hebrew Bible as a thoroughly patriarchal construct, and developing a strategy of response and resistance, and in some cases counter–reading. J. C. Exum argues: 'a feminist critique must, of necessity, read against the grain'.[46] Like Bal, she approaches the text as a 'cultural artifact', not as a religious object. Therefore, her 'intention in this book is neither to recover affirmations of women in the Bible nor to attack the Bible as a sexist document'.[47] Instead, she attempts to 'construct feminist (sub)versions of biblical narratives'. Moreover, most of the feminists for instance consider 'in-

---

[43] *Postmodern Bible,* p. 275.

[44] Ibid., p. 302.

[45] J. Fetterly, *The Resisting Reader: A Feminist Approach to American Fiction* (Bloomington: Indiana University Press, 1978), p. xxii, as cited by Culler, *On Deconstruction,* p. 53.

[46] J. C. Exum, *Fragmented Women: Feminist (Sub)versions of Biblical Narratives* (JSOTS 163; Sheffield: JSOT Press, 1993), p. 11.

[47] Ibid., p. 9.

terpretation to be a *reader's response,* necessarily based on the *reader's* personal input, assumptions, and biases'.[48]

Danna Nolan Fewell, Associate Professor of Old Testament at Perkins School of Theology, Texas, has a keen interest in reading Old Testament narrative texts in literary perspective. Throughout her work one can observe the ideological dimension of narratological interpretation. She has written most of her writings with David M. Gunn in the feminist area.[49]

Athalya Brenner writes at length as a Jewish woman both in Hebrew and in English. She is also the editor of the *Feminist Companion* series being published by Sheffield Academic Press.[50] She examines the social roles of Israelite women by a literary narrative approach. Her study reveals the various roles taken by women in the Old Testament period. She concludes that women always had a secondary status in Israelite society.[51]

2.2.4 Other feminist writers

In addition to the above writers many other feminist scholars have contributed to the feminist readings of the Bible. The American feminist writers have jointly published *The Women's Bible Commentary* covering both the Testaments. Almost all contributors are teaching scholars in the American universities or seminaries. It is an elaborate work with particular attention

---

[48] I. Rashkow, *The Phallacy of Genesis: A Feminist–Psychoanalytic Approach* (Louisville: W/JKP, 1993), p. 110; emphasis original.

[49] Danna Nolan Fewell, 'Feminist Criticism of the Hebrew Bible: Affirmation, Resistance, and Transformation', *JSOT* 39 (1987), pp. 39–65; Fewell & David M. Gunn','Controlling Perspectives: Women, Men, and the Authority of Violence in Judges 4 and 5', *JAAR* 56 (1990), pp. 389–411; 'Tipping the Balance: Sternberg's Reader and the Rape of Dinah', *JBL* 110 (1991), 193–211; *Gender, Power, and Promise: The Subject of the Bible's First Story* (Nashville: Abingdon, 1993); 'Feminist Criticism', in *To Each its Own Meaning: An Introduction to Biblical Interpretations and Their Applications* (eds.) S.L. Mckenzie *et.al.* (Louisville: W/JKP, 1993); 'Genesis 2–3: Women, Men and God', in *Narrative in the Hebrew Bible* (Oxford: OUP, 1993).

[50] See Athalya Brenner, *A Feminist Companion to the Bible* (Sheffield: Sheffield Academic Press, 1993–). Now all 10 volumes are published as follows: *A Feminist Companion to the Song of Songs* (FCB vol. 1., 1993 with an introduction to the series by A. Brenner, the editor), *A Feminist Companion to Genesis* (FCB vol. 2., 1993), *A Feminist Companion to Ruth* (FCB vol. 3., 1993), *A Feminist Companion to Judges* (FCB vol. 4., 1993), *A Feminist Companion to Samuel and Kings* (FCB vol. 5., 1994), *A Feminist Companion to Exodus to Deuteronomy* (FCB vol. 6., 1994), *A Feminist Companion to Esther, Judith and Susanna* (FCB vol. 7., 1995), *A Feminist Companion to the Latter Prophets* (FBC vol. 8., 1995), *A Feminist Companion to Wisdom Literature* (FCB vol. 9., 1995), *and A Feminist Companion to the Hebrew Bible in the New Testament* (FCB vol. 10., 1996).

[51] See Brenner, *The Israelite Woman*; see also Brenner, 'Who's Afraid of Feminist Criticism? Who's Afraid of Biblical Humour? The Case of the Obtuse Foreign Ruler in the Hebrew Bible', *JSOT* 63 (1994), pp. 38–55.

given to feminist concerns. The editors write: 'The *Women's Bible Commentary* is the first comprehensive attempt to gather some of the fruits of feminist biblical scholarship on each book of the Bible in order to share it with the larger community of women who read the Bible.'[52] Different methodological devices are employed in the reconstruction of feminist stories of the Bible in this work.

Mention must be made about the British and European Scene. Already reference has been made to Mieke Bal in the Netherlands. Fokkelien van Dijk–Hemmes taught Hebrew Bible and Women's Studies at Rijksuniversiteit Utrecht. She has written on feminist issues.[53] Mary Hayter, the Deacon at Holy Trinity Church in Cambridge, has expressed a balanced viewpoint in her scholarly work, *The New Eve In Christ: The Use and Abuse of the Bible in the Debate about Women in the Church.* Both Mary Evans and Grace Emmerson have also expressed their moderate stance on feminist concerns in their respective works.[54]

2.2.5 Womanist writers

Mention must be made of another stream within the broader feminist movement who call themselves 'womanist' rather than feminist. Womanists are black feminists who critique main line white feminists for race and class oppression. 'Womanist critics have pointed out that not all men have access to the same kinds of power nor have all women historically embraced each other as sisters, but rather some have been responsible for the oppression of others.'[55] In womanist readings of the Bible, they bring into focus mainly racial and class concerns.

Interpretations of Numbers 12, for example, show how feminists and womanists read the same text with different agenda. In feminist readings Miriam is the victim due to her challenging of Moses' (male) authority.[56] However, in womanist readings Moses' black Cushite wife is the victim and Miriam is the oppressor who opposes Moses because of his marriage to

---

[52] C. A. Newsom and S. H. Ringe (eds.), *The Women's Bible Commentary,* p. xv.

[53] See 'Tamar and the Limits of Patriarchy: Between Rape and Seduction (2 Samuel 13 and Genesis 38)', in *Anti–Covenant: Counter–Reading Women's Lives in the Hebrew Bible* (JSOTS 81; BALS 22), (ed.) M. Bal (Sheffield: Almond Press, 1989).

[54] Mary Evans, *Women in the Bible;* Grace I. Emmerson, 'Women in Ancient Israel', in *The World of the Ancient Israel: Sociological, Anthropological and Political Perspectives,* (ed.) R.E. Clements (Cambridge: CUP 1989), pp. 371–394.

[55] *The Postmodern Bible,* p. 238.

[56] Laffey, *Wives, Harlots and Concubines,* pp. 54–55; Trible, 'Bringing Miriam out of the Shadows', *BibRev* 5 (1989), pp. 14–25 and p. 34.

the black woman.[57] Weems writes: 'But the new woman in the camp was more than an outsider; for Miriam, she was a threat. The Ethiopian woman threatened Miriam's position among her own people.'[58] On the other hand, Trible notes: 'As the people journey to a new site, the power struggle rages. Miriam enters the fray, and for the first time she lacks the company of women. Aaron is her companion, yet in a supporting role.'[59] But Weems argues that Miriam could have found a friend in her Cushite sister–in–Law, if she had made an effort to build a relationship. Probably both readers have over interpreted this passage in order to express their concern. However, my effort here is not to judge the soundness of their exegesis; rather to show how feminists and womanists read the same text with different focus.

Conclusion

Our survey of the history of feminist interpretation of the Bible shows that it predates recent trends in biblical hermeneutics, and is in fact a hermeneutical strategy which began at least two centuries ago. Feminists used many methods beginning with 'feminist proof–texting' to 'feminist critical assessment' and finally reached feminist reinterpretation, in the manner of Willard and Stanton.

In recent decades feminist criticism has grown to be a scholarly discipline. Now it is very conspicuous that there is no single monolithic feminist methodological approach to the Bible. Moreover, our survey reveals that Feminist scholarship is a thoroughly complex hermeneutical approach which consists of various methods and perspectives both on the text and its interpretation.

---

[57] Renita J. Weems, *Just a Sister Away: A Womanist Vision of Women's Relationships in the Bible* (San Diego:Luramedia, 1988), pp. 71–83; see also J. Weems, 'Reading Her Way through the Struggle: African American Women and the Bible' in *The Bible and Liberation: Political and Social hermeneutics*, revised, (eds), Gottwald *et al.,* 1993, pp. 31–50. Womanists do not like to use the term 'feminist'.

[58] Ibid., p. 76.

[59] Trible, 'Miriam out of the Shadows', p. 21.

PART TWO

FEMINIST READINGS OF GENESIS 1–3

CHAPTER 3

Feminist Literary–Readings of the Creation Narratives (Gen. 1–3)

Introduction

In this core section of our work we will analyse feminist readings of Genesis 1–3. The prominent feminist biblical scholars, Phyllis Trible, Carol Meyers and Phyllis A. Bird, will be discussed at considerable length in this section. The above three represent three prominent methodological perspectives, namely literary, social–scientific and historical–critical. We will begin with Trible for two reasons. First of all, Trible is the first feminist biblical scholar who published a full–length study of the creation narratives. So her work has become a classic foundational study in feminist hermeneutics. Secondly, many of the feminist scholars after Trible interact with and build upon her readings. For instance, although Meyers approaches the text from a totally different perspective, she takes on board many of Trible's exegetical conclusions. Bird too interacts with Trible on various issues.

In addition to the above three major feminist biblical scholars, we will also bring the contributions of other minor feminist scholars. For the sake of convenience, they are grouped with the above three. Although they do not strictly share the exact methodological presuppositions of the main writers with whom they are classified, they share to a certain extent some general methodological characteristics of those writers. In some cases, the similarity is superficial, and I admit that the minor writers could have been classified differently. Yet I think, no strict categorisation is possible due to the eclectic and trans–disciplinary nature of feminist readings.

One could further observe that most of the shorter feminist readings are grouped with Trible, under literary readings. This categorisation itself reveals that most of the contemporary feminist readers make use of literary and similar post–modern approaches in order to read the text feministically. In other words, more than the traditional methods, the contemporary hermeneutical approaches have become increasingly useful in facilitating the 'readerly intentions' of feminist as well as other ideological readings.

3.0 Preliminary Remarks

The literary paradigm and the social science paradigm are two of the most important approaches to biblical studies in recent decades. I will be dealing with the second paradigm in our examination of Carol Meyers' work.[1] In this chapter, however, I will look at the first with a special focus on rhetorical criticism, which comes under the generic rubric of literary criticism. In our present nomenclature contemporary literary criticism has nothing to do with the *Literarkritik,* the older paradigm in biblical scholarship. In order to avoid this sort of scholarly confusion, contemporary literary criticism has been termed the 'new literary criticism' in present usage.[2]

3.1 Rhetorical Criticism and the Old Testament

3.1.1 Definition of rhetorical criticism

Rhetorical criticism is as old as Aristotle. Rhetoric is basically the art employed by a speaker to persuade his/her audience. According to Aristotle rhetoric is 'the faculty [power] of discovering in the particular case what are the available means of persuasion'.[3] But in contemporary usage 'rhetoric' has many nuances. Some rhetorical critics for instance are interested in the stylistic or the formal features of a text whereas others will focus on the aspect of 'persuasion' in a text. Yehoshua Gitay defines the study of rhetoric as:

> a pragmatic method of analysis that integrates the three dimensions of a literary work: the author, the text itself, and the audience. The author/speaker establishes his or her thematic goal through the transmission of his or her thought into a text (speech). The listener's/reader's situation, ways of perception, and set of mind are also taken into considera-

---

[1] For a detailed discussion of these approaches see Norman K. Gottwald, *The Hebrew Bible: A Socio–Literary Introduction* (Philadelphia: Fortress Press, 1985), pp. 6–34.

[2] See J. Cheryl Exum and David J. A. Clines, *The New Literary Criticism and the Hebrew Bible.* For a distinction between the two see R. Detweiler and V. K. Robbins, 'From New Criticism to Poststructuralism: Twentieth–century Hermeneutics', pp. 225–226.

[3] Aristotle, *The 'Art' of Rhetoric,* (trans.) H.E. Butler, as cited by Yehoshua Gitay in *To Each its Own Meaning,* p. 136. For a historical review of rhetoric since Homer see Phyllis Trible, *Rhetorical Criticism: Context, Method, and the Book of Jonah,* (ed.) Gene M. Tucker (Minneapolis: Fortress Press, 1994), pp. 5–23. For a survey of the various categories of "Rhetorical Criticism' in the study of the Old Testament see David. M. Howard Jr., 'Rhetorical Criticism in Old Testament Studies', *BBR* 4 (1994), pp. 87–104.

tion by the author/speaker. The discourse is structured and shaped thematically and stylistically in order to capture the audience's interest.[4]

In short, for Gitay rhetorical method is a trilogue between the author, text and the audience. With the above general definition of rhetoric we will move to biblical rhetorical criticism in particular. One of the most comprehensive definitions of the Old Testament biblical 'rhetorical criticism' is given by Alan J. Hauser, in his book *Rhetorical Criticism of the Bible*. He defines rhetorical criticism as:

> a form of literary criticism which uses our knowledge of the conventions of literary composition practised in ancient Israel and its environment to discover and analyse the particular literary artistry found in a specific unit of Old Testament text. This analysis then provides a basis for discussing the message of the text and the impact it had on its audience.[5]

According to this definition, rhetorical critics are expected to comprehend the literary artistry of the biblical writers in order to interpret properly the Old Testament text. We now consider the method of rhetorical criticism in more detail.

3.1.2 Method of rhetorical criticism

The eclectic nature of rhetorical criticism gives room for accommodating different methods. However, 'close reading' of a text is seen as a common feature in every method. Rhetorical critics are interested in the poetical function of the text rather than referential function. So 'the literary work serves as an end in itself— it is valued primarily for its own sake'.[6]

In rhetorical critical readings of the Old Testament, the final form of the text tends to be considered as an entity in itself, with much less attention paid to its previous history or its literary sources or composition. In his presidential address delivered at the annual meeting of the Society of Bibli-

---

[4] Yehoshua Gitay, 'Rhetorical Criticism', in *To Each its Own Meaning,* p. 136. Gitay uses the terms 'rhetorical study' or 'rhetorical analysis' instead of rhetorical criticism.

[5] See Duane F. Watson and Alan J. Hauser, *Rhetorical Criticism of the Bible: A Comprehensive Bibliography with Notes on History and Method* (BIS 4; Leiden: E. J. Brill, 1994), p. 4; see also Martin Kessler, 'A Methodological Setting for Rhetorical criticism', in *Art and Meaning: Rhetoric in Biblical Literature,* (eds.) David J. A. Clines *et al.* (JSOTS 19; Sheffield: JSOT Press, 1982), pp. 1–19.

[6] See M. A. Powell, *The Bible and Modern Literary Criticism,* p. 6. M. H. Abrams in his literary theory classifies the poetical function under 'objective theory', where he analyses the work 'as a self–sufficient entity constituted by its parts in their internal relations, and sets out to judge it solely by criteria intrinsic to its own mode of being'. See M. H. Abrams, *The Mirror and the Lamp,* p. 29.

cal Literature in 1968, James Muilenburg broke fresh ground in the field of
rhetorical criticism. He also showed its *modus operandi* with regard to the
Old Testament texts. He pointed to two important tasks of rhetorical critics.
The first was to 'define the limits or scope of the literary unit, to recognise
precisely where and how it begins and where and how it ends'.[7] This
would enable one to recognise the rhetorical devices in the text. The second concern was to 'recognise the structure of a composition and to discern
the configuration of its component parts... and to note the various rhetorical
devices that are employed for marking... the shifts or breaks in the development of the writer's thought'.[8] In addition to these, other literary features
like theme or plot, chiastic structures, acrostics, word play, inclusio and me-
tonymy would also be taken into consideration.[9]

Now the successors of Muilenburg or the 'Muilenburg School' practise
rhetorical criticism, *mutatis mutandis,* following Muilenburg's original proposal. Though all rhetorical critics focus on literary artistry and on rhetorical devices in a text, there is considerable difference of opinion concerning
the meaning of a text. To some, meaning is the same as authorial intention,
but for others meaning is found in the text, and for still others meaning is
articulated by the readers.[10] For instance, in Muilenburg's proposal there is
scope for grasping the writer's intent and meaning whereas his successors
underscore the need for plurality of meaning in a text.[11] To them 'content
is not author's intent, but only the unique configuration of details that an interpreter would impose on a text'.[12] Moreover, Muilenburg's methodology
is a blend of diachronic and synchronic approaches, a complement to form
criticism, whereas his followers treated it purely as a synchronic discipline.
This change has been effectively noted by Dozeman. Hence he writes:

---

[7] See James Muilenburg, 'Form Criticism and Beyond', *JBL* 88 (1969), p. 9. Gitay
rightly notes that Muilenburg concentrates only on the stylistics of the text, that is just
one aspect of rhetoric, see *supra*.

[8] Ibid., p. 10.

[9] For details see Watson and Hauser, pp. 9–14. See also George A. Kennedy, *New Testament Interpretation through Rhetorical Criticism* (North Carolina: University of
North Carolina Press, 1984), pp. 33–38. Trible provides useful guidelines for the practice of rhetorical criticism.. She lists the following factors: beginning with the text,
background readings, acquaintance with rhetorical terms, close examination of the features of the text (like beginning and ending, repetition of words, phrases, and sentences,
types of discourse, design and structure, plot development, character portrayals, syntax,
particles etc.). See *Rhetorical Criticism*, pp. 101–106.

[10] For a discussion of various types of rhetorical criticism see Trible, *Rhetorical Criticism,* pp. 55–84.

[11] See Muilenburg, p. 9; see also Trible, *God and the Rhetoric*, pp. 8–11. For a detailed
comparison and contrast between Muilenburg and his followers see Thomas B. Dozeman, 'O.T Rhetorical Criticism', in *ABD* vol. 5 (Auckland: Doubleday, 1992), pp. 714–
715.

[12] See Dozeman, p. 714.

By shifting rhetorical criticism away from form criticism and placing it under literary criticism, the 'Muilenburg school' abandons the tradition–historical aspect of Muilenburg's work, so that rhetorical criticism becomes a method which only examines the present or final form of biblical texts.[13]

From the above distinction we can broadly classify the present rhetorical criticism under literary or 'new criticism'. At present, rhetorical criticism is increasingly moving towards a reader–oriented approach. Accordingly, M. A. Powell considers rhetorical criticism to be 'a pragmatic approach to literature that seeks to understand the means through which literary works achieve particular effects on their readers'.[14] Trible has classified the various types of rhetorical criticism under five perspectives. They are: the traditional perspective (discovering the means of persuasion), the experiential perspective (focusing on the experiences, insights and judgements of the critic), the dramaturgical perspective (focusing on symbol as the core of rhetoric–shift from persuasion to motive), the sociological perspective (focusing on the interrelationship between society and communication), and the post modern perspective (focusing on the plurality of meanings).[15]

There are a considerable number of works which have employed rhetorical criticism in analysing the Old Testament texts. Phyllis Trible, a student of Muilenburg, is known to be one of the most effective practitioners of rhetorical criticism among feminist writers on the Old Testament. Both of her books[16] have been widely read and attracted scholarly attention. Her latest work, *Rhetorical Criticism,* provides an excellent rhetorical analysis of the book of Jonah along with an elaborate discussion on different models of rhetorical analysis. These days almost all literary critics pay attention to the artistic and rhetorical aspects of the text even if they are not themselves primarily regarded as rhetorical critics. So the scope of the rhetorical reading of the text has been greatly increased during recent decades.[17]

---

[13] Ibid.

[14] M. A. Powell, p. 10. See also p. 6. Here he comments on the development of literary criticism at the beginning of the twentieth century from an expressive mode of criticism focusing on the author in the creation of meaning, to a pragmatic reader–oriented mode of criticism at the end of this century.

[15] Trible, *Rhetorical Criticism,* pp. 57–61. Trible points out that all the above discussed perspectives have been employed in biblical rhetorical criticism..

[16] Trible, *God and the Rhetoric* and *Texts of Terror.*

[17] For a collection of essays covering the whole Hebrew Bible with rhetorical methods, J. J. Jackson and M. Kessler, *Rhetorical Criticism: Essays in Honor of James Muilenburg* (Pittsburgh: Pickwick, 1974). See also R. Alter, *The Art of Biblical Narrative*; M. Sternberg, *The Poetics of Biblical Narrative.* See for different rhetorical readings of the

3.1.3 Strength and weakness of this method

Rhetorical criticism is classified under the wider umbrella of literary criticism. Since rhetorical criticism shares major features of literary criticism[18] in general, the strengths and weaknesses of both the methods are by and large the same. Powell summarises the important strengths and weaknesses of literary criticism.[19]

The most important strength of literary criticism is its emphasis on the final or the canonical form of the biblical text. It enables the biblical interpreter to concentrate on the given text without having to pay attention to literary layers and sources before its composition. Moreover literary criticism can bring many insights which are normally not available through the historical critical method, due to its focus on the poetical function of the language. It can also serve 'communities of faith' who regard the final form of biblical texts as their authority while maintaining dialogue with the academic world outside the community of faith due to its emphasis on the artistic and stylistic features of the text rather than the religious dimension.

Despite its strength, objections are also raised to this approach. The main weakness of modern rhetorical criticism is its concentration more on stylistic features at the expense of other aspects of rhetorical analysis. We will note the important objections below. It is alleged to be anachronistic since 'literary criticism of the Bible seeks to impose on ancient literature concepts derived from the study of modern literature'.[20] The objection is that devices made for the study of fiction may not be suitable for interpreting the Bible. Another major problem with modern literary criticism is its disregard for the referential function of biblical texts, a difficulty keenly felt by those who are concerned for the 'historical witness of scripture'. As D. Patrick and A. Scult aptly pointed out, in many cases the ultimate object of enquiry becomes merely 'the form and shape on the surface of the text itself'.[21] Commenting on R. Alter's work, *The Art of Biblical Narrative,* they write:

> the Bible is obviously not just a great work of literature, but also claims
> to embody a great spiritual vision. We therefore maintain that, as diffi-

---

biblical texts, *The Bible as Rhetoric: Studies in Biblical Persuasion and Credibility,* (ed.) Martin Warner (London/New York: Routledge, 1990).

[18] Though both literary criticism and rhetorical criticism are concerned with the poetics of the text, the slight difference could be noted. In literary criticism normally the author is perceived as 'poetic maker' whereas in rhetorical criticism the author is a persuader. See Martin Warner (ed.) *The Bible as Rhetoric,* 1990, p. 4.

[19] Powell, *The Bible and Modern Literary Criticism,* pp. 16–19.

[20] Ibid., p. 16.

[21] Dale Patrick and Allen Scult, *Rhetoric and Biblical Interpretation,* (JSOTS 82; BALS 26; Sheffield: Almond Press, 1990), p. 19.

cult as it might be to do so without losing scholarly objectivity, the interpreter must somehow engage the spiritual and theological truth claims of the Biblical text in order to understand it rightly. A rhetorical perspective must recognise the artful form– the rhetorical shape–of the Biblical text as the essential vehicle through which its truth claims are communicated.[22]

There is strength in the view that the theological claims inherent in biblical texts should not be overlooked even if they exhibit spectacular artistic qualities. In the quest for discovering the literary and stylistic features of the text the literary critic, arguably, should not lose sight of the spiritual or religious dimension. This is because the biblical texts are 'intended to function as texts in readers' and hearers' lives, ideas and actions, both in the past and now'.[23] This concern, furthermore, may involve trying, as far as possible, to find out what the text meant when addressed to its original readers. At the same time we cannot overlook the rich insights which have been gained through the literary readings of the texts in their final form. Robert C. Culley also underscores the importance of combining various approaches 'to explore the richness and diversity of the biblical material'.[24] In short, I suggest that we should maintain a proper balance between historical analysis and literary interpretation. Bearing these aspects in mind, we move now to the text of Genesis.

3.2 Trible's Reading

3.2.1 Life and work

Phyllis Trible, Baldwin Professor of Sacred literature at Union Theological Seminary in New York since 1981, received her B.A. (magna cum laude) from Meredith College, North Carolina, and Ph.D. from Union Theological Seminary and Columbia University. After receiving her doctorate, she served as Assistant and Associate Professor of Religion at Wake Forest University from 1963 to 1971. From 1971 to 1979 she worked as Associate Professor and Professor of Old Testament at Andover Newton Theological School. Before becoming the Baldwin Professor of Sacred Literature, she

---

[22] Ibid., p. 18.

[23] See Ellen van Wolde, *Words Become Worlds,* p. 161.

[24] Culley, *Themes and Variations,* p. 7. He aptly points out that the Bible deserves special treatment compared with many other texts, as it has many rare features. He pinpoints three characteristics: first, the Bible is an ancient collection of various types of materials, second, it is literary in nature comprising prose and poetry; and third, the Bible has served as scripture for both Jews and Christians for centuries.

had served as the Professor of Old Testament at Union Seminary since 1979.

She has often travelled abroad to give lectures at colleges, universities, seminaries, and international gatherings. Her trips include Australia, Canada, England, Japan, Jerusalem, Korea, Scotland and New Zealand. In the United States Trible has lectured at more than 150 academic institutions. Her books, *God and the Rhetoric of Sexuality* and *Texts of Terror* have been translated into Dutch, German, and Japanese.

Trible's sound scholarship and her international reputation led her to be elected president of the Society of Biblical Literature for the year 1995. Trible's ecclesiastical background is Southern Baptist.

3.2.2 Hermeneutical Presupposition

For many feminist interpreters, the Bible, the corner stone of the Judaeo–Christian tradition, is shaped in a patriarchal and androcentric culture. As a result they believe that the Bible has been used in the past and the present to legitimate subordinate roles of women in church and society. In other words, gender and sex have been used as weapons to advocate male domination and female subordination throughout history. Feminist interpreters of the Bible are involved in a process of identifying sexism and freeing the biblical texts from patriarchal domination. Underscoring the importance of feminist interpretation, Trible writes: 'For centuries church, synagogue, and academy have advocated patriarchy as the way things are and ought to be. In exposing their bias, feminism evokes a different hermeneutic.'[25] Trible finds 'hermeneutics functioning within scripture'. She explains: 'Depatri-archalising is not an operation which the exegete performs on the text. It is a hermeneutic operating within Scripture itself. We expose it; we do not impose it.'[26]   According to this statement, her reading is 'recuperative'. She writes: 'The Bible is a pilgrim wandering through history to merge past and present.'[27] For Trible, 'this inner hermeneutics of scripture is a clue to the pilgrimage of the Bible in the world'.[28]   Trible believes that feminist perspectives emerged out of the Bible and the Bible has been benefited by the feminist perspective. Hence she writes: 'the Bible informed a feminist perspective, and correspondingly, a feminist perspective enlightened the Bible'.[29] She concludes: 'the Bible is a potential witness against *all* our in-

---

[25] Trible, 'Treasures Old and New: Biblical Theology and the Challenge of Feminism', in *The Open Text,* pp. 36–37.
[26] Trible, 'Depatriarchalising in Biblical Interpretation', *JAAR* 41 (1973), p. 48.
[27] Trible, *God and the Rhetoric*, p. 1.
[28] Ibid., p. 5.
[29] Ibid., p. 202.

terpretations, for the pilgrim named scripture wanders through history to merge past and present on its way toward the future'.[30]

So she attempts to depatriarchalise the text through her reading, thereby making Scripture a positive experience for women. Trible calls this hermeneutical process 'depatriarchalisation'. Moreover in her readings, she also attempts to recognise the case against women in the text, to reinterpret the texts and to retell the stories of terror about women in the text.[31] Trible explores the cases of inferiority, subordination and abuse of women in scripture, for instance, Lot's offering of his daughter to protect male guests (Gen. 19), and Jephthah's sacrifice of his daughter to fulfil his foolish vow (Jud. 11).[32] At the same time, she highlights neglected texts and reinterprets familiar ones. She tries to unearth feminine images of God from the Scripture and to portray deity where possible as female.

She also exposes the conditions of women as persons oppressed due to their sex. She tries to show women's oppressed conditions in patriarchal culture. For instance, the betrayal, rape, murder and dismemberment of the concubine in Judges 19. Trible entitles this task: 'tales of terror *in memoriam*'. She undertakes sympathetic readings of abused women to remember women's stories of terror in biblical accounts.

Trible is the first feminist biblical scholar to propose a feminist Old Testament theology. Her feminist biblical theology begins with creation theology, an ideal of mutuality and equality, not with covenant theology. Moreover, it recovers the hidden history of women, and it investigates the language of God. Finally, it grapples with the issue of biblical authority.[33]

3.2.3 Methodology

Phyllis Trible is a pioneer in the second wave of feminist hermeneutics who has done an extensive analysis of Genesis 2–3.[34] She is considered as one of the most influential contemporary feminist biblical scholars. Her book *God and the Rhetoric of Sexuality,* has become a classic in feminist interpretation of the Bible. Trible finds three clues to interpret the text: topical, methodological and hermeneutical. She describes her methodology as follows:

---

[30] Ibid.

[31] See For details, 'Feminist Hermeneutics and the Biblical Studies', *The Christian Century,* (3–10 Feb. 1982), pp. 116–118.

[32] For a detailed study see Trible, *Texts of Terror.* This a literary feminist readings of Hagar, Tamar, Jephthah and the unnamed concubine in the book of Judges.

[33] See for details, Trible, 'Treasures of Old and New: Biblical Theology and the Challenge of Feminism', pp. 48–49.

[34] We will consider Gen. 2:4b–3:24 as Gen. 2–3.

Within the scripture, my topical clue is a text: the image of God male and female. To interpret this topic, my methodological clue is rhetorical criticism. Outside scripture, my hermeneutical clue is an issue: feminism as a critique of culture.[35]

TOPICAL CLUE

Employing the theory of metaphor from I. A. Richards' work, *The Philosophy of Rhetoric*, Trible differentiates between the vehicle and the tenor of a metaphor. She applies this metaphor to interpret Gen. 1:27. Trible takes the 'image of God' in Gen. 1:27 as a metaphor parallel to 'male and female' in the same verse. She postulates that 'the formal parallelism between the phrases "in the image of God" and "male and female" indicates a semantic correspondence between a lesser known element and a better known element'.[36] She treats 'the image of God' as the tenor and 'male and female' as its vehicle, postulating that '[t]he vehicle is the base of metaphor, the better known element, while the tenor is its underlying (or overarching) subject, the lesser known element'.[37] She explains: 'vehicle and tenor may call attention to each other equally, or one may highlight the other...Together they produce new meanings that are not available through the individual elements'.[38] Drawing on this, she suggests that the parallelism between האדם (*hā–'ādām*) and 'male and female' indicates equality, not hierarchy. Then noting the use of pronouns in Gen. 1:27, and the shift from singular to plural, she infers that האדם (*hā–'ādām*) is not a single creature but two separate creatures, one male and one female. Hence she writes 'created simultaneously, male and female are not superior and subordinate. Neither has power over the other; in fact, both are given equal power'.[39] The implica-

---

[35] Trible, *God and the Rhetoric,* p. 23. For an elaborate analysis of her methodology see pp. 1–30

[36] Ibid., p. 17.

[37] Ibid.

[38] Ibid. For a working definition of metaphor see Janet Martin Soskice, *Metaphor and Religious Language* (Oxford: Clarendon Press, 1985), p. 15. She defines that 'metaphor is that figure of speech whereby we speak about one thing in terms which we are seen to be suggestive of another'. For an explanation for the terms 'vehicle' and 'tenor', see Peter Cotterell and Max Turner, *Linguistics and Biblical Interpretation,* p. 300.

[39] Trible, p. 18. For a similar reading see Ilona N. Rashkow, *Upon the Dark Places: Anti–Semitism and Sexism in English Renaissance Biblical Translation* (Sheffield: Almond Press, 1990). She treats Adam in Gen. 1:27 as an androgynous being because of the use of the singular pronoun 'him'. However she admits that though Adam is a generic term for humanity which has two subtypes namely male and female since the plural pronoun 'them' is used in the second part of the verse. Hence she writes: 'Both of

tion of her topical clue is that both the male and female are created equally in the image of God.

METHODOLOGICAL CLUE

In her adoption of James Muilenburg's, rhetorical criticism as a method of reading texts, Trible treats the final shape of the particular text as a literary unit, with more stress on rhetorical devices and poetics and other literary artistry in the text. In Trible's words 'the major clue to interpretation is the text itself'.[40] Accordingly she focuses on the form and structure of the text in order to articulate its meaning. So the external aspects of the texts like historical background, archaeological data, authorial intention, sociological setting or 'theological motivation and result' are beyond the scope of this methodology. Although Muilenburg treated rhetorical criticism as a complement to form criticism, Trible places it purely under literary criticism with scope for multiple readings of the same text. Hence she advocates that, 'since all methodologies are subject to the guiding interests of individual users, the application of a single one may result in multiple interpretations of a particular passage'.[41] This, as we have seen, is a departure from Muilenburg's original proposal, since his aim was to locate the authorial intention, in other words, Muilenburg had focused on author and text. According to Trible, in contrast, the author's intention alone does not determine the meaning of a text. She asks: 'To what extent does the reader's intention, imposed upon a text, decide the author's intention?'[42] In short, in Trible's rhetorical methodology the text and the reader are at work, giving more than a single meaning. Thus, in Trible's method readers are active in the process of making meanings.

HERMENEUTICAL CLUE

Trible takes feminism as a hermeneutical clue to discuss the 'rhetoric of sexuality'. According to Trible feminism is not 'a narrow focus upon women, but rather a critique of culture in light of misogyny. This critique affects the issues of race and class, psychology, ecology, and human sexuality'.[43] She believes that the biblical hermeneutics of feminism emerge from biblical passages such as the creation accounts, certain Levitical laws, the Song of Songs, the wisdom literature and other similar New Testament accounts.

---

them, *together* and *equally* therefore, are to rule over other creatures and there is no dominion of male over female' (p. 81; emphasis original).

[40] Trible, *God and the Rhetoric*, p. 8.

[41] Ibid. p. 11.

[42] Trible, *Rhetorical Criticism*, p. 96.

[43] Trible, *God and the Rhetoric*, p. 7.

3.3 Trible's Reading of the Creation Narrative (Gen. 2–3)

The creation narrative of Gen. 2:4b–3:24 is the important foundational text within the Old Testament which deals with the creation of humanity. The apostles, church fathers, reformers, theologians and other Bible interpreters have used these texts to elucidate the man–woman relationship and their separate roles and place in the church and society. Yet the same text has been used by different interpreters to advocate the inferior, the superior and the egalitarian status of woman. This text has been one of the most interpreted, reinterpreted and misinterpreted texts within the Old Testament. Even after centuries of interpretation, analyses and readings of it are numerous. Furthermore, the status of woman in the creation narrative has ever been a widely debated issue. So there is no wonder that the creation narrative of Genesis 2–3 has now become one of the most frequent areas of feminist investigation.

First of all, I will present Trible's case in her own terms, evaluating her argument in the light of the particular text. I will also make use of scholarly responses to feminist readings in the process of our evaluation. In her reading of the creation narrative, Trible believes that the problem lies not with the text *per se* but with the centuries–old patriarchal misinterpretations. According to Trible, this story is the development of a drama between love (Eros) and death (Thanatos). Regarding the structure of the story, she finds three short scenes. The first scene is the development of Eros (2: 7– 24), the second is the act of disobedience (2: 25– 3: 7) and the third is the disintegration of Eros (3: 8–24).[44] As a method, she first presents the traditional reading of the narrative, and then offers an alternative reading with a critique of it. These are:

> A male God creates first man (2: 7) and last woman (2: 22); first means superior and last means inferior or subordinate.

> Woman is created for the sake of man: a helpmate to cure his loneliness (2:18–23).

> Contrary to nature, woman comes out of man; she is denied even her natural function of birthing and that function is given to man (2: 21–22).

> Woman is the rib of man, dependent upon him for life (2:21–22).

> Taken out of man (2:23), woman has a derivative, not an autonomous, existence.

---

[44] Ibid., p. 74.

Man names woman (2:23), and thus has power over her.

Man leaves his father's family in order to set up through his wife another patriarchal unit (2:24).

Woman tempted man to disobey and thus she is responsible for sin in the world (3:6); she is untrustworthy, gullible, and simpleminded.

Woman is cursed by pain in childbirth (3:16); pain in childbirth is a more severe punishment than man's struggles with the soil; it signifies that woman's sin is greater than man's.

Woman's desire for man (3:16) is God's way of keeping her faithful and submissive to her husband.

God gives man the right to rule over woman (3:16).[45]

Trible points out that the above specifics are taken against woman to depict male superiority and female inferiority. She argues that 'not one of them is altogether accurate and most of them are simply not present in the story itself'.[46] In her readings, Trible attempts to rebut all the above arguments by her own analysis. In the following discussion we look at how Trible counters the traditional readings.

3.4 Eros Created (Gen. 2:7–24)

In this section Trible shows how Eros is created by the creation of the earth creature and later the woman.

3.4.1 הָאָדָם: (hā–'ādām) an earth creature

In Genesis 2:7 we read that
'then the LORD God formed man from the dust of the ground,...'

Trible challenges the generally accepted translation and meaning of the term הָאָדָם (hā–'ādām). In her ground–breaking article published in 1973[47] she postulates that הָאָדָם (hā–'ādām) is basically androgynous until the differentiation of male and female in Gen. 2: 21–23.[48] Later in her book she

---

[45] Ibid., p. 73.

[46] Ibid.

[47] Trible, 'Depatriarchalising in Biblical Interpretation', pp. 30– 48.

[48] Ibid., p. 35; cf. Rashkow, *Upon the Dark Places*, p. 86. She thinks that until Gen.2:23 אדם is a generic term and אישׁ (man) *and* אשׁה (woman) are socio–sexual terms.

drops the term androgynous because she thought the term androgyny connoted sexuality. She takes האדם (*hā–'ādām*) as a common noun with the definite article ה. So she translates it as an 'earth creature' or a creature from the earth (האדמה– *hā–'ādāmāh*).[49] She goes on to argue that this 'earth creature' is neither a particular person nor a typical person, 'it' is not the male or 'the first man', but only a sexually undifferentiated earth creature.[50] In Trible's reading האדם (*hā–'ādām*) has three different meanings in Gen. 2–3: first, a sexually undifferentiated earth creature, then the male after the sexual distinction, and finally as a generic title, humanity. Before examining the reading of Trible, it is worth looking at other feminist readings which share the same viewpoint.

Mieke Bal, a narratologist, reads Genesis 2–3 with an interdisciplinary approach. In many respects she shares the conclusion of Trible in her readings.[51] Bal also thinks of האדם (*hā–'ādām*) as a sexless creature. She writes: 'From 2:7 to 2: 20 this creature has no name, no sex and no activity'.[52] Following the same logic as Trible, she also argues that האדם (*hā–'ādām*) is not a proper name, since it carries the definite article, but rather a common noun.[53]

Mary Hayter also supports Trible's explanation of the term.[54] Accordingly she considers האדם (*hā–'ādām*) as undifferentiated humanity rather than a male. Approaching the text from a sociological and historical perspective, Carol Meyers arrives at almost the same conclusion as Trible: 'the first creature is not inherently gendered...'[55] So Meyers translates the text as: 'Then God Yahweh formed an *earthling* of clods from the *earth* and breathed into its nostril the breath of life; and the *earthling became* a living being.'[56]

---

[49] Trible, *God and the Rhetoric,* p. 80. In fact, Trible is indebted to Professor Prescott Williams for the translation 'earth creature'. She has also drawn insights from E. A. Speiser; see Trible, p. 140 note no. 7.

[50] Trible, p. 80, cf. Hanne Köhler, '1. Mose 2, 4b–3, 24: Die Erdkreatur' in *Feministisch gelesen,* (ed.) Eva Renate Schmidt *et al.,* pp. 17–24 [p. 18].

[51] Like Trible, Bal considers Gen. 2–3 as a love story. Generally her readings are very similar to that of Trible. Yet she disagrees totally with her in certain respects.

[52] Mieke Bal, 'Sexuality, Sin, and Sorrow: The Emergence of the Female Character', in *Lethal Love: Feminist Literary Readings of Biblical Love Stories* (Bloomington: Indiana University Press, 1987), p. 112.

[53] Bal, p. 113.

[54] Mary Hayter, *The New Eve in Christ: The Use and Abuse of the Bible in the Debate about Women in the Church* (London: SPCK, 1987), pp. 96–98.

[55] Carol Meyers, *Discovering Eve: Ancient Israelite Women in Context* (Oxford: OUP, 1988), p. 82.

[56] Meyers, p. 81.

David M. Gunn and Danna Nolan Fewell think that Trible's reading of האדם (*hā–'ādām*) as 'a sexually undifferentiated creature has merit'.[57] They underscore Trible's claim by noting a suggestion of the tenth–century Jewish Commentator Rashi that 'the first human was male on one side and female on the other and that God simply divided the creation in half'.[58] Interestingly they acknowledge that this interpretation may not be supported by the grammar of the text. But they take the structural device of binary logic to support this reading. The assumption is that we know something by its opposites; in this instance, we know male because we know female. Some Asian feminist theologians like Sun Ai Park also accept Trible's viewpoint.[59]

3.4.2 Woman a corresponding companion

From the above verse some consider that woman was created as an afterthought with secondary status, being the helper to the man. The Hebrew phrase עזר כנגדו (*'ezer kenegdô*) has been translated differently in English translations: KJV translates it as 'help meet for him', RSV 'a helper fit for him', NRSV 'a helper as his partner', and NIV 'a helper suitable for him'. Many feminist interpreters think that the above renderings have a pejorative sense in English. Trible writes:

---

[57] David M. Gunn and Danna Nolan Fewell, *Narrative in the Hebrew Bible,* p. 194.

[58] Ibid. Something similar to the above readings is also proposed by an Indian feminist theologian. Drawing on Hindu religious tradition, Padma Gallup offers an interpretation of Godhead in Genesis 1:27–28 based on the image of the Hindu god *Sivam* (Siva) in which Siva seems to be half–male and half–female. She writes: 'If Godhead created humans in its image, then the Godhead must be a male/female, side by side, non dualistic whole', See P. Gallup, 'Doing Theology—An Asian Feminist Perspective', in *Commission on Theological Concerns Bulletin* (Christian Conference in Asia, 4, 1983), p. 22 as cited by Kwok Pui Lan, 'Discovering the Bible in the Nonbiblical World', in *The Bible and Liberation: Political and Social Hermeneutics,* p. 23. Padma's reading is supported by R. S. Sugirtharajah, 'The Bible and its Asian Readers', *Biblnt* 1 (1993), p. 60. The difference between Gunn' s and Fewell' s reading and Gallup's is only that one divides the human being into male and female and the other divides the Godhead into male and female. However, this interpretation does not do justice to the biblical materials which may have been written polemically against the existing creation mythlogies. For polemical aspects of Genesis creation, see John H. Walton, *Ancient Israelite Literature in its Cultural Context: A Survey of Parallels Between Biblical and Ancient Near Eastern Texts* (Grand Rapids, Michigan: Zondervan Publishing, 1989), pp. 19–38; David Atkinson, *The Message of Genesis 1–11: The Dawn of Creation* (BST; Leicester: IVP, 1990), pp. 20ff.

[59] See Sun Ai Park, 'Understanding the Bible from Women's Perspective', *Voices from the Third World* x (June 1987), p. 70.

the English word *helper* suggests an assistant, a subordinate, indeed an inferior, while the Hebrew word *'ezer* carries no such connotation. To the contrary, in the Hebrew scriptures this word often describes God as the superior who creates and saves Israel.[60]

Before feminist interpreters pointed out the ambiguity of this translation, many scholars had already recognized the difficulty of the traditional translation. Accordingly, S.R. Driver in the beginning of this century indicated that 'to speak of woman (as is sometimes done) as man's "help–meet" (absolutely) is an error implying strange ignorance of the English Language'.[61] John Skinner, another prominent Old Testament Scholar of this century, translated this as a helper, 'corresponding to him'.[62] Moreover, modern commentators like Speiser have also corrected this mistranslation as 'an aid fit for him' or 'corresponding to him', acknowledging that the traditional rendering ('help meet to him') is subject to confusion.[63]

It is worth mentioning here the work of Anastasius Sinaita of the late seventh century AD, and how he interpreted the term. According to him the equivalent Greek word *boēthos* in the Septuagint version of Gen. 2:18, usually translated as helper or helpmate, 'must be a stronger one, in no way needing help'. He defined *boēthos* as 'helper in dangers and in adversities as one who repels adverse forces'.[64]

Following Trible, many other feminist interpreters have explained the term in a similar fashion. Marsha Wilfong explains the aloneness of man as a 'predicament' because there was only one living creature or human being created at the beginning. Like Trible, she also cites the occurrences of the term *'ezer* in the Old Testament and accordingly she interprets: 'Whether human or divine, the help to which *'ezer* refers is (a) deliverance from a

---

[60] Trible, p. 90. We need to note here that in her previous article, she had a different nuance regarding the use of the term. Hence she wrote, ' ... *'ezer* is a relational term; it designates a beneficial relationship; and it pertains to God, people, and animals. By itself the word does not specify positions within relationships; more particularly, it does not imply inferiority'. See 'Depatriarchalizing in Biblical... ', p. 36.

[61] S. R. Driver, *The Book of Genesis,* 10th ed. (London: Methuen & Co. Ltd., 1916), p. 41. note 2.

[62] John Skinner, *Genesis,* (ICC), 2nd ed. (Edinburgh: T&T Clark, 1956), p. 67; see also U. Cassuto, *A Commentary on the Book of Genesis: From Adam to Noah,* Part 1, (trans.) Israel Abrahams (Jerusalem: Magnes Press, 1961). He also translates it as 'a helper corresponding to him', p. 132.

[63] E. A. Speiser, *Genesis,* p. 17.

[64] Cited by Jean M. Higgins, 'Anastasius Sinaita and the Superiority of the Woman', *JBL,* 97 (1978), p. 255. She notes that of the forty–five occurrences of the word in the LXX, forty–two refer to help from 'a stronger one in no way needing help' (p. 255).

predicament of danger or need, (b) by a powerful individual or group.'[65] In her reading, woman functions as a 'deliverer' of man from his aloneness from which he needs rescue. She also considers woman as equal. Hence she writes:

> Far from presenting woman as a creature subordinate to man, the author of this creation story describes her as a deliverer, a political and military ally, equal (that is, not superior) to man only because the little word *kenegdo* modifies the powerful '*ezer*![66]

Along with Trible and Wilfong, most feminists underscore the fact that the phrase עזר כנגדו (*'ezer kenegdô*) does not have any connotation of inferiority or subordination; rather it stresses equality.[67]

Many male scholars who are sympathetic to feminist concerns have also supported the above readings. In his book, *Till the Heart Sings: A Biblical Theology of Manhood and Womanhood*, Samuel Terrien reveals this concern. To explain עזר כנגדו (*'ezer kenegdô*) he takes the root עזר (*'ezer*) from which the noun is derived. He thinks the verb עזר (*'ezer*) means 'to succour' (at the existential level of being), 'to save from extremity' or 'to deliver from death'. He explains: '[I]n some other Semitic languages, the cognate describes the action of someone who gives water to a person dying of thirst or who places a tourniquet on the arm of a bleeding man, thereby saving his life.'[68] So woman is a saviour of man according to Terrien. In his *Old Testament Ethics*, W. C. Kaiser interprets עזר כנגדו (*'ezer kenegdô*)

---

[65] Marsha M. Wilfong, 'Genesis 2: 18–24', 42 (1988), p. 59; see also Ilona N. Rashkow, *Upon the Dark Places*, p. 83.

[66] Ibid., p. 60.

[67] Katharine D. Sakenfeld, 'The Bible and Woman: Bane or Blessing?', *TToday* 32 (1975), p. 224; Hayter, *The New Eve in Christ*, pp. 101–102; Mary Evans, *Women in the Bible*, pp. 16–17; Rashkow, *Upon the Dark Places*, p. 83; Mieke Bal, *Lethal Love*, p. 115; Carol Meyers, *Discovering Eve*, p. 85; Grace I. Emmerson, 'Women in ancient Israel', p. 390; Alice Ogden Bellis, *Helpmates, Harlots, Heroes: Women's Stories in the Bible* (Louisville: W/JKP, 1994), pp. 45–66; Joy Elasky Fleming with J. Robin Maxson, *Man and Woman in Biblical Unity: Theology From Genesis 2–3* (Minnesota: Saint Paul, 1993). This is an abstract of J.E. Fleming's doctoral dissertation entitled *A Rhetorical Analysis of Genesis 2–3 With Implications for a Theology of Man and Woman*, submitted to the University of Strasbourg, France, 1987; Katherine C. Bushnell, *God's Word to Women: One Hundred Bible Studies on Woman's Place in the Divine Economy*, published in 1923 by Ray Munson, New Jersey, (n.p & n.d.), see paragraphs 18ff; Corona Mary, 'Woman in Creation Story', *Jeev* 21 (1991), pp. 95–106. For an opposite viewpoint, see Clines, *What Does Eve Do to Help*, pp. 25–48.

[68] Samuel Terrien, *Till the Heart Sings: A Biblical Theology of Manhood and Womanhood* (Philadelphia: Fortress Press, 1985), p. 10. For a similar sympathetic male reading of creation narrative see Trevor Dennis, *Sarah Laughed: Women's Voices in the Old Testament* (London: SPCK, 1994), pp. 8–33.

as 'equal power or strength'. Following David R. Freedman,[69] he translates
it as 'a power (or strength) equal to him'.[70]

3.4.3 Woman as culmination of creation

In traditional readings, woman is portrayed as a secondary creation since
she is created from the rib of האדם (*hā–'ādām*). Feminist interpreters counteract this notion in their treatment of this passage. Trible thinks that the
creation of woman by Yahweh Elohim from the rib of man is the culmination of the entire movement. She also argues that her creation is a unique
one since she is not created from the earth, like other creatures; rather
'Yahweh God *builds* the rib into woman'.[71] As the 'earth creature' is put
under deep sleep, in the creation of woman, 'it' is neither a participant nor
even a spectator. Therefore 'woman is no weak, dainty, ephemeral creature. No opposite sex, no second sex, no derived sex—in short, no
"Adam's rib." Instead, woman is the culmination of creation, fulfilling
humanity in sexuality'.[72]

In her earlier work, 'Depatriarchalising in Biblical Interpretation', she
points out that ' the Yahwist account moves to its climax, not its decline, in
the creation of woman. She is not an afterthought; she is the culmination'.[73]
She explains it as an *inclusio* device used in Hebrew literature, where the
main theme of a unit often appears at the beginning and the end. Accordingly she argues that the creation of man first and woman last is a ring
composition where the two are parallel.[74] The creation of man and woman
is a sequential act consistent with an egalitarian status of women in the
creation order. Accordingly she argues that woman is the culmination of
creation in order to balance the creation of the male first. However, in her
book *God and the Rhetoric of Sexuality,* she suggests that the creation of
man and woman is a simultaneous act, thereby avoiding the priority of man

---

[69] David R. Freedman, 'Woman, a Power Equal to Man', *BARev* 9 (1983), pp. 56–58.

[70] Walter C. Kaiser, *Toward Old Testament Ethics* (Grand Rapids, Michigan: Zondervan publishing House, 1983), p. 182, note 1. Freedman suggests that there were two
Hebrew roots for the noun עזר one 'to help' and the other 'to be strong'. He also notes
that כנגדו appears only here in 2:18 and that is translated 'equal' in later Hebrew; 'a
power (or strength) equal to him' is the resulting translation (cited by Kaiser, p. 154,
note 6).

[71] Trible, *God and the Rhetoric,* p. 102. She contends that the Hebrew verb בנה connotes considerable labour to achieve desired results. It is used for building towns, tow-
ers, altars and fortifications etc. For a similar reading see Cassuto, *A Commentary on
the Book of Genesis part 1*, p. 135; see also Rashkow, *Upon the Dark Places*, p. 84.

[72] Ibid., cf. Emmerson, p. 390.

[73] *Art. Cit.,* p. 36.

[74] Ibid.

in creation. In other words, in both Trible's readings the woman is given equal footing in creation, whether it is sequential or simultaneous.

3.4.4 Naming of the woman

In the Old Testament the act of naming a person or a place is traditionally understood as a demonstration of exercising authority over that person or place. Von Rad, for instance, writes: '[N]ame–giving in the ancient Orient was primarily an exercise of sovereignty, of command.'[75]

Trible rejects the above implication of the naming motif. She argues that there is a naming formula consisting of the verb קרא (*qr'*–'call') and the noun שם (*šem*–'name') (Gen.4:17; 4:25; 4:26a; 4:26b). She continues to argue that the verb קרא (*qr'*) alone does not indicate naming.[76] She points out that the naming formula is present in 2:19 where האדם (*hā-'ādām*) names the animals, and in 3:20 where man names his wife Eve. But it is absent in 2: 23. 'The noun *name* is strikingly absent from the poetry. Hence in naming the woman, the man is not establishing power over her but rejoicing in their mutuality.'[77] Trible's interpretation is also shared by other feminist writers such as Sakenfeld, Evans and Hayter.[78]

3.4.5 Woman not a derivative

Trible refutes the traditional argument that woman is a derivative since she is taken from man. She advocates that 'the raw material, not the woman herself, is taken from the earth creature... to be taken from man is to be differentiated from him...'[79] She explains that the phrase 'taken from' is poetic license which links איש (*'îš*) and אשה (*'iššâ*) only to create a pun but not to give information about the creative activity. Moreover, life for both the earth creature and the woman originates only with God. Yahweh God himself builds בנה (*bnh*) the rib into woman with considerable labour. Hence, 'woman is the culmination of creation,... Equal in creation with the

---

[75] Von Rad, *Genesis* (London: SCM Press, 1961), p. 81.

[76] Trible, *God and the Rhetoric*, pp. 99–100.

[77] Ibid., p. 100.

[78] Sakenfeld, 'The Bible and Woman: Bane or Blessing?', *TToday* (1975), p. 225; Evans, 1983, p. 16; Hayter, 1987, p. 100.

[79] Ibid., p. 101. Interestingly, in their rhetorical reading of the narrative, Dale Patrick and Allen Scult arrive at the opposite conclusion. They point out Adam's participation in the completion of creation. They show how woman was built with a part of him as God provided the Man with a part of himself. See *Rhetoric and Biblical Interpretation*, p. 110.

man...'[80] Now the sexually undifferentiated earth creature is transformed into a sexual being. So the development of Eros is completed.

3.5 Eros Contaminated (Gen. 2:25–3:7)

In this section Trible points out that the Eros created in the previous section has been contaminated due to the disobedience of the human couple. Her main argument in this section is to show that both the man and the woman are equally responsible for the disobedience.[81] By arguing this way, she tries to refute the traditional allegation against woman's sole responsibility for humanity's 'fall'.

3.5.1 *Woman a spokesperson*

In the conversation between the serpent and the woman (3:1–5), Trible treats woman as a spokesperson, since the serpent initiated the conversation with her, using a plural verb form. Moreover, Trible comments on the woman's capability in discussing theology with the serpent, and her hermeneutical skills. The latter are shown by the woman's addendum to the original command 'you shall not touch it'. According to Trible, the woman's addendum to Yahweh's original command is building 'a fence around the Torah'. She explains: 'If the tree is not touched, then its fruit cannot be eaten.'[82] By this on the one hand, Trible incidentally negates the woman's disobedience of the commandment and on the other hand, she establishes that woman is more intelligent than man. To Trible, woman is a theologian, ethicist, hermeneut, and rabbi. In addition, Trible also notes the woman's act of independence from man: 'seeking neither his [man's] permission nor his advice'.[83]

3.5.2 *Man as passive*

If the woman is intelligent, the man is passive in the whole disobedience scene. Trible underscores the presence of the man during the dialogue be-

---

[80] Ibid., p. 102.

[81] Contra David Jobling, *The Sense of Biblical Narrative: Structural Analyses in the Hebrew Bible* (JSOTS 39; Sheffield: JSOT Press, 1986), pp. 41–42. He goes for an 'asymmetry of the offences' and argues that the woman sinned first and incited him to sin.

[82] Trible, p. 110. For a similar literary reading see James G. Williams, *Women Recounted: Narrative Thinking and the God of Israel* (BALS 6; Sheffield: Almond, 1982), pp. 67ff. He writes: 'the literary fact that she does not repeat Yahweh Elohim's injunction verbatim is a sign of the ability to refract and expand what has been communicated' (p. 68).

[83] Ibid., p. 113.

tween the woman and the serpent in noting the Hebrew adverb עמה (*'im-māh*–'with her') in Gen. 3: 6. Trible accuses the man of not speaking up for obedience. She complains that 'He does not theologise; he does not contemplate; and he does not envision the full possibilities of the occasion. Instead, his one act is belly–oriented, and it is an act of acquiescence, not of initiative'.[84] So by implication, she emphasises both woman's sagacity and man's equal participation in the disobedience.

3.6 Eros Condemned (Gen. 3:8–24)

Because of the disobedience of the human couple the developed Eros between them begins to disintegrate. Trible notes how the solidarity and equality between them are lost. The man tries to betray the woman and begins to blame God for giving her as his partner. The woman confesses her guilt more quickly than the man and without blaming either God or the man.

3.6.1 The judgement for the disobedience

Trible notes the sequence and the length of the trial and judgement of the serpent, the woman and the man. She argues that the accusatory formula כי (*kî*–'because') is absent when God addresses the woman, though the same formula is used with regard to the man and the serpent. Moreover the specific word 'curse' is not employed in the woman's judgement, though the serpent and the ground (because of man) were cursed by God. The brevity of God's judgement upon the woman is another noted feature. Trible argues strongly that what we have in Gen. 3:16 is not a curse, rather 'the particular *consequences* that disobedience has brought to her [woman's] existence'.[85] However she admits that the woman is equally responsible for the disobedience.

3.6.2 Man's ruling—the consequence of disobedience

Following Speiser, Trible takes the two objects in Gen. 3:16 עצבונך (*isse-bônek*) and הרנך (*heronek*) as a hendiadys, and translates it as 'pain in child birth'. She finds support from the resultant parallelism in the succeeding

---

[84] Ibid. For a similar viewpoint see Rashkow, *Upon the Dark Places*. She finds Adam more guilty than woman as he heard the command directly from God. p. 90; cf. Susan Niditch, 'Genesis', in *The Women's Bible Commentary*, pp. 12–14. She considers the man utterly passive like a baby.

[85] Ibid., p. 127. Emphasis mine. Cf. Mieke Bal, *Lethal Love*, p. 126. Bal also thinks that woman is not cursed and like Trible that Yahweh's words are only the depiction of reality rather than the consequences of the sin.

line, 'in pain you will bring forth children'. Hence she writes: 'The more she gives birth, the more her pain increases.'[86] The real issue for her is not the pain in childbirth *per se,* as Meyers proposes, rather the reason for the pain. Though woman yearns for the original unity through her 'desire', '[t]he man will not reciprocate the woman's desire; instead, he will rule over her'.[87] Now there is hierarchy rather than mutuality. However, she argues: 'His supremacy is neither a divine right nor a male prerogative. Her subordination is neither a divine decree nor the female destiny. Both their positions result from shared disobedience.'[88] Trible thinks that by naming the woman Eve, the man exercises the rule which the deity had pronounced. She explains: 'in effect, the man reduces the woman to the status of an animal by calling her a name'.[89]

3.6.3 The disintegration of eros

God's judgement upon the man and the woman resulted in the disintegration of Eros. The equality between the sexes is lost as a result of disobedience. Trible argues that until the disobedience took place there was complete equality between the man and the woman. The equality and harmony were lost as a result of their shared disobedience. Now the erotic desire of woman is not reciprocated by man; instead, he starts to rule over her. This ruling over the woman is not the intention of God, but rather the consequence of the disobedience. 'The tree of life, available in Eros, is denied in Thanatos. The man shall not live forever.'[90] He has to return to the earth as the last act of disintegration. She concludes: 'Estranged from each other,

---

[86] Ibid., Contra Meyers, *Discovering Eve,* p.105. For another interpretation see Susan Foh, 'What is the Woman's Desire?', *WTJ* 37 (1975), pp. 380–81. She argues that the man's case is similar to Cain's, sin's desire is to enslave him but he has to overpower sin. Similarly, 'as a result of the fall, man no longer rules easily; he must fight for his leadership'(p. 382).

[87] Ibid., p. 128. For a different reading see Rashkow, *Upon the Dark Places,* She argues that in the structure of Hebrew poetry the second line repeats the same idea of the first line. Accordingly 'In pain you shall bring forth children' duplicates 'your pain in childbearing'. Likewise, 'he shall rule over you' parallels 'your desire shall be for your husband' (pp. 92–93). So the husband's 'rule' is to be seen in relation to the wife's need for her husband with respect to bearing children. So this is not an abstract command concerning the subordination of woman to man in all relationships. We need to note in this context the LXX rendering. There is no sexual desire in LXX (Gen. 3:17) as in Hebrew. It reads 'your turning back'. John W. Wevers suggests that 'what the translator probably meant was that though 'in pains you will bear children' yet 'your return will be to your husband', i.e. 'you will keep coming back to him...', see John W. Wevers, *Notes on the Greek Text of Genesis,* Atlanta (Scholars Press: 1993), p. 45.

[88] Ibid.

[89] Ibid., p. 133.

[90] Ibid., p. 136.

the man and the woman are banished from the garden and barred forever from the tree of life. Truly, a love story has gone awry.'[91]

3.7 Genesis 1:27 and Feminine Imagery in the Old Testament

By employing her 'metaphor' of God as male and female (Gen. 1:27), Trible attempts to unearth the feminine aspects in the Godhead. Talking about the nature of God in the Old Testament, Trible locates both androcentric and gynomorphic images.[92] According to Trible there are evidences in the text to show the gynomorphic images to depict God. They are: texts dealing with feminine activities or emotions of God such as Yahweh the midwife (Ps. 22:9), God as a woman in labour pain (Deut. 32:18) and God a nursing mother (Is. 49:15; 66:9, 12–13; Ps. 131:2; Num. 11:12).[93] Secondly, Trible notes the use of words having feminine roots to depict God's nature. For instance, the Hebrew noun רחם (*rehem*–womb) has the broader meaning of 'love' 'compassion' and 'mercy' in its plural form רחמים (*rahamîm*). She argues that the metaphor רחם (*rehem*–womb) deals with a physical organ unique to the female. And thus she claims that the biblical concept of God as merciful and compassionate is derived from the feminine symbolism of the womb.[94] She concludes:

> God conceives in the womb; God fashions in the womb; God judges in the womb; God destines in the womb; God brings forth from the womb; God receives out of the womb; and God carries from the womb to grey hairs. From the uterine perspective, then, Yahweh molds life for individuals and for the nation Israel. Accordingly, in biblical traditions an organ unique to the female becomes a vehicle pointing to the compassion of God.[95]

רחום (*rehem*–womb) therefore, is not a term meant for a father but for a mother, 'who creates by nourishing in the womb'. She also finds gynomorphic language in Gen. 49:25 where God is portrayed as אל שדי (*'el saddāy*). Following F.M. Cross she too thinks that שדי (*shady*) had the original meaning of 'feminine breasts'. So in Trible's translation אל שדי (*'el shady*) is

---

[91] Ibid., p. 139.

[92] Trible, 'God, Nature of, in the OT', *IDBS* (Nashville: Abingdon, 1976), pp. 368–369.

[93] See Trible, '*Depatriarchalizing...*', pp. 30–48; see also Ibid., p. 368.

[94] Trible, *God and the Rhetoric*, pp. 33ff; cf. 'God, Nature of...', pp. 368–69. Here also she makes use of her metaphor. Accordingly 'womb' is the vehicle and 'compassion', the tenor.

[95] Ibid., p. 38.

'God with breasts'.[96]   Hence, Trible writes: 'The God of the breasts gives the blessings of the breasts.'[97]   Through this analysis, Trible has depicted female metaphors for God, especially the feminine organs womb and breasts.

3.8 Genesis 1–3 and Feminist Old Testament Theology

Trible has proposed an Old Testament feminist theology in the light of her readings of the creation narratives.[98]   Unlike the systematic–covenant model of Eichrodt or the tradition–historical model of Von Rad, Trible's Old Testament theology focuses upon 'the phenomenon of gender and sex in the articulation of faith.'[99]   She suggests that feminist theology should begin with the creation stories (Gen. 1–3).[100]   She explains that 'it might use the phrase 'image of God male and female', as leitmotif for the entire project, relating it positively to Genesis 2 and negatively to Genesis 3'.[101] She also proposes that Old Testament feminist theology can recover the hidden history of woman and could also investigate the language of God. She suggests further that it can grapple with models and meanings for biblical authority.[102]   The implication of her proposal is that feminist theology

---

[96] Trible, *IDBS*, p. 368; *God and the Rhetoric*, pp. 60–71, cf. Hos. 9:14.

[97] Ibid. For a critique of Trible see Francis Martin, *The Feminist Question: Feminist Theology in the Light of Christian Tradition* (Grand Rapids, Michigan: William B. Eerdmans, 1994), pp. 234–241; John W. Miller, 'Depatriarchalizing God in Biblical Interpretation: A Critique,' *CBQ* 48 (1986), pp. 609–616.

[98] See Trible, 'Five Loaves and Two Fishes: Feminist Hermeneutics and Biblical Theology', *TS* 50 (1989), 279–95; 'Treasures Old and New: Biblical Theology and the Challenge of Feminism', in *The Open Text: New Directions for Biblical Studies,* pp. 32–56.

[99] Ibid., p. 292.

[100] Cf. Rolf Rendtorff, *Canon and Theology: Overtures to an Old Testament Theology,* (trans & ed.) Margaret Kohl (Edinburgh: T&T Clark, 1993), pp. 91ff. Here Rendtorff underscores the rationale for creation as the starting point for the theology of the Old Testament. He also points out the error of subordinating the creation theology to the doctrine of election or redemption, as Von Rad and other earlier scholars had done. Rendtorff argues that each pentateuchal tradition had its own history before its formation. 'This means that the traditions about creation were first formulated and worked out independently of the traditions about the patriarchs, the exodus from Egypt, the giving of the law on Sinai, and so forth, all of which now follow the creation accounts in the Pentateuch' (p. 96). This demonstrates an increasing tendency among Old Testament scholars to treat the creation theology in its own right. However, we also note that, like Trible, Rendtorff has in this place a definite agenda in his thinking about the Old Testament namely the possibility of a Christian–Jewish Old Testament Theology.

[101] See Trible, 'Treasures Old and New: Biblical Theology and the Challenge of Feminism', p. 47.

[102] Ibid., pp. 47– 48.

replaces the hierarchical model of covenant theology with a mutual and equal model of creation theology which undercuts patriarchy.

3.9 Observation, Discussion and Evaluation

3.9.1 Strength of Trible's reading

Trible's reading of the creation narrative is a remarkable contribution to the understanding of Genesis 1–3. In many respects Trible's reading has widened our horizon of understanding. She reads the text with a theological motive and her purpose seems to be recuperative. She highlights many overlooked aspects in the narrative and is able to challenge many misogynist and male–biased readings established by certain Church fathers and certain commentators in the past. Trible's reading also redresses some centuries–old male–biased interpretations.

An example is the portrayal of the woman as a 'temptress' in the narrative. It is widely held that the woman tempted the man. Von Rad observes: 'The one who has been led astray now becomes a temptress'.[103] Although it is true that the woman was tempted by the serpent, it is not appropriate to argue that the woman is a temptress. While it is true that the woman gave the fruit to the man, the man could have avoided eating it, since he was already commanded by the Lord not to eat from that tree. The text does not tell us that the woman made him eat or tempted him. It only says, 'she also gave some to her husband'. We should also bear in mind that of the actors in the drama only the serpent was directly cursed by God, not the man or the woman (although the ground is cursed because of the man).

Trible's readings of the creation narratives have a wide and far reaching influence upon biblical interpreters and feminist writers. Trible is probably the most influential feminist biblical scholar in generating an interest in and momentum for feminist issues in the cross section of biblical scholarship.[104] In almost all scholarly materials today, there are references to feminist interpretations, especially to Trible's exegesis. In a way, Trible's work has

---

[103] Von Rad, *Genesis,* p. 87. For a similar view see Eugene Maly, 'Genesis', in *The Jerome Biblical Commentary, JBC* (London: Geoffrey Chapman, 1968). Maly writes: 'The woman is tempted and falls first; she then tempts man'., p. 13; A similar viewpoint is maintained in the new edition. See Richard J. Clifford & Roland E. Murphy, *'Genesis'* , NJBC, (London: Geoffrey Chapman, 1989), pp. 8–43. They note: 'At the snake's deceptive assurance, the woman eats and persuades her husband to eat' (p. 12).

[104] Cullen Murphy notes her influence on the academy: 'Ask graduate students in their twenties or established scholars in their thirties or forties how an interest was awakened in women's issues and biblical studies, and the answer will often turn out to involve an article or a book by Trible', see C. Murphy, 'Women and the Bible', *AM* (Aug 1993), p. 48.

promoted feminist readings as a scholarly discipline. Her reading has enabled biblical scholars to a certain extent to rethink the position of woman in the creation narrative and this has resulted in rectifying certain chauvinistic attitudes. So in many ways Trible's readings have functioned as socio–critical hermeneutics exposing male domination and at the same time have attempted to liberate both woman and the biblical texts from dominant male traditions.[105]

Trible has established that encounter with the biblical text may still be a positive experience for women despite alleged patriarchal orientation. We need to note here that before Trible both Simone de Beauvoir and Kate Millet had argued that the Bible is permeated with patriarchy. Their caption was 'patriarchy has God on its side'.[106] In fact Trible's reading in the first place suggested that this was not the case. This is vital, when many feminist readers are leaving the Christian and Jewish traditions because of the alleged patriarchal nature of the text.

3.9.2 Problems of Trible's reading

Despite the various strengths and influence of Trible's reading, it also raises various difficulties. Here we will take up some of the most important issues with regard to her readings. I will mainly examine her methodological presuppositions, exegetical arguments and hermeneutical options.

METHODOLOGICAL PROBLEMS

Trible's topical clue

As we have already noted in describing her methodology, Trible's whole argument is based on her topical clue of Gen. 1:27. She argued that since both the man and the woman are created in the 'image of God', as male and female, they are equal and there is no question of superiority or subordination.

According to Trible, as we have already discussed, 'male and female' functions in the text as the vehicle of the metaphor and 'the image of God' as its tenor. In this connection, Trible makes use of I. A. Richards' theory of 'the principle of metaphor'. That is 'when we use a metaphor we have two thoughts of differing things active together and supported by a single

---

[105] For the meaning and function of 'socio–critical hermeneutics' see Thiselton' see Thiselton, *New Horizons*, pp. 379–409. Thiselton defines socio–critical hermeneutics as 'an approach to texts (or to traditions and institutions) which seeks to penetrate beneath their surface–function *to expose their role as instruments of power, domination, or social manipulation*', p. 379; emphasis original. See our discussion in Part One.

[106] See Kate Millet, *Sexual Politics*, p. 51.

word, or phrase, whose meaning is a resultant of their interaction'.[107] In other words the interaction of the two elements of metaphor (vehicle and tenor) creates new meaning. Trible explains: 'vehicle and tenor may call attention to each other equally, or one may highlight the other'.[108]

There are many issues involved here; how does she know whether the two thoughts in the verse call attention to each other or whether one is highlighting the other? Explaining metaphor Cotterell and Turner write: 'Metaphorical language is like any other manifestation of real language in that it is to be understood only in a context'.[109] Moreover one also has to have a thorough knowledge of the meaning of the term both in its cotext and its context.[110] Trible pays less attention to explaining what the 'image of God' means, and instead she explains the terms 'male and female' by means of 'the image of God'. However, there is no evidence for the two expressions interacting with each other in this way. James Barr rightly shows: 'If phrase X is followed at once by phrase Y, it is only one among many possible functions of Y that it should be the explanation of X; it could equally well be the sequel or the consequence of X, or an addition of a new factor to X, or indeed a qualification or modification of X'.[111] Trible has considered only one option. 'The image of God' could function as the vehicle and 'male and female' as its tenor. Moreover, in my view, the term 'male and female' interprets more logically האדם rather than 'image of God'. That is humankind is created as male and female.

Commenting on Trible's analysis of Gen. 1:27, Phyllis Bird, another feminist biblical scholar writes that Trible's interpretation 'rests on a faulty syntactical analysis which isolates vs. 27 as a unit of speech/thought. The metaphor is the creation of the interpreter'.[112] The above considerations show us that Trible's treatment of the verse has linguistic and exegetical problems.

Trible postulates the egalitarian ideal not only as a starting point for reading the creation narrative but also in order to articulate an Old Testament feminist theology. We need to examine this claim from various per-

---

[107] I.A. Richards, *The Philosophy of Rhetoric* (Oxford: OUP, 1936) as cited by Soskice, p. 39.

[108] Trible, *God and the Rhetoric,* p. 17.

[109] Cotterell & Turner, p. 301.

[110] The cotext is 'the sentences, paragraphs, chapters, surrounding the text and related to it', whereas the context is 'the sociological and historical setting of the text', ibid., p. 16.

[111] James Barr, *Biblical Faith and Natural Theology: The Gifford Lectures for 1991 Delivered in the University of Edinburgh* (Oxford: Clarendon Press, 1993), p. 160. Here Barr is evaluating Karl Barth's analysis of the *imago Dei* in Gen. 1:26–27. This critique is equally applicable to Trible since she reads the passage in a similar way to Barth.

[112] Bird, 'Sexual Differentiation and Divine Image in the Genesis Creation Texts', p. 29, note 19. Cf. also Hayter, *The New Eve in Christ,* p. 23.

spectives. She argues: 'Created simultaneously, male and female are not superior and subordinate. Neither has power over the other; in fact, both are given equal power.'[113] From this statement, at the outset of her thesis, it may appear that Trible seems to have formulated her conclusion before the reading.

Although Trible's concern for reading the text from this perspective is quite valid, we need to examine closely whether the text allows such a reading. While there is no doubt that in the priestly account of creation in Gen. 1 both the man and the woman are created simultaneously, we do not know whether the phrase 'image of God' refers to 'gender equality' of the sexes as Trible and others propose.[114] It is quite legitimate to seek the meaning of the text in its own cultural context, especially when we deal with an ancient text, before we impose our own concerns on it. In other words, first of all we must try to understand how the particular text would have been understood by an Israelite reader,[115] to see whether he or she would have understood it as a text promoting the egalitarian status of the sexes. We have seen that Trible's whole thesis concerning the equality of the sexes is centred around this verse. But the P writer cites the same theme in Genesis 5:1–2 when dealing with the genealogy of Adam. Here the issue is not equality but sexuality and reproduction. Trible limits the various possible meanings of Gen. 1: 27 to the egalitarian ideal and furthermore, pays little attention to the rest of the unit. This reveals her selectivity in her attempt to prove her case.

Contrary to Trible's argument, Phyllis Bird argues more convincingly that the Hebrew terms זכר (*zakār*–male) and ונקבה (*neqebâ*–female) are 'biological', rather than 'sociological terms signifying equality'.[116] She ex-

---

[113] Trible, *God and the Rhetoric*, p. 18.

[114] For the gender equality view, see J. P. Fokkelman, 'Genesis', in *The Literary Guide to the Bible*, (eds.) Robert Alter and Frank Kermode (London: Collins, 1987), pp. 44–45; see also Alter, *The Art of Biblical Narrative*, p. 141.

[115] This point has been explained theoretically by both J. W. Rogerson and Mark G. Brett. According to Rogerson's sociological theory this factor is called 'description'. In Brett's linguistic explanation this aspect is called 'emics'. For details see J.W. Rogerson, 'The Use of Sociology in Old Testament Studies' (*VTS* 36; Leiden: E. J. Brill, 1985), pp. 250ff; Mark G. Brett, *Biblical Criticism in Crisis?: The Impact of the Canonical Approach on Old Testament Studies* (Cambridge: CUP, 1991), pp. 15–18. See also Brett, 'Four or Five Things to do with Texts: A Taxonomy of Interpretative Interests', in *The Bible in Three Dimensions*, pp. 359–365.

[116] Bird, 'Genesis I–III as a source for a contemporary theology of sexuality' *Ex Audi* 3 (1987), pp. 31–44, here p. 33; cf. 'Male and Female He Created them', pp. 129–59; and see also David J. A. Clines, *What Does Eve Do to help?*, pp. 25–48; see also Adela Yarbro Collins, 'The Historical–Critical and Feminist Readings of Genesis 1: 26–28', in *Hebrew Bible or Old Testament?: Studying the Bible in Judaism and Christianity*, (eds.) Roger Brooks *et al.* (Notre Dame: University of Notre Dame Press, 1990), pp. 197–199. Carol Meyers also shares Bird's view; see Meyers, *Discovering Eve*, p. 86.

plains that the same terms are used by the P writer in the flood narrative in
the context of the pairs of animals brought to the ark by Noah (Gen. 6:19;
cf. 7:9). Thus she summarises her argument concerning the Priestly account of creation:

> It [Priestly account of creation] says nothing about the image that relates
> humankind to God, nor about God as the referent of the image. Neither
> does it qualify the notion of human dominion over the creatures (or of
> subjugating the earth, vs. 28). It relates only to the blessing of fertility,
> making explicit its necessary presupposition. It is not concerned with
> sexual roles, the status or relationship of sexes to one another, or mar-
> riage. It describes the biological pair, not the psycho–social pair; male
> and female, not man and woman or husband and wife.[117]

The above argument has much strength.[118] In the light of the above arguments Trible's fundamental thesis concerning gender equality based on
Gen. 1: 27 is insecure.

Another problem arises when Trible treats the two texts, the Priestly and
Yahwistic creation accounts, from a single perspective. She does not ask
whether there might be a difference between the two. It is well known that
the Yahwistic writer portrays the narrative from an entirely different perspective. Robert Alter rightly notes that 'the two accounts are complementary rather than overlapping, each giving a different *kind* of information
about how the world came into being'.[119] Trible's major problem with her

---

[117] Bird, 'Genesis I–III as a Source for a Contemporary Theology of Sexuality', p. 36.
For an elaborate and extended discussion of the same theme see her other essays, 'Male
and Female He Created them', pp. 129–159; 'Bone of my Bone and Flesh of my Flesh',
TToday 4 (1994), pp. 521–534; 'Sexual Differentiation and Divine Image in the Genesis
Creation Texts', in *Image of God and Gender Models in Judeo–Christian Tradition*,
(ed.) Kari Børresen (Oslo: Solum Forlag, 1991), pp.11–34; cf. Gordon J. Wenham,
Genesis 1–15 (WBC), p. 33. He comments: 'The expression 'male and female' is most
frequent in legal texts, and highlights rather the sexual distinctions within mankind and
foreshadows the blessing of fertility to be announced in v. 28'.

[118] Cf. Clines, 'What Does Eve Do to help?', p. 44. His argument is similar to Bird's.
Accordingly, he takes what immediately follows verse 27 as decisive in contrast to
Trible who takes what immediately precedes the verse. He negates the notion of equality of the sexes in the text. However he accepts equality in some respects, like the to-
getherness in creation, the humanness of both, the inclusiveness of both male and female
in '*adam*. Despite these points Clines argues that 'while the woman is fully human, she
is definitely subordinate to the man' (p. 44). For a comparison between Trible's and
Bird's position see Jo Ann Hackett, 'Women's Studies and the Hebrew Bible', in *The
Future of Biblical Studies: the Hebrew Scriptures*, (eds.) Richard Elliott Friedman and
H. G. M. Williamson (Georgia: Scholars Press, 1987), pp. 141–164 (here pp. 142–43).

[119] Alter, *The Art of Biblical Narrative*, p. 141, emphasis original. See also John F.A.
Sawyer, 'The image of God, The Wisdom of Serpents and the Knowledge of Good and

methodological approach is her treatment of both the stories of creation from a single perspective, ignoring the differences.[120] Although the Priestly narrative seems to provide a simultaneous creation of the sexes, the Yah-wistic account according to Alter 'imagines woman as a kind of divine af-terthought, made to fill a need of man, and made, besides, out of one of man's spare parts'.[121] So Alter sees two 'ostensibly contradictory accounts of the same event' as a narrative technique of the Hebrew writer, to provide a 'tension of views'. Accordingly, we see 'woman as man's equal sharer in dominion, standing exactly in the same relation to God as he; then, woman as man's *subservient helpmate*, whose weakness and blandishments will bring such woe into the world'.[122]

Although Alter's attempt to resolve the seeming contradictions of the creation accounts is commendable, his treatment of Gen. 1:27 seems to be similar to Trible's, especially when it comes to the meaning of the phrase 'male and female he created them'. At one point he also falls prey to for-malism. Accordingly he assumes that Gen. 1:27 is an egalitarian account of creation. We have already noted that the phrase more likely denotes bio-logical function rather than sociological function. It is true that the woman was a simultaneous creation and the sharer of dominion with the man since

---

Evil', in *A Walk in the Garden* (eds.) Paul Morris & Deborah Sawyer (Sheffield: JSOT Press), pp. 64–73. Sawyer argues that the two accounts of creation are not contradictory, rather 'the Garden of Eden story in Genesis is an expansion of the "image of God" story in ch.1... the two stories say the same things about human nature, the one in rather stark theological language, the other more in the style of a myth or fable', here p. 64.

[120] The two accounts differ in many respects such as language, style and form. The order of creation for instance, is considerably different. In the first account (P), the order is light, firmament–heaven, dry land, vegetation, heavenly bodies, birds and fishes, ani-mals and finally the human kind. In the Yahwistic account (J), the order is man, vegeta-tion, animals and finally woman. Cf. also Bird, 'Genesis I–III as a source for a contem-porary theology of sexuality', pp. 36ff.

[121] Alter, p. 141. Alter thinks that this is because the writer is a member of a patriarchal society in which women had only a limited role in legal and institutional matters. So the 'social convention' attributes to woman a subsidiary position to man (p. 146); for a similar cinematic interpretation of the creation accounts cf. Larry J. Kreitzer, *The Old Testament in Fiction and Film: On Reversing the Hermeneutical Flow* (Sheffield: Shef-field Academic Press, 1994), pp. 126–138; see also A. Brenner, *The Israelite Woman: Social Role and Literary Type in Biblical Narrative* (Sheffield: JSOT Press, 1985, p. 124; S. S. Lanser, 'Feminist Criticism in the Garden: Inferring Genesis 2–3', *Semeia* 41 (1988), 67–84; Ann Gardner, 'Genesis 2:4b–3: A Mythological Paradigm of Sexual Equality or the Religious History of Pre–exilic Israel?', *SJT* 43 (1990), pp. 1–18.

[122] Ibid., p. 146, emphasis mine, Cf. Bar–Efrat, *Narrative Art in the Bible*, Sheffield, Almond, 1984, p. 99. He observes the concept of 'measure for measure' with regard to the punishment of the man and the woman for their disobedience. He writes: 'the sin of eating gives rise to the punishment of eating ("In the sweat of your face you shall eat bread"), the woman's tempting of the man leads to the man's supremacy over the woman ("... and he shall rule over you")'.

האדם (*hā–'ādām*) is a generic term and the parallel line includes both sexes, yet it does not follow that there is equality between them. Another difficulty arises with Alter's interpretation of J's account, where he sees the woman as a subservient helpmate to the man. Here Alter seems to exaggerate the case. As we have seen in the narrative the woman is created as 'a helper fit for him', not as a secondary helper.[123] Westermann also argues:

> "a helper fit for him" refers neither to the sexual nature of woman (so Augustine) nor to the help which she could offer to the farmer. Any such limitation destroys the meaning of the passage. What is meant is the personal community of man and woman in the broadest sense— bodily and spiritual community, mutual help and understanding, joy and contentment in each other.[124]

From this we can conclude that the help which the woman provided to the man is not merely procreative help as Clines now argues. At the same time Trible opted for the other extreme, placing the woman in the centre of the narrative, emphasising only the equality and overlooking the differences.[125] The truth seems very likely to lie somewhere in between. Here the traditional reading seems likely to be more appropriate. As Von Rad comments: 'God designed a help for him, to be "corresponding to him" (כנגדו–*kenegdô*)–she was to be like him, at the same time *not identical with him*, but rather his counterpart, *his complement.*'[126] In the light of J's perspective it is very doubtful whether the J narrative portrays the woman as being the same as the man in every role and function. On the other hand, the text does not assign a secondary role to the woman since only with the creation of woman did the act of creation reach its culmination. The man welcomes her as the 'bone of my bones and flesh of my flesh'. Here Trible overemphasises the case by ignoring the complementary aspect of woman's help for which she was created. Her main concern is to emphasise the ideal

---

[123] Von Rad, *Genesis*, p. 80.

[124] Claus Westermann, *Genesis 1–11, A Commentary,* (trans.) John J. Scullion (London: SPCK/Minneapolis: Augsburg, 1984) , p. 232; see also Werner Neuer, *Man and Woman in Christian Perspective,* (trans) Gordon Wenham (London: Hodder and Stoughton, 1990), pp. 69ff (original *Mann und Frau in Christlicher Sicht,* Giessen and Basle, Brunnen Verlag, 1988).

[125] For a discussion of the differences between the sexes, see Neuer, pp. 69ff.

[126] Von Rad, *Old Testament Theology: The Theology of Israel's Historical Traditions,* vol. 1, (trans) D.M.G. Stalker (London: SCM Press, 1975), p. 149, emphasis mine. Cf. Bird, who argues that J's account is a complement to P, providing a psycho–social meaning of sexuality which includes companionship, the sharing of work, mutual attraction and commitment. See 'Sexual Differentiation and Divine Image in the Genesis Creation Texts', p. 23.

unity of the man and the woman. This seriously affects her proposal for an Old Testament feminist theology based on the creation narratives.

Another problem with Trible's reading is her superficial treatment of other important aspects within the narrative. She reads the narrative mainly as 'A love story gone awry', and in doing so she pays very little attention to other important themes such as prohibition, transgression and punishment.[127] Although Trible's readings broaden our understanding of the narrative, we need to ask again the descriptive question first; namely, how the narrative would have been understood by its first readers, whether as a love story or as something else. And from this perspective, it is hard to eliminate the dimension of humankind's first transgression of the divine commandment. Bruce Vawter rightly observes: '... since the perspective is of the first man and woman, it can be viewed as the first sin and first transgression-'[128]

EXEGETICAL DIFFICULTIES

The meaning of האדם (hā–'ādām)

Now we need to examine the details of Trible's exegesis. Her interpretation of האדם (hā–'ādām) as a sexually undifferentiated earth creature raises many exegetical difficulties. According to her interpretation the 'man' did not exist before the woman and both came into being simultaneously at the sexual differentiation of male and female in Gen. 2: 21–23. There are a number of problems with this view.

First, האדם (hā–'ādām) is a complete human being even before the creation of the woman, with the capacity to till and work the ground and also with the power to name the animals which the Lord created. We also see the human characteristics of solitary feelings in האדם (hā–'ādām). Second, the terminology does not change after the creation of the woman; rather the term האדם (hā–'ādām) continues to be used with the article (Gen. 2: 25; 3:8, 9, 2, 20).[129]

---

[127] Cf. Robert C. Culley, *Themes and Variations,* pp. 122ff.

[128] Bruce Vawter, *On Genesis: A New Reading* (New York: Doubleday & Company, Inc, 1977), p. 79. For a similar view see Speiser, *Genesis;* George W. Coats, *Genesis with an Introduction to Narrative Literature* (Grand Rapids: Michigan, William B. Eerdmans, 1983); C. Westermann, *Genesis 1–11; Creation,* (trans) John J. Scullion (Philadelphia: Fortress Press/London: SPCK, 1974); Von Rad, *Genesis*; Victor Hamilton, *The Book of Genesis Chapters 1–17* (NICOT; Grand Rapids, Michigan: William B. Eerdmans, 1990); Wenham, *Genesis 1–15* ; David Atkinson, *The Message of Genesis 1–11* (BST; Leicester: IVP, 1990).

[129] Childs points out that the Massoretic tradition treats the term 'man' as a proper name before the creation of woman. Here in 2:20b, the noun אדם is used without an article. He also finds support in the Septuagint tradition where in both places in Gen. 2: 20 אדם

On the view of Trible and Bal, after the creation of woman האדם (*hā–'ādām*) should have been rendered without an article. So the presence or the absence of the definite article is not an absolute criterion in determining whether the particular usage signifies a common noun or a proper noun. After the creation of the 'man' (male) and the 'woman' (female), האדם (*hā–'ādām*) does not disappear. Trible and Bal thus cannot satisfactorily explain what happened to the 'earth creature' after what they see as the creation of sexuality. Contrary to their argument, and following the evidence of the text, האדם (*hā–'ādām*) never ceased to exist; rather the term is used continuously in the narrative to depict the man. In this respect, Anne Gardner rightly observes that 'there is no creation of the male analogous to that of the female'.[130]

Trible thinks that האדם (*hā–'ādām*) became a sexual being only after the differentiation of איש (*'îš*) and אשה (*'iššâ*) in Gen. 2:21–24. So she argues that Yahweh made woman from the earth creature. However, she does not explain how the earth creature became a sexual being. It is noteworthy that Yahweh brought the woman to האדם (*hā–'ādām*), not to the איש (*'îš*). This means the status of the man is not changed after the creation of woman, as Trible argues. It is also important to note the response of האדם (*hā–'ādām*) from the narrative. 'Then the man said, 'This at last is bone of my bones and flesh of my flesh; this one shall be called Woman, for out of Man [איש *'îš*] this one was taken'. Though it is a pun, the issue here is whether the woman was taken from the 'earth creature' or from the איש (*'îš*–male). Trible does not explain this. According to her male and female are created from the earth creature as an evolutionary process. If we apply the same logic of Trible, it is also plausible that Yahweh first created איש (*'îš*) from the earth creature and then אשה (*'iššâ*) from the איש (*'îš*).

Trible's interpretation has been challenged by both feminist and non–feminist biblical scholars. Richard Hess argues with the help of ancient Near Eastern background material and linguistics. In Akkadian texts of the second millennium BC, the logographic sign *lu´* was used for 'man' or 'human being'. It was prefixed in syllabic cuneiform to names of offices and functions. For instance, to refer to the 'leader of the city of Kumidu', *lu´ Uru Kumidi* was used.[131] Hess compares the usage of the Hebrew term אדם (*'ādām*) in Gen. 2–4 with the *lu´* sign, as both refer to the West Semitic world of the second millennium BC. He argues that 'both *'dm* and the *lu´* sign have a similar semantic range in their usage in the written languages in

---

is used as a proper name. See Brevard S. Childs, *Old Testament Theology in a Canonical Context,* pp. 190–91.

[130] Anne Gardner, 'Genesis 2: 4b–3: A Mythological Paradigm of Sexual Equality or of the Religious History of Pre–exilic Israel', *SJT* 43 (1990), p. 7.

[131] R. S. Hess, 'Splitting the Adam: The Usage of *'ādām* in Genesis I–V', in *Studies in the Pentateuch,* (ed.) J. A. Emerton (VTS 41; Leiden: E. J. Brill, 1990), p. 6.

which they occur. They each carry meanings "man", "human being", and "humanity" in general'.[132] In other words, the same term carries different shades of meaning. So in their respective contexts both the above terms (*'dm* and *lu´*) 'refer to a particular individual who has or is given responsibility for the care and maintenance of a particular geographical area, be that a city, a city state, a region, or a garden'.[133] Hess also notes the development of אדם (*'ādām*) from a generic term or title to a personal name.[134] Hence in the light of semantic, linguistic and functional similarities, he asserts that אדם (*'ādām*) is used as a title in the opening chapters of Genesis. This explanation shows how a different line of enquiry regarding the text may produce a different result. It points to the limited nature of Trible's angle.

Applying another different line of enquiry, namely speech act theory, to Genesis 2–3, Susan Lanser challenges Trible's and Bal's readings. In her paper she questions the egalitarian readings proposed both by Bal and Trible. She contends that the traditional reading of Gen. 2–3 'is consistent with the model of communication proposed by speech act theory, whereby meaning always depends on specific contexts of language use in which the process of inference plays a powerful role'.[135]

She argues that אדם (*'ādām*) is a male in the creation narrative because 'when a being assumed to be human is introduced into a narrative, that be-

---

[132] Ibid., p. 7.

[133] Ibid.

[134] See Hess's summary here: 'As a description of humanity in general, *h'dm* in ch. i refers to all people who have existed and will ever exist. It has the sense of humanity in general. In ch. ii, *h'dm* as a title carries the sense of the male who is set in the Garden of Eden to take care of it. Here it is placed within a temporal context and therefore does not serve as a generic reference. Instead, it refers to that male who is responsible for the Garden of Eden', (p. 9).

[135] Susan S. Lanser, '(Feminist) Criticism in the Garden: Inferring Genesis 2–3', *Semeia* 41 (1988), pp. 67–84 [67]. Lanser makes use of the speech act model of communication developed by J. L. Austin, H. P. Grice and John R. Searle. She argues: that 'Meaning is... a function of the *context* in which linguistic communication is performed' (p. 70). She points out that Trible uses 'language as a code or system of signs, in which meaning is a function of semantic, grammatical, and phonological or orthographical properties and communication a process of encoding and decoding sentences' (Lanser. p. 70). The main difference seems to be that Trible is involved in decoding signs but Lanser takes into account contextual inferences. So for Lanser the meaning of a text is derived from its given context. So the 'Speech act theory offers the means to orient literature away from various formalisms which detach the text from its historical and social matrix, toward its concrete context, without engulfing it once again in the psychological, social and historical conditions of its production'. See Hugh C. White, 'Introduction: Speech act theory and Literary Criticism', *Semeia* 41 (1988), p. 2.

ing is also assumed to have sexual as well as grammatical gender'.[136] Accordingly in the narrative she treats האדם (*hā–'ādām*) as a man (male) from whom the woman is created. Thus in a quite different way from Hess, Lanser has broadened the context of enquiry compared with Trible, locating the meaning of a text in the light of context and inference.

In her semiotic analysis of the narrative, Ellen van Wolde emphasises the importance of the communicative context, the experience of life, and the reading experience of the reader in the generation of meaning or *semiosis*. Accordingly she notes that the common name Adam in Genesis 2–3 functions as an individual and it denotes 'both the individual human being and the individual male human being'.[137]

Anne Gardner, interpreting Gen. 2–3 against its ancient Near Eastern mythological context, disputes Trible's claim that both the man and woman were equal since both of them were made from raw material processed by God. Gardner raises the point that this itself implies male and female, so goes against Trible's own claim that האדם (*hā–'ādām*) was sexually undifferentiated until the appearance of the female. She points out that there was no male creation analogous to that of the female. She supports the idea of woman being taken from Adam's rib with the ancient mythology of the male giving birth.[138]

Contrary to Trible's conception, Phyllis Bird who reads the text with literary–historical methods with an intention 'to recover the author's intention', understands האדם (*hā–'ādām*) as both the 'genus and the first individual, who appears as male and not androgynous, though the woman is formed from him'.[139] In her latest work, she translates אדם (*'ādām*) as 'the human' and understands him as a term or a title for the species. She argues that, as per the ancient Hebrew social norms and linguistic conventions האדם (*hā–'ādām*) is understood as male. In addition to the grammatical

---

[136] Lanser, p. 72. See also for a similar reading, Elizabeth Achtemeier, 'The Impossible Possibility: Evaluating the Feminist Approach to Bible and Theology', *Int* 42 (1988), p. 51.

[137] Ellen van Wolde,*Words Become Worlds,* p. 16; for her detailed analysis of Genesis 2–3 see *A Semiotic Analysis of Genesis 2–3: A Semiotic Theory and Method of Analysis Applied to the Story of the Garden of Eden* (Assen: van Gorcum, 1989); see also Julie Galambush, ''*ādām* from '*adāmâ*, '*iššâ* from '*îš* : Derivation and Subordination in Genesis 2. 4b–3. 24', in *History and Interpretation: Essays in Honour of John H. Hayes,* (eds.) M. Patrick Graham *et al.* (Sheffield: JSOT Press, 1993). She rightly points out that the term '*îš* indicates *ādām's* 'manliness', and it is used in relation to '*iššâ* (Gen. 3:6, 3:16), p. 36.

[138] Anne Gardner, 'Genesis 2:4b–3: A Mythological Paradigm of Sexual Equality or of the Religious History of Pre–exilic Israel?', p. 7.

[139] Phyllis A Bird, 'Images of Women in the Old Testament', p. 287 note 88; cf. also, Ilana Pardes, *Countertraditions in the Bible: A Feminist Approach* (Cambridge, MA: Harvard University Press, 1992), p. 23.

convention, he is portrayed as 'a peasant cultivator representing the typical occupation of the ancient Israelite male...'[140]

Brevard S. Childs, holds the view that on many grounds Trible's position cannot be sustained. He from a literary perspective, notes that Genesis 2 has a different narrative movement from chapter one about the creation of male and female. Hence the woman is formed from the sleeping אדם ('*ādām*) and formed into a אשה ('*iššâ*). Childs says:

> There is no indication that '*ādām* was split into an '*îš* and a[n] '*iššah*, but rather the '*iššah* is derived from the '*îš*. There is no sign of a simultaneous creation of sexuality. The description of the woman being formed from a portion of the man is given in a way which is not parallel to the creation of '*ādām* in ch. 1.[141]

Secondly, he examines Trible's argument that האדם (*hā–'ādām*–the earth creature) is differentiated into an איש ('*îš*) and אשה ('*iššâ*) in 2:18–23–that is as male and female human beings. However, against Trible's thesis, the term אדם ('*ādām*) continues to be used as a parallel for איש ('*îš*). Hence, he says, her argument cannot be sustained linguistically.

Many other readers who employ modern methodological devices also read this narrative, but cannot reach the conclusion which Trible proposes. Alan J. Hauser, for instance, treats man as an individual in the narrative and his intimate relationship with woman and their inter–dependence.[142] James G. Williams also considers האדם (*hā–'ādām*) as both humankind and a man in the story.[143] By using the same method as Trible (rhetorical criticism), J.T. Walsh reads האדם (*hā–'ādām*) as male from the beginning of the narrative.[144] Similarly J. Rogerson considers Trible's readings as doubtful.[145]

Feminist readers may allege that male writers who criticise Trible do so due to their gender bias. On the other hand we also need to acknowledge that feminist readers themselves oppose Trible's reading and support the traditional rendering of האדם (*hā–'ādām*) as male in the narrative. It is conspicuous from Trible's reading that her main intention is to counter all the traditional arguments. That is why she negates the sequential creation of

---

[140] Bird, 'Bone of my bone and flesh of my flesh', *TToday* 4 (1994), 523.

[141] Childs, *Old Testament Theology in a Canonical Context*, p. 190.

[142] Alan J. Hauser, 'Genesis 2–3: The Theme of Intimacy and Alienation', in *Art and Meaning: Rhetoric in Biblical Literature*, pp. 20–36.

[143] James G Williams, *Women Recounted*, p. 70; cf. also David Jobling, *The Sense of Biblical Narrative: Structural Analysis in the Hebrew Bible* (Sheffield: JSOT Press, 1986), p. 41.

[144] J.T. Walsh, 'Genesis 2:4b–3:24: A Synchronic Approach', *JBL* 96 (1977), pp. 161–177.

[145] J. Rogerson, *Genesis 1–11*, OTG (Sheffield: JSOT Press), 1991, pp. 49–50.

man and woman and tries to establish a simultaneous creation of man and woman and thereby bring an egalitarian ideal. Although Trible's effort is important, in the light of the whole context of the text, her reading should be resisted. Trible has in fact over–interpreted the word האדם (*hā–'ādām*) and made him, or 'it', a senseless creature.

We have examined various readings of the term האדם (*hā–'ādām*). Both the traditional historical critical methods and the modern approaches, such as speech act and semiotic models, understand האדם (*hā–'ādām*) as ambiguous in the narrative. In other words, האדם (*hā–'ādām*) is seen as a complete human being with solitary feelings even before the creation of woman. He represents both generic humanity and a male human being in the narrative. Our examination of the text and of several other readings point strongly to this conclusion.

The meaning of עזר כנגדו (*'ezer kenegdô*)

Trible's explanation of עזר כנגדו (*'ezer kenegdô*) is also not new. Already before Trible, a similar explanation was suggested by traditional biblical scholars. For instance, the connotation of the word עזר (*'ezer*) being a superior was already proposed by Clarence J. Vos.[146] Trible's interpretation of עזר כנגדו (*'ezer kenegdô*) as 'a companion corresponding to it' is not unique.[147] But interestingly most of the modern readers quote Trible for this explanation of the term as if she had proposed this rendering for the first time.[148]

We have already seen how the term עזר כנגדו (*'ezer kenegdô*) has been translated as one which does not carry any inferior sense but rather indicates an egalitarian status along with the man. Recently, in his literary reading of this passage, David J. A. Clines has argued that the woman was in fact taking an inferior role in the narrative and her role was to help man in the process of procreation. For that purpose alone man needs a helper.[149] His argument seems to be that 'though superiors may help inferiors, strong may help weak, gods may help humans, in the act of helping they are being "inferior". That is to say, they are subjecting themselves to a secondary, subordinate position'.[150] So the one helped is the superior and the helper is

---

[146] See Clarence J. Vos, *Woman in Old Testament Worship* (Amsterdam: N.V. Verenigde Drukkerijen Judels & Brinkman–Delft, 1968), p. 18.

[147] Trible, p. 90, cf. her translation with the above translations.

[148] See Gunn and Fewell, *Narrative in the Hebrew Bible*, p. 194.

[149] Clines, *What does Eve Do to Help?*, pp. 25–48; cf. Bird, who in her recent work also supports Clines' reading and suggests that the woman's primary role in being a helper to the man is in childbearing, see 'Bone of my bone and flesh of my flesh', *TToday* 4 (1994), p. 525.

[150] Ibid., pp. 30–31.

the inferior. This principle he applies to the narrative and accordingly he reads עזר in the narrative as an inferior.

Clines' argument is not fully convincing. His argument cannot be applied to all situations. Some help may be superior and other inferior. It is not necessary when you help somebody always to take a subordinate role, as Clines argued. Let me cite an example close to home: when I am preparing this dissertation, I am being helped by my supervisors. I never think that they are taking an inferior role, rather the opposite. When I help others I feel some sense of superiority because I think that I have the capacity to help them in some way in which they are not able to manage by themselves. So Clines' argument is subjective and hard to establish.[151] Responding to Clines' argument, Lyn M. Bechtel, pursuing a structuralist methodology, argues that the word עזר does not carry any sense of superiority or inferiority built into it. She aptly notes: 'When a suzerain helps a vassal, the suzerain remains politically superior. When a vassal helps a suzerain, the vassal remains inferior. It is the cultural context that determines superiority and inferiority, not the act of helping.'[152]

Now the question remains, is the woman inferior or superior to the man or an equal with man? Since the word כנגדו (*kenegdô*) is a *hapax legomenon,* it is difficult to find the true meaning of this Hebrew adverb. The adverb נגד (*ngd*) is used in the Old Testament in various ways. It can be translated as 'in front of', 'before', 'opposite to', 'over against' or 'toward'. BDB translates the whole phrase as 'a help *corresponding* to him, i.e. equal and adequate to himself'.[153] In the Old Testament generally the word עזר (*ezer*) is used mainly in relation to God as the helper in a superior sense. But Vos rightly observes that 'the expression "fit for him"[כנגדו] here modifying [עזר] makes this unlikely'.[154] On the other hand woman is in no way inferior to the man in the creation account. So the question of woman either as an inferior or a superior does not arise out of the content. Does the text then say that she is his equal? In this connection, it is to be noted that she is created in the process of the search for a suitable companion for man in the narrative, and this could be regarded as an equal complement. This aspect had already been noted by Delitzsch back in the last century. According to him the term meant, 'one who by relative difference and essen-

---

[151] Contra Clines, see van Wolde, *Words Become Worlds,* p. 18. She argues that the term עזר does not have any sense of superiority or inferiority on the part of the person giving or receiving the aid; cf. also W. Vogels, 'It is not good that the "Mensch" should be alone; I will make him/her a helper fit for him/her', *Eg T* 9 (1978), pp. 25–35.

[152] See L. M. Bechtel, 'Rethinking the Interpretation of Genesis 2.4B–3.24', in *A Feminist Companion to Genesis,* p. 113.

[153] *BDB,* p. 617.

[154] C. J. Vos, *Women in Old Testament Worship,* p. 16.

tial equality should be his fitting complement'.[155] He argued that this is why the term כנגדו is used rather than the term כמוהו (*kemoho*–like him) in the narrative. Gordon Wenham also advocates the idea of complementarity rather than identity.[156]

In the light of the above discussion it is doubtful whether Trible's conclusion concerning the phrase עזר כנגדו ('*ezer kenegdô*) is unequivocal. She undermined at the outset the aspect of help the woman provided to the man in being a עזר ('*ezer*). Moreover, Trible herself pointed out that the term עזר has been used in relation to God as a 'superior one'. Generally in relation to God עזר (*ezer*) is translated as 'helper'[157] in the Old Testament. If that is the case we do not need to change from a 'suitable helper' to a 'corresponding companion'. If God can be the helper of human beings why may not the woman be a helper to the man? I think van Wolde's rendering of כנגדו עזר ('*ezer kenegdô*) as 'a corresponding help' or 'a helper corresponding to him' would be more true to the text in the light of the wider context of the Old Testament.

I do not agree with Clines that Adam needs woman's help only for fulfilling God's divine command in Gen. 1:28, that is to procreate. He argues that Church Fathers like Augustine and Aquinas were right in advocating this viewpoint. But we need to note that first, the help is needed to remove the solitariness of man, and then it is needed in tilling the earth (2:15). So the 'Woman saves the human both from loneliness and from mortal danger, because she saves him from the threat of non–survival... It is God who sees the need for differentiation, because what he has in mind is a life in perpetuity and a continual tilling of the earth.'[158] So woman's role as a helper to the man is not merely procreative. Procreation is linked with the broader purpose of אדם ('*ādām*) in the world.

From the above discussion we can conclude that the phrase עזר כנגדו ('*ezer kenegdô*) neither connotes superiority nor inferiority in the creation status. However, Trible's rendering of it as 'companion corresponding to him' entirely eclipses the aspect of help which the woman provides to the man. In other words, though the woman seems to be a 'corresponding companion' in status and rank, in the narrative she functions as a 'corresponding helper' to the man. Westermann rightly observes: '2:18 is looking to the mutuality of the relationship, the complementarity of the companionship. This does not exclude a relationship of subordination: one could

---

[155] Franz Delitzsch, *A New Commentary on Genesis* vol. 1, (trans) Sophia Taylor, (Edinburgh: T&T Clark, 1888), p. 140.

[156] Wenham, *Genesis 1–15*, p. 68; cf. B. S. Childs, *Old Testament Theology in a Canonical Context*, p. 192.

[157] See Ex. 18:4 'The God of my father was my help' (בעזרי), see also Pss. 33:20; 70:5(6); 115; 9, 10, 11.

[158] Van Wolde, *Words Become Worlds*, p. 19; see also p. 18.

not say in 2:18 that man is created as a helper for the woman'.[159] Moreover, there is linguistic difficulty in translating the term עזר (*'ezer*) as companion in the light of other Old Testament passages. So it is better to understand the phrase as a 'corresponding helper'. A recent translation of this
passage by a female scholar reads: 'I will make for it a help as its counterpart.'[160]

Both Trible and Clines unduly emphasise only one aspect of the term עזר
(*'ezer*). Trible overlooks the helping aspect in the story; Clines the other aspects of help apart from procreative help for which the woman is created by
God. It seems to me that procreation is only one aspect of their companionship and that the equality which Trible proposes is also not there in the narrative.

The naming formula

Trible's conclusion regarding the naming seems to be unclear. It is not
necessary that in all cases the verb קרא *(qr')* should be joined to the noun שם
(*šem*) to form a naming formula as Trible argued. Contrary to her own argument we read in Gen. 35:18 that ' as her soul was departing (for she
died), she called his name Ben–Oni; but his father called his name Benjamin' (RSV). It is to be noted that in the Hebrew text the noun שם (*šem*) is
used in one place only. Hence the second part of the verse should read:
'but his father *called him* Benjamin'. Trible cannot say that it is not a naming formula due to the absence of the noun since in Old Testament society
fathers exercise more power over children than mothers. So it is not necessary for the verb and the noun to go together to make a naming formula.
Since the context in Gen. 35:18 is naming the son, it is not necessary to repeat the noun again. But it is very clear from the context that his father also
called his *name,* though the text only says 'but his father *called* him Benjamin'. We also need to note that in the context of God's creation in Gen. 1,
the verb קר *(qr')* alone is constantly used in relation to naming the things
which God created (vv. 5, 8, 10).[161]

In the light of the above argument, it is only the context which decides
whether a situation is name–giving or not. The presence or the absence of
the formula is not an absolute rule. The creation of woman is in the context
of man naming the animals, birds and beasts. Although man named the

---

[159] Westermann, *Genesis,* p. 262.

[160] See Mary Phil Korsak, *At the Start... Genesis Made New: A Translation of the Hebrew Text,* Kessel–Lo, Van der Poorten Press (Printed for the European Association
for the Promotion of Poetry), 1992, p. 6. This book is a translation of the whole book of
Genesis. It follows the Hebrew original very literally.

[161] Cf. Clines, 'What Does Eve Do to help', pp. 38–40.

animal kingdom, he could not find a suitable helper among them.[162] In this context, the Yahweh God made woman for man. Then the man said, 'This shall be called woman' (Gen. 2:23). So this also is a naming situation, even though the above form is not repeated. Trible acknowledges that by naming the animals the 'earth creature' was establishing power over the animals. But if so, the naming of woman indicates the same. This observation can be supported by modern hermeneutical insights.

Employing speech act theory, Lanser points out the situation 'in which ordinary discourse abbreviates syntactic forms in a context where a clear inference can be presumed'.[163] In the light of this she argues that in Genesis 2:19–22 a sequence has been set up where האדם (*hā-'ādām*) has been authorised to name. Hence she asserts: 'the text has already generated the context in which "call" may be inferred to mean "call the name of," despite the abbreviated surface form. Repetition of *haššem* is not needed'.[164]

Lanser's conclusion seems convincing and true to the context. Clines also argues that Gen. 2:23 is a naming formula. He rightly points out that 'in Genesis 1 all the naming has gone on exclusively by means of the verb "call", without the "name" ever being used. So it cannot be denied that "calling" is a perfectly acceptable Hebrew way of describing naming....'[165]

In the light of the above evidence, Trible's thesis concerning the naming is highly doubtful. Trible rightly acknowledges that 'through the power of naming, animals are subordinated to the earth creature;'[166] so, by the same token, is the woman subordinated to the man. The point has again been established by considering a variety of approaches to the text.

The meaning of עמה (*'immāh*)

Trible's treatment of ותאכל ותתן גם לאישה עמה ויאכל (And she ate and gave also to her husband who was with her and he ate–(My translation) deserves special attention. Trible argues that the term עמה points out the man's real

---

[162] See Thomas E. Boomershine, 'The Structure of Narrative Rhetoric in Gen. 2–3', *Semeia* 18 (1980), p. 116. He observes a parallelism between God bringing the animals to the man (2:19) and the bringing of woman by God to man (2:22). My only intention here is to show the possible connection between the two.

[163] Lanser, 1988, p. 73.

[164] Ibid. Cf. Howard N. Wallace, *The Eden Narrative* (Georgia: Scholars Press, 1985), p. 147. He rightly notes that the woman was named in the context of man's naming of other creatures. For a different viewpoint concerning the aspect of name giving, see George W. Ramsey, 'Is Name-giving an Act of Domination in Gen. 2:23 and Elsewhere?', *CBQ* 50 (1988), pp. 24–35. To him the naming of woman 'is an act of discernment rather than an act of domination' (p. 35). He also points out that the meaning of naming is commonly determined by the circumstances. I agree with the second suggestion, but the first seems to be unconvincing.

[165] Clines, *What Does Eve Do to Help?* p. 38.

[166] Trible, p. 92.

presence in the disobedience scene. The phrase 'with her' is omitted in modern translations though it is retained in KJV, the Jerusalem Bible and in the New American Bible. Other feminists have also argued that the man was present when the woman conversed with the serpent.[167] The use of the plural verbs in the narrative like לא תאכלו (You shall not eat), נאכל (we may eat), לא תאכלו (you shall not eat), לא תגעו (you shall not touch), תמתון (you shall die), ונפקחו עיניכם (your eyes will be opened), והייתם (you will be like) shows the presence of the man. Yet the plural verb does not necessarily mean that the man was present in person, since the serpent already knows that the woman knows the original commandment which was given to the man only, and it also assumes it was binding on both of them. If that is the case the serpent can use the plural verb to represent both members of the couple. Moreover, the narrator's use of the verbal forms seems to me inconsistent in the narrative. For instance, he only tells us that God sent out the man (וישלחהו–and he sent him out [singular]) from the garden; we know that the woman was also sent out, though the text is silent. Arguments, therefore, from the use of singular or plural in the narrative are inconclusive.

Now we need to examine the meaning of the term עמה (*'immāh*). This is considered to be the strongest argument for the presence of the man in the conversation with the serpent. This can be interpreted in both ways as 'an actual presence' or 'mere association'.[168] Lange argued that 'with her' is adverbial, modifying the verb 'gave'. Then it should be read as 'she took it and ate, and also (besides feeding herself alone) gave it to her man along with herself'.[169] We do not know whether the term here means actual presence or mere association. If we take it as actual presence then Trible is right, 'the man is passive, brutish, and inept' and the woman is 'intelligent, sensitive and ingenious'. But the naming of the animals by the man in the scene before the creation of the woman does not present the man as dull and stupid. Moreover we need to explain the man's silence here. He responds quickly enough throughout the rest of narrative (e.g. man's naming of all the animals, man's response when the woman was brought to him, man's hiding when he heard the sound of the Lord after eating the fruit, his response to the Lord's question, Adam's naming of his wife). The question remains why the man did not enter into conversation with the serpent at least at the point when the serpent distorted the original command, if he was

---

[167] See Elizabeth Cady Stanton, *The Woman's Bible*, p. 26; Katherine Doob Sakenfeld, 'The Bible and Woman: Bane or Blessing', *TToday* 32 (1975), p. 225; Jean M. Higgins, 'The Myth of Eve: The Temptress', *JAAR* 44 (1976), pp. 645–647; van Wolde, *A Semiotic Analysis of Genesis 2–3,* p. 180, note 73; see also *Words Become Worlds,* p. 22; Fleming, *Man and Woman in Biblical Unity,* p. 22.

[168] See Higgins, 'The Myth of Eve', p. 646.

[169] Lange, *A Commentary on the Holy Scriptures* as cited in 'The Myth of Eve', p. 646.

present. These concerns also have to be taken into consideration before we jump to any conclusion.

Woman's intelligence or man's passivity

Both Trible and Bal argue that the woman is more intelligent than the man and functions as spokesperson in the narrative. Here they are reading too much into the text. Although the serpent treated the woman as the spokesperson, the Lord God asked the man first regarding the transgression, even though the woman initiated the disobedience. In his examination of the plot of the narrative, Shimon Bar–Efrat notes the importance of the man in this regard: 'The man's special importance is indicated by the fact that he is the first and the last character to whom God speaks'.[170] If the woman was the spokesperson, we could expect her to be interrogated first concerning this. Moreover, she could answer more logically than man since the man is passive according to Trible's contention. In relation to the woman's response to God, Trible also argued that the woman did not blame the man as he did her, rather she confessed 'The serpent beguiled me' (not 'us')'.[171] If the woman was more intelligent than the man, we would never expect her to be deceived by the serpent.

Differently from Trible, Gerhard Von Rad writes in this context that 'the woman confronts the obscure allurements and mysteries that beset our limited life more directly than the man does. In the history of Yahweh–religion it has always been the women who have shown an inclination for obscure astrological cults'.[172] Richard S. Hess attempts to answer the question why the serpent approached the woman rather than the man. He suggests through close reading that by naming the snake the man would have discerned the shrewdness of the creature, but the woman was not party to this information and hence became vulnerable to the snake's 'persuasive powers' rather than man.[173] Both von Rad and Hess thus come to very different conclusions from Trible. Yet all three have probably read more into the text than can be justified. The fact is that we are not told why the serpent talked to the woman rather than to the man. Rather we see the strength of preconception in interpretation.

God's judgement: descriptive or prescriptive

Trible argues that the woman was not cursed by God although the serpent and the man (indirectly) were cursed by God. She also points out the comparative brevity of the judgement of the woman to show the lesser respon-

---

[170] Shimon Bar–Efrat, *Narrative Art in the Bible*, p. 99.

[171] Trible, *God and the Rhetoric*, p. 120.

[172] Von Rad, *Genesis*, p. 88.

[173] Richard S. Hess, 'The Roles of the Woman and the Man in Genesis 3', *Them* 18 (1993), p. 16.

sibility of the woman in the transgression. Though the judgement of the woman seems to be short, we cannot overlook the constant enmity between the serpent and the woman's offspring, that is the whole human race. In that respect, God's judgement of the serpent will be binding on the woman also. In this case the curse on the serpent relates also to the woman, though the woman was not cursed by God.

Susan S. Lanser argues that though the accusatory formula ('Because you have done this') is absent in relation to woman's judgement, 'the formula "Because you did this" simply carries over from the address to the serpent in 3:14 and is confirmed by the address to the man in 3:17'.[174] So the woman becomes the object of God's curse directly and indirectly. Now the question remains whether God's word to the woman in Gen. 3:16 is a punishment or a consequence of disobedience. Lanser rightly points out that Trible's and Bal's readings here reach the 'impasse, silence, that unravels their argument'. She points out that 'finally neither can explain why male dominance should be the particular consequence of a transgression for which both man and woman are equally, as they argue, responsible'.[175] So she argues that their readings have broken down. Then she goes on to comment that 'everyone brings cultural and personal contexts to the act of reading... they operate as a kind of grid that obscures certain meanings and brings others to the foreground'.[176]

We need to ask whether the subordination of the woman to the man in the narrative (Gen. 3: 16) is the original divine intention or the result of her disobedience. We need to acknowledge at the outset that a concrete answer to this question is not an easy task. Scholars have argued this case in both ways. A number have said that the woman's subordination is a result of the disobedience. Julie Galambush relates the suffering and subordination of both the man and the woman to their 'substance of origins', that is man to the ground from where he was taken and the woman to her husband from whom she was taken. However, she writes that the subordinate status 'is not a prescription for the world but a description of the world in which the

---

[174] Susan S. Lanser, '[Feminist] criticism in the Garden: Inferring Genesis 2–3', p. 74. Trible assumes 'a theory of language as formal code, in which meaning is a function of surface propositions and their semantic and grammatical properties' whereas Lanser makes use of 'the model of communication proposed by speech act theory, whereby meaning always depends on specific contexts of language use in which the process of inference plays a powerful role,' p. 67; cf. also Hugh C. White, *Narration and Discourse in the Book of Genesis* (Cambridge: Cambridge University Press, 1991), pp. 142–143. He also treats it as a 'curse'; cf. also Thomas E. Bommershine, 'The Structure of Narrative Rhetoric in Genesis 2–3', *Semeia* 18 (1980), p. 119.

[175] Lanser, p. 75.

[176] Ibid., p. 77.

author lived'.[177]   On the other hand, the traditional argument considers the subordination of woman as prescriptive. There are problems with both positions. 'If the woman were now punished with subjection under the man, he would be given an advantage which he least deserved at this point.'[178] Since the man is more responsible than the woman for the disobedience because he was given the original prohibition, he could not be given any privilege over the woman at this juncture. So man cannot be an executor of the punishment over the woman. At the same time it also cannot be descriptive as Lanser pointed out (see above); why should male dominance over the woman be a particular consequence for one of them, as both of them are equally responsible?   Hence there is no justification for such a consequence.

We need to resolve this from another angle.   Neuer attempts to resolve this difficulty by arguing that the subordination of the woman is a part of creation ordinance and not a result of sin.   He interprets the woman's initiative in the disobedience act as a ruling of the woman over her husband that is contrary to the divinely intended subordination.   So the rule of the man announced in Gen. 3:16 is only a move towards the original ordinance.   At the same time he notes that the מָשַׁל (*masal*) in 3:16 does not have any negative connotation as it is used in a positive sense in the Old Testament (Isa: 40:10; Ps. 22:28).   He writes: 'In Old Testament thinking man's rule and the subordination of women is not something negative. It is therefore questionable to start out with modern presuppositions and see Genesis 3:16 as bemoaning the oppression of women.'[179]   The difficulty with Neuer's conclusion is that the assumed subservience he proposed is not clearly spelled out in the creation narrative; rather it could only be inferred from the fact that the woman was created as a helper to the man.   Similarly in his close literary readings of the narrative, Jerome T. Walsh observes character relationships in the creation order.   Yahweh God has superior authority, the man has authority over the animals and the woman since he names them.

---

[177] Julie Galambush, ''ādām from 'adāmâ, 'iššâ from 'îš', p. 45. Moreover she argues that the subordination status is just like 'crop failure' in agriculture for men. So the situation in Gen. 3. 8–24 is not what God intended for the world; see also Walter Brueggemann, *Genesis: A Bible Commentary for Teaching and Preaching* (Atlanta: John knox), p. 51 and Westerman, *Genesis 1–11, A Commentary*, p. 262. Most feminist writers also argue in the same way. However, B. J. Stratton, quite recently argued that 'patriarchy is inscribed' in the story from the beginning and '[t]he man exercises his authority over her not only after the fruit–eating incident, but also before by naming her in 2. 23'. See B. J. Stratton, *Out of Eden: Reading, Rhetoric, and Ideology in Genesis 2–3* (JSOTS 208; Sheffield: Sheffield Academic Press, 1995), p. 101.

[178] B. Jacob, *Das erste Buch der Tora* , as cited in *Man and Woman in Christian Perspective,* p. 79.

[179] Neuer, *Man and Woman in Christian Perspective*, p. 80. For a similar view see Westermann, p. 262.

He summarises the hierarchy among the characters: 'Yahweh God is supreme; the man is the highest of the creatures, with the woman closely associated but subordinate to him; least of all are the animals.'[180]

Since none of these options is entirely satisfactory we must attempt another explanation. Gen. 3: 16 has to be understood in relation to verses 14–19, where it is clearly prescriptive judgement rather than a descriptive situation. The prescriptive punishment of the woman is not the ruling of the man over her but the number of conceptions and the pain in giving birth to children. Nevertheless, she still desires sexual union with him and he responds to this. The man's rule over the woman in this respect cannot be treated as authoritarian, since the man only responds to the woman's desire. The text doesn't say that the man will rule over the woman other than in the area of sex. Though the woman desires her husband for sexual union, the resulting conception and childbirth becomes painful for the woman. As a social norm, the woman in the ancient world cannot but continue to give birth to children. Carol Meyers aptly notes in this context: 'because she [woman] experiences desire and yearning for the man, such male control would not be experienced as oppressive'.[181] So I do not think this verse speaks about the man's supremacy over the woman in every sphere of life.[182] The man is not given any privilege in ruling over the woman. This line of interpretation enables us to view the passage as a prescriptive judgement of God upon the woman for her disobedience; at the same time man cannot enjoy general dominance over the woman as he is equally or even more responsible for the disobedience.

---

[180] Jerome T. Walsh, 'Genesis 2: 4b– 3: 24: A Synchronic Approach', *JBL* 96 (1977), p. 174.

[181] See Meyers, *Discovering Eve*, p. 116. However, I disagree with Meyers when she postulates that the social and economic necessities force the woman to have sexual relationship with the man frequently in order to meet the demand for more labour force in the highland economy of the Palestine. For an elaborate discussion of these issues see the chapter on Carol Meyers. Cf. the Jewish interpretation of this verse in *Genesis Rabbah: The Judaic Commentary to the Book of Genesis, A New American Translation, Parashiyyot One through Thirty–Three on Genesis 1:1 to 8: 14* , vol. I, (trans) Jacob Neusner (BJS 104; Atlanta: Scholars Press, 1985). It states: 'When a woman sits down on the birthstool, she says, "I shall never again have sexual relations with my husband". Then the Holy one, blessed be he, says to her, "you will return to your lust, you will return to having lust for your husband"', chapter XX: VII:2 (p. 221).

[182] So Robert B. Coote and David Robert Ord, *The Bibles's First History* (Philadelpia: Fortress Press, 1989), see p. 63.

HERMENEUTICAL DIFFICULTIES

Complexity of the feminist approach

It is not an easy task to evaluate feminist hermeneutics as it adopts various hermeneutical methods and holds different approaches to the text. In many cases a single author even applies divergent approaches to the text using the same methodology. However, we will make use of some of the hermeneutical criteria discussed in Part One to evaluate this section. Although *God and the Rhetoric of Sexuality* and *Texts of Terror* are companion volumes of Trible, the two books have opposite concerns. In her own words: 'The two volumes share a feminist perspective, a literary critical methodology, and the subject matter of female and male in the Hebrew scriptures. Yet the studies differ in emphasis and spirit. The first is a time to laugh and dance; the second, a time to weep and mourn.'[183] Even she finds positive and negative within a single work. In one place she reads the 'creation narrative' as an egalitarian text, and in another, she finds in the 'Ruth narrative' that Naomi and Ruth 'struggle for survival in a patriarchal environment'.[184] In modern literary terminology Trible's readings deconstruct themselves on some occasions. I have touched the above issues to show the complexity of feminist approaches.

While Trible with the qualification just made and some others[185] read the creation narrative positively as an egalitarian text, still other feminists read it negatively as a patriarchal text. I will illustrate. We read: 'Therefore a man leaves his father and his mother and cleaves to his wife, and they become one flesh'. According to Trible this is the consummation of Eros where 'the man does not leave one family to start another; rather, he abandons (*'zb*) familial identity for the one flesh of sexuality'.[186] On the other hand, it shows the 'woman's independence' and 'the woman stands alone,' according to Trible.[187] Applying similar literary method, Danna Nolan Fewell and David M. Gunn comment on the same verse:

> Implicit is a claim that the man's desire is the defining norm. He is the one leaving and cleaving. The woman is the point of gravity, the object

---

[183] Trible, *Texts of Terror,* p. xiii.

[184] Trible, *God and the Rhetoric,* p. 166.

[185] British feminist scholars also read the creation text in a positive manner along with other American feminist hermeneuts like Alice Laffey, *Wives, Harlots, and Concubines;* see Mary Hayter, *The New Eve in Christ;* Mary Evans, *Woman in the Bible;* Grace Emmerson. 'Women in Ancient Israel', in *The World of Ancient Israel,* pp. 371–394. Also see Meyers, *Discovering Eve.*

[186] Trible, *God and the Rhetoric,* p. 104.

[187] Trible, 'Treasures Old and New', p. 42.

to be acquired. She, by contrast, is allowed (at this point in the plot) no desire and no attachments to parents or children.[188]

In both readings a general literary approach has been employed. How might a reader decide which of the above readings of the text is true? Why are there diametrically opposite conclusions for the same text with the same feminist perspective?

Katharine Doob Sakenfeld in her essay on 'Feminist Interpretation'[189] points out the methodological problems inherent in feminist hermeneutics. Sakenfeld views 'unresolvable disputes' over the result of feminist writers who employ different approaches. Referring to another feminist reading Sakenfeld writes: 'Trible reads Genesis 2 as a celebration of the equality of male and female' whereas Rebecca Clouse thinks that 'the same kinds of formal literary criteria have been used to argue that the chapter is in fact a "text of terror" that displays subordination of the woman.'[190] Sakenfeld rightly notes that any method might be used 'in support of the silence and subordination of women– or in support of their voice and equality'.[191] What we can conclude from the above examples is that feminists can read any text either way, positively or negatively. B. J. Stratton is right in saying that '"what we know depends on where we stand", in terms of both our life experiences and our practical agendas'.[192] In hermeneutical terms, this is a typical example of an *intentio lectoris*, i.e. the reader's intention to make use of the text to serve her purpose. The conclusions of the readings considerably vary according to their perspectives to the text. This subjectivity has become a serious problem in feminist hermeneutics. The problem is seen more intensely among interpreters who use a formal literary approach for reading texts.

Complexity of feminist methods

Trible's hermeneutical method has its own problems. In Trible's method her interest is to find out what is 'in front of the text'. In her own words

---

[188] Danna Nolan Fewell and David M. Gunn, *Gender, Power, and Promise,* p. 29. Gunn is a male feminist and has co–authored with Fewell in most of her feminist readings.

[189] Katharine Doob Sakenfeld, 'Feminist Biblical Interpretation', *TToday* 46 (1989), pp. 154–168. This is a slightly modified version of her previous essay entitled 'In the Wilderness, Awaiting the Land: The Daughters of Zelophehad and Feminist Interpretation', *PSB* 19 (1988), pp. 179– 196.

[190] Sakenfeld, 'In the Wilderness ...,' p. 190. See also note 15. Rebecca Clouse prepared this paper for a Feminist Hermeneutics Course at Yale Divinity School in October 8, 1985 with the title 'Considering Speech and the Structures of Reality: Gen. 2: 18–24'.

[191] Ibid., p.191.

[192] See Stratton, *Out of Eden,* p. 252.

'Proper analysis of form yields proper articulation of meaning'.[193] Accord- ing to this method the meaning of text is determined by what is in the text. But in another place she writes: 'A single text appears in different versions with different functions in different contexts... What it says on one occa- sion, it denies on another. Thus, scripture in itself yields multiple interpre- tations of itself'.[194] What does she mean by saying what scripture says one occasion it denies on another? Is this not a form of deconstruction? If so, how can Trible reconcile this with her above assumption of articulating meaning within the text? This is another complexity of her method.

Yet another complexity with Trible's hermeneutics is her assumption of indeterminacy of the meaning of the text. Her first book was written in 1978 and the second six years later. Over these years major changes were witnessed in the realm of biblical hermeneutics. Having been influenced by general trends in the fields, Trible now adopts a reader–oriented approach in her readings. Concerning meaning she writes: 'In the interaction of text and reader, the changing of the second component alters the meaning and power of the first.'[195] From the above statement one could infer that read- ers determine the meaning of any text. Now she advocates that 'No reading is objective, so every reading is equally valid'. This assumption leaves no room for her readings to be criticised by others. However, in her first book, she suggested that 'Not all interpretations are valid, and not all valid inter- pretations are equally so. Methodology is one major criterion for evalua- tion.'[196]

On Trible's earlier hermeneutical stance, Lanser pointed out in the light of hermeneutical theory that Trible's use of the theory of language was not adequate and she failed to give attention to the 'multi–functional nature of the language'.[197] Accordingly Lanser rightly observes that 'meaning is cre- ated not only by decoding signs but by drawing on contextual assumptions to make inferences'.[198] In other words, Trible overlooked the function of other aspects of the language such as context and inference. Her main fo- cus was on the formal aspect of the language such as semantics, grammar and phonology.

Moreover, Trible's methodology is only a synchronic approach to the text without taking into account any referential function. We have noted in our first section that rhetorical analysis of a text with focus on the three di- mensions of a literary work, namely author, the text and the reader could bring better results. In Trible's reading the authorial and the historical di-

---

[193] Trible, *God and the Rhetoric,* p. 8.

[194] Ibid ., p. 4.

[195] Trible, 'Feminist Hermeneutics and Biblical Theology', *TS* 50 (1989), p. 294.

[196] *God and the Rhetoric*, p. 24 (note. 10).

[197] Lanser, 'Feminist Criticism in the Garden', p. 70; see also Thiselton, p. 454.

[198] Ibid.

mensions are completely lacking. Trible has not taken into account 'the communicative context of the text' in her reading and that limited its scope. This is because Trible overemphasises and exaggerates aspects which relate to the woman in order to counteract the traditional readings and undermines and overlooks other important aspects in the narrative. Here John Goldingay's criticism of 'those who pretend to be objective and critical and who then find their own concerns in the texts they study'[199] can be applied to Trible's reading.

Trible is also attacked by other feminist scholars for her formal literary approach. Pardes treats Trible's method as 'ahistorical' because she neglects the difference between the Yahwistic and the Priestly accounts by treating them homogeneously. At the same time Fiorenza also directs similar criticism against Trible. She shows that although Trible's definition of feminism is a 'critique of culture in light of misogyny', in practice 'she does not engage in such a feminist critique of Scripture's misogynist stamp and character as a document of patriarchal culture because her method allows her to abstract the text from its cultural–historical context'.[200] Fiorenza comments: 'a method divorcing the language and text of the Bible from its socio–cultural patriarchal conditions cannot provide a model for the reconstruction of women's history as members of biblical religion'.[201] Fiorenza asks whether the female imagery and traditions are only 'remnants' of patriarchal repression (Trible's view) or feminist 'countervoices'.

The problem of Trible's formal literary approach is evident in her treatment of the feminine imageries of the Old Testament. She has failed to note the function of imageries in their socio–religious contexts; rather she claimed them as examples of a 'depatriarchalizing' principle operating in the Scripture. Susanne Heine shows the difficulty in appealing to feminine features 'as a counterbalance to a long tradition of one–sided stress on the masculinity of God'.[202] She asks: '[W]hether that is honest and meaningful .... it is dangerous and contrary to basic feminist interests when a division of the male and female properties of God gives a boost to the usual stereotyping of roles'.[203] She argues that such a reading will lead to the notion that loving care, oversight, clothing, feeding, the household are seen as 'typically' feminine and justice, law, anger, punishment, power, as 'typically' masculine. She also points out that the maternal features which feminists bring out come from a tradition which is polemical towards 'goddess myths

---

[199] John Goldingay, 'How far Do Readers Make Sense?: Interpreting Biblical Narrative', *Them* 18 (1993), p. 7.

[200] Fiorenza, *In Memory of Her,* p. 20.

[201] Ibid., p. 21.

[202] Susanne Heine, *Christianity and the Goddesses: Can Christianity Cope with Sexuality?* (London: SCM Press, 1988), p. 28.

[203] Ibid.

and cults' (Hosea, Jeremiah, Deutero–Isaiah, Trito–Isaiah, Deuteronomy, the Priestly Writing). 'It is obvious what they want to say. Why do you need a mother goddess? Yahweh, the father, judge and warrior hero, can also give birth, breast feed, care for and have mercy.'[204]

In this discussion we must also ask why the Old Testament does not commonly use feminine imageries for God as it does male metaphors to depict God. Tryggve N. D. Mettinger rightly points to the sexuality of gods in the ancient near Eastern mythologies, particularly in Mesopotamia and Canaan. He shows that '[i]n Israel, by way of contrast, matters were different ... God was conceived as standing above the genders of the created world, that is, that God was held to be asexual'.[205] Further, he points out that androcentric metaphors are 'thematically neutral with respect to gender'. However, they are used to show 'the role that God plays in such texts'. He explains:

> God is neither male nor female, that God is above and beyond that distinction, and that the divisions of gender belong to the created world. What is at stake in texts that use metaphors of the sorts ... is not divine gender. Rather, the point is the necessity to express certain aspects of God's being, such as his care, protection, compassion, and so forth. Some of these traits are best expressed by metaphors deriving from human females, others by metaphors derived from males of one and the same humanity.[206]

The study of P. D. Hanson throws light on the fact that the presence of female metaphors of God does not guarantee the liberated position of women in a particular society.[207] He shows that in Babylon, although the 'Herodotus of the mother goddess' was a prominent feminine metaphor, women were treated as merely a sex object, with the presentation of fertility plaques. Moreover he points out that this goddess cult was still a part of the male–dominated society.[208]

From the above discussion we can come to the conclusion that the unequal distribution of feminine imageries in the Bible is not due to any gen-

---

[204] Ibid., pp. 28–29. For a detailed discussion on the use of feminine and masculine imagery in the Old Testament see Hayter, *The New Eve in Christ,* pp. 21–44.

[205] T. N. D. Mettinger, *In Search of God: The Meaning and Message of the Everlasting Names* (Philadelphia: Fortress Press, 1988), p. 205.

[206] Ibid., p. 207; for a similar view see Wolfhart Pannenberg, 'Feminine Language of God?', *ATJ* 48 (1993), pp. 27–29. Cf. George Caird, *The Language and Imagery of the Bible* (London: Duckworth, 1980), pp. 18–19.

[207] See P. D. Hanson, 'Masculine Metaphors for God and Sex Determination in the Old Testament', *EcR* 27 (1975), pp. 316–24.

[208] Ibid., p. 318.

der bias nor due to a desire to perpetuate the patriarchal androcentric world–view of the biblical writers as some feminists think. If that is the case, Trible's attempt to depatriachalise the image of God may not entail significant results. In short, Trible's treatment of the biblical text merely from a formal literary perspective has created many difficulties. We have already seen earlier that a single hermeneutical approach is inadequate to explore all the hermeneutical possibilities in a text.

Complexity of presupposition

Although feminist theology shares generally with other liberation theologies (Black and Latin American) the same concerns, much feminist hermeneutics sees the Bible itself as the cause for women's oppression due to its patriarchal nature.[209] In other words, generally in other liberation theologies, God functions as a Liberator from oppression and exploitation (Exodus tradition) but for feminists a patriarchal God himself sides with their oppressors, the males. So in feminist hermeneutics, both the patriarchal God and the texts themselves are often seen as part of the oppression. Sandra M. Schneiders writes:

> because the biblical text is not purely and simply a text of liberation for women but is itself a part of the problem, the transformational agenda of feminist hermeneutics involves not only the liberation of the oppressed through the transformation of society but also the liberation of the biblical text itself from its own participation in the oppression of women,...[210]

The above aspects of feminist hermeneutics make it different from other liberation hermeneutics. Now the question remains; If God himself sides with the oppressors, how can that patriarchal God and the text function for the liberation of Woman? So nowadays there is an increasing trend among feminist scholars to move from socio–critical hermeneutical model to socio–pragmatic models. Thiselton points to the seriousness of the problem: 'pragmatic hermeneutics is *diametrically opposed in practice* to the deepest theoretical concerns which lie behind liberation hermeneutics: those whose readings of texts win the day can only be the power groups: the most militant, the most aggressive, the most manipulative'.[211] The result is that no transcendental or transcontexual critique is possible and this model can only

---

[209] See Trible, *Texts of Terror,* p. 16. Trible argues that the God one who delivers his people out of Egyptian bondage 'identifies with the oppressor...' (here the context is the expulsion of Hagar).

[210] S. M. Schneiders, 'Feminist Hermeneutics', in *Hearing the New Testament: Strategies for Interpretation,* (ed.) Joel B. Green (Grand Rapids: Michigan, William B. Eerdmans, 1995), p. 350.

[211] Thiselton, *New Horizons,* p. 603; emphasis original.

serve the dominant group. Trible's recent proposal for more reader– oriented hermeneutics is a recipe for socio–pragmatism. In every model of feminist hermeneutics, the starting point is the 'hermeneutics of suspicion': Feminists always assume that the Bible legitimises male oppression. If they could start from some other more neutral ground, then more objectivity could probably be achieved. Kathleen A. Farmer (Professor of Old Testament at United Theological Seminary, Dayton, Ohio) seems to start with a balanced pre–understanding. She writes: 'Taken as a whole, the Scriptures proclaim the value and validity of female as well as of male aspects of human experience. Taken as a whole our canon of faith upholds the dignity, the value, and the worth of every human being.'[212]

Complexity of feminist ideology

Trible's major concern was to establish an egalitarian reading of the text. We noted earlier concerning the creation of the woman that in her original article she admitted that the woman was a sequential creation to the man. She attempted to establish the 'woman as the culmination of creation' to counter the traditional argument based on the point that the man was created first. In her book, however, she argued for the simultaneous creation of the man and the woman. Here also Trible's concern is to establish an egalitarian reading. This is evident in her choice of Gen. 1:27 as her topical clue. From this we notice that following either kind of argument she comes to the same conclusion: that is the equality of the man and the woman in the creation narrative. Richard Bauckham reminds us of the dangers of interpreting the text in the context of our contemporary world. He notes: 'One is the danger of manipulating the text to support our preconceived attitudes and projects'.[213] He further illustrates: 'we must recognise that revolutionary interpretations of Scripture can be as ideological as interpretations by those in power, just as feminist interpretations can be as ideological as patriarchal interpretations'.[214] To overcome these sorts of perils, Bauckham advocates the study of the text in its historical context.

In many cases, Trible seems to be more occupied with her feminist agenda than with consistent argument to rebut the traditional readings. In order to counterbalance the misogynist renderings she advocates gyno–centred readings. Examining Trible's work, Ilana Pardes with her interdisciplinary approach criticises Trible's ideology. She observes: 'In Trible's hands the Bible almost turns into a feminist manifesto, where every detail

---

[212] Kathleen A. Farmer, *Who Knows What is Good?: A Commentary on the Books of Proverbs & Ecclesiastes*, ITC (Grand Rapids/Edinburgh: Wm.B. Eerdmans and the Handsel Press, 1991), p. 11.

[213] Richard Bauckham, *The Bible in Politics: How to Read the Bible Politically* (London: SPCK, 1989), pp. 18–19; here p. 18.

[214] Ibid.

suspiciously ends up supporting woman's liberation.'[215] A typical example
is her reading of the man as passive and the woman as more intelligent in
Genesis.

Although Trible started her readings with the intention of correcting the
misogynist readings, ultimately she too became a prey to partisan readings.
As a result she also became liable to the criticism that 'the oppressed take
up the tools of the oppressors'.[216] Although her readings started with a
socio–critical theoretical approach in order to liberate the text from male
biased, oppressive interpretations, she has finished in socio–pragmatic hermeneutics. Trible has used the same tools which the male oppressors had
used. Her socio–pragmatic approach is very evident throughout her exegesis.

Complexity of faith versus post–modernism

An apparent tension between Trible's Christian confession and her post–
modern hermeneutical outlook can be observed from her writings. Trible's
high regard for the Scriptures is evident in her writings, especially her effort
in articulating an hermeneutics out of the Scriptures. This is presumably
due to her ecclesiastical background. As we noted, she comes from Southern Baptist tradition, although she does not make it known in her work.
Her high regard for scriptural authority and function has resulted in her being severely criticised by other feminist scholars.

Fiorenza charges that Trible's hermeneutical process is rooted in neo–
orthodox theology.[217] Pardes thinks that Trible's approach is problematic
since 'Trible remains on God's side–exempting Yahweh from critique.'[218]
She thinks it as an 'idyllic reconciliation between Biblical faith and
women's liberation'.[219] In the same vein Bal also alleges that Trible is
'taken in by her religious feelings, which make her overrate the character of
Yahweh'.[220] Recently Phyllis Bird suggests that Trible's view of biblical
authority 'appeals readily to Evangelicals in the role she assigns to the Bible for faith and in her emphasis on the Bible's transhistorical character and
the experience of the reader/believer'.[221] These criticisms interestingly reveal a spectrum in feminist biblical interpretation. Yet they also do not do
justice to Trible's work taken as a whole. For as we have seen in the sec-

---

[215] Ilana Pardes, *Countertraditions in the Bible,* p. 24.

[216] For details see Thiselton, *New Horizons,* p. 450. I am indebted to Thiselton for the
hermeneutical terms which I use here.

[217] See Elisabeth Schüssler Fiorenza, *In Memory of Her,* pp. 19–21.

[218] Ilana Pardes, *Countertraditions in the Bible,* p. 21.

[219] Ibid., p. 3.

[220] Mieke Bal, *Lethal Love,* p. 124.

[221] Bird, *Feminism and the Bible: A Critical and Constructive Encounte: the J. J. Thiessen Lectures* (Winnipeg, Manitoba: CMBC, 1994), p. 61.

tion on 'complexity of feminist method', we can observe an iconoclastic outlook in Trible's work itself, when she advocates a post–structuralist, reader–oriented approach, where 'contexts *alter texts*, liberating from frozen constructions'.[222]

Towards a plausible solution

Nowadays there has been an increasing awareness among male and female scholars that the biblical texts should be interpreted in their historical and social contexts without losing sight of their literary character. In other words, the world of the text and the world of the interpreter should be brought together in articulating the meaning of the text. Katharine Doob Sakenfeld calls this method 'culturally cued literary reading'. In this method, the text is read as the product of its own culture. She explains: 'interpretive constraints of what would be imaginable or probable for speakers and hearers in a particular ancient patriarchal culture are thus to be given considerable weight in assessing literary design, as well as in deciding which textual clues to focus on and how to assess their significance and meaning'.[223] Another feminist biblical scholar Alice Ogden Bellis (Assistant Professor of Old Testament Language and Literature, Howard University School of Divinity, Washington DC.) has also expressed this concern very recently in her evaluation of feminist readings.[224]

Some male scholars who are interested basically in literary analysis of the text also point to the need for a synthesis of historical and literary aspects. Meir Sternberg suggests 'a closer interworking of text and context' which he called 'discourse oriented analysis'.[225] Yehoshua Gitay looks for three dimensions in reading, namely 'the author', 'the text', and 'the audience'. He rightly points out that style is merely one aspect. He calls his method 'Rhetorical analysis'.[226] The same concern is expressed in detail in Grant Osborne's *The Hermeneutical Spiral*, in which he calls for 'a trialogue between the author, the text and the reader'.[227]

The above concern has been expressed in the speech act theory of language which could incorporate both historical and literary dimensions for better results. This model was proposed by the Oxford philosopher John L. Austin and developed and popularised by his student John R. Searle. In this model attempts have been made to rectify the problems of both a historical method (detaching the past from the present) and a literary formalist approach. In this model language (speech or word) functions as an act it-

---

[222] Trible, *God and the Rhetoric*, p. 202; emphasis mine.

[223] See Sakenfeld, p. 187.

[224] Alice Ogden Bellis, *Helpmates, Harlots, Heroes* (1994), pp. 10–20.

[225] See Meir Sternberg, *The Poetics of Biblical Narrative*, pp. 7–23.

[226] Gitay, 'Rhetorical Criticism', pp. 136–37.

[227] Osborne, *The Hermeneutical Spiral*, p. 411.

self with the power to achieve something. Austin finds three different dimensions in the use of a sentence or language, which he terms as 'locutionary act', 'illocutionary act', and 'perlocutionary act' respectively.[228] Moreover, the speech act is rooted in socio–historical context in which the language or the speech is uttered.[229] Examining the value of the speech–act model of language to biblical interpretation, Hugh C. White writes:

> By treating language itself as an act, the dichotomy between literary
> word and historical fact is eliminated at the theoretical level. The mean-
> ing of language is understood neither in terms of a logical (or existential)
> system, nor its correspondence to empirical fact, but in terms of the con-
> ditions which govern its use. The division between word and event, be-
> tween the theoretical and factual, is thus overcome in principle.[230]

As we have discussed earlier in our first chapter, the biblical text has a 'communicative function' as it functions as the 'speech act of God' (Van Wolde), therefore it cannot be merely treated as a literary work. It is a religious text aimed to achieve something in the recipients. So communicative context is important to understand the total meaning of the text. Trible's formal approach appears not to have been compatible with this understanding of meaning.

Trible's treatment of the creation narrative as an 'autonomous'[231] text independently from the text's socio–historical contexts led her to many methodological and hermeneutical complexities. Her concentration was mainly on the stylistics and literary artistry of the text. That aspect is only one among many factors in the articulation of meaning. One of our main contentions has been that texts should be interpreted in their original socio–historical contexts. Moreover, in Trible's method there is no scope for the 'fusion of horizons' according to the hermeneutical theory of Gadamer.[232]

---

[228] See J. L. Austin, *How to do Things with Words* (Oxford: OUP, 1973), p. 108 (original, HUP, 1955). He explains 'the illocutionary act which has a certain *force* in saying something; the perlocutionary act which is *the achieving* of certain *effects* by saying something'. (p. 120) , emphasis original.

[229] For an elaborate discussion of speech act and its use in Biblical criticism, see *Speech Act and Biblical Criticism, Semeia* 41 (1988).

[230] Ibid., P. 54.

[231] The notion of 'autonomous' texts was proposed by Paul Ricoeur. Ricoeur writes: 'Writing renders the text autonomous with respect to the intention of the author. What the text signifies no longer coincides with what the author meant'; see Paul Ricoeur, 'Hermeneutical Function of Distanciation', in *Hermeneutics and the Human Sciences,* (ed. and trans.) John B. Thompson (Cambridge: CUP, 1981), p. 139.

[232] Hans–Georg Gadamer, *Truth and Method.* According to Gadamer, for a proper understanding of the present, it is necessary to understand the past. He writes: 'it is part of the hermeneutic approach to project an historical horizon that is different from the hori-

She concentrated only on the single horizon of the present text, overlooking its historical dimension.

THEOLOGICAL PROBLEMS

Feminist readings and biblical authority

If the text does not allow an egalitarian reading in the sense in which Trible claims how might this text become meaningful for women: Does it mean that the text sanctions patriarchy? Both male and female interpreters have attempted to resolve this issue from various angles. Some of them like David J. A. Clines, David Jobling,[233] and Pamela J. Milne argued that the Bible is irredeemably patriarchal and that depatriarchalisation is a vain attempt. But Trible found both positive and negative aspects concerning woman in the biblical narrative. Though she reads the creation narrative positively, in her later book, *Texts of Terror*, she shows how patriarchal these texts are. Her book is a literary reading of the stories of the abuse of Hagar, the rape of Princess Tamar, the dismemberment of an unnamed woman and the sacrifice of the daughter of Jephthah. Here Trible 'recounts tales of terror *in memoriam* to offer sympathetic readings of abused women'.[234] In fact one's hermeneutical approaches to the text determine the view of the text's authority. For instance, while Milne and Danna Nolan Fewell[235] consider the creation narrative to be irredeemably patriarchal, Trible attempts to redeem it from the patriarchal interpretation through her readings. In other words, a text is authoritative to some feminists but not to others. So the various hermeneutical stances make our evaluation complex.

In her 1973 essay 'Depatriarchalising in Biblical Interpretation', Trible argues that only the interpretations are patriarchal and chauvinistic not the text *per se*. So she writes: 'I affirm that the intentionality of biblical faith, as distinguished from a general description of biblical religion, is neither to create nor to perpetuate patriarchy but rather to function as salvation for

---

zon of the present', p. 273. A fusion has to take place between the horizon of the text and the interpreter. For a better understanding of a text its socio–historical aspects are vital.

[233] Clines, *What Does Eve Do to Help,* pp. 25–48; David Jobling, *The Sense of Biblical Narrative,* p. 42; Pamela J. Milne, 'Eve and Adam—Is a Feminist Reading Possible?', *BibRev* IV (June, 1988), pp. 12–21, 39 see also 'The Patriarchal Stamp of Scripture: The Implications of Structuralist Analyses for Feminist Hermeneutics', *JFSR* 5/1(1989), pp. 17–34, reprinted with postscript in *A Feminist Companion to Genesis,* pp. 146–172.

[234] Trible, *Texts of Terror,* p. 3.

[235] See Danna Nolan Fewell and David M. Gunn, *Gender, Power, Promise;* see the chapter 'Shifting the Blame (Genesis 1–3)'. They read the text as thoroughly patriarchal..

both women and men.'[236] The main purpose of that essay was to undercut the patriarchal interpretations alien to the text, but not to depatriarchalise the text as such. However, in her later work she notes: 'the patriarchal stamp of scripture is permanent. But just as clearly, interpretation of its content is forever changing, since new occasions teach new duties and *contexts alter texts*, liberating them from frozen constructions'.[237] According to her later view, she argues that patriarchy is embedded in the text itself, and consequently she raised objections towards a fixed canon.

At the same time she negated the trend of making a 'canon within the canon' as Rosemary Radford Ruether and Elisabeth Schüssler Fiorenza do when they deal with the issue of authority. For instance, whatever promotes the full humanity of women is taken to be holy, as the authentic message of redemption according to Ruether,[238] whereas for Fiorenza only the non–sexist and non–androcentric traditions of the Bible have authority. Forenza thinks that authority lies not in the 'special canon of texts' but in 'the experience of women', thereby creating a 'canon outside the canon'. Fiorenza believes that since the biblical texts are patriarchal products '[a] feminist hermeneutics cannot trust or accept the Bible and tradition simply as divine revelation'.[239] At the same time she finds the Bible to be a resource in the struggle against every oppression. However, she does not consider the Bible as archetype but rather as prototype because of violence and domination.[240] If experience takes the place of the revealed canon as Fiorenza

---

[236] Trible, 'Depatriarchalizing in Biblical Interpretation', p. 31.

[237] Trible, *God and the Rhetoric,* p. 202; emphasis mine. The patriarchal bias of the text itself is advocated by most contemporary feminist scholars. For an elaborate discussion on the authority of the Bible in feminist readings see Mary Ann Tolbert, 'Defining the Problem: The Bible and Feminist Hermeneutics', *Semeia* 28 (1983), 113–126; 'Protestant Feminists and the Bible: On the Horns of a Dilemma', in *The Pleasure of Her Text: Feminist Readings of Biblical and Historical Texts,* (ed.) Alice Bach (Philadelphia: Trinity Press International, 1990), pp. 5–23; Phyllis A Bird, *Feminism and the Bible,* pp. 19–87; 'The Authority of the Bible' in *The New Interpreter's Bible* (NIB), vol. 1 (Nashville: Abingdon Press, 1994), pp. 33–64, especially pp. 61–63.

[238] See Rosemary Radford Ruether, *Sexism and God Talk* (London: SCM Press, 1983), p. 19. Ruether considers the Old Testament prophetic tradition as the biblical basis where God vindicates the poor and oppressed (Amos 8:4–6; Is. 10:1–2, 61: 1–2); see further Ruether, 'Feminism and Patriarchal Religion: Principles of ideological critique of the Bible', *JSOT* 22 (1982), pp. 54–66.

[239] See Elisabeth Schüssler Fiorenza, *Bread Not Stone: The Challenge of Feminist Biblical Interpretation* (Boston: Beacon Press, 1984), p. X; see further for an elaborate treatment of every aspect of feminist readings her collection of essays in her book entitled *Discipleship of Equals: A Critical Feminist Ekklesia–logy of Liberation* (London: SCM Press, 1993).

[240] Fiorenza, *Bread Not Stone,* p. 61. See also *In Memory of Her,* p. 33. She explains archetype as 'an ideal form that establishes an unchanging timeless pattern' whereas a prototype is 'critically open to the possibility of its transformation'.

suggested, then the feminist authority will have to stand on subjective feelings of the women. John Goldingay rightly reminds us: 'The tension between our religious experience and that of which we read in scripture is resolved not by reinterpreting scripture in the light of our experience but by seeking to have our experience conformed to that of which scripture speaks..[241]

Now we come back to Trible. What Trible proposed above in her book has been spelled out clearly in her later work. She affirms: 'A fixed, unchangeable text is neither possible nor desirable. For better or worse, be it conscious or unconscious, the text is always being changed'.[242] According to this viewpoint the text can be altered according to new emerging situations and occasions. When she began her feminist re–reading of the text her hermeneutical focus was on the text itself as we have seen in her essay but later she moved towards a more reader–oriented hermeneutics. Accordingly, she advocated that '*authority* centres in readers... In the interaction of text and reader, the changing of the second component alters the meaning and power of the first'.[243] From the above statement one can presume that the readers determine the meaning and authority of the text. So the shifting of authority from the text to readers seems to be theologically problematic.

If the readers begin to change the texts in order to cope with the emerging contexts, then the texts can no more offer any judgement or critique on us; rather we may go on changing the text to legitimise our conduct and belief. The lack of an external criterion to judge our faith and conduct carries the potential consequence of anarchy. This has special significance in the context of theology and the life of the Church. Anthony Thiselton aptly points out the need in our hermeneutics for some external criteria to judge our self–assertions. He writes: 'the cross and resurrection stand not only as a critique of human self–affirmation and power, but also as a *meta–critique which assesses other criteria, and which transforms the very concept of power*'.[244]

Employing structuralist methods in reading the text David Jobling challenges Trible's claims for depatriarchalising the texts, though he is sympathetic to feminist concerns. He uses structural analysis (deep structure) to read the story whereas Trible focuses on the surface structure of the story.

---

[241] John Goldingay, *Models for Scripture* (Grand Rapids, Michigan: William B. Eerdmans /Carlisle: Paternoster Press, 1994), p. 194.

[242] Trible, 'Post Script: Jottings on the Journey', in *Feminist Interpretation of the Bible*, (ed.) Letty M. Russel (Oxford: Basil Blackwell, 1985), pp. 147–149, here p. 148.

[243] Trible, 'Feminist Hermeneutics and Biblical Theology', in *The Flowering of OLd Testament Theology*, (eds.) Ben. C. Ollenburger *et al.* (SBTS 1; Winona Lake: Eisenbrauns, 1992), p. 463. Cf. Trible, 'Treasures Old and New', pp. 48–49.

[244] Thiselton, *New Horizons*, p. 615, emphasis original.

Jobling asks: 'Who, in a patriarchal culture, composed the feminist story which she takes the text to be; and how was it received, by a patriarchal culture, as its basic myth of origins?'[245] He sees the 'positive features' found in the text with regard to the woman not as an 'expression of a feminist consciousness', but as a result of the 'patriarchal mindset' in order to support their assumptions.[246] In short, Jobling reiterates that the Bible is patriarchal.

Jobling's, Clines' and Lanser's structuralist and post–structuralist readings of the creation narrative as basically a patriarchal text led Pamela J. Milne to raise doubts about 'the potential effectiveness' of the reading strategy of Phyllis Trible as a feminist reformist.[247] Hence the option that remains for feminists according to Milne is the following: 'We can either accept the patriarchal biblical text as sacred and content ourselves with exposing its patriarchy ...or we can expose its patriarchy and reject it as sacred and authoritative.'[248] In addition, she also assumes that 'if the biblical authors are all or mostly male, then it seems reasonable to expect the literature they produce to be "male" literature insofar as the fictive world it presents is male–imaged'.[249] So she thinks that women's counter reading will not make it women's literature.

While Milne thinks that the Bible is basically a patriarchal literature, promoting patriarchal interests, another feminist, Ilana Pardes finds 'the tense dialogue between the dominant patriarchal discourses of the Bible and counter female voices which attempt to put forth other truths'[250] in the Scriptures. Her basic argument seems to be that 'Naming is not only Adam's prerogative... Eve is no exception to the rule.'[251] Eve also begins naming from Genesis 4 onwards, thereby challenging the patriarchal trends in the Bible. Pardes admits that her intention is not 'to turn the Bible into a feminist manifesto but rather to show that, while the dominant thrust of the Bible is clearly patriarchal, patriarchy is continuously challenged by antithetical trends'.[252] I agree with Pardes that though there is patriarchal

---

[245] Jobling, *The Sense of Biblical Narrative*, p. 42. For a parallel between Bultmann's method of 'demythologising' and Trible's method of 'depatriarchalizing' see Thiselton, *New Horizons,* pp. 452–456.

[246] Ibid., p. 43.

[247] Milne, 'The Patriarchal stamp of Scripture', in *A Feminist Companion to Genesis*, p. 168. We have noted above that though Trible began as a reformist, later she adopted more a radical step in suggesting altering the text.

[248] Ibid., p. 167.

[249] Ibid., p. 171.

[250] Ilana Pardes, *Countertraditions in the Bible,* (reprint) in *A Feminist Companion to Genesis,* 'Beyond Genesis 3: The Politics of Maternal Naming', pp. 173–193.

[251] Ibid., pp. 174–175.

[252] Ibid., p. 185.

dominance in the Bible there are also counter female voices. But I disagree with her assumption that patriarchy was continuously challenged by anti-thetical trends during the biblical period itself. Pardes seems to assume that there were feminists at work from the very beginning of the biblical tradi-tions. Here Pardes is imposing on the Scripture her own modern ideology. If feminists were at work from the beginning, then the situation of women would have been considerably different. Rather, her 'counter voices' merely reflect a situation that prevailed in the biblical period where both the parents exercised authority over their children by naming and disciplining. The book of Proverbs may be a typical example illustrating this sharing as-pect of parental power.

As we have seen, Susanne Heine rightly shows that the feminine im-agery in the Bible is not there because of any feminist traditions working within the texts but rather as a check against the prevailing goddess cults by depicting Yahweh, the father, Judge and warrior, who can also give birth and breast–feed.[253] The feminists like Trible and Pardes might argue that this is an indication of a 'depatriarchalising' principle or an 'antithetical trend' in the Scripture. In my view, Pardes' notion seems to be anachronis-tic.

I think it can be argued that the Bible is not irredeemably patriarchal, promoting only male interests contrary to Clines, Jobling and Milne.[254] Nevertheless, I do acknowledge that the Biblical culture was also patriar-chal, as are most modern cultures. It can certainly be held that some of the Church fathers and Reformers were chauvinistic, and I would regard this as a cultural factor rather than a theological sanction. But their main problem was theologising their cultural mores as divine oracle. Since the enlight-enment, we have seen many of these misconceptions rectified. Most of the scholarly commentaries written on the text of Genesis during the last cen-tury by male scholars pointed out the difficulties of many male–biased ren-derings and arrived at similar conclusions which Trible and other contem-porary scholars propose. I have cited some of these in this chapter. In short, many of the serious misreadings had already been recognised before the rise of feminist interpretation.

Mary Ann Tolbert as a Protestant feminist approaches this issue from another angle. She remains in the Christian tradition because she believes that the Bible 'is not only a book that has justified slavery, economic ex-ploitation, and sexual oppression; it also a book that has informed libera-tion, the infinite worth of the individual, and the call to fight against

---

[253] Cf. Susanne Heine, *Christianity and the Goddesses,* pp. 28–29.

[254] See John Barton, *What is the Bible?* (London: SPCK, 1991); especially the chapter 'Is the Bible Sexist?', pp. 125–142.

evil.'[255] In other words the Bible is both liberative and enslaving. Tolbert suggests that the patriarchal authority in the Bible should be defeated by using the Bible as liberator.

Phyllis A. Bird also finds authority in the text at a different level though she deplores its pervasive androcentrism. Concerning the authority of Scripture she writes:

> The authority of Scripture does not depend on infallible words or model behavior but in the ability of its words to confront readers with the story and the presence of a God who redeems sinners by assuming their weakness, and empowers the weak and the silent (or silenced) with visions and with speech.[256]

From the above discussion it is clear that the feminist scholars have difficulty in accepting the authority of the biblical texts due to its patriarchal nature. At the same time they also find the text as a resource for claiming their liberation. So for the feminists the authority of the Bible functions in two ways, positively and negatively. Hitherto feminists have widely held the view that the biblical texts are a patriarchal product as we have discussed above. But feminists' recent agenda is to 'gender' the texts thereby 'searching for women's texts within the Hebrew canon...'[257] The basic conclusion of their study seems to be that women had made a contribution to the oral 'literature' of ancient Israel. If Brenner and van Dijk–Hemmes are correct then the view of the Bible as being totally in a patriarchal mould is to be questioned.

From the above discussion we can conclude that many feminists still consider the Bible as normative. We have already seen that Clines argues that Gen. 1–3 cannot be redeemed from patriarchal orientations. Nevertheless he suggests that the Bible can still become meaningful to women if one thinks about the *'function'* of the Bible rather than its nature. He thinks:

> The authority of a text has to do with its nature, we want to be saying things about the Bible that have to do with its *function*. We want to be saying, not so much that the Bible is right, not even that the Bible is wrong, but that its impact for good upon people... despite its handicaps,

---

[255] Tolbert, 'Defining the Problem', p. 120; cf. Paul Joyce's discussion of 'positive' and 'negative' themes about woman in the Old Testament: P. Joyce, 'Feminist Exegesis of the Old Testament: Some Critical Reflections', in *After Eve: Women, Theology and the Christian Tradition,* (ed.) J.M. Soskice (London: Collins, Marshal Pickering, 1990), pp. 1–9.

[256] Bird, 'The Authority of the Bible', p. 62.

[257] See A. Brenner and Fokkelien van Dijk–Hemmes, *On Gendering Texts: Female and Male Voices in the Hebrew Bible* (BIS 1; Leiden: E.J. Brill, 1993), here p.1.

despite the fact that it has misled people and promoted patriarchy, it has an unquenchable capacity—when taken in conjunction with a commitment to personal integrity—to inspire people, bring out the best in them and suggest a vision they could never have dreamed of for themselves. Think of it as a dogma and you will at times, as over the matter of men and women, either be wrong or get it wrong. Think of it rather as a resource for living which has no authority but which nevertheless manages to impose itself powerfully upon people.[258]

I agree in his assertion of the Bible's impact upon people for good and its capacity to bring out the best in them. When we talk about the patriarchal nature of the Bible, no doubt, it was born and bred in a patriarchal culture, though talk of 'misleading' is emotive, may be itself misleading. In this context, John Barton rightly observes: 'when seen against its cultural background, in a society where the dominance of men was taken for granted, the Bible turns out to be less sexist than one might expect'.[259] A similar sort of judgement is also made by Westermann in the context of the creation of the woman in Genesis. Hence he writes: '[t]he narrative in Gen 2 reflects a stage in civilisation which was aware of the great importance of the role of woman in the existence of humankind. Gen 2 is unique among the creation myths of the whole of the Ancient Near East in its appreciation of the meaning of woman,...'[260] The biblical narratives precisely record the life of the people who had failed to fulfil God's will in their lives. As a result we see how they oppressed the weaker ones, including the women. But that was not the ideal situation which God intended for them. I may borrow the feminist terminology here to illustrate this. The patriarchal dominance was not prescriptive but it was only descriptive. In other words patriarchal dominion was not normative. The feminist writers have to make this distinction. Despite the patriarchal nature of the biblical texts, Letty M. Russell still reiterates the authority of the scripture. She writes:

> The Bible has authority in my life because it makes sense of my experience and speaks to me about the meaning and purpose of my humanity in

---

[258] Clines, 'What Does Eve do to Help?', p. 48; For a superficial critique of Cline's reading see Deborah F. Sawyer, 'Resurrecting Eve? Feminist Critique of the Garden of Eden', in *A Walk in the Garden: Biblical Iconographical and Literary Images of Eden,* (eds.) Paul Morris and Deborah Sawyer (Sheffield: JSOT Press, 1992), pp. 287–288. She rates Clines with the radical feminists like Mary Daly because he thinks that the Bible is irretrievably patriarchal.. Moreover, she ironically states that 'in engaging with Eve, feminists are in danger of using the "master's tools" since Eve has been the possession of male commentators since the time of her creation'. I wonder why Sawyer did not interact with Clines on exegetical grounds.

[259] Barton, *What is the Bible,* p. 131.

[260] Westermann, *Genesis,* p. 232.

Jesus Christ. In spite of its ancient and patriarchal world views, in spite of its inconsistencies and mixed messages, the story of God's love affair with the world leads me to a vision of New Creation that implies my life.[261]

Though some have denied the authority of the Bible, Russell and others still find the Scripture authoritative in their lives due to its function, and despite its patriarchal nature.

PRACTICAL PROBLEMS

Feminist readings and interpretative community

Even after this lengthy discussion how do we know which of the interpretations we have discussed is more true to the text? Rogerson put forward a viable solution to resolve this type of 'confusion of tongues'. He aptly notes the great increase of the 'interpretative communities' during the last two decades, (as against the single interpretative community which was composed of the Church, Universities and colleges at the end of the nineteenth century) to respond to the challenges put forward by natural sciences, especially Darwinism.[262] According to Rogerson the concern of the 'feminist interpretative communities' 'is to make the biblical text a partner in the struggle against sexism, so that a new and appropriate understanding can emerge of the respective contributions of males and females to the business of living as human beings',[263] whereas the former interpretative community's concern was to depict the human being as thinking and rational beings. New interpretative communities, like the 'liberationist' and 'feminist', address other concerns such as social, political, economical and even gender.

Rogerson notes that within the interpretative communities norms are set for acceptable readings. He pointed out that for a 'university interpretative community', the main concern is academic and academics may not have sympathy with other concerns if their readings rely on 'impossible translations of the Hebrew or implausible reconstructions of the social and historical background to the text'.[264] We can employ Rogerson's criterion for evaluating Trible's readings. Trible's readings have wider acceptance among the 'feminist interpretative communities'; however, her readings are challenged by other academic communities. Nevertheless Rogerson does not undermine the need for listening to the readings of different interpretative communities and he thinks of the 'diversity of approaches' not as a threat but as an opportunity. Rogerson rightly comments: 'in every genera-

---

[261] Letty M. Russell, 'Authority and the Challenge of Feminist Interpretation', in *Feminist Interpretation of the Bible*, p. 138.

[262] For a full discussion see Rogerson, *Genesis 1–11*, pp. 50–52.

[263] Ibid., pp. 50–51.

[264] Ibid., p. 51.

tion, differing interpretations are part of a continuing struggle to hear the text of the Bible addressing communities as the Word of God'.[265] I hope my interaction with Trible and others will lead to a similar result.

Conclusion

In the first section of this chapter we have discussed the method of 'new literary criticism', with a special focus on 'rhetorical criticism' and its possibilities in enhancing our understanding of the biblical texts. We have also examined its strengths and weaknesses. Then we have presented the main hermeneutical assumptions of feminist interpretation and particularly Trible's methodology.

In the main section, we have presented Trible's important arguments and claims based on creation narratives as such. In the final section, we have discussed in detail her major claims and interacted with her on major issues. In our study of Trible we have seen the positive contribution of Trible's readings and her influence on Old Testament biblical scholarship. Indeed Trible has succeeded in offering a feminist reading of the creation texts, in the sense that her readings of the text have broadened the horizon of our knowledge of the text and stimulated much scholarly discussion on the issue of male and female and gender. We have seen that Trible could redress some of the centuries old patriarchal interpretations; yet despite the merits of her readings, many of her major assumptions and claims are prone to criticism in a wider context.

First of all, we have examined her methodology, we have seen that Gen. 1:27 cannot function effectively as a 'topical clue', to establish an egalitarian reading of creation narratives. Her attempt to read back human sexuality–male and femaleness–to God seems to be problematic. Again, Trible's attempt to base her case on a part of a single verse ('male and female he created them') led her into various methodological and exegetical difficulties. A single phrase was not adequate to establish her case. Contrary to the generally held opinion that this text functions sociologically to depict the equality of the sexes, we have seen that it is more likely that the text deals with biological function. That seems to be the more appropriate meaning of the phrase in the context. So Trible cannot postulate an egalitarian reading based on this text. We have seen that her conclusion was predisposed by her starting point. As a result not only her readings of the creation narrative, but also the proposal for her Old Testament theology based on this narrative have become problematical.

Secondly, we noted the problems with Trible's formalism, overlooking the historical dimension of the text. Trible paid very little attention to the

---

[265] Ibid., p. 52.

historical dimension, and thereby failed to ask how the narrative would
have been understood in its own context. She overlooked the difference between the two creation accounts and treated them similarly. As a result,
Trible argued that there was perfect equality between the man and the
woman before the disobedience of the couple. That was lost only after their
disobedience. But our examination of the text reveals that in the Yahwistic
narrative there is not an ideal unity between the man and the woman even
before the disobedience. The woman was created to be a helper in every respect. In this connection, however, we questioned the concept that the
woman's help is required only in the area of procreation.

Thirdly, we have found difficulty with her exegetical conclusions which
are affected by the lack of a historical context. As a result some of her readings seem to be fanciful. Moreover, generally her exegesis is rather atomistic without taking into consideration the whole context of the narrative.
Our close reading of the narrative with the help of historical critical, socio–
literary, ANE mythological, semiotic, and speech–act theory principles
questioned many her assumptions. A typical example is her reading of האדם
as an undifferentiated earth creature before the creation of the woman. We
have seen that the man functions both as a male and a generic human being
in the narrative. There is agreement on this across a variety of methodological approaches. We also found difficulty with many of her other exegetical conclusions and suggested other alternatives. In our reading we
have suggested that in spite of the judgement of God on humanity, there is
still room for man and woman to live in harmony and peace without the
subjugation or ruling of woman by man.

Fourthly, we have seen that Trible's hermeneutical theory of language
was not adequate to prove her case. She only concentrated on the 'form'
and 'surface' of the text and neglected the deeper aspects such as 'the spiritual and theological truth claims of the Bible'. She concentrated much on
the romantic aspect of the couple and neglected other important aspects. In
her reading she had only limited concern for the religious dimension,
though her general aim was reformist. Due to her feminist commitment,
she attempted to acquit Eve of her rebellion and she tried to ease her responsibility, thereby promoting to her a higher rank.

Fifthly, we have also seen apparent inconsistencies in her hermeneutical
assumptions. According to her presupposition, some texts are redeemable
but others not. In one place, she finds only the interpretations are patriarchal but in another place, she asserts 'the patriarchal stamp of scripture is
permanent'. In this context, Thiselton's observation of the tension of positive and negative in feminist hermeneutics can be true in the case of
Trible's readings also. He notes: 'While androcentric tradition is destruc-
tive, it is urged, many aspects of tradition including women's "lost" place in

it should be "retrieved."'[266] Later, she shifted her hermeneutical focus from the *text* to the *readers*. Now for Trible the authority lies in the hands of the readers.

Sixthly, we have observed that the main line biblical scholarship was not misogynist as Trible complained. We have shown that many traditional scholarly readings pointed out the difficulty with existing interpretations and suggested alternatives. To a certain extent, Trible is also dependent upon them for her exegetical conclusions. In some cases Trible's arguments are diverted by non–issues. Her documentation of the belief that 'Woman is the rib of man, dependent upon him for life' is a case in point (see her documenting of traditional prejudiced readings which responsible scholars today would not seriously advocate).

Finally, we have argued that the Bible is not irredeemably patriarchal as many feminist and male scholars propose. We have also negated the notion that any 'antithetical feminist trend' or a depatriarchalising principle is at work in the biblical text since that cannot be expected in a patriarchal culture. Instead, we suggested that though the biblical culture was patriarchal, there was a place for harmony and exercising of power for both man and the woman at different levels. We also noted that even granted the patriarchal nature of the text, the Bible can be still authoritative and meaningful to women.

In the light of our reading of the passage we can conclude that *eros* is only one of the themes in the narrative. But Trible has highlighted this aspect at the expense of other prominent themes in the narrative.

Before we conclude we need to ask how far Trible's readings have offered a social critique, unmasking oppression at a broader level, rather than affirming the interests of feminist readers through her rereading. I doubt how far Trible has been successful in this aspect. As we have already seen she has become more prone to socio–pragmatic trends. Ruether clearly reminds us of the holistic dimension of hermeneutics. I think it is worth quoting at length:

> ...women cannot just reverse the sin of sexism. Women cannot just blame males for historical evil in a way that makes themselves only innocent victims. Women cannot affirm themselves as created in the image of God and as subjects of full human potential in a way that diminishes male humanity. Women,... must reach for a continually expanding definition of the inclusive humanity: inclusive of both genders, inclusive of all social groups and races. Any principle of religion or society that

---

[266] Thiselton, *New Horizons*, p. 431.

marginalizes one group of persons as less than fully human diminishes us all.[267]

Other Writers

3.10 Joy Elasky Fleming: Rhetorical–Theological Reading

Joy Elasky Fleming is a graduate of Trinity Evangelical Divinity School, Deerfield, Illinois. She earned a Ph.D. in the Old Testament from the University of Strasbourg, France, in 1987. Fleming was a missionary with the Evangelical Free Church Mission and taught at the Bangui Evangelical School of Theology in Bangui in Central African Republic.

Like Trible, Fleming utilises rhetorical methodology to read the creation narratives. While Trible's concept of rhetorical style is artistic, Fleming's is mathematical, with charts and diagrams.[268] Her main intention seems to be to interpret the passage in its canonical context. Together with Trible, she affirms that the biblical text is positive to woman and only interpretations are biased. Fleming is probably the first feminist interpreter who reads the creation narrative within the framework of a traditional 'fall from grace' understanding. While Trible reads the creation narrative as a 'love story', Fleming reads with the theological intention of showing that the corporate disobedience of the human couple in the breaking of the divine command resulted in the subjugation of woman by man. Her arguments are found in her doctoral dissertation, *Rhetorical Analysis of Gen. 2–3.*[269]

Fleming's readings are similar to Trible's in many respects.[270] Like Trible, the main purpose of her reading also seems to be to refute misogynist interpretations. Accordingly, she tries to show that the woman is not 'a rib of man' and hence secondary and subordinate. Like Trible, she argues that עזר כנגדו (*'ezer kenegdô*) does not signify any inferiority, but an equal in all respects. Following Trible, she also argues that the woman is not a derivative from the 'rib' of man, rather a special creation of Yahweh. Her view of the naming of woman by man in Gen. 2:23 is also very similar to Trible. Like Trible, she also posits that no distinctive naming formula is

---

[267] Rosemary Radford Ruether, 'Feminist Interpretation: A Method of Correlation', in *Feminist Interpretation of the Bible*, p. 116.

[268] She follows Isaac M. Kikawada's 'rhetorical methodology'. For details see Kikawada, 'The Shape of Genesis 11:1–9', in *Rhetorical Criticism: Essays in Honor of James Muilenburg*, (eds.) J. J. Jackson and M. Kessler (Pittsburgh, Pennsylvania: 1974), pp. 18–32.

[269] Joy Elasky Fleming, *A Rhetorical Analysis of Genesis 2–3 with Implications for a Theology of Man and Woman*; see also, *Man and Woman in Biblical Unity: Theology from Genesis 2–3.*

[270] Fleming, *Man and Woman*, pp. 1–44.

used here. She points out the presence of the man in the transgression of God's commandment, and shows that the serpent is the tempter, not the woman. So the woman is not the temptress and the seducer of the man.

Like Trible, Fleming also notes that 'no curse is levied on the woman', and only the serpent is cursed. She too thinks that the man's rule over the woman is not prescriptive but descriptive and like Trible, she notes that although the woman desires her husband, he will not reciprocate; 'instead he will misuse her for his own selfish purposes'.[271]

There is also some dissimilarity with Trible, however, for whom this is a 'love story gone awry'. Unlike most of the feminists, Fleming reads Gen 3 as the story of transgression and fall, finding rebellion and sin to be clear motifs in the narrative. She finds in Gen. 2 'God at work', and in Gen.3, 'sin at work'. Fleming emphasises the importance of divine commandment in Gen. 2:16–17 and its violation by 'eating' the fruit which God told them not to eat. She notes the occurrence of the verb אכל (*'kal*) in each line and argues that it is an injunction on "eating".[272] Unlike other feminist readers, she underlines this as transgression and sin.

She takes a point of departure from others in her interpretation of Gen. 3:16. Following KJV, she translates 3:16a as two things, avoiding hendia-dys. So her translation of the verse is: 'I will greatly multiply thy *sorrow* and "I will greatly mutiply thy *conception*"'.[273] She notes that the phrase הרון (*heron*) means 'conception' or 'pregnancy', not childbirth. Fleming argues in relation to Gen. 1:28 (the command to be fruitful and multiply) that 'I will greatly multiply your *conception*' is similar to 'I will greatly multiply your *seed*'. So she considers it as a 'message of hope' to the woman. She writes: 'God adds a new promise to the original creation blessing. God personally ensures that she will conceive. God will "greatly multiply" her "conception"'.[274] In short, Fleming reads Gen. 3:16 as a promise. Fleming views the man's rule over the woman in relation to man's deliberate sin of eating the fruit (she thinks woman's sin was not de-liberate as she was deceived by the serpent) which resulted in man seeking independence 'by setting himself up as the new emperor. His new kingdom will be <u>her</u>! In so doing he will take the place of God and claim to be her new lord'.[275] She also argues that in his ruling he would misuse the woman and treat her as he used to treat the animals.

In her zeal to refute the chauvinist readings, Fleming also has over-stated the case in many instances. For instance, her interpretations of Gen.

---

[271] Fleming, *A Rhetorical Analysis,* p. 355.

[272] Ibid., p. 195. Contra Meyers.

[273] Fleming, *Man and Woman,* p. 32. Cf. Meyers.

[274] Ibid., p. 35. She finds the notion of *protoevangelium* in this promise.

[275] Fleming, *A Rhetorical Analysis*, p. 352. Cf. Trible; on this particular aspect Fleming is very much dependent on Trible.

114 Eve: Accused or Acquitted?

3:16 as a promise and of 'man's ruling of woman', are problematic. Here she reads too much into the text. As I have elsewhere argued, this ruling may only be in relation to sexual union, not beyond that. In Gen. 2:23 the man leaves his father and mother and becomes one flesh with his wife. Now the woman turns to her husband in her desire for union. If we read the text in this perspective, the woman's desire and the man's rule are not at all negative. In the rest of the chapters in Genesis or other parts of the Bible we never see men ruling women like animals as Fleming suggested. In some cases, she attempts a Christian reading of the text by bringing the concept of *protoevangelium* into play.

Fleming's reading is an example of a committed theological feminist reading, exploiting the modern literary approach. However, her reading reflects dual commitments, that is, feminist and conservative. Precisely because of this, at some points her interpretations tend to be strained.

3.11 Alice Laffey: Literary Reading:

Alice L. Laffey, an American Roman Catholic is the first woman to receive a Doctorate from the Pontifical Biblical Institute in Rome, Italy. She is the Associate Professor of Old Testament at the College of the Holy Cross, Worcester, Massachusetts, USA. Her *An Introduction to the Old Testament: A Feminist Perspective* first appeared in 1988.[276] Laffey offers a literary reading of the biblical text with the presupposition that 'women are equal to men. It insists that all texts be interpreted by this principle. Since the biblical texts are historically conditioned and were produced by a patriarchal society, they are patriarchal in character'.[277] She approaches the text with some suspicion due to its patriarchal bias. Like the later Trible, Laffey finds 'patriarchal prejudices' of the biblical authors as well as its interpreters. Although the text is permeated with patriarchal bias she does not want to reject the text outright because she finds a liberative thread in the Old Testament struggling for 'women's liberation' in the ancient culture.[278]

She reads Genesis 2–3 from a feminist perspective.[279] She considers this narrative as an 'aetiology' 'to explain the present situation, why things are the way they are'.[280] Through her readings she wanted to show that to malign Eve as the cause of sin in the world is an injustice to textual interpretation and that is out of a patriarchal bias. She thinks woman is an equal

---

[276] Laffey, (Philadelphia: Fortress Press 1988). This book was published in Great Britain by SPCK, London in 1990 with the title, *Wives, Harlots and Concubines: The Old Testament in Feminist Perspective*. Our reference is from this edition.
[277] Ibid., p. 2.
[278] Ibid., pp. 3–4.
[279] Ibid., pp. 21–27.
[280] Ibid., p. 25.

helpmate for אדם (*'ādām*) and in no sense an inferior. Moreover, she does not find any literary significance in the woman's eating of the forbidden fruit first. At the same time she acknowledges her role along with the man and the serpent in disobeying God and thus the punishment each of them received. However, she notes that 'the present reality of female submission' is contrary to the situation of 'man's equal helpmate' in Gen. 2.[281] In relation to their punishment, Laffey treats man's act as 'greater wrong' and his punishment more severe: tilling the soil and human death, 'the punishment of the more significant offender. His punishment extended not to a situation peculiar to his state—like the serpent's and the woman's—but to one which affects all the living'.[282]

Laffey's reading is in many respects similar to Trible's. Both aim to counteract male chauvinistic readings. The woman is equal to the man in both readings. The woman's subordination is seen in relation to her disobedience by both authors. However, Laffey considers man's punishment as more severe.

There are many inconsistencies in her reading. I would like to examine one of her main assumptions in her readings. She notes that 'the character Eve has a minor role in the story as a result of the patriarchal culture in which the text was produced. She speaks very little; the dialogue which takes place between Yahweh and the man is both more copious and more significant'.[283] This evaluation is odd in view of Eve's speaking role in Genesis 3 and it is especially striking because of the contrast with Trible at this point. While Trible's interpretation needs qualification, she has seen the prominence of Eve's dialogue with the serpent. If it was a thoroughly patriarchal restrictive culture, arguably the woman never would have conversed with the serpent.[284]

Laffey's conclusion depicting man's punishment as more severe cannot hold true. In addition to the 'great pain' (Laffey's term), she also has to undergo death like man, and she was also driven out from the garden along with man. Moreover, woman also has to share all the punishments which are given to man. In that case woman's punishment seems to be more severe.

---

[281] Ibid., p. 27.

[282] Ibid.

[283] Ibid., p. 26.

[284] There is a factual error in her treatment of the serpent. She writes: 'serpent is feminine in Hebrew' and accordingly she uses feminine pronouns for the serpent in their readings. See pp. 23–24.

3. 12 Ellen Van Wolde: Semantic Reading:

The Dutch scholar Ellen van Wolde provides very valuable insights in the understanding of the creation text in relation to many feminist issues. Although she does not approach the text with a feminist 'pre–commitment', she indirectly addresses many feminist concerns.

Van Wolde provides a detailed discussion of the various aspects of semiotic methodology and its application to biblical exegesis.[285] In her approach there are many factors involved in the process of *semiosis* or generation of meaning. According to Van Wolde the semiotic interpretation of a biblical text is mainly based on two processes of generation of meaning. The first she calls 'the process of the text', which 'is concerned with the biblical text as the outcome of experienced interaction between God, humanity and the world'.[286] The second one is the reader. 'The interaction between the reader's life and thought and the text enables the reader to attribute meanings to the biblical text'.[287] In this process mainly the reader locates iconicity or similarity between many aspects within the text.[288] Because of the possible ambiguities of the language, she takes into consideration, unlike other literary readers, the 'contextual relationships' within the text to specify the meaning. She writes: 'To do justice to the semantic world of the Hebrew Bible stories a study of the elements of meaning in the stories must be focused on the context of the elements within a text, and must therefore be a text semantics.'[289] In her readings, she also recognises the role of the reader. So the reader needs to choose between many possible meanings with the help of literary and linguistic markers in the text.[290] In short, in her reading, meaning is generated as a result of an interaction between the Hebrew language code, the text and the reader.

Van Wolde makes an important observation concerning the relational nature of the human being. That is 'in his relation with woman, אשה, the human no longer refers to himself as אדם as a being differentiated from the אדמה but as איש as a being differentiated in man and woman'.[291] Along with Vogels, she also notes: 'As a human he derives his identity from his relation

---

[285] Ellen Van Wolde, *Words Become Worlds*, pp. 113–209. She sets apart around half of her work to discuss theoretical aspects. Van Wolde defines semiotic analysis as 'a normal reading process in which the reader enters into a relation with the text and attributes meaning to the text.' See E.J. Van Wolde, *A Semiotic Analysis of Genesis 2–3*, p. 56.

[286] Ibid., p. 203.

[287] Ibid., p. 204.

[288] These similarities include phonetic, morphemic, sememic (resemblance between word and stem), and syntactic levels. For a detailed discussion, see Van Wolde, *A Semiotic Analysis of Genesis 2–3*. pp. 130–31.

[289] Van Wolde, *Words Become Worlds*, p. x.

[290] Ibid.

[291] Van Wolde, *Words Become Worlds*, pp. 16–17.

with the earth, as a male human being he derives his identity from his relation with woman.'[292] So one could argue that no change takes place as far
as the human being is concerned, rather he is only aware of his role in relation to woman.

Along with most of the feminists, Van Wolde does not see any inferiority or superiority in the term עזר ('*ezer*) either on the part of the person giving or receiving the aid.[293] She emphasises the role of woman as man's
perfect partner as the one who saves man from loneliness and from mortal
danger.[294]

Van Wolde interprets Gen. 3:16 and v. 20 in the light of phonetic, morphemic and lexemic iconic relations of the text, Gen. 2–3. First of all, she
notes the phonetic relations between אדם-אדמה ('*ādām*–'*ādmāh*) and איש–
אשה ('*îš*–'*iššâ*). The second resemblance, the morphemic, is between the
feminine forms אדמה and אשה ('*ādmāh*–*iššâ*). She notes the life giving
function of both. אשה ('*iššâ*) brings forth children in Gen.3:16a and 3:20
and אדמה ('*ādmāh)* is the source of life in Gen. 2:7, 19, 23; 3:19, 24.[295] She
explains: 'the morpheme or the female suffix –ה in (אדמה and אשה) shows in
which sense both terms are similar, namely in the sense of bringing forth
life; it expresses the female, in this case the life–giving function'.[296] The
third similarity is lexemic,[297] that is, the similarity between the basic or root
forms. She offers text–semantic relations between אדם-אדמה ('*ādām*–
'*ādmāh*) and אשה-איש ('*îš*–'*iššâ*) in Gen. 2–3. She elucidates:

> Gen. 3:16b describes אשה as someone who yearns for איש, while איש,will
> rule over אשה, Gen. 3:17–18 and 3:23 describe the אדם as something
> which because of the tilling by the אדם can bring forth plants. As the
> אדמה depends on the husbandry of the אדם, so the אשה depends on the
> management of the איש.[298]

In short, according to Van Wolde the feminine forms describe the life–
giving and the masculine the managing function in Gen. 2–3. She dia-
gramatically shows this connection as follows:[299]

---

[292] Ibid., p. 17. Cf. Vogels, pp. 29–30.

[293] Ibid., p. 18. Contra Clines.

[294] Ibid., p. 19. Cf. Terrien.

[295] Ibid., pp. 25–26. Here אדם is brought forth by the אדמה and איש is brought forth by
אשה . Cf. Gen. 2:7 and 4:1.

[296] Ibid., p. 26.

[297] Cf. Cotterell and Turner, p. 21.

[298] Van Wolde, *Words Become Worlds*, pp. 26–27.

[299] Ibid., p. 27.

אדמה :אדם
——————————————— = management : giving life
אשה :איש

Because of the above correlation, she finds both continuity and disconti-
nuity between the man and the woman and between the human and the
earth. She finds a mutual dependence between the man and the woman.
Man has to depend on earth as it is his beginning and end, also his food
source, and on the woman because she is the one who bears new life. Similarly, the woman needs to depend on the earth as it is also her beginning
and end and food supply. She is also dependent on 'man's management,
care and protection'.[300] In short, 'the dependence of the woman with respect
to the man can therefore not be separated from the man's dependence with
respect to woman, nor can it be separated from the relation of mutual dependence between the human and the earth'.[301]

Van Wolde's reading is significantly different from other feminist readings. Her reading avoids all domination and the subjugation of man over
woman; rather the relation between man and woman is 'a partnership based
on similarities and differences. In this partnership the woman is responsible
for new life and so for the survival of the human being, while the man is responsible for management, care and protection'.[302] This line of interpretation is inevitable, especially in the present context where the readers find either unequivocal unity, undermining the essential differences, or dominant
subjugation without any room for reciprocal relationships between man and
woman.

Some commentators and a few feminist interpreters unduly praise the
serpent as a hero in telling the truth.[303] Van Wolde's exegesis on this aspect is more logical in the context of the whole text. She rightly observes
the role of the serpent as a deceiver. Although many things which the serpent told the woman come true,[304] the rest of the chapter clearly gives us the
picture that the serpent did not give the woman the whole truth. She points
out that although there was no immediate death, in the following episode
God showed the couple that there was death after life.[305] She explicates:

---

[300] Ibid.

[301] Ibid., p. 28. She notes earth needs tilling for the production of vegetation.

[302] Ibid., pp. 28–29.

[303] For instance, James Barr, *The Garden of Eden and Hope of Immortality* (London:
SCM Press, 1992); Fewell and Gunn, *Gender, Power and Promise.*

[304] The man and the woman did not die after eating the fruit, their eyes were opened,
they became like God in knowing good and evil (3:22).

[305] Van Wolde, *Words Become Worlds*, p. 10.

The serpent removes all differences and proclaims an absolute equality denying the differences: a life without death, no distinction between the human being and God, pure knowledge, no difference between the human being and serpent.... The serpent's deception is the totalitarian principle, the denial of differences and limits.[306]

Van Wolde also points out the difference between Yahweh God and the human. יהוה–אלהים [*yahweh elohim*] both creates and lives forever; the human does not live forever but can only survive as a result of his procreative capacity...the human being who lives temporarily acknowledges יהוה אלהים (*yahweh elohim*) who is timeless and lives and creates in continuation'.[307]

Her methodological concern for the contextual aspects has much strength. Van Wolde's method makes an important contribution to the feminist readings of the creation narrative, although it does not attempt to deal with all the feminist issues, and perhaps it cannot. But that was not the main intention of her reading.

3.13 Mary Phil Korsak: Philological Reading

Mary Phil Korsak, a British born and educated Roman Catholic, working in a catholic parish (Paroisse Libre) in Brussels contributed to feminist scholarship through her scholarly retranslation of the whole book of Genesis from the Hebrew text.[308] The purpose of her study is to find 'a word in the target language capable of corresponding to a given Hebrew word in all its contexts'.[309] She has learnt modern languages both at Oxford and Paris and taught in England, France and Belgium. She also pursued biblical studies. Her semantic study of the first chapters of Genesis gives an explanation about her translation, especially in relation to feminist scholarship.[310] She thinks feminism 'must benefit both women and men by helping to restore harmony where it has been lost'.[311]

Korsak's approach is positive as far as feminist issues are concerned. She finds the text positive to woman in its original and she locates the problem mainly with androcentric translations. We would take on board only the terminologies which are relevant to feminist thinking. Throughout her work, she translates אדם (*'ādām*) as 'groundling' in line with אדמה (*'ādmāh*), 'ground'. Following Trible, she avoids the third person masculine pronoun 'he' for אדם (*'ādām*) as it represents the 'potential human couple'

---

[306] Ibid.

[307] Ibid., p. 47.

[308] Korsak, *At the Start...Genesis Made New: A Translation of the Hebrew Text*, 1992.

[309] Korsak, 'Genesis: A New Look', in *A Feminist Companion to Genesis*, p. 42.

[310] Ibid., pp. 39–52.

[311] Ibid., p. 52.

and instead she uses 'it' until the sexual distinction of אדם (*'ādām*) in Gen.
2:23. In other words, Korsak uses 'it' whenever it represents couple in a
collective sense.[312] For instance, she translates:

> It is not good for the *groundling* to be alone
> I will make for *it* a help as *its* counterpart (2:18) [emphasis mine]

Likewise, she translates צלע (*selah*) not as 'rib' but as 'side'.[313] Accordingly the woman is made from the side of the groundling not from the
'rib' with the further implication of them being side by side. She finds the
basic equality of human beings in this 'Genesis myth'. She thinks that the
myth focuses on another issue that 'archetypal woman is said to be born of
archetypal man, the deeper implication being that of a man's relationship
with his woman companion is not to be confused with his relationship to his
mother'.[314] So here the man–woman relationship substitutes child–parent
relationship.

Her translation of Gen. 3:20 is significant for a feminist point of view.
Contrary to common feminist assumptions, Korsak finds something positively remarkable in this name 'Life'. She explains: 'By giving her the
name Life, Genesis pays a great tribute to woman. This name is linked
through its root to the tetragrammaton.'[315] Moreover, she views the
woman's 'breeding' of a son (Gen. 3:16) as a 'positive experience' in the
Hebrew world though it involves labour. In a similar vein, she suggests,
'the longing' (desire) of woman to her man as 'sexual desire'. She interprets man's rule intertextually, comparing the rule of 'two great lights' in
Gen. 1:16–18 for ruling the day and the night. Obviously the intended implication is that there is no negative aspect intended in man's ruling of
woman.

Korsak's retranslation and philological explanations of the key terms of
Genesis once more reiterate that the creation narratives can still become
meaningful to woman if the androcentric interpretations could be rectified.
She locates the problem not in the text but only with the interpretations.

---

[312] Ibid., p. 46. She assumes that the term האדם involves both male and female.

[313] Cf. Cassuto, *A Commentary on the Book of Genesis.* He thinks woman is not made
from the rib alone. Cassuto notes: 'He [God] did not take the bone alone, as the exe-
getes usually understand the verse; the hard bone would not have been suitable material
for the fashioning of the tender and delicate body of the woman. The meaning of the
text is that the Creator took together with the bone also the flesh attached to it, and from
the flesh He formed the woman's flesh, and from the bone her bones. Proof of this we
find in the words of the man (v. 23)', p. 134.

[314] Ibid., p. 49.

[315] Ibid., pp. 49–50.

3.14 Ilana Pardes: Heteroglossia

Ilana Pardes did her doctorate on feminist readings at the University of California, Berkeley. Now she works at the Princeton Theological Seminary, New Jersey. In her literary reading of the creation narrative, Ilana Pardes tries to identify many voices in the same text. She calls this methodology heteroglossia. Her reading is found in her book, *Countertraditions in the Bible*.[316]

Pardes belongs to the third wave of feminist biblical criticism. In our survey of scholarship, we saw the emergence of the first wave of feminist criticism in the last century. Elizabeth Cady Stanton was the main figure in this wave. The second wave acquired momentum in 1970's led by Phyllis Trible, with the intention of redeeming the texts from patriarchal bias. They found the texts to be more positive to women and the problem they saw was mainly with translations and interpretations. In the third wave of feminism, not only the male interpretations of the Scriptures but also the biblical texts and male characters, including Yahweh/God are subject to criticism. In other words, no distinction is made between the human characters and God. In many instances Yahweh himself is a villain for feminists, promoting male interests. Biblical texts, then are not in themselves positive to women. However, almost all these writers are perplexed by the fact that, although they proclaim the text is negative to women, there are many positive elements in relation to women. Most of the third wave feminists explain these positive traits either as an 'antithetical trend' within the Bible or as irony or counter voices. Athalya Brenner uses the term 'female voices'.

Pardes' reading of the biblical texts draws insights from feminist theory, literary criticism and psycho–analysis. The main goal of her work 'is to explore the tense dialogue between the dominant patriarchal discourses of the Bible and counter female voices which attempt to put forth other truths'.[317] Pardes starts with the presupposition that there were 'counter female voices' in the biblical text raised against the 'dominant patriarchal discourses' of the Bible. Her readings 'call for a consideration of the heterogeneity of the Hebrew Canon, for an appreciation of the variety of socio–ideological horizons evident in this composite text'.[318] She argues that 'the analysis of Genesis 4–11 and especially of Genesis 4–5 is essential to the understanding of both the Priestly and Yahwistic treatments of femininity in Genesis 1–3'.[319] Contrary to other feminist readers, Pardes thinks that in

---

[316] Ilana Pardes, *Countertraditions in the Bible: A Feminist Approach.*

[317] Ibid., p. 4.

[318] Pardes, *Countertraditions,* p. 3.

[319] 'Beyond Genesis 3: the Politics of Maternal Naming', in *A Feminist Companion to Genesis*, p. 174, This article has been reprinted here from her above book.

both creation accounts (Priestly and Yahwistic) 'patriarchy reigns'. She assumes that the Priestly account of creation is a 'reinterpretation of the Yahwistic one....'

Pardes' readings of the creation accounts stretch beyond Genesis 3. Her argument mainly revolves around Genesis 4:1b:

ותאמר קניתי איש את יהוה (I have produced' a man with the help of the LORD).

Following Cassuto, she translates it as 'I have created [קניתי] a man[איש] equally with the Lord (את ה)[320] Moreover, she argues that Eve, previously the object of naming, now becomes the subject, and Pardes treats this text as 'the ground for maternal naming–speeches in the Bible'.[321] Her basic presupposition is that naming is not only the prerogative of men in the Bible but also of women and she takes Eve as a prime example. She views Eve not only as a name–giver but also as a creatress, questioning 'the preliminary biblical tenet with respect to (pro)creation—God's position as the one and only Creator'.[322] She claims that Eve's naming–speech in Genesis 4:1 is a 'first rebellion against the Father'.[323] Pardes notes another important implication of Eve's naming speech. She writes: '[Her] speech is a critique not only of monotheistic principles, but also of the underlying patriarchal presuppositions of monotheism'.[324]

Moreover, Pardes sees in Eve's naming 'a response to Adam's naming of woman; it is a response to his almost dream–like reversal of the order of things, to his indirect claim to have created woman out of his body, to his celebration of the generative capacity of his flesh and bones'.[325] Here Pardes is clearly referring back to the creation of woman from man, and to his speech. Further she notes how the woman responds: 'It is not you who created woman out of man (with divine help), she seems to claim, but it is I who created you (*'iš*) together with YHWH!.[326] Therefore, she goes on to suggest that Eve is not merely Cain's mother, but also the 'bearer' of Adam

---

[320] Cf. Cassuto, who interprets קניתי איש את־יהוה (Gen. 4:1) as Eve's creative power similar to the Divine creative power. 'The Lord formed the first *man* (ii 7), and I have formed the second *man... I stand together* {i.e. *equally*} WITH HIM *in the rank of creators*', see Cassuto, *A Commentary on the Book of Genesis,* p. 201; emphasis original; see also pp. 198–99.

[321] Pardes, p. 174. Pardes argues that Eve's speech follows 'the formal conventions of biblical naming speeches; it links the name "Cain" and the *qānâ* (create) by means of a pun', (p. 178).

[322] Ibid., p. 181.

[323] Here Pardes takes Eve and God as daughter and Father as in Freudian psychology.

[324] Pardes, 'Beyond Genesis 3', p. 181.

[325] Ibid., p. 182.

[326] Ibid.

and even the 'ex–consort of YHWH'.[327] Pardes notes down some changes with regard to her first and second naming speech in Gen. 4:25 where God becomes the subject 'the one who "grants" [שׁת] a seed'. She proposes that 'this fall between Eve's first and second naming–speeches be added to the long list of Yahwistic stories of pride/crime and punishment in primeval history'.[328] Pardes also points out that Eve's naming speech is an indicator to show that 'Eve never fully acknowledges Adam's rule...'[329] She adds that, even if Eve accepts divine authority in her second naming–speech, 'this does not mean that her daughters will refrain from calling God's authority into question'.[330]

Although Pardes assumes that the main thrust of the Bible is patriarchal, she argues: 'patriarchy is continuously challenged by antithetical trends'.[331] Pardes argues that through the naming of her sons, Eve tries 'to dissociate motherhood from subordination'. Moreover, 'by taking pleasure in her creativity she attempts to undo God's punishment in Gen. 3:16....'[332] Pardes argues that Gen. 1:27 does not 'prescribe equality between the sexes' in the light of Gen. 5:1–3. She thinks that although the Priestly narrative acknowledges 'a certain symmetry between male and female on the cosmic level,... when dealing with the social realm, procreation turns out to be the perpetuation of male seed in male seed'.[333]

There are many problems with Pardes' reading. First of all, Gen. 4:1 is not a naming speech in a strict sense of the term. Although there is assonance[334] between the name קין (*qyn*) and the verb קניתי (*qnyty*), this alone does not make this speech a naming speech. Almost every naming speech consists of קרא (*qr'*) with שׁם (*šem*) or at least קרא (*qr'*) with an object. Even the biblical maternal naming–speeches which Pardes cites as examples follow the above rule, except Gen. 4:1 where neither שׁם nor קרא is present. The only reason Pardes finds for treating this as a naming speech is the phonetic link between the name קין (*qyn*) and the verb קנה (*qnh*) by means of a pun. However, in my judgement, the mere presence of a pun

---

[327] Ibid., p. 183.

[328] Ibid., p. 187. Pardes thinks that the tragic death of her son (Abel) 'as a retributive deflation of her hubris' because of her "(pro)creative pride" in challenging God's prerogative of procreation.

[329] Ibid., p. 188.

[330] Ibid.

[331] Ibid., p. 185.

[332] Ibid., p. 189.

[333] Ibid., p. 190. She further posits that Gen. 5: 3 is a misreading of Gen. 4:1 with the purpose of refuting the theomorphic begetting by females (see p. 191).

[334] Driver distinguishes *assonance* from etymology. In *assonance* 'the name is explained not by the word from which it is actually *derived,* but by a word which it *resembles* in sound', *The Book of Genesis* (London: Methuen & Co., 1906), p. 63.

does not rule out the need for the above elements of naming (see Gen. 2:23;
3:20; 4:25; 5:29; 16:11; 29: 32, 33, 34, 35; 30:6, 8, 11, 13, 18, 20, 24,
41:51, 52; Exod. 2:22; 18:3–4; 1 Sam. 1:20, 4:21). In other words in every
naming speech above, one or another of the above naming elements is present in addition to the pun.

In his study of naming speeches, George W. Ramsey identifies four
types of naming formulas.[335] The most common type of naming speech contains the verb קרא (*qr'*) and the noun שם (*šem*),[336] with an explanation of
the name introduced by לאמר (*lemor*) and כי (*ki*). In the second type the explanation precedes the naming clause (Gen. 30:13). The third category provides a basis for the name first and then the naming itself in an על כן (*'al
ken*) clause (Gen. 29:34–35; Exod. 15:23). The fourth is an abbreviated
form without the explanation of naming (sometimes given after the naming
– Gen. 4:26, 30:21).[337]

In the light of the above discussion, Gen. 4:1 cannot be treated as a naming formula. It seems very likely that Gen. 4: 1 could be a kind of praise after the birth of a child in the light of other intertextual evidences. Contrary
to Pardes' argument, in most of the births the woman gives credit to the
Creator God either in terms of thanksgiving praise or prayer (Gen. 4:25;
16:11; 21:6–7; 29: 32,33, 35; 30: 18–20, 23, 24; I Sam. 1:20; 4:21–22).[338]
The biblical women are not in opposition to Yahweh; rather they acknowledge that Yahweh is the one who gives the fruit of the womb (Gen. 21:1–2;
30:1–2,22). Terence E. Fretheim comments on Gen. 4:1, in the context of
Eve's speech:

> Her [Eve's] cry expresses no more a prideful boast than does that of the
> man. Eve's response appears similar to that of Leah and Rachel (29:32–
> 30:24), expressing gratitude to Yahweh (a woman first speaks this name)
> for the child and acknowledging divine participation, which probably re-

[335] See Ramsey, 'Is Name–giving an act of Domination in Genesis 2:23 and Elsewhere?', *CBQ* 50 (1988), pp. 26–29.
[336] Cf. Trible, *God and the Rhetoric*, pp. 99–100; cf. Gen. 4:17, 25, 26a, 26b; 5:29;
29:32.
[337] Ramsey, p. 28. Ramsey also notes in some cases, instead of the noun שם as the object of the verb קרא the proposition ל attached to the pronominal suffix of the noun in
naming formulas (1 Sam. 4:21, 2Kgs. 18:4, 1 Sam. 23:28, Gen. 35:18). In any case,
קרא is important in the naming formula.
[338] It is to be noted that no praise or prayer is offered to God when Lot's daughters
named their children, probably because they were born through incestuous relationship
with their father (Gen. 19:37–38). The lack of theological explanation here is probably
due to God's disapproval in this affair. It was also common for men to ascribe credit to
God at the birth of a child, either in terms of praise or prayer (Gen. 5:29; 41:51,52;
Exod. 18:4).

fers generally to God's blessing of fertility and child–bearing capability.[339]

If the speech of Eve in Gen. 4:1 was a first rebellion against the Father, it would have been followed by some kind of punishment as we often witness in the primeval history. For instance, in the story of the Tower of Babel, people seemed to be challenging the prerogative of God, and this was followed by divine punishment.[340] Moreover, it is quite unlikely that Eve was attempting again to challenge God so soon after her expulsion from the Garden for rebellion.

Secondly, there is difficulty in determining the meaning of this enigmatic verse. Von Rad notes: 'Every word of this little sentence is difficult.'[341] One could literally translate it as: 'I have gained or acquired a man with the Lord' (if ת is the preposition) or 'I have gained a man the Lord' (if את is the definite object indicator). Nonetheless, Isaac. M. Kikawada's comparative study of this verse in the light of the Babylonian version of the Atra–hasis epic seems to have resolved many of these problems. He notes the following parallels between the creatress Mami and Eve. First, both Mami and Eve are involved in the creative process.[342] Second, a parallel between the phrases *itti Enkima* and *'et–Yhwh* is noted, and finally a similar motif is seen in both cases, that is, Mami and Eve are themselves inadequate in their 'creative ability', 'both of them requiring male divine help for their success'.[343] Kikawada further notes: 'If we understand Gen 4:1 in this light, the traditional translation, "I have gained a man *with the help of Yhwh*", would make good sense as a humble expression of the mother Eve'.[344] So the implication of his study is that as Mami cannot create without the help of Enki, Eve cannot procreate with out the help of YHWH. Moreover, it is not a challenging naming speech as Pardes argues but only a 'humble expression of mother Eve'.

There is no considerable difference between the content of Eve's speech in Gen. 4:1 and 4:25 as Pardes argues. In both instances YHWH or the

---

[339] Terence E. Fretheim, 'The Book of Genesis: Introduction, Commentary, and Reflections', in *NIB* vol. I (Nashville: Abingdon Press, 1994), p. 372; see also Trevor Dennis, *Sarah Laughed: Women's Voices in the Old Testament*, p. 32; cf. Westerman *Genesis*, p. 289. He also thinks that this sentence is a 'cry of triumph or praise'.

[340] For rebellion–punishment sequences see Clines, *The Theme of the Pentateuch* (JSOTS 10; Sheffield: JSOT Press, 1986).

[341] Von Rad, *Genesis*, p. 100; cf. Wenham, *Genesis*, p. 101.

[342] See I. M. Kikawada, 'Two Notes on Eve', *JBL* 91 (1972), p. 37.

[343] Ibid.

[344] Ibid., emphasis original.

Elohim is the provider of the child.[345] The main difference is that Eve's first speech is not a naming speech rather only an explanation of the name, whereas the second one is a clear naming speech. I disagree with Pardes' contention that Eve's acknowledgement of God's power in Gen. 4:25 is a result of Eve being punished for her hubris by killing her son (Abel). Even a cursory reading of the text shows that Eve acknowledges the role of God in granting a child to her in both instances.[346] Pardes' attempt to undermine the role of God and Adam in the process of procreation is not only true to the text, but also violates the natural principal of human birth, since a woman cannot produce a child alone. It is not contentious to say human beings are procreators with God. However, the texts acknowledge that God is the one who opens the womb and grants the child.

We have elsewhere argued that the changing of the generic אדם in Gen. 5:1–2 into a proper name in 5:3 is not due to any gender reasons but only a narrative strategy to introduce the genealogy. We would argue that the repetition of Gen. 1:27 ('male and female he created them in the image') in 5:1–2 is a reassertion of this fact that both male and female are created in God's image/likeness. So before the narrator gives the genealogy of Adam in 5:3, he reiterates in the preceding verse (5:2) that both male and female are in God's image.[347] Although the biblical narratives give mainly male genealogies, they also name all the patriarchs' wives. In some cases indeed the names of the sons are omitted and only the names of the daughters are given (Job: 42:13–15).[348]

In short, Pardes' readings seem to overrate the male orientation of the texts, and 'feminine voices' are misconstrued as conscious counter–voices.

3.15 Ilona N. Rashkow: Psycho–Analytic Reading

Ilona N. Rashkow works in the Department of Comparative Studies in the State University of New York at Stony Brook, New York. She provides two diametrically opposite feminist readings of the creation narratives. Her

---

[345] Ellen Van Wolde aptly observes a correlation between איש and אשה. She writes: 'As the אדמה brings forth an אדם together with YHWH (2:7), the אשה brings forth an איש together with YHWH (4:1),' *Word Become Worlds*, p. 26.

[346] The Parallels between these two speeches are noted by Cassuto. While I disagree with Cassuto's description of the first speech as a naming speech, I find his parallels vey convincing. The most important parallel to be noted is, in both places Eve explains the name of the child in reference to deity.

[347] Cf. Emmerson, 'Women in Ancient Israel', p. 390, contra Watson, Bird.

[348] We read the story of Zelophehad's daughters (all their names are given) and their demand for their father's inheritance and the Lord's approval in this matter. This could be an indication that even in that patriarchal culture, women's rights were protected by Yahweh to a certain extent (Num. 27:1–12).

earlier readings are given in her book entitled *Upon the Dark Places*.[349] Although her main intention in this work is to expose anti–semitism and sexism in 'English Renaissance Biblical Translation', she also addresses feminist issues in the course of her work. She has attempted to show the failure of Renaissance translators in undermining 'the ambiguities of the Hebrew Bible'. In this work, in many areas she often agrees with Trible. Like Trible, Rashkow translates עזר כנגדו ('*ezer kenegdô*) as a 'helper to match him', meaning an equal counterpart to Adam. She argues that the term עזר ('*ezer*) 'designates a relationship which implies no inferiority on the part of the helper. In fact, the helper is *necessary* to continue the very existence or well–being of the person being assisted'.[350] Again like Trible, she argues that the verb בנה (*bnh*) in relation to the creation of woman signifies a 'unique creation of Woman', thereby avoiding the common notion that woman is inferior as she was created from Adam's rib. Similarly to Trible, she also argues that Adam was present and passive when the woman took the fruit. She thus relieves the woman of the role of the tempter of Adam.

Rashkow's interpretation of Gen. 3:16 is to be noted carefully as it is considerably different from other feminist interpreters. Taking into account the structure of Hebrew poetry, she argues that in Gen. 3:16 "'In pain you shall bring forth children" duplicates "your pain in childbearing". Likewise, "he shall rule over you" parallels "your desire shall be for your husband"'.[351] So for Rashkow, 'the husband's "rule" would seem to lie either in the wife's need for her husband because of her desire to have children, or the strength of his sexual attraction for her'.[352] Through this reading she tries to show that this statement does not mean the subordination of Woman to Man in all relationships. In this work, Rashkow has succeeded in exposing many sexist translations in the English Renaissance. She shows that the source text is free from sexual bias and only the translations are sexist.

In her recent book, *The Phallacy of Genesis*,[353] Rashkow employs psycho–analytic literary theory to read the text. However, her hermeneutical stance is clearly reader–response, that is she considers 'interpretation to be a *reader's response*, necessarily based on a *reader's* personal input, as-

---

[349] Rashkow, *Upon the Dark Places: Anti–Semitism and Sexism in English Renaissance Biblical Translation* (BALS 28; Sheffield: Almond Press, 1990), pp. 75–96.

[350] Ibid., p. 83; cf. Terrien, *Till the Heart Sings: A Biblical Theology of Manhood and Womanhood* (Philadelphia: Fortress Press), 1985, p. 11; contra Clines, *What Does Eve do to Help?*, p. 30.

[351] Ibid., p. 93.

[352] Ibid.

[353] Rashkow, *The Phallacy of Genesis: A Feminist–Psychoanalytic Approach*, (Louisville: W/JKP, 1993). The argument of this book has been re–iterated in her work, 'Daughters and Fathers in Genesis... or What is Wrong with this Picture?', in *The New Literary Criticism and the Hebrew Bible*, pp. 250–265.

sumptions, and biases'.[354] So she takes her 'feminist stance' as an explicit starting point. In her own words: 'Meaning does not stand waiting to be uncovered behind a text, but evolves in front of it, actualised by readers and interpreters who produce new possibilities.'[355] Rashkow adapts psycho–analytical insights in her reader response readings. In this approach 'the reader and a text work together'. She explains: 'a reader imitates a psycho-analyst by looking beyond the literal story to relate its structure and con-flicts to a drama within some *theoretical* human mind, a mind ambiguously located between the fictional characters of the text and that of the reader'.[356] In this reader–oriented approach, objectivity is not at all a guiding principle in interpretation. The basic assumption of reader–response critics is that 'a narrative has no meaning before it is read, there can be no distinction be-tween what is "in" a narrative and what is "in" a reader. Hence, neither a text nor a reader can be "objective."'[357] Moreover, meaning does not have any existence 'outside the mind of a reader'.

Using Freudian psychology, Rashkow focuses on the sexual nature of the narrative. She thinks the creation story consists of two 'interwoven sub-texts'. According to Rashkow Gen. 1–3 is a story of an 'unacknowledged daughter's rebellion by means of her appropriating the forbidden fruit that stands "erected" at the centre of the enclosed garden'.[358] She argues against Trible that Gen. 1 is not an 'authorisation for women's equality', because she thinks that 'Every authorisation of equality in Genesis 1 is sub-sequently repressed and erased by chapters 2–3'.[359]

The juxtaposition of two creation accounts is explained as 'the shad-owed family construct'. She explains: 'The syntax in Gen 1:26–27, which implies man and woman are created simultaneously, constructs Adam and Eve as son and daughter'.[360] However, she argues that this narration neces-sitates a re–narration because of the deity's fatherly role 'who authorises his children's implicitly incestuous union (i.e., brother–sister incest)...'[361] So she argues that in the re–creation of man and woman in Gen. 2, the deity avoids the role of the 'parentage of the woman' and removes the incestuous relationship. She also notes that in this story Adam, 'the acknowledged son, becomes the father', as a result of Eve's derivation from Adam's side.[362]

---

[354] Ibid., p. 110; emphasis original.
[355] Ibid., p. 22.
[356] Ibid., p. 19.
[357] Ibid., p. 21.
[358] Ibid., p. 75.
[359] Ibid., p. 76.
[360] Ibid., p. 77.
[361] Ibid.
[362] Ibid.

Rashkow treats Gen. 3 as the daughter's rebellion against the father 'to acquire the father's knowledge and power through the (phallic) sign that has been denied her, and dramatises the threat to patriarchy which daughters represent'.[363] Moreover Eve's offering of the 'seed–bearing fruit' to Adam indicates 'the daughter's ultimate dispossession of her father, and may thus reveal the daughter as *the* dangerous threat to paternal power...'[364] This violation resulted in a permanent separation between the father and the daughter.

One of the main problems with Rashkow's reading is her effort in criticising other feminist writers who read the same text from other perspectives. For instance, she criticised Trible for providing a reading which underlines the equality of women in Gen.1. Another problem for any reader is to decide which of her conclusion concerning the status of woman in the creation account is to be considered. Again, by raising questions about the validity of other readings Rashkow showed the weakness of her methodology. What right has she got to criticise other readings when her reader–response approach validates every reading equally? The other main serious concern we need to be aware of in this method is the tendency to reflect our own value–system in our reading of the ancient text. Rashkow is not free from this flaw either.

3.16 Athalya Brenner:Socio–Literary Reading

Athalya Brenner, one of the most prominent feminist critics of the Hebrew Bible, is Senior Lecturer at the Technion, Haifa, Israel, and Professor of Feminism and Christianity at the Catholic University of Nijmegen, the Netherlands. In addition to her writings, she also serves as the editor of *A Feminist Companion to the Bible*. Her recent book, *On Gendering Texts: Female and Male Voices in the Hebrew Bible*,[365] co–authored with Fokkelien van Dijk–Hemmes, aims to gender texts by locating women's voices in the Bible, and seems to be a new agenda in feminist hermeneutics.

In her previous work, *The Israelite Woman*,[366] Brenner provides a reading of biblical women against the 'literary and sociological framework of biblical thoughts and times'. In this work she also deals with the creation narratives of Gen. 2–3,[367] combining literary and psychological insights to read the narrative about man and woman. Like Trible and Bal she portrays the woman as more intelligent and capable than man. Basing her argu-

---

[363] Ibid., p. 78. From a Freudian perspective, she considers 'the seed bearing fruit' on the father's tree as 'father's self', the father's phallus itself.

[364] Ibid., p. 79.

[365] Brenner (BIS I; Leiden: E.J. Brill, 1993)

[366] Brenner, *The Israelite Woman*.

[367] See pp. 123–131.

ments on psychology, she argues that the rebellion of man and woman is an independent, courageous act in order to escape from the dominant tyrannical control of the divine parent. She also sets the creation of woman in this context. As the man is bored with the parent [God], he needs more company. Brenner thinks that was why God created first animals, then the woman.[368]

She does not consider 'the fall of mankind', to be the result of the woman's initiative nor that this is the *leitmotif* of the Garden story. Rather she casts the woman, not as as a temptress or villain, but as a heroine. Her act of eating the fruit is portrayed as an effort towards maturity and civilisation. So in this respect woman was the instigator of human growth, and her act a struggle to lead an independent life.[369] She writes: 'The serpent approaches the woman, knowing not only that she would listen but also that she would understand that God has lied to his child in order to prevent the child from leaving him.'[370] Moreover, she notes that in the first creation story (Gen.1–26–27) similarity to Godhead is bestowed upon man [through creating in God's image] whereas in the Garden story, 'it is acquired through temptation, deceit, and disobedience'.[371] In this connection, she points to the divine characteristics the human couple had achieved after eating the fruit, and sees this as a positive gain.

She also thinks that the woman is stronger than man. 'the celebrated matriarchal saying' of Gen. 2: 24 (man leaving father and mother to become one flesh with the woman) in this patriarchal story reflects the idea that 'woman was the stronger and dominant partner; and that she forfeited this position by behaving badly. Man gained his dominance over woman not by his own strength, but because woman's punishment dictates that he sujugates (sic) her'.[372] She leaves the questions to readers to decide whether the state of knowledge is preferable to the state of innocence and whether painful maturity is preferable to pleasant childhood.

Brenner's reading of the creation account is another typical example of a resistant reading, challenging the givenness of the text and its interpretation.

3.17 Danna Nolan Fewell and David M. Gunn: Narrative Reading

Danna Nolan Fewell is Associate Professor of Old Testament at Perkins School of Theology, Southern Methodist University, Dallas, Texas, and

---

[368] Ibid., p. 126.

[369] Ibid., p. 128.

[370] Ibid., p. 127.

[371] Ibid. Contra Straumann who links Gen.2: 18 with Gen. 1: 26–7. She thinks that by eating the fruit, they acquired certain divine qualities.

[372] Ibid., p. 128.

David. M. Gunn is Professor of Old Testament at Columbia Theological Seminary, Atlanta, Georgia. Unlike other feminist writers, Fewell co–authors her writings with a male feminist writer, David M. Gunn. They represent third wave of feminist criticism. Fewell and Gunn are not interested in reconstructing an ancient 'history', rather they construct 'a story world in which questions of human values and belief find shape in relation to our own (and our likely readers') worlds'.[373] They draw insights from literary theory, sociology and anthropology to interpret the texts. They present the aim of their readings in their own words: 'The primary concern we bring as contemporary readers of this ancient story is a commitment to see a radical reformation in gender relations in our own society.'[374] In this line the main question they ask of the text is 'Whose interest does this text serve?'[375] They begin with the presupposition that the subject of the biblical texts is Israelite men and the stories are geared to serve their interests. Moreover, throughout their work they look for opportunities to see women as subjects of the stories and they 'deliberately read the text as a story of women'.[376] Like Bal and Pardes, Fewell and Gunn also take 'God's function as a character in the story'. Hence, they write: 'unless the character of God is subject to the same kind of critical scrutiny as all other characters, we are not really reading the text'.[377]

They read creation stories from a different perspective from other feminist interpreters. After reviewing other feminist readings, they provide their own readings. They think that meaning is derived through the interaction between text and reader.[378] They also assume that the Bible is 'a product of a culture'. So they believe ancient cultural notions are encoded in the text and they attempt to identify those notions. They also presuppose that 'texts are not objective representations of reality, but representations of particular value systems'.[379] The crux of their argument is that the text promotes only the interests of the male.

They begin to read the Genesis story with the observation that in the past commentators were reticent about the character of YHWH. So they regard YHWH as being on a par with the human characters in the story. As a re-

---

[373] Danna Nolan Fewell and David M. Gunn, *Gender, Power, and Promise*, p. 12.

[374] Ibid., p. 13.

[375] Ibid., p. 18.

[376] Ibid.

[377] Ibid., p. 19. See also Fewell, 'Reading the Bible Ideologically: Feminist Criticism', in *To Each its Own Meaning*, p. 246. For a similar male resistant reading see Philip R. Davies, *Whose Bible is it Anyway?* (JSOTS 204; Sheffield: Sheffield Academic Press, 1995), pp. 84–94.

[378] Danna Nolan Fewell and David M. Gunn, *Narrative in the Hebrew Bible,* OBS (Oxford: OUP, 1993), p.193.

[379] Ibid., p. 191.

sult criticisms are mainly levelled against the character YHWH and for his responsibility in putting the tree in the garden.[380] They also depict God as the one who did not tell the couple the whole truth. Therefore, in their analysis, God is to be blamed for the woman's actions. They note: '... though God readily redirects his question from the man to the woman, the serpent's mouth he stops first with words and then with dust'.[381]

Commenting on Gen. 2:24, they write that man's desire is the 'defining norm'. 'He is the one leaving and cleaving. The woman is the point of gravity, the object to be acquired'.[382] They argue that woman's eating of the fruit is a result of her exploratory and adventurous spirit.

With regard to 3:16 they note that the control of woman's sexuality is denied to her: 'the man shall rule over her. Thus both sex and eating end up in the domain of the man. The woman becomes subordinate, the man subjugator'.[383]

Feminist readers of the Bible struggle with the positive and negative aspects of women in the Bible. In the past, some feminists have emphasised the positive and a few others the negative. Nonetheless, it is a matter of fact that there are both positive and negative elements relating to women in the Bible.[384] So the wide range of diverse materials makes feminist readings problematical. Together with Pardes and Tolbert, Fewell and Gunn try to resolve 'negative' and 'positive' traits. Pardes as we saw, understands the positive as an 'anti–thetical trend', challenging the male ideology, and they also come to more or less similar conclusion. They write: 'The Bible shows us not merely patriarchy, élitism, and nationalism; it shows us the fragility of these ideologies through irony and counter–voices'.[385] So in addition to the obvious mandatory patriarchal characteristics of the texts, they also see another world–view within the text. They write:

> They [texts] may be uncovering a world in need of redemption and heal-
> ing and a world–view much in need of change. This is the kind of read-
> ing that can transform us. If we realise that the world of the Bible is a
> broken world, that its people are human and therefore limited, that its so-

---

[380] Fewell and Gunn, *Gender, Power and Promise*, p. 28–29.

[381] Ibid., p. 33.

[382] Ibid.,p. 29. Contrary to this assumption, most of the feminists consider the man's leaving and cleaving more positively as we have seen in other readings.

[383] Ibid., p. 36. They further comment that women's sexual desire for men is named and not men's, and this desire subordinates women.

[384] See P. Joyce, 'Feminist Exegesis of the Old Testament,' in *After Eve,* (ed.) J. M. Soskice (London: Collins, Marshall, 1990), pp. 1–7.

[385] Gunn and Fewell, *Narrative in the Hebrew Bible*, p. 204. Cf. Edwin M. Good, *Irony in the Old Testament* (Sheffield: Almond Press, 1981). Good finds ironic themes scattered in the creation narrative, pp. 81–84.

cial system is flawed, then we might start to see more clearly our own broken world, our own human limitations, our own defective social systems.[386]

There is an obvious methodological problem with this kind of reasoning. How can there be positive and negative within the same text? If the text intentionally promotes patriarchy how can there be another world–view in the text? Who has placed that world–view there? In other words, what they have said about the mandatory negative patriarchal nature of the text has been deconstructed by the positive 'counter–voices and ironies'. If there are counter–voices in the same text, then how could it be purely a patriarchal text, serving only the male interests? In short, the patriarchy of the text is under deconstruction.

In some instances their arguments are iconoclastic. For Gunn and Fewell there is no distinction between the divine (sacred) and secular (human). Like many other literary readers they uproot the biblical text from its original historical–religious setting, and find in it their own interest and concerns. As we have said before, the religious dimension of the biblical text cannot be escaped. Yet in this, as in a number of other feminist readings, the religious dimension of the text has been completely eclipsed.

3.18 Mieke Bal: Semiotic Psycho–Analytic Reading

Mieke Bal was trained in the Netherlands and she teaches Comparative Literature and Art History at the University of Rochester, USA. Since each feminist method is similar to, and different from, the others, it is imperative to note down the similarities and differences. Mieke Bal's reading in many respects is in line with Trible's. Many of Bal's exegetical conclusions are similar to those of Trible although she employs narratological and semiotic insights to read the text.[387] However, her hermeneutical presuppositions are entirely different from Trible. She combines literary theory, feminism and narrative theory in reading the text. The main difference between the two is Bal's indifference to religious traditions and she attacks Trible precisely for the latter's commitment to these. Bal asserts: 'I do not claim the Bible to be either a feminist resource or a sexist manifesto. That kind of assumption can be an issue only for those who attribute moral, religious, or political authority to these texts, which is precisely the opposite of what I am interested

---

[386] Ibid., p. 205.

[387] See Mieke Bal, 'Sexuality, Sin and Sorrow: The Emergence of Female Character: A Reading of Genesis 1–3', in *The Female Body in Western Culture*, (ed.) Susan Rubin Suleiman (Cambridge, MA: HUP, 1986), pp. 317–338. A revised version of this article has appeared in her book *Lethal Love: Feminist Literary Readings of Biblical Love Stories* (Bloomington: Indiana University Press, 1987), pp.104–130.

in.'[388]   She rather considers it as 'one of the most influential mythical and literary documents of our culture'.[389] It is worth quoting in length the purpose of her alternative reading:

> The alternative readings I will propose should not be considered as yet another, superior interpretation that overthrows all the others. My goal is rather to show, by the sheer possibility of a different reading, that "dominance" is, although present and in many ways obnoxious, not unproblematically established. It is the challenge rather than the winning that interests me. For it is not the sexist interpretation of the Bible as such that bothers me. It is the possibility of dominance itself, the attractiveness of coherence and authority in culture, that I see as the source, rather than the consequence, of sexism.[390]

Contrary to the historical critical reading,[391] she focuses on the linearity of reading and she takes Gen. 1–3 together. Accordingly, she treats the text as a semiotic object and argues: 'it [text] creates not the world, but narrative. It presents an account of the making of humanity within a progressive development of character'.[392]   Bal's argument in this line fits very well here, since her whole argument is geared to project 'the emergence of female character' (here Eve), from a sexually undifferentiated 'earth creature' (so Trible) to man and woman. So Bal argues that the creation narrative of Gen. 2 does not contradict with Gen. 1. She argues: 'it provides a specified narration of what events are included in the idea that "God created them male and female". This synecdochical composition turns Genesis 1–2 into one coherent creation story'.[393]

Like Trible, Bal challenges Eve's secondary character and her temptation. Rather, she finds in the story 'the equality of the simultaneous creation of man and woman out of a non–gendered first being, Eve's wisdom in her acceptance of the human condition, and her guiding of man...'[394] and so

---

[388] Bal, *Lethal Love*, p. 1.

[389] Ibid.

[390] Ibid., p. 3.

[391] Bal thinks that the historical critics' treatment of these two creation accounts separately is a 'retrospective fallacy'. She explains this as an ideologically motivated reading strategy which is responsible for the 'production of the sexist myth of "Eve"' (p. 109). So Bal argues that due to this 'retrospective fallacy' 'readers project the accomplished characters Adam and Eve, who appear at the very end of the third story, on to their previous stages of particularisation. Hence, the concept of character is at once a cause of the sexist myth ... ' (p. 112). However, Bal takes these separate creation stories as a progressive development of human character, but not as a gloss or a later account.

[392] Ibid., p. 112.

[393] Ibid., p. 119.

[394] Ibid., p. 2.

on. Since Western society aims at 'equal rights and emancipation', she adopts an egalitarian reading of the text.

Bal considers האדם (*hā–'ādām*) merely as a *clod* without any individuality. She posits 'the clod is still a puppet; entirely passive, it is put into the garden among the trees to grow'.[395] She writes: 'From 2:7 to 2:20 this creature has no name, no sex, and no activity'. She views the principle of differentiation and semiotic principle at work in the creation of 'the earth creature', because האדם (*hā–'ādām*) is differentiated from a larger environment.[396] She supports her arguments with intertextual evidence from Gen. 1:26–27 where she finds the 'androgynous image of the deity'.

Bal underscores 'Eve's wisdom in her acceptance of the human condition, and her guiding of man'[397] and so on, in much the same vein as Trible. With regard to the creation of woman, she thinks the deep sleep resulted in unconsciousness and thereby the death of the earth creature. The woman was formed first according to the semiotic principle, then only the man, and he is merely what is 'left over'.[398] Here Bal applies the semiotic principle[399] of differentiation whereas Trible emphasises the equality and unity in creation. Bal explains that woman being 'taken out' of man does not mean 'made out of' but 'taken away from' in the sense of 'differentiated from'. So the man is the son of האדם (*hā–'ādām*) and the woman the daughter. She also attempts to resolve the philological problem in Gen. 2:23. Here the text says that woman is taken from איש (*'îš*) rather than from האדם (*hā– 'ādām*). Here she responds with a psycho–analytical explanation.[400] In the disobedience narrative Bal praises the woman and accuses Yahweh of tricking the woman as the serpent does. She considers the woman's disobedience as the 'first independent act, which makes her powerful as a character. Not only has she the power to make the man eat, hence to make him know (her) and disobey in his turn'.[401] Moreover, Bal further thinks that woman's disobedient act also resulted in providing the Almighty God of Genesis 1, the creating spirit, with a body walking down in the garden 'with *equal status, equal features, equal feelings* to others'.[402] So Bal's reading

---

[395] Ibid., p. 113.

[396] Ibid., p. 113.

[397] Bal, *Lethal Love*, p. 2.

[398] Ibid., 116.

[399] The word semiotics is derived from the Greek word *semeiotikos*, meaning theory of signs or an interpreter of signs. For a detailed analysis and discussion of this method in biblical hermeneutics see Thiselton, *New Horizons*, pp. 80– 141.

[400] See Bal, 'Sexuality, Sin and Sorrow,' p. 324. She writes: 'in allotropy, the change of properties within the same substance, the man retrospectively assumes that he always had this sexual identity. He focalises his earlier version from his actual state' (p. 324).

[401] Bal, *Lethal Love*, p. 125.

[402] Ibid; emphasis mine.

results in equal status not only between the man and the woman but also their equal status with God.

Bal's indifferent attitude to the authority of biblical texts and her lack of theological interest are evident throughout her ideological readings. As we have noted above, her aim is to read the biblical texts in the context of western egalitarian ideals. So she fails to do proper justice to the biblical texts. Moreover, Bal's use of the semiotic principle and psycho–analytical explanations is also problematic. Her decoding of the sign in the text is faulty when she assumes that האדם (*hā–'ādām*) is an 'undifferentiated earth creature', put in the garden to grow among the trees as a passive puppet. But the text clearly gives the sign that האדם (*hā–'ādām*) is not a passive puppet among the trees; rather a male creature to tend the trees in the garden. In addition, the text does not say that the אשה (*'iššâ*) came first; it only says that the אשה (*'iššâ*) is taken from איש (*'îš*). In this case it is very likely that either אשה (*'iššâ*) and איש (*'îš*) are created together or the איש (*'îš*) is created first. Her psycho–analytical explanation concerning the use of איש (*'îš*) is also contradictory. How can the man assume that he always had this sexual identity since he was a 'leftover' after the creation of the woman as Bal reads? I do not attempt to interact with Bal in detail as our evaluation of Trible's work could indirectly respond to Bal's reading also.

Bal also falls into etymological fallacy and accordingly she interprets the *rib* of man as an euphemism which stands for 'womb'.

Although Bal does not ascribe any authority to the text, she makes use of the biblical text to support her feminist view points. So finding support from the biblical text is in reality a way acknowledging biblical authority. That is one of the apparent tensions in her readings.

Her reading is not a comprehensive reading. In her own words: 'My readings present an alternative to other readings'.[403] Both Bal and Trible have emphasised this at the expense of the main theme of the story. A proper reading should do justice to all or most of the details in a narrative. Most of the feminist scholars have failed in this area and thereby fail to deal with the important exegetical, hermeneutical and theological issues.

Although Bal does not consider the Bible either as a 'sexist manifesto' or as a 'feminist resource', like Trible, Bal also begins with the presupposition that 'the mainstream of biblical ideology is obviously patriarchal'. And she also finds the *problematisation* of 'man's priority and domination' in the Bible, including the Genesis account.[404] Another presupposition is based on the Western egalitarian ideology and emancipation. So she expects 'an evolution from a sexist text to more "equal" readings'. Since Bal has read the text from these assumptions, her readings are not at all neutral

---

[403] Ibid., p. 132.
[404] Ibid., p. 110; emphasis original.

as she claimed. Eventually, she supports a clear feminist case in her readings.

3.19 Pamela J. Milne: Structuralist Reading

Pamela J. Milne makes use of structuralist methods to read the creation stories. Having examined the various feminist readings of the creation narrative, she comes to the conclusion that the patriarchal character of the biblical text cannot be overcome by feminist rereading as patriarchy lies in the 'deep structures' of the text. As the text cannot be redeemed positively for women, her reading is a resistant reading. In this context she writes: 'We are now forced to come to terms with the idea that the sacred text is patriarchal and continues to communicate patriarchal values both directly on its surface and indirectly through its deep structures and narrative strategies'.[405] This stance raises an important question about the Bible's authority for women.

Milne takes Trible's 'reformist' feminist reading of Gen. 2–3 as a case for discussion and she tries to show mainly with the help of David Jobling's and other structural exegesis, that Gen. 2–3 is a 'male mythology' and a patriarchal document.[406] So she argues that 'the "reformist" feminist goal of reclaiming the Bible from its own patriarchal biases, and from those of its interpreters through the centuries, is simply not a viable one'.[407] In her view, the patriarchal culture produced the text and as a result the encoded value system of the Bible is also patriarchal. As a result, she thinks, the Bible cannot be read positively for women. Therefore the options that remain for feminists according to Milne are:

> We can either accept the patriarchal biblical text as sacred and content ourselves with exposing its patriarchy ... or we can expose its patriarchy and reject it as sacred and authoritative. But if we are looking for a sacred scripture that is not patriarchal, that does not construct woman as 'other' and that does not support patriarchal interpretations based on this

---

[405] Milne, 'Eve and Adam——Is a Feminist reading Possible?', *BibRev* IV (June, 1988), p. 39.

[406] See, Milne, 'The Patriarchal Stamp of Scripture: The Implications of Structuralist Analyses for Feminist Hermeneutics', in *A Feminist Companion to Genesis*, pp. 146–172, reprinted from *JFSR* 5/1 (1989), pp. 17–34. Walter Vogels reads the creation account using structuralist insights and comes to an opposite conclusion to that of Milne and other structuralists. Vogel's conclusions are similar to Trible's in most cases, though his methodology is different. See Vogels, 'It is not good that the "Mensch" should be alone; I will make him/her a helper fit for him/her', *Eg T* 9 (1978), pp. 9–35. For a positive structuralist feminist reading see Lyn M. Bechtel, 'Rethinking the Interpretation of Genesis 2. 4b—3. 24', pp. 77–117.

[407] Ibid., p. 168.

otherness, we are not likely to find it or to recover it in texts such as Genesis 2–3. If we want an authoritative sacred Scripture that does not make it possible to believe that women are secondary and inferior humans, it appears that we need to make new wine to fill our new wine-skins.[408]

---

[408] Ibid., p. 167.

CHAPTER 4

Feminist Social–Scientific Readings of the Creation Narrative: Carol Meyers

4.0 Preliminary Remarks

Sociological interpretation of religion is not a new phenomenon in the realm of interpretation. Even before the development of sociology as a full scientific discipline, there were instances where sociological principles had been used to assess religious matters. Josephus in his *Antiquities* had used sociological judgements to evaluate the situation of early Israel.[1] Hugh of St. Victor (d. 1141) had used sociological criteria in interpreting the biblical texts. Similarly the great Jewish interpreter, Rashi (1040–1105) had stressed the significance of literal interpretation which resulted in the use of sociological observation as part of the interpretive process.[2] Some of his disciples also adapted his insights. Seventeenth and eighteenth century interpreters too were aware of comparative methods.[3]

4.1 Sociology and Old Testament Interpretation

In the dawn of this century, in his famous essay, 'Die protestantische Ethik und der Geist des Kapitalismus' Max Weber, the founder of modern social sciences, showed how Calvinism with its doctrine of 'predestination' led to the emergence of Capitalism in Western Europe. Weber too had studied

---

[1] See J. W. Rogerson, 'The Use of Sociology in Old Testament Studies', in *Congress Volume, Salmanca, 1983*, ((ed.) J. A. Emerton (VTS 36; Leiden: E. J. Brill, 1985), p. 245. Assessing the situation of Israel during the period of Judges, Josephus writes: 'they suffered their aristocracy to be corrupted also, and did not ordain themselves a senate, nor any other such magistrates as their laws had formerly required....' See *The Antiquities of the Jews* Book V, Chapter, ii, 7 in *The Works of Josephus* (trans) William Whiston (Peabody: Hendrickson, 1992). The above observation is made by Clines. Rogerson comments on this: 'Clearly, for Josephus, Roman models of government were necessary for any people that was to be properly organised' (p. 245).

[2] See Robert R. Wilson, *Sociological Approaches to the Old Testament* (Philadelphia: Fortress Press, 1984), p. 2.

[3] Ibid., p. 3.

ancient Israel from a sociological perspective.[4] Also at the beginning of this century, Louis Wallis analysed sociologically the material and social situations of early Israel in his book, *Sociological Study of the Bible.* He notes that 'only through a long struggle with materialistic and social problems was Israel fitted to see God'.[5] In recent decades we have seen a fresh reawakening among biblical scholars to the application of social–scientific principles to interpreting biblical history and religion.[6] My main intention here is to show the influence of sociology in interpreting the sacred text.

4.1.1 *The Definition of method*

Norman K. Gottwald, who pioneered sociological study of the Old Testament, defines this approach as follows:

> Sociological exegesis tries to situate a biblical book or subsection in its proper social setting—taking into account the literary and historical relations between the parts and the whole. It further attempts to illuminate the text according to its explicit or implicit social referents, in a manner similar to the historical–critical method's clarification of the political and religious reference points of texts.[7]

From his definition we can understand that sociological criticism is interested in social referents as historical criticism focuses on political and religious reference points. So in a way this method is complementary to historical criticism. This revival of interest in socio–scientific methods in biblical religion is due to many factors as explained below.

The previous method of articulating the history of Israel was mostly from the biblical texts. All the main biblical histories have been written from this perspective. There is a growing belief among biblical scholars that 'the study of the history of Israel needs to be released from the constraints imposed on it by the methodological priority accorded to the biblical texts'.[8] For instance, Whitelam points out that the 'text based' picture

---

[4] Max Weber, *Ancient Judaism* (New York: Charles Scribener's Sons, 1952), cited in Wilson, p. 15.

[5] Louis Wallis, *Sociological Study of the Bible,* 1912, Chicago, p. 298, cited in Jack M. Sasson, 'On Choosing Models for Recreating Israelite Pre–Monarchic History', *JSOT* 21 (1981), p. 11.

[6] For the study of prophecy in Israel using this methodology see R. R. Wilson, *Prophecy and Society in Ancient Israel* (Philadelphia: Fortress Press, 1980); D. L. Petersen, *The Roles of Israel's Prophets* (JSOTS 17; Sheffield: JSOT Press, 1981).

[7] Norman K. Gottwald, *The Hebrew Bible: A Socio–Literary Introduction*, 1985, pp. 28–29.

[8] See Keith W. Whitelam, 'Recreating the history of Israel', *JSOT* 35 (1986), p. 59.

of conquest or infiltration is problematic in the light of archaeological data. Moreover, he also thinks that 'the study of literary remains such as the Vedas, the Confucian classics or the Hebrew Bible often reveal[s] only the self perceptions of an intellectual elite rather than the wide diversity of social reality'.[9] So he suggests that the early history of Israel needs to be explained with the help of archaeological evidences, comparative history and anthropology.[10] Hence the main thrust of 'Biblical sociology' is 'to extract social data from the Bible and to assess its import for understanding Hebrew society and culture'.[11]

The sociological principles of Max Weber, Emile Durkheim and Karl Marx have been employed to analyse biblical texts. Their theories have been used to interpret the social changes in societies. There are mainly two sociological traditions, namely the conflict tradition and the functionalist tradition. The conflict tradition views 'society as consisting of "groups and individuals trying to advance their own interests over others, whether or not overt outbreaks take place in this struggle for advantage"',[12] whereas in the functionalist tradition 'society is the prior reality which determines the individual, materially, mentally and spiritually. The collective consciousness which imposes itself on the individual comprises those beliefs and sentiments common to the members of a given society'.[13] Both these traditions have been used in the study of the Old Testament.[14]

In recent decades many biblical scholars have attempted to reconstruct the history and life of ancient Israel with the help of social–scientific disciplines.[15] They contend that the existing political history and textual evi-

---

[9] Ibid., pp. 59–60.

[10] Ibid., p. 60. We cannot make a sharp distinction between anthropology and sociology since they are complementary and interdependent disciplines.

[11] See Sasson, p. 11.

[12] R. Collins, *Three Sociological Traditions* (Oxford: OUP, 1985), p. 47 cited in 'Sociology and the Old Testament' by Andrew D. H. Mayes, in *The World of Ancient Israel,* p. 40.

[13] Ibid., pp. 41–42.

[14] For a detailed discussion see Mayes, pp. 39–63.

[15] A complete documentation of the works is not possible here. For the most important works that focus on the early origins of Israel and on the formation of Israelite society see George. E. Mendenhall, 'The Hebrew Conquest of Palestine', *BA* 25 (1962), pp. 66–87; Mendenhall, *The Tenth Generation: The Origins of the Biblical Tradition* (Baltimore: Johns Hopkins University Press, 1973); Norman K. Gottwald, *The Tribes of Yahweh: A Sociology of the Religion of Liberated Israel, 1250–1050 B. C. E.* (London: SCM Press, 1980); Gottwald, *The Hebrew Bible: A Socio–Literary Introduction*; David Noel Freedman & David Frank Graf (eds.), *Palestine in Transition: The Emergence of Ancient Israel* (SWBA 2; Sheffield: Almond Press, 1983); Niels Peter Lemche, *Early Israel: Anthropological and Historical Studies on the Israelite Society before the Monarchy* (VTS 37; Leiden: E.J. Brill, 1985); Lemche, *Ancient Israel: A New History of Israelite Society* (Sheffield: JSOT Press, 1988); Frank S. Frick, *The Formation of the*

dence are quite inadequate to articulate the real life situation during the pre–monarchic period.[16] They also argue that a thorough knowledge of the social situation of the period is a *sine qua non* in reconstructing the history of Israel.

4.1.2 The contributions and limitations of the social–scientific approach

Robert R. Wilson writes about the contribution of sociology to the study of the Old Testament.   He points out that social–scientific insights can broaden our horizon of the Old Testament in many ways.[17] Here we will note the most important of these. First of all social scientific methods will enable us to make useful analogies which can help us discover the author's world. This can be done through linguistic and literary studies, especially oral tradition, which in its turn can throw light on Old Testament literary conventions.[18] Modern cultural analogies can also help us to grasp the social structures and cultural institutions of ancient Israel to a certain extent. Although there is a wide gap between ancient Israelite society and modern industrialised societies, 'a social scientific approach can bring us closer to the world of the biblical writers than would be possible if we relied on our own cultural experiences'.[19] At the theological level, social sciences can shed more light on Israelite faith and its religious components. This is possible because sociological research suggests that religious phenomena in various societies may share common structural patterns and functions.

State in Israel: A Survey of Models and Theories (Sheffield: Almond Press, 1985); Robert B. Coote, *Early Israel: A New Horizon* (Minneapolis: Fortress Press, 1990); Robert B. Coote & Keith W. Whitelam, *The Emergence of Early Israel in Historical Perspective* (SWBA 5; Sheffield: Almond Press, 1987); David C. Hopkins, *The Highlands of Canaan: Agricultural Life in the Early Iron Age* (SWBA 3; Sheffield: Almond Press, 1985); Hopkins, 'Life on the Land: The Subsistence Struggles of Early Israel', *BA* 50 (1987), pp. 178–191; Volkmar Fritz, 'Conquest or Settlement?: The Early Iron Age in Palestine', *BA* 50 (1987), pp. 84–100; Israel Finkelstein, *The Archaeology of the Israelite Settlement* (Jerusalem: Israel Exploration Society, 1988).

[16] For a theoretical basis for this method, See Norman K. Gottwald, 'Sociological Method in the Study of Ancient Israel', in *The Bible and Liberation: Political and Social Hermeneutics,* rev. (eds.) Gottwald & R.A. Horsley (New York: Orbis /London: SPCK, 1993), pp. 142–153; Gottwald, 'Sociology of Ancient Israel', in *The Anchor Bible Dictionary,* hereafter (ABD) vol. 6 (Auckland: Doubleday, 1992), pp. 79–89. For a comprehensive analysis of the use of sociological methods in Old Testament Studies, see Rogerson, 'The Use of Sociology in Old Testament Studies', pp. 245–56; Rogerson, 'Anthropology and the Old Testament', in *The World of Ancient Israel*, pp. 17–37; A. D. H. Mayes, 'Sociology and Old Testament', pp. 39–63; see also Mayes, *The Old Testament in Sociological Perspective* (London: Marshall Pickering, 1989).

[17] See Wilson, *Sociological Approaches to the Old Testament*, pp. 1–9.

[18] Ibid., p. 6.

[19] Ibid., p. 7.

However, we need to be cautious in using comparative evidences to interpret Israelite faith and religion, because of the special nature and function of Israelite faith.

We have discussed some of the contributions of the social–scientific model. Despite its usefulness in unearthing the social world behind the biblical texts, many limitations have been noted. The following are some of the major criticisms levelled against this method.

The question has often been raised how far we can apply the same tools which have been used to analyse modern organisations, societies or groups to a group or a society (here ancient Israel) in antiquity. So the method is alleged to produce anachronistic results.[20]

Another major problem with this method is 'circular reasoning'. In this case, the criticism is that one begins with a social–scientific model and '[finds] that the model is strangely self–authenticating, especially when the evidence is fragmentary'.[21] As a result the whole text is interpreted using these parameters, on the assumption that this is *the* interpretation for that particular text.[22]

In this connection we need to be aware of some of social science's theoretical assumptions such as positivism, relativism and determinism[23] and their basic presuppositions. Positivism is defined 'as the desire to emulate the empirical methods of natural science in the quest for knowledge'.[24] According to this assumption, reason has the central role and human sciences become the only valid form of knowledge. 'In such an intellectual climate, many scholars trained in the more "subjective" approaches of the humanities (history, theology and philosophy) may come to believe that the "more objective" social sciences [*per se*] can render a more accurate picture of what was "real" in ancient Israel.'[25] Herion defines *relativism* and *determinism*

> as the assumption that issues of morality and religion can never be considered truly right or wrong in any "absolute" sense, rather that they vary with (or are "relative" to) persons, societies and cultures. In conjunction

---

[20] For a comprehensive discussion of the problems of social–scientific models, see S. C. Barton, 'Social–scientific Approaches to Paul', in *Dictionary of Paul and His Letters*, (ed.) Gerold F. Hawthorne *et al* (Leicester: IVP, 1993), pp. 894–95.

[21] Ibid., p. 894.

[22] See also David M. Gunn and Danna Nolan Fewell, *Narrative in the Hebrew Bible*, 1993, pp. 7–8.

[23] For a detailed discussion of these concepts, see Gary A. Herion, 'The Impact of Modern and Social Science Assumptions on the Reconstruction of Israelite History', *JSOT* 34 (1986), pp. 3–33.

[24] Ibid., p. 6.

[25] Ibid.

with this, *determinism* may be defined as the general tendency to think that human values, choices and actions are caused (or "determined") by certain variables in the social and cultural environment.[26]

Barton points to the roots where social sciences lie:

Their roots lie in post–Enlightenment atheism and the hermeneutics of suspicion, according to which theology and religion have an epiphe- nomenal status only as the products of other forces and interests, whether the human unconscious (Freud), class conflict (Marx), the maintenance of society (Durkheim), the legitimation of patriarchal domination (femi- nism) or whatever.[27]

Due to the above secular bent there is a tendency to assign secondary importance to the religious and confessional matters in these models be- cause they assume that social–scientific knowledge is the *summum bonum*. So 'it is necessary for the reader to become conscious of personal predispo- sitions and understandings so as not to impose them on the text'.[28]   One must also avoid the danger of forcing biblical Israel into a modern socio- logical mould.[29]

4.2 Carol Meyers' Reading of the Creation Narratives

4.2.1 Life and work

Carol Meyers, Professor in the Department of Religion at Duke University, Durham, North Carolina since 1990, received her A.B. (B.A.) from Welles- ley College, and M.A. and Ph.D. (in Near Eastern and Judaic Studies) from Brandeis University. Meyers has been in academic and related professional services ever since her education. From 1975–1977 she worked as an Old Testament Lecturer (part–time) in the Department of Religion at the Uni- versity of North Carolina at Chapel Hill and visiting Lecturer at Duke Uni- versity during 1976–77. She served as Assistant Professor in Duke Univer- sity from 1977–1984. In 1984, she became Associate Professor in the same

---

[26] Ibid., p. 8.

[27] Barton, 'Social–scientific Approaches...', p. 895. According to the positivist theory of sociology, religion is an 'institutionalised ignorance, a vestige of man's primitive past doomed to disappear in an era of scientific rationalism' (see Herion, p. 8.).

[28] Wilson, *Sociological Approaches to the Old Testament*, p. 4.

[29] Ibid., p. 9.

University and served in that capacity until 1990 when she became Professor.

In addition, she also served the 'Women's Studies Programme' of Duke University in various capacities. She maintains very close links with the Holy Land. Her association with Israel dates back to 1964 with Hebrew Union College Biblical and Archaeological School, Jerusalem. Almost every year for the last thirty years, Meyers has engaged in archaeological excavations and related activities in the Middle East.

Meyers is a prolific writer who has published many books and articles not only related to gender issues but also archaeological and theological works. Some of her important titles include: *The Tabernacle Menorah: A Synthetic Study of a Symbol from the Biblical Cult* (Cambridge: American Schools of Oriental Research, Dissertation Series 2, and Missoula, Montana: Scholars Press, 1976); *Discovering Eve: Ancient Israelite Women in Context* (New York/Oxford: OUP, 1988); *Haggai, Zechariah 1–8* (AB 25B), with E. Meyers (Garden City, New York: Doubleday, 1987); *Zechariah 9–14* (AB 25C), with E. Meyers (New York: Doubleday, 1993); *Sepphoris,* with E. Netzer and E. Meyers (Winona Lake, Indiana: Eisenbrauns and the joint Sepphoris project, 1992).

Her *curriculum vitae,* running to twenty six pages (May 1994), shows her multiple roles as an archaeologist, academician, administrator, writer, editor, biblical scholar and teacher. She has travelled widely in and outside the United States in connection with her academic career. She has memberships in the American Academy of Religion, American Schools of Oriental Research, Archaeology Society of Jordan, British School of Archaeology in Jerusalem, Society of Biblical Literature, Israel Exploration Society, Centre for Cross–Cultural Research on Women (Oxford) etc.

She is married to Eric. M. Meyers, Professor in the Department of Religion also at Duke University and they have two children. Her religious background is Jewish.

4.2.2 Methodological presuppositions

Norman Gottwald, one of the main proponents of the sociological method, makes use of the macro–sociological tools of Durkheim, Weber and Karl Marx in his *magnum opus, The Tribes of Yahweh,* to explain the pre–monarchic history of Israel. In this work he adapts a historical cultural material model which includes techno–environmental and techno–economic elements such as the topography of the Israelite highlands, the use of iron tools, the introduction of water cisterns and the use of terracing in agriculture.[30] The basic presupposition of his argument is that

---

[30] Gottwald, *The Tribes of Yahweh,* p. xxiii.

early Israel was an eclectic formation of marginal and depressed Canaanite people, including "feudalized" peasants (*hupshu*), '*apiru* mercenaries
and adventurers, transhumant pastoralists, tribally organised farmers and
pastoral nomads (*shosu*), and probably also itinerant craftsmen and disaf-
fected priests.[31]

Carol Meyers has employed many of Gottwald's sociological assumptions and principles in her feminist reading of biblical texts. Meyers is the
first feminist biblical scholar who has employed social–scientific methods
to read the biblical texts from a feminist perspective.
    She argues that the textual evidences are totally inadequate in under-
standing the real situation of women in ancient Israel. She believes: 'The
Israelite woman is largely unseen in the pages of Hebrew Bible. To presume to locate her in biblical narrative would be to commit a fundamental
methodological error.'[32] So she attempts to explore the condition of Israelite women during the period of Israel's origins (c. 1200–1000 B.C.E.) with
the aid of interdisciplinary methods such as socio–history, cultural anthropology and archaeology. Meyers is mainly interested in 'social reality
rather than textual representation'.[33] So the biblical texts have only secondary importance in her analysis. This is evident in her words: 'For centuries
we have looked at Eve through the distorting lenses of patriarchal, Judeo–
Christian tradition. Now perhaps we can examine her in the clear light of
her own world'.[34] Hence she tries to recover the *Sitz im Leben* of the Iron
Age for reconstructing the situation of ancient Israelite women. Her methodological assumptions are clearly set out in her work.[35] The third chapter
of her book deals with the methodological issues.
    In order to reconstruct the gender relations in early Israel, she tries to
unearth the productive and procreative roles which women played in society. So in order to reconstruct the status of Israelite women she thinks that
'The Bible as a primary source is unreliable' and hence she chooses a
multi–disciplinary approach. Here she advocates the need for articulating a
social history rather than a political history as proposed by Mendenhall and
Gottwald. In order to reconstruct Israel's character, and to understand the

---

[31] Ibid., p. xxiii.

[32] Meyers, *Discovering Eve*, p. 5.

[33] Personal interview with Carol Meyers at Duke University, USA in November 1994.

[34] Meyers, *Discovering Eve*, p. 5.

[35] See Carol Meyers, 'Procreation, Production and Protection: Male–Female Balance in
Early Israel', *JAAR 51* (1983), pp. 569–593; see also Meyers, 'Gender Roles and Genesis 3.16 Revisited', in *The Word of the Lord shall Go Forth,* (eds.) Meyers and M.O.
Connor (Winona Lake: Eisenbrauns, 1983), pp. 337–354. The same essay is reprinted
in *A Feminist Companion to Genesis,* pp. 118–141.

role of ideology in that community, she opts for an integrated approach with archaeology and sociology supported by literary and textual analyses.

She also assumes that the female contribution in the basic productive task is an important factor in determining the status of women. So she argues: 'The task of discovering Eve thus begins with an examination of the material conditions that were the basis of Israel's existence and hence integral to Israel's distinct social and cultural formations.'[36] To her, to explore the material world of early Israel the following three aspects are to be taken into consideration:

i. The pioneer status of Israel as a society.
ii. The specific demands of Palestinian highland agricultural subsistence economy.
iii. The demographic situation during the early Iron Age.[37]

In recent scholarship, there have been, broadly speaking, three schools of thought in the attempt to explain the origin of Israel.[38] They are the conquest model, the peace infiltration model and the revolt model. Carol Meyers adopts the last of these proposed by Mendenhall and developed and popularised by Gottwald. According to this view, there was a peasant revolt within Canaan against the city rulers around 1200 B.C.E. which was joined by a nuclear group of infiltrators from the desert.[39] They had slowly moved to the highland regions of Palestine from the cities (recently

---

[36] Meyers, *Discovering Eve*, p. 49.

[37] Ibid., p. 50.

[38] According to the traditional account, the people of Israel emerged as a community due to the unified military conquest of Canaan by Israelites. This model was developed by William F. Albright and G. E. Wright. The main sources of evidence are found in the conquest accounts of biblical texts in the early chapters of Joshua. The main problem with this method is that in many instances the recent archaeological evidence does not corroborate the biblical conquest account of Canaan. The second model was proposed by Albrecht Alt and developed by Martin Noth and his followers. According to them the origin of Israel is a result of peaceful infiltration of nomadic people from outside Canaan. The main difficulty with this model is that it does not have much direct support in the O.T. This theory has been accepted nevertheless, by many prominent European and a few American scholars. For a survey of the various models see Manfred Weippert, *The Settlement of the Israelite Tribes in Palestine* (London: SCM Press, 1971), pp. 5–62; Marvin, L. Chaney, 'Ancient Palestinian Peasant Movements and the Formation of Pre–monarchic Israel', in *Palestine in Transition,* pp. 39–90; I. Finkelstein, 'The Process of Israelite Settlement: Archaeological Evidence and the Schools of Scholarship', in *The Archaeology of the Israelite Settlement,* 1988, pp. 293–314; Gösta W. Ahlström, *The History of Ancient Palestine from the Palaeolithic Period to Alexander's Conquest* (JSOTS 146; Sheffield: JSOT Press, 1993). pp. 334–370.

[39] See Gottwald, *The Tribes of Yahweh*, p. 210. For a critique of the other two models and a detailed discussion of the revolt model see pp. 192–219.

Gottwald renamed his theory 'social revolution' since he thinks that 'peasant revolt' is too narrow to explain the social revolution which occurred).[40] Meyers accepts the above hypothesis as a starting point for her methodology. Concerning the origin of early Israel, she also thinks, along with Gottwald, that it was a result of political revolution. Hence she writes:

> Traditionalists tend toward the theological, echoing the Bible's claim that divine promise and election brought displaced Israelites to a home land. Social historians now see the beginning of widespread settlement in the hill country as in fact constituting a social or even a political revolution.[41]

Moreover, like Gottwald, she also assumes that the people who escaped from Canaanite and Egyptian exploitation formed an egalitarian society in the hill country.[42] Following Gottwald she also attempts to recover the *materiality* of Israel's life and thought in order to understand the religion of Israel.[43] In her work she sets apart one chapter for 'Setting the highland environment of Ancient Israel', thereby determining the methodology. So she explores the three broad material aspects of early Israel which we have noted above.[44]

According to Meyers the above three aspects of the material world determine 'Eve's social role during the pre–monarchic period of Israel'. While men were involved in arduous tasks like felling trees and hewing out cisterns, Meyers thinks: 'Females would have had to perform certain regular productive tasks that otherwise might have been relegated to males alone.'[45] In short she claims that the early occupants of the Palestinian highland were peasants who had to work hard to make the land arable and productive. It involved the construction of terraces which 'not only provided level surfaces for crops, but the removal of stones needed for terrac-

---

[40] See Gottwald, *The Hebrew Bible in its Social World and in Ours* (Atlanta: Scholars Press, 1993), p. 90.

[41] Meyers, *Discovering Eve,* p. 52.

[42] Ibid., pp. 52–53.

[43] Ibid., p. 49. Gottwald assumes that a full understanding of the materiality is essential for the proper understanding of Israel's spirituality. See *Tribes of Yahweh*, p. xxv.

[44] Ibid., p. 50. For a similar viewpoint see Gottwald, 'Domain Assumptions and Societal Models in the Study of Pre–monarchic Israel', in *Congress Volume, Edinburgh, 1974* (VTS 27; Leiden: E. J. Brill, 1975), pp. 89–100. He writes: 'Israel's economy was a form of intensive rain agriculture with animal husbandry, an economy which capitalised on the recent introduction into the highlands of Canaan of iron implements for clearing and working the land...' (p. 95). He also notes the significance of iron implements for clearing the land, slaked lime plaster for water–tight cisterns and the art of rock terracing for effective agriculture. See also Gottwald, *The Tribes of Yahweh,* pp. 655–660.

[45] Ibid., p. 56.

ing exposed a layer of cultivable soil'.[46] This also prevented the crops and soil from erosion. The construction and the maintenance of terraces required a huge effort which involved the collective responsibility of both men and women. Along with this task they also had to clear the forest and cut cisterns resulting in more pressure on individual members of the society. 'For women, the increased labour needs had a double impact: more work meant women became more involved in production; in addition, increased labour needs required a larger work force, which in turn called for larger families.'[47]

She also points out another factor which resulted in pressure towards a larger family. According to Meyers, during the Bronze Age (thirteenth century B.C.E) there was widespread depopulation due to pestilence, famine and diseases in Canaanite–city states. With the help of biblical and extra–biblical evidence such as comparative studies, anthropology, archaeology and other extra–biblical textual sources she accounts for a loss of population during that period. She points to some biblical references which deal with pestilence and plague (Jer. 14: 11–12; Exod. 32: 5 and other biblical pasages which allude to similar situations in Num. 16, 21 and 25). She argues: 'Several lines of evidence point to an equally devastating outbreak of plague ... in the thirteenth century BCE, which marked the end of Bronze Age civilization in the ancient world.'[48] She even finds reference in the Amarna letters to death from pestilence and disease.[49] She also observes archaeological evidence suggesting severe destruction showing a thick layer of ashes during the Late Bronze Age.[50] As a result, in order to meet the labour demand of the pioneer highland situation, Israelites had to opt for a big family.[51] She assumes that due to the above factors, there was a balanced division of labour in ancient Israel.

With this explanation of the environment of ancient Israel, she attempts to place Israelite women in their time and in particular, it serves as the background for her study of Genesis 2–3.[52]

---

[46] Ibid., p. 60.

[47] Ibid., p. 61.

[48] Ibid., p. 66.

[49] Ibid., p. 68.

[50] Ibid., p. 69.

[51] Ibid. See also pp. 64–71.

[52] Meyers, 'The Roots of Restriction: Women in Early Israel', in *The Bible and Liberation: Political and Social Hermeneutics*, (ed.), pp. 289–306 (reprint from *BA* 41 (1978), pp. 91–103); Meyers, 'Procreation, Production and Protection: Male–Female Balance in Early Israel', *JAAR* 51 (1983), pp. 569–93; Meyers, 'Everyday Life: Women in the Period of the Hebrew Bible', in *The Women's Bible Commentary*, pp. 244–251.

4.3 The Creation Narrative in Feminist Perspective

4.3.1 Preliminary considerations

As a method, first of all, we will present Meyers' readings of the creation
narrative, highlighting the important issues which she brings out in her
readings. In the last part of this chapter we will make a critical evaluation
of her readings. As we have seen, Meyers attempts to read the creation narrative of Genesis 2–3 against the social context of ancient Israel in its be-
ginnings. Meyers considers the creation narratives of Genesis as the most
important biblical passage which deals with the concept of sexual balance.[53]
In *Discovering Eve,* she sets apart two chapters for reading the creation narrative. In another work, there is also elaborate discussion of gender roles
based on Gen. 3:16.[54] Meyers thinks that these two chapters of Genesis
have had more influence than any other part of the Bible in determining
gender roles and identity in the western world.

4.3.2 The social setting of the Eden narrative

According to Meyers the Eden narrative is not a story of the 'fall of Eve'
but a literary reflection of the particular conditions of highland life meant
for the agrarian Israelite society.[55] She thinks that the portrayal of this narrative as a story of human sin and suffering is a later creation of post–
biblical religion.[56] With this perspective, she wants to recover the pristine
Eve.

GENESIS 2–3 AS A 'CREATION MYTH'
She treats Gen.2–3 as two genres of folk literature,[57] namely, 'creation
myths' and 'etiologies'. She thinks that Genesis 3 also contains a 'wisdom
parable'. As a 'creation myth' 'Genesis 2–3 is a tale dealing with origins;

---

[53] See Meyers, 'Procreation, Production, and Protection, pp. 570–71.

[54] See Meyers, 'Gender roles and Genesis 3:16 revisited', pp. 337–354.

[55] Meyers, *Discovering Eve,* pp. 77–78.

[56] Like Meyers, D. R. G. Beattie had also found the social setting of the story as a peasant economy and he also negated the notion of sin in the narrative. See 'What is Genesis
2–3 About?', *Exp Tim* 92 (1980/81), p. 9. Similarly, negating the concept of 'sin and
fall' interpretation, another feminist Lyn M. Bechtel argues that the theme of the Genesis creation story is the process of human maturation from 'infancy' to adulthood, see
Bechtel, 'Genesis 2.4b–3.24: A Myth about Human Maturation', *JSOT* 67 (1995), pp.
3–26.

[57] Ibid., p. 79.

as such it is a tale meant to help human beings come to grips with the nature and meaning of their own existence'.[58] Then she shows that

> Etiology helped pre–scientific people answer the perennial questions about how they fit into the natural and social worlds; and it also helped them to accept the answers. Etiologies thus cannot be read as statements of historical or scientific causality.[59]

Through this assumption Meyers negates the traditional reading of the narrative as a story of the origin of sin and woman's part in the fall. According to Meyers, the concept of sin is a later development. She lists the following reasons for this:

i. There is no explicit reference to sin in the narrative.
ii. The aetiological nature of the narrative reduces the human theme of disobedience.
iii. There is no vocabulary of sin.
iv. The *genre* of the narrative deals with daily living.[60]

According to Meyers the biblical narratives in Genesis 2–3 are myths of origins, and '[t]he characters [man and woman] in the creation story present the *essential* (archetypal) features of human life, not the *first* (prototypical) humans in a historical sense'.[61] She argues that only 'prototypes',[62] such as the Exodus event, in contrast, will have influence on subsequent generations. Hence she writes that the characters in the creation narrative do not have *prototypical* value effective for subsequent generations, but only show an *archetypal* feature of human life.[63] Nonetheless, Meyers thinks that the archetypal creation stories are 'cast as prototypes by virtue of their place at the fore of what is the first great historical tradition ever recorded'.[64] By

---

[58] Ibid.

[59] Ibid., p. 80. Meyers also finds counterparts for the 'creation myth' in Babylon, Egypt, Athens, and Rome. She cites the Roman historian Sallust in order to establish that 'A myth has never happened. It happens every day' (p. 80).

[60] See Meyers, 'Gender Roles and Genesis 3.16 revisited', in *A Feminist Companion to Genesis*, pp. 126–128. See also *Discovering Eve*, p. 86ff.

[61] Meyers, *Discovering Eve* , pp. 80–81; emphasis original. For an explanation of the term 'archetype', see Sproul, B.C., *Principal Myths: Creating the World* (San Francisco: Harper and Row, 1979), p. 27. Sproul says that archetypes 'reveal and define form, showing how a truth of a moment has the same structure as an absolute or eternal one', cited by Meyers, p. 80.

[62] Meyers defines prototypes as 'formative events that happen in time and influence subsequent generations' (see p. 80).

[63] Ibid., pp. 80–81.

[64] Ibid., p. 80.

this distinction she suggests that the creation narrative in Genesis does not have any binding authority on succeeding generations as generally believed.

'ĀDĀM AS EARTHLING

Meyers translates Gen. 2:7 as 'Then God Yahweh formed an *earthling* of clods from the *earth* and breathed into his nostrils the breath of life; and the *earthling* became a living being'. She argues that the traditional rendering of אדם *('ādām)* as man in the creation narrative is to attribute a priority to male existence and to ignore the word–play. Since אדם *('ādām)* is taken from אדמה *('ādmāh)* which is ground or earth, *it* is an *earthling* rather than a man. By this rendering she tries to avoid the gender nuanced tone of the word.[65]

Her rendering of אדם *('ādām)* as *earthling* fits well in her ancient Israelite agrarian setting. Hence she writes: 'The term *'adam* tells us the essence of human life is not its eventual classification into gendered categories but rather its organic connection to the earth.'[66] So Meyers argues that there is an agrarian orientation at work in the shaping of the creation narrative.[67] In Gen. 2:5–9 she points out that two situations prevailed: one without rain or workers and the other with the temporary availability of food provided by God. 'Because the creation of humanity occurs centrally to this arrangement, this passage is telling us that human existence is inextricably caught up with concern for sustenance. The Israelite highlanders, [were] confronted with the daily reality of intensive labor...'[68]

WOMAN AS SUITABLE COUNTERPART [69]

Having pointed out the pejorative tone in the traditional rendering of woman as a 'help meet for man', Meyers renders it as 'suitable counterpart'. She contends that the relationship between the woman and the man in the narrative is non–hierarchical because the prepositional phrase in Gen. 2:18 and 20 means 'opposite', or 'corresponding to' or 'parallel with' or 'on a par with'.[70] Along with some other feminist writers Meyers also

---

[65] Ibid., p. 82. She also provides an alternative translation where she substitutes *human* for *earthling* and *humus* for earth. This translation is in line with Trible. So Bechtel, p. 9.

[66] Ibid.

[67] She picks up many words and phrases from the creation account which have association with agricultural life, such as *bush of the field, land, grains of the field,* etc (Gen. 2: 5).

[68] Meyers, p. 84.

[69] Meyers' treatment of this theme is very similar to Trible's.

[70] Ibid., p. 85. Unlike other feminist writers, here she offers a balanced treatment of the Hebrew noun עזר. Generally feminist readers including Trible consider that this phrase makes woman superior.

thinks that only by the creation of women are the gendered human beings, male and female, introduced into the narrative.[71] Hence she writes: 'The creation of humanity in its sexually nuanced form brings to an end the sequence of creation begun when God took up a formless clod of earth and formed a human being.'[72]

MALE AND FEMALE FOR PROCREATION

She affirms that the creation of humanity into male and female (Gen. 1:26–27) is for procreation. Modern feminist interpreters, in common with their nineteenth–century predecessors, have considered this verse to emphasise sexual equality.[73] She criticises other feminists who see it in terms of social relations rather than having biological significance.[74]

4.4 Genesis 3 in a Highland Setting

4.4.1 Preliminary remarks

Meyers believes that the traditional reading of Genesis 3 with the focus on sin and punishment is a distortion. Though she recognises the aspect of disobedience and its consequences in the story, for Meyers there are other important aspects which are equally important.[75] In this way she prepares for her interpretation of Gen. 3:16–19 against the background of early Iron Age Palestine. She also finds thematic and linguistic parallels with other texts that speak of the early experience of Israel.[76]

---

[71] Here Meyers agrees with Phyllis Trible and Mieke Bal. See our chapter on Phyllis Trible, where we have discussed this aspect in detail.

[72] Meyers, p. 85. Though she employs the term "human being" here, she advocates that before the creation of woman אדם was not inherently gendered. In other words the first creature was not a male.

[73] From Elizabeth Cady Stanton to Trible this was the case. However, Meyers agrees with Phyllis Bird. See Bird, ' "Male and Female He created Them": Gen. 1:27b in the context of the Priestly account of Creation', *HTR* 74 (1981), pp. 129–159.

[74] Meyers, p. 86.

[75] Ibid., p. 87. She points out that the first occurrence of 'sin' is in Gen. 4:7 in the Cain and Abel episode. She also argues that the Israelite prophets who condemned the sinful behaviour of the Israelites never mentioned Eve or Adam.. So she thinks that it is very difficult to deal with this narrative primarily in terms of sin.

[76] See Meyers, 'Gender Roles and Genesis 3.16 revisited', pp. 139–140. She cites Pss. 127, 128 and the Song of Hannah (I Sam.2:1–10). In these texts too she finds the activities of reproduction, subsistence, and defence.

4.4.2 Gen. 3 as a setting of Israel's formative period

On literary and contextual grounds she sees the garden setting of Genesis 3 as reflecting a situation of human life in the highlands of Palestine. She maintains that since Gen. 3 belongs to the oldest 'Yahwist'(J) tradition,[77] it predates the tenth century and hence belongs to the formative period of Israel's existence. She argues that the poetic oracles (Gen.3:14–19) aim to explain the life setting. She further claims that neither the man nor the woman is cursed by God, but only the ground, in the context of God's word to the man.[78] So God's oracle to the man 'to work it and to keep' the 'Garden of Eden', is in reality an oracle that helps come to terms with the accursed ground. In her own words:

> The human meant "to work the earth" and so to bring forth the "grains of the field" (2:5 and 3:18) for bread (3:19) has at last entered the environment where such tasks constitute the core of the agrarian routine. But the earth resists; without significant human intervention only the tough and inedible "thorns and thistles" (3:18) sprout forth. The famous phrase, "by the sweat of your brow" (3:19), has captured for all time the intense labor required to grow cereals in that environment.[79]

She also asserts that this situation is that of a highland agrarian economy where tree and vine do not need laborious toil once they are planted, but only the field crops need much attention.[80] So there is a command to work and keep the garden. Its interpretation, according to Meyers, is that human beings are expected 'to work the earth' and so produce the 'grains of the field', for bread.[81] Then she applies the highland situation to every man and every woman, that being the case for God's word to the first man.

By setting Genesis 3 in an ancient (pre monarchic) Palestinian highland situation, Meyers attempts to counter the prevailing traditional theological understanding of the narrative as an explanation of the origin of sin and in that line woman's role in the disobedience narrative.

---

[77] Contrary to the general understanding of J as a male writer, David Rosenberg and Harold Bloom argue that J was a woman writer, 'either a princess of the Davidic royal house or else the daughter or wife of a court personage...', see D. Rosenberg and H. Bloom, *The Book of J* (London: Faber and Faber, 1991), pp. 34ff.

[78] Meyers, p. 92, so Trible.

[79] Ibid., p. 93.

[80] Ibid. The laborious toil such as ploughing, sowing, weeding, and harvesting is needed.

[81] Ibid. She cites verses Gen. 2:5, 3:18 and 19 to support her above argument.

4.4.3 Eating and sustenance as the main theme

She points out that the most prominent 'theme word' in the narrative is the Hebrew root אכל (*akal*) from which both the verb 'eat' and the noun 'food' are formed. She shows that this is one of the most frequent repetitive elements of vocabulary in the narrative. 'This striking repetition and placement carries its own message; it tells us that the beginning of human existence coincides with a concern for food.'[82] Hence the commandment of God to Man (human being) in Gen.2:16 concerning the eating of the fruits in the garden shows the existence of the supply of food. So Meyers links this with the situation of highland Palestine where she sees the pressing concern for food to the farmers. Hence she reiterates: 'Eating in this scheme is not simply or primarily a vehicle for introducing the concept of disobedience. It is a central issue in itself...The daily, central, interminable concern of the farmer in the highlands of Palestine has shaped the movement, focus, and vocabulary of the Eden narrative.'[83] According to Meyers the oracle to the man in Gen. 2:15 is the material basis for human life. That is, man is placed in the garden 'to work *it* and to keep *it*'.[84]

4.4.4 Gen. 3 As part af a wisdom tale

Meyers also notes wisdom traits in the narrative. She thinks that it 'belongs to the speculative type of wisdom, that highlights the paradoxes and harsh facts of life'.[85] After setting the *genre* she calls attention to the woman's dialogue with the shrewdest of all the wild animals and her desire to possess wisdom. Here she regards woman as wiser than man in the narrative. She asserts that 'the woman's dialogue with the prudent reptile should be considered not a blot on her character but rather a comment on her intellect'.[86] She also points out the personification of Wisdom as a woman in the Book of Proverbs.

4.5 Genesis Paradigms for Female Roles

4.5.1 Meyers' exegesis of Genesis 3:16

In this part, Meyers offers a lengthy literary–philological explanation of Gen. 3:16 for providing an alternative interpretation to the text. In her

---

[82] Ibid., p. 89.

[83] Ibid., p. 90.

[84] Ibid., p. 93; emphasis original.

[85] Ibid., p. 91.

[86] Ibid., p. 92. By and large the same conclusion is drawn by Phyllis Trible and Mieke Bal from the same passage.

words 'Perhaps no single verse of scripture is more troublesome, from a feminist perspective, than is the divine oracle to the woman in Genesis 3:16.'[87] She shows how this text has been carried over from LXX to English translations so as to convey two persistent ideas about female existence. That is, women are condemned to severe pain in childbirth, and they are put in a subordinate relationship to men. So she re–examines the Hebrew text, focusing on particular aspects of syntax and lexical nuance. At the end of the section, she tries to link this text with the ancient Palestinian context.

4.5.2 Gen. 3:16—A close reading

'I will greatly increase your pangs in childbearing; in pain you shall bring forth children.'(Gen. 3:16)

She has discussed at very considerable length the above verse both in previous and in her present work with slight changes. She translates the Hebrew text (MT) as follows:

> I will greatly increase your toil and your pregnancies;
> (Along) with travail shall you beget children.
> For to your man is your desire,
> And he shall predominate over you.

We need to note here that her earlier interpretation of the same verse is different at certain points. In that work she translates it as follows:

> I will greatly increase your work and your pregnancies;
> (Along) with toil you shall give birth to children
> To your man is your desire,
> And he shall predominate over you.[88]

In her present work she has adapted 'toil' instead of 'work' in the first line. And in the second line 'travail' has been substituted for 'toil'. Again in the second line 'you shall give birth to children' is replaced by 'shall you beget children'. In the third line she has added the causative preposition 'for' before 'to'. The rest of the rendering is almost the same.

She points out that the common rendering of 'greatly multiply' is misleading as a translation of the Hebrew text. She reminds that the use of the infinitive absolute before the verb רבה *(rabah)* is to emphasise the action of the verb.[89] She points out that in English translation the syntactic doubling

---

[87] Ibid., p. 95. For Meyers' older reading see 'Gender Roles and Genesis 3:16 Revisited', pp. 337–354.

[88] Meyers, 'Gender Roles...', p. 130.

[89] Meyers, *Discovering Eve*, p. 99.

of the verb is not possible as in Hebrew. Hence this intensification can be reproduced with an addition of an adverb. So 'greatly increase' is preferable as it could avoid the concept of pain in quantitative terms as in the case of 'multiply'.[90]

Meyers calls attention to the way the noun הרון (*heron*) is translated. Quoting other passages from the Old Testament (e.g. Jer. 20:14–18) she argues that it means 'pregnancy' or 'conception' (Gen. 16:4) rather than the process 'childbirth'. So she rejects the common translation of 'childbirth' for הרון (*heron*). She points out that the word which connotes the birth process occurs only in the following parallel line as a form of complementary parallelism developing the above idea. The terms are not synonymous.[91] So in Meyers' rendering, the Hebrew noun הרון (*heron*) is pregnancy, not childbirth as in traditional translation. Therefore, according to Meyers God's oracle to the woman implies 'greatly increasing a female's conceptions or pregnancies'.

Then she challenges the traditional translation of the other noun עצבון (*'itsabon*) as 'pain' in common rendering. She points out that this noun is derived from the verb עצב (*'atsab*) which means 'to upset, to grieve'. She argues that the concept of 'physical pain' is not meant here. So the most appropriate interpretation of the noun עצבון (*'itsabon*) is 'physical labour' rather than distress or 'physical pain'.[92] So she rejects the rendering of the term as 'pangs', 'pain', or 'sorrow', as in many translations. According to Meyers physical labour or 'toil' sets forth woman's role in the agrarian setting in addition to her increased procreative role (pregnancy). So 'God's oracle to the woman does not assign her a new aspect of existence but rather intensifies what was seen as an intrinsic part of existence, namely human labour.'[93] In short, the destiny of woman is not to deliver children in increasing pain, rather she is required to be involved in physical labour along with her conceptions. In Meyers' words:

> Just as pregnancy or conception in the first stich is presented as an entity
> separate from toil, the parallel member here deals with labour— again

---

[90] Ibid., 100. She calls attention to the range of usages of the term רבה (*rabah*), she says, in most cases it has a meaning of numerical increase (see Gen. 16:10 and 22:17). Hence she asserts that it is used in relation to countable things. In our case 'pain' is not used in quantitative terms.

[91] Meyers, *Discovering Eve*, p. 103.

[92] See Gen. 3:17, God's decree to man, where the same noun עצבון (*'itsabon*) is used. See also Gen. 5:29; Judg. 19:16; Exod. 23:16; Hag. 2:17; Prov. 14:23. She also argues that the two objects of the verbal constructs are independent concepts; one referring to woman's *productive work* and the other to her *procreative role*. See Meyers, 'Gender roles and Genesis 3:16 revisited', pp. 344–45.

[93] Meyers, *Discovering Eve*, p. 105.

not the labour of the birth process but rather the labour of the subsistence realm—distinct from childbirth.[94]

In Gen. 3:16 the two nouns עצבון (*'itsabon*—'pain or toil') and הרון (*heron*—usually rendered in English translations as 'childbearing') are treated as a hendiadys by scholars.[95] Meyers pointed out that according to the order of the two nouns 'pain' appears first, hence it should qualify 'childbirth', thereby providing a translation "I will greatly increase your painful childbirths". Although she admits that hendiadys is possible grammatically, she thinks it is not necessary in this context.[96]

Then she analyses the use of the verb ילד (*yld*) in biblical usage. She points out that this verb has a wide range of meanings rather than merely 'childbirth'. She explains that this verb is also used as the general term for having children.[97] Here she makes the distinction that when the verb is in the transitive form it refers to the status of parenthood, while in the intransitive it points to the birth process. In the case of Gen. 3:16 the verb is transitive, so '[t]he emphasis is consequently not on labour and parturition but rather on the more abstract notion of becoming a parent, of having children.'[98] According to Meyers it is not at all a reference to physical childbirth in a personal sense rather it is the social dimension of contributing to family growth. Hence her resulting translation: 'shall you beget children".

The noun עצב (*'itsabon*) in the second line is translated as 'travail' recognising both the nuances of physical work as well as emotional distress. This word denotes the stressful aspects of hard work and the psychological toll of the physical condition.[99] Here also she rejects the notion of 'pain', as the word is usually rendered.

The preposition ב in the second line is usually translated with the accompanying noun 'pain' or 'travail' as 'in pain' or 'with travail'. Meyers

---

[94] Meyers, 'Gender roles...', p. 345.

[95] See Speiser, E., *Genesis,* p. 24. Hendiadys is 'a method where usually two formally co-ordinate terms—verbs, nouns, or adjectives—joined by "and" express a single concept in which one of the components defines the other.' (Speiser, p. LXX). For instance, Gen.1:2, where 'unformed and void' means 'a formless void'. See also, Westermann, *Genesis,* p. 262 and Wenham, *Genesis,* p. 81. They also treat it as hendiadys. Wenham translates it as 'Your pains of pregnancy'.

[96] Meyers, *Discovering Eve*, pp. 100–101. She shows that LXX and KJV do not take it as a hendiadys. But other standard English translations treat it as such (e.g. RSV; NIV; NRSV). It is also commonly interpreted as 'pain in childbearing', see Skinner, *Genesis,* p. 82; S.R. Driver, *The Book of Genesis,* pp. 49–50; U. Cassuto, *Genesis I,* p. 163; and Westermann, *Genesis,* p. 262.

[97] Meyers, *Discovering Eve,* p. 106. For instance, biblical genealogies in Gen. 5:10 and I Chr. 1 where the use of 'begat' for this term.

[98] Ibid.

[99] Ibid., p. 108.

translates it as 'along with travail' because she argues that in this case ‫ב‬ is comitative rather than instrumental which means that 'one thing accompanies or goes together with another thing'.[100]

WOMAN'S DESIRE

In this section Meyers treats the last two lines of her rendering of the verse 3:16

> For to your man is your desire,
> And he shall predominate over you

She recognises that these are related to the above lines. Although she acknowledges the lexical nuances of the term ‫איש‬ as both 'man' and 'husband' she prefers to translate it as 'man' since 'husband' conjures up the image of marriage, which does not fit the archetypal literary setting of the Eden story'.[101]

The biblical scholars have no consensus regarding the meaning of the term ‫תשוקה‬ (*teshuqah*) in Gen. 3:16.[102] Meyers thinks that 'the "desire" that the woman has for her companion is an attraction that already exists and is not part of the divine prescription of the oracle'.[103] In the light of the usage of this term in Song of Songs, she understands it as a term for mutual sexual desire. In the peasant mode of life woman has an intensification of two roles: an increase in her work load, and in her reproductive role. A high rate of procreation was also inevitable due to the high death rate in pre–monarchic Palestine because of pestilence and disease. On the other hand, her work load would have militated against her having a large family. In that situation 'How does a woman overcome an understandable reluctance to have many children? The natural sexual and emotional desire that she

---

[100] Ibid.

[101] Ibid., p. 110.

[102] It is usually translated as 'sexual desire' which the woman has for her husband. See Driver, *The Book of Genesis*, p. 49, Skinner; cf. *Genesis,* p. 83. The word ‫תשוקה‬ (*teshuqah*) appears only three times in the Old Testament (Gen. 3:16, 4:7b and Song of Solomon 7:10). Contrary to this interpretation, by comparing Gen. 3:16 with Gen. 4:7 Susan Foh writes that as sin's desire is to enslave Cain in Gen. 4:7, the woman's desire is to control her husband. See Susan Foh, 'What is the Woman's Desire?', *WTJ* 37 (1975), pp. 376–383. According to Walter Kaiser, there is no sensual desire or *libido* in the word ‫תשוקה‬ (*teshuqah*). He proposes that the word is from the verb ‫שוק‬ (*shuq*— 'to run') then it means 'a turning' (toward her husband). He says LXX , Syriac, Peshitta, Samaritan, Old Latin, Ethiopic, Sahidic and Arabic Versions translated all the three occurrences as 'turning'. See Walter C. Kaiser, *Toward Old Testament Ethics,* pp. 204–205.

[103] Meyers, p. 110. She writes: 'The mutual attraction of the couple is not simply a sexual meeting, because their physical union apparently follows a day's work'.

experiences toward her mate is the answer.'[104]   So the 'desire' which woman has for her husband is seen in the light of the demands of life in highland conditions.

MAN'S RULE NOT AN ABSOLUTE IMPOSITION

The last part of the verse 'he shall rule over you' is very problematical from a feminist point of view because of its absolute and hierarchical concept of the dominance of man over woman. Therefore, Meyers argues that though the verb מָשַׁל (*msl*— 'rule') means 'rule or control' in almost all cases, she thinks it is not necessary that it always means the same thing. She suggests that the verb מָשַׁל (*msl*) refers to an extension of Israelite dominion beyond its primary locus in a political sense.[105] Accordingly, she translates it as 'he shall predominate over you...which preserves the concept of rule (dominion) yet allows for the less than absolute imposition of male will'.[106] Her intention of this rendering is to diminish the connotation of authority.

4.6 The Eden Oracle in Context

After a literary analysis of verse 3:16, Meyers attempts to offer a social milieu in which this verse can be applied. She negates the traditional understanding of Genesis 3 as the account of 'The story of the fall'[107] and she reiterates:

> the Eden story is a strong testimony to the essential human task of subsistence, ... "Eating" is not simply or only a symbolic vehicle for the concept of disobedience. It is a central issue. One can sense the profound anxiety about life, about food necessary to sustain life, in the pivotal usage of '*kl* . What else would have been the central, daily interminable concern of the Palestinian peasant?[108]

We have already seen in our discussion of Meyers' methodology, how she sets the Eden context in a highland situation in pre–monarchic Palestine. She argues that in Genesis 3:17–19 we see man's lot as an unceasing and tiring toil to make the inhospitable land productive and suitable for ag-

---

[104] Ibid., p. 113. See also pp. 111–12.

[105] Ibid., p. 115. She quotes 1kgs. 5:1; Josh. 12:5. She argues that when Solomon rules beyond the territory of Israelite kingdom; he 'has dominion' over those kingdoms.

[106] Ibid., p. 117.

[107] Meyers, 'Gender roles...,' p. 342. See von Rad, *Genesis*, 1961, pp. 83–99,

[108] Ibid., p. 343.

riculture.[109] She claims that this can be well attested with the help of archaeology, historical geography, and the study of ancient agriculture.[110]

Through the above reading Meyers attempts to show that during the formative period (pre–monarchic period) of the biblical world the women had an equal participation in the productive role. By the monarchy, this situation was gradually being changed in favour of male domination.[111]

4.7 The Gender Roles of Women in the Rest of the Old Testament

Although our primary interest is in the Old Testament narrative texts, it is important to relate the implications of Meyers' readings of the narrative texts to other parts of the Old Testament. In the rest of her book she argues that women had a considerable status in pre–monarchic Israel. This was because the family was the important social structure during this period, and women played a vital role in the economic and social functions of the family. She also notes that women had the crucial role in the family in socialising and educating the children and the young.[112] She refers to the conceptualisation of wisdom in the Bible to show women's role, especially in the Proverbs' personification of wisdom as a woman.[113] She also finds women's role in the musical, literary and theological life of early Israel,[114] and points to the mutuality of love in the Song of Songs as an example of gender relationships during the pre–monarchic period.[115]

Meyers argues that under the monarchy woman's life changed due to the shifting of power from household to nation–state.[116] As a result 'the locus of power moved from the family household, with its gender parity, to a public world of male control'.[117] In short, Meyers establishes that during the pre–monarchic period there was a balanced gender role prevailing in Israel and this situation was changed by the advent of the monarchy.

---

[109] Meyers, *Discovering Eve*, p. 118. Before Meyers, David C. Hopkins also advocates a similar view. He writes that the high view of work in the 'creation epic of Genesis 2–3' well fits with the highland village situation where there was great demand for agricultural labour. See Hopkins, *The Highlands of Canaan: Agricultural Life in Early Iron Age*, p. 274.

[110] See her chapter on 'Setting the Scene: The Highland Environment of Ancient Israel', (chapter 3).

[111] See Meyers, 'The Roots of Restriction: Women in Early Israel', in *The Bible and Liberation*, p. 303.

[112] See chapters 6 and 7; see also Meyers, 'Women and the Domestic Economy of Early Israel', pp. 275 ff; 'The Creation of the Patriarchy in the West', p. 16.

[113] Ibid., p. 152.

[114] See pp. 154–164.

[115] Ibid., pp. 177–79; see also 'Gender Imagery in the Song of Songs', pp. 209–223.

[116] Ibid., p. 188.

[117] Ibid., p. 190.

4. 8 Observation, Discussion and Evaluation

In this section, we will evaluate every aspect of her arguments from various perspectives. Before considering weaknesses in many of the methodological and hermeneutical strategies, we will first highlight the strength of her arguments.

4.8.1 The strength of Meyers' reading

Meyers' reading of the creation narrative is a formidable essay in the reconstruction of the socio–cultural situation of women during Iron Age I. Through her study she has tried to reduce the historical lacunae between the biblical world and the modern world. Unlike many modern interpreters of the ancient text (Hebrew Bible) she is well aware that in order to get a clear picture of the situation of women in the ancient period one needs to unearth their social and cultural milieu. This methodological outlook is significant at a time when *the readers* of the text are widely held to determine meaning; in her view social and historical contexts determine the meaning. This is potentially one of the major methodological contributions of her study. In this aspect her study could be a check against extreme forms of contemporary reader response theory where little or no relevance is attributed to the social and historical milieu of the text.

Meyers' study rejects the assumption of the third wave of feminist interpreters that the Bible is irredeemably patriarchal. Through her analysis she shows that women had a favourable footing with men in the formative period of Israel, though the situation changed eventually. So in her treatment she prefers a 'revisionist' approach, at least at the surface level, making the biblical tradition positive to women rather than rejecting them altogether. Concerning the contribution of her work Grace I. Emmerson writes:

> The book does succeed in discovering Eve, bringing into focus the hitherto indistinct figure of ancient Israelite woman, seen now to be not the downtrodden subservient creature so often supposed but robust, influential and indispensable in the interdependence of a pioneer agrarian economy.[118]

Her specific contribution to the realm of feminist hermeneutics comes from her study of gender roles and sexual balance. When most of the modern feminist writers and male writers who are sympathetic to feminist concerns attempt to establish an egalitarian ideal, Meyers tries hard to bring out the gender roles and male-female balance in ancient Israel.

---

[118] Grace I. Emmerson, Book review of *Discovering Eve* in *Theology* 93 (1990), p. 67.

Her study of the biblical narrative texts generated a momentum among contemporary biblical scholars to look afresh at the text and rectify certain androcentric notions that have been carried to our period from the period of Church fathers and Rabbinic interpreters. Her study provides an atmosphere in which to address those issues among all scholars. There is no doubt that her study stimulated scholarly discussion.

In addition to her sociological explanation of the narrative, some aspects of her literary insight of the text are illuminating. Those aspects we will take up later. As a whole, Meyers' contribution to the field of biblical interpretation and especially to feminist hermeneutics is very significant.

4.8.2 The problems of Meyers' reading

Despite its strength, her readings have many methodological, exegetical and theological problems. Whether she has achieved her broader aims remains to be seen, but many specific aspects of her methodology, ideology and exegesis need to be challenged.

METHODOLOGICAL PROBLEM

First of all, we need to remember that the methodology that Meyers employs to reconstruct the situation of women in Israel is only one of the viable alternatives in biblical hermeneutics. As a result there are a wide range of opinions among scholars about taking technological factors as parameters for reconstructing the pre–monarchic Israelite history. The sociological theory on which her study is based still remains a hypothesis. George E. Mendenhall, its first proponent, himself pointed out in his later writings the problems inherent in this method of reconstructing an ancient society.[119] Contrary to an egalitarian society, Mendenhall himself points out that in ancient Israel, there were social distinctions between the affluent and the poor, and indeed the practice of slavery also prevailed.

Gottwald's view of technological innovations (i.e. introduction of iron tools, terracing and waterproof cisterns) and egalitarian ideals has also been challenged from various quarters,[120] and this too has implications for Meyers' study.[121] Now we will look at some of the objections.

---

[119] See George E. Mendenhall, 'Ancient Israel's Hyphenated History', in *Palestine in Transition*, pp. 91ff.

[120] Ibid., see pp. 92ff. For a detailed critique of Gottwald, See A. J. Hauser, 'Israel's Conquest of Palestine: A Peasants" Rebellion?', *JSOT* 7 (1978), pp. 2–19; Lemche, *Early Israel: Anthropological and Historical Studies on the Israelite Society Before the Monarchy,* pp. 407–410; J. W. Rogerson, 'Was Early Israel a Segmentary Society?', *JSOT* 36 (1986), pp.17–26; Gösta W. Ahlström, *Who were the Israelites?* (Wi-

In his work[122] on agricultural life in the Early Iron age, Hopkins raises objections to the three factors (forest clearing, water cisterns and terrace building) which have been used by scholars to reconstruct early Israelite settlement. These three factors are the basis on which Meyers reconstructed the situation of women and their intensive role in the productive task in highland situations in the early settlement. Hopkins points out 'the vegetational state of the Highland evergreen forest and maquis and [assumes] that fire was a more significant land–clearing tool than axe,...'[123] He also shows that the archaeological evidences from the occupational sites are not very supportive of the water cisterns. Moreover, the evidence for widespread terracing is also very limited.[124]

In our discussion of methodological issues we need to examine one of the important works on the Israelite settlement in the light of recent archaeological findings. Finkelstein invalidates the role of the above factors said to have contributed to the settlement during the Iron Age period I in the Palestinian highlands.[125] His archaeological findings reveal 'that terraces must have been built already during the Middle Bronze period, if not earlier' because settlement was not possible without constructing terraces.[126] So his findings show that terrace–building was not a special feature of Iron Age settlement. Moreover, in the light of recent archaeological surveys he shows:

> [T]he earliest Israelite Settlements turned out to be located in the very areas where terraces were less essential, while the classic terraced regions were practically devoid of Settlement sites..., terraces were obviously in use long before Iron I, at least since the beginning of relatively dense occupation in the hill country in MB II, ...the need to build terraces was simply a function of topography and population growth.[127]

Many theories and solutions are offered to explain the emergence of early Israel. From the above discussion one thing is very clear, no theory is

---

nona Lake: Eisenbrauns, 1986), pp. 5–9. Ahlström points out that the peasant revolt model is not supported by any textual evidence.

[121] See Meyers, *Discovering Eve*, pp. 52–63. She has also emphasised the development of technological factors during the Iron Age.

[122] Hopkins, *The Highlands of Canaan: Agricultural Life in Early Iron Age*

[123] Hopkins, p. 265.

[124] Ibid., p. 266. He also calls attention to the other challenges which the highland settlers confronted. See pp. 266–275.

[125] Israel Finkelstein, *The Archaeology of the Israelite Settlement*. This work provides solid evidences regarding the settlement of ancient Israel.

[126] Ibid., p. 202.

[127] Ibid., p. 309. For a thorough critique of the sociological school in the light of recent archaeology, see pp. 306–314.

adequate to explain the complex nature of Israelite origins.[128] So we need to be very careful in interpreting the existing data.

The same tools which Meyers applies to reconstruct the pre–monarchic Israelite history can also be used to study the monarchic period. In her review of Meyers' work, Diana Edelman raises important objections to her methodological scheme. Contrary to Meyers' claim that the social organisation of Israel is better known during the pre–monarchic period, Edelman points out that the monarchic era in Judah is better known than the pre–monarchic era because of the availability of reliable biblical and extra–biblical texts.[129] She also points out that the work which Meyers frequently employed to rework the statistics and understanding of the pre–monarchic period was mainly based on the monarchic period. Hence she writes:

> Her decision to restrict the time frame to Israel's formative period obscures the equal validity of her results for the later monarchic and restoration periods, when the demands of pioneer village life gave way to equally strong demands for villagers to produce more food with which to pay taxes to the royal regime.[130]

This observation seems to be valid.

Meyers' statistical data are also problematical. In her discussion about the highland settlement, she argued that during the beginning of the Iron Age period there was an increase in the occupied sites. She wrote 'At the beginning of the Iron Age, 114 sites were inhabited, with almost 100 of those being entirely new settlements.'[131] She also argued that the archaeological findings of the early Iron Age settlements reveal only one kind of architectural structure, that is domestic buildings. She also pointed out that there were no public buildings like granaries, temples, stables, markets, or water systems.[132] From this she infers that 'the absence of public works supports the idea that the full range of productive, cultural, and regulatory functions that served the highland settlers was carried out largely within the household unit'.[133] Her interpretations of the statistical data are misleading. Diana Edelman points out that 'Based on available information, we have no

---

[128] For recent reviews of all these theories concerning the origins of Israel in Canaan, see Rogerson, 'Anthropology and the Old Testament', (1989), pp. 17–37; John J. Bimson, 'The Origins of Israel in Canaan: An Examination of Recent Theories', *Them* 15 (1989), pp. 4–15.

[129] See Diana Edelman, *Discovering Eve; Ancient Israelite Women in Context* (book review) in *BA* 53 (1990), pp. 43–45.

[130] Ibid., p. 44.

[131] Meyers, p. 52.

[132] Ibid., p. 140.

[133] Ibid.

way of knowing how many of those sites were settled in the first or second half of the era, or how many were occupied simultaneously.'[134] She also calls attention to the fact that her conclusion concerning the domestic layout in the highland settlement cannot be decisive, since less than 30 percent of the settlement area has been excavated because of cost and time restrictions.

Meyers argued that the loss of population due to plague, disease and famine especially during the late Bronze Age, encouraged and promoted a large family. She cited examples from the biblical texts referring to the plague. However, her theory is not convincing in socio–economic terms. According to the Malthusian theory of population, human beings increase in geometrical progression (multiplication) while the resources increase only in arithmetic progression: if the population is not checked it must outstrip the resources. Otherwise natural checks like disease, war and misery would keep the population within its means of subsistence.[135] If this was the case it would actually have encouraged a small family since they had to work hard to produce their livelihood from such a hostile high land situation without the help of modern agricultural technology and techniques such as we have today. Meyers cannot demonstrate that her proposal is more persuasive than its converse.

Meyers said that women's involvement in production tasks resulted in their high status in ancient Israel. But can we take women's involvement in the productive process as an indicator of their social status? It is not clear how we might know this with certainty. Even in a modern society, women's participation in agricultural and other similar productive processes does not bring increased status in family and society. So the role of women in the productive task cannot be taken necessarily as a positive factor. In a Western setting, the women's role in production does indeed bring independence, power and status. But even today in an Asian agrarian setting, women are forced to work for their sustenance. The fate of the majority of women in Asian cultures is not only to rear children and manage the home, they are also necessarily involved in very laborious work which they cannot avoid. Even where the working situation and the climatic conditions are not at all tolerable, they have to work for their subsistence. I would like to illustrate the above situation with the help of some data on Indian women.

---

[134] Edelman, p. 44.

[135] See *The Family in Contemporary Society* (London: SPCK, 1958), p. 4. In this connection, an interesting parallel may be found in Atrahasis, where overpopulation is stated as the reason for the flood. See John H. Walton, *Ancient Israelite Literature in its Cultural Context: A Survey of Parallels between Biblical and Ancient Near Eastern Texts* (Grand Rapids: Zondervan Publishing House, p. 1989), p. 41.

In their work, *Women and Work in India: Continuity and Change,*[136] Joyce Lebra and Joy Paulson discuss the situation of women in India. Their study provides an entirely different picture of the status of women in an agrarian rural setting. Though we can draw direct parallels between ancient Israelite society and a modern society only with great caution, their insights regarding the relationship between work and status are significant. Lebra and Paulson point out that 'most women in rural India work because of necessity, not by choice'.[137] They need to work in order to support their families. If they do not work their family will starve. To be unemployed is a luxury for a toiling rural Indian woman.[138] To them, work is neither a status symbol nor a right, but a hardship.

Veena Das also calls attention to the important fact that 'the participation of women in the subsistence economy, is not sufficient for either ensuring their control over the products of their labour, or for a high social evaluation of their participation.'[139] This is mainly because women do not have much claim on the ownership of the land. Even if women work on their own land, agricultural labour is treated as non–work and it does not bring any positive credit to their status.[140] We know that agricultural labour is not paid labour. 'Not being paid, the agricultural work of the family labourer is no more "proper" work than washing the dishes.'[141] Moreover, in an Indian setting women consider housework as a more appropriate, satisfying and feminine work than agricultural work.[142]

If this is the fate of women in a modern world, what would have been women's status in a patriarchal ancient society? In the light of the prevailing situation in India, I am very dubious about the conclusion of Meyers concerning the high status of ancient Israelite women due to her increasing role in the productive task. In the light of the above analogy, one can even argue that the Israelite women were forced to work hard in addition to their procreative role as a result of exploitation of women by men. The Indian scene which I illustrated above is only to show that there is another side to Meyers' argument. From this comparative evidence one can understand how Meyers brings into the text her modern Western idea of the equal par-

---

[136] *Women and Work in India: Continuity and Change,* (eds.) Joyce Lebra *et al.* (New Delhi: Promilla & Co, 1984).

[137] Ibid., p. 20.

[138] Ibid., p. 289.

[139] Veena Das, 'Indian Women; Work, Power and Status', in *Indian Women: From Purdah to Modernity,* (ed.) B.R. Nanda (New Delhi: Vikas Publishing House, 1976), p. 142.

[140] See Ursula Sharma, *Women, Work, and Property in North–West India* (London/New York: Tavistock Publications, 1980), p. 123.

[141] Ibid., p. 124.

[142] Ibid., p. 127.

ticipation of both sexes in the productive process and thereby postulates an egalitarian status for woman in every aspect of life. My intention here is not to show that women are inferior or subordinate, rather what I suggest is that it is quite difficult to reconstruct the original status of women in ancient Israel with this sort of reasoning. Critiquing Gottwald's reconstruction of Israel's origins (on which Meyers heavily depends) Normal C. Habel asks: 'Is it possible to reconstruct, with any degree of certainty, the specific social orders that developed in Israel's history, especially in Israel's early history?'[143] This is a penetrating question and a challenge.

Meyers' premonarchic dating of the J source is also problematic. Even though most of the Old Testament scholars dated this source back to the 10th century B.C,[144] in recent decades scholars tend to argue for a later dating. George Mendenhall argued that the linguistic and historical milieu from which Genesis 3 originated was the wisdom literature and he thinks that it comes from a 'wisdom tradition', which he dates this to the sixth century BC.[145] His conclusion of this study is that 'Gen 3 is a work stemming from the period of exile, when there was a great ferment of agonising and recrimination concerning the question: "what happened—and why?"'[146] It is important to note that though Meyers acknowledges this work to show Genesis as a wisdom tale, she still dates the passage to the monarchic period. Both Luis Alonso–Schökel and Joseph Blenkinsopp draw attention to the literary aspects of the creation narrative. They point out that the Eden narrative is not referred to in any pre–exilic text.[147] Blenkinsopp also points out many sapiential and other vocabulary links of Gen. 2–3 with Proverbs, Ecclesiastes, Job, Psalms and Ezekiel, thereby suggesting a later dating.[148] There are also other scholars who argue for a later dating.[149] In a

---

[143] N. C. Habel, 'The Future of Social Justice Research in the Hebrew Scriptures: Questions of Authority and Relevance', in *Old Testament Interpretation: Past, Present, and Future* (G. M. Tucker Festschrift), (eds.) J. L. Mays *et al.* (Edinburgh: T & T Clark, 1995), pp. 277–291 [p. 278].

[144] See Von Rad, *Genesis,* p. 23; Speiser, *Genesis*, p. xxviii ff.

[145] George E. Mendenhall, 'The Shady Side of Wisdom: The Date and Purpose of Genesis 3', in *A Light unto My Path: Old Testament Studies in Honor of Jacob M. Meyers*, (eds.) Howard N. Bream *et al.* (GTS IV; Philadelphia: Temple Univ. Press, 1974), pp. 319–334 [327–28]; cf N. Wyatt, 'Interpreting the Creation and Fall Story in Genesis 2–3', *ZAW* 93 (1981), pp. 10–21.

[146] Ibid., p. 329.

[147] Cited in Joseph Blenkinsopp, *The Pentateuch: An Introduction to the First Five Books of the Bible* (Auckland: Doubleday, 1992), see pp. 22ff and pp. 63–67. See Ezek. 28:13; 31:9, 16,18; 36:35; Isa. 51:3; Joel 2:3)

[148] Ibid., pp. 65–67, see Gen. 2:6 cf. Job 36:27; 2:9; 3:6 cf. Ps. 19:11; Pro. 21:20; Gen. 3:7 cf. Ezek. 13:18; Job 16:15; Eccl. 3:7; Gen.3:16 cf. Ps. 127:2; Prov. 5:10; 10:22; 14:23; 15:1. For wisdom themes Gen. 3:1 cf. Prov. 12:16; Job 5:15; 15:5; Gen. 3:6 cf. Pro 13:12; Job 33:20.

recent historical–critical feminist reading of the creation narrative, Helen Schüngel–Straumann also argues for a later dating of the J source on historical grounds.[150] She finds a one–to–one relationship of man and woman in this narrative. During the period of Solomon, in contrast, polygamy was the rule. So she finds it problematical to date Gen 2–3 so early. Moreover, she notes how the J writer relegates the serpent to a subordinate position. In her view this is due to 'the latest interpretation of the serpent as a symbol of the Canaanite fertility cult, which also symbolises the Canaanite Baal and his sexual potency...'[151] She also notes the dispute with the Canaanite cults as another reason for her later dating. Whether we are convinced of a post–monarchic dating for the J or not, Meyers' thesis is handicapped by the current lack of consensus on the date of J, and of Gen. 2–3 in particular.

We have already noted that Meyers finds balanced gender roles for women in the Book of Proverbs and in the Song of Songs. Although she notes the difficulty in dating these books, she assumes that this situation would have emerged in the pre–monarchic period. However, we need to acknowledge that scholars have reached no consensus regarding the dating of these books. There is no doubt that it is safer to date them to a later period than the monarchic, mainly due to their linguistic and literary features.[152] The Song of Songs is probably post exilic.[153] By the discussion of these books one can just as well argue that the gender roles and the status of women during the later period of Israel's history were also not bad.

Another question remains: namely, how can a text which was produced by the royal élites, who were said to promote only the male interest and suppress the woman's role, write something favourable to women? Even in

---

[149] See Rolf Rendtorff, *The Old Testament: An Introduction* (London: SCM Press, 1985), pp. 157–63; John Van Seters, *Abraham in History and Tradition* (New Haven: Yale Univ. Press, 1975). For a detailed discussion of the composition and dating the source see Hamilton, *Genesis*, pp. 11–38.

[150] Helen Schüngel–Straumann, 'On the Creation of Man and Woman in Genesis 1–3: The History and Reception of the Texts Reconsidered', in *A Feminist Companion to Genesis*, pp. 53–76.

[151] Ibid., p. 168, see also p. 167, note 1.

[152] For a discussion about the dating and composition of Proverbs, see, J. A. Emerton, 'Wisdom', in *Tradition and Interpretation: Essays by Members of the Society for Old Testament Study,* (ed.) G. W. Anderson (Oxford: Clarenden Press, 1979), pp. 214–237; see also William McKane, *Proverbs*, OTL (London: SCM Press, 1970), pp. 1–10.

[153] Modern scholarship dates this to post–exilic period, see Roland E. Murphy, ' Song of Songs, book of', in *ABD* vol. 6., pp. 150–155; Michael D. Goulder, *The Song of Fourteen Songs*, JSOTS 36 (Sheffield: JSOT Press, 1986), pp. 72–74; John G. Snaith, *Song of Songs*, NCBC (Grand Rapids: William B. Eerdmans, 1993), pp. 8–9. See also A. Brenner, *The Song of Songs*, OTG (Sheffield: JSOT Press, 1989), pp. 17–18. For an elaborate discussion of the question of dating the Song of Songs, see Marvin H. Pope, *Song of Songs: A New Translation with Introduction and Commentary,* AB (New York: Doubleday, 1978), pp. 22–33 [p. 26].

her treatment of Proverbs, I wonder why Meyers omitted the so–called advice to young men to avoid the wicked woman. The depiction of wisdom
as feminine in Hebrew neither supports nor devalues the status of women.
In many instances Meyers assumed that women had a balanced gender role
during the pre–monarchic period, and a changed situation in the succeeding
period. But this cannot be shown to be true. So before we conclude our
discussion, mention must be made of the condition of women during monarchic and post–exilic periods in the history of Israel.[154] Challenging Meyers, Tamara C. Eskenazi recently argues:

> conditions similar to premonarchic Israel recur in the post–exilic era. If,
> as Meyers holds, the emphasis on family in premonarchic Israel meant
> more equitable distribution of power for women, then the re–emergence
> of the family as the significant socio–economic unit in the post–exilic era
> likewise leads to greater power for women than was available during the
> monarchy.[155]

Though the references are scanty, we see at least certain roles performed
by women in the post–exilic Israelite community. Women were involved in
rebuilding the wall with Nehemiah, and they were also part of the covenant
community (Nehemiah 8: 2–3; 10:29–30). Regarding the status of women
during the post–exilic period, Claudia V. Camp writes: 'Inferences from
scattered biblical references reveal an explicit inclusion of women in the
economic, religious and political spheres.'[156] Again, the prophet Malachi
emphasised the importance of loyalty to one's own partner (Malachi 2:10–
16). From the above discussion it is clear that reconstruction of the situation of women in ancient Israel remains an unresolved task. Here we need
to hear to the caution which another Old Testament feminist scholar, K. D.
Sakenfeld suggests, that we cannot make 'generalisations about one thou-
sand years of culture that are based on fragments of indeterminate origin'.[157] This caution is also relevant in reconstructing the status and role of
ancient Israelite women.

---

[154] For a comprehensive and balanced treatment of the status of women in Israel, see
Grace I. Emmerson, 'Women in ancient Israel', pp. 371–394, especially for their status
during the monarchy, see pp. 373–74.

[155] T. C. Eskenazi, 'Out from the Shadows: Biblical Women in the Post–exilic Era',
JSOT 54 (1992), pp. 25–43 [p. 33].

[156] Claudia V. Camp, *Wisdom and the Feminine in the Book of Proverbs* (BALS 11;
Sheffield: Almond, Press, 1985, p. 259); cf. also Tamara C. Eskenazi for the favourable
status of women during the post–exilic period. She argues that the status of women during the post–exilic age was also the same as pre–monarchic period.

[157] K. D. Sakenfeld, 'Old Testament Perspectives: Methodological Issues', *JSOT* 22
(1982), p. 14.

HERMENEUTICAL PROBLEMS

In Meyers' interpretation, she is pre–occupied with assumptions and pre-suppositions from the social sciences. So in her analysis, the biblical texts have only epiphenomenal status due to the alleged androcentric orientation of the Hebrew Bible. Hence she writes: 'Its androcentric bias and also its urban, élite orientation mean that even the information it contains may be a distortion or misrepresentation of the lives of women removed from urban centres and bureaucratic families.'[158] Moreover she is also very much governed by the social science assumptions such as positivism, relativism and determinism.[159] I think Meyers was too much pre–occupied with this assumption in her reconstruction of the situation of the status of women in early Israel. That is why she asserted that 'the Bible as primary source is unreliable in reconstructing Israel's history...' (p. 48)

Herion points out the impact of the above assumptions on the reconstruction of pre–monarchic Israel by Gottwald. The crux of Gottwald's assumption is that in order to understand ancient Israel's *spirituality*, her full *materiality* is to be grasped (see Gottwald p. xxv. See also the early section of the present chapter). As a result he centres his argument around technological innovations, 'providing a new basis for social relations among now relative equals; and this in turn, engendering an "egalitarian" ethic in early Israel...'[160] Carol Meyers followed these assumptions in the reconstruction of the situation of women in Israel. Hence she wrote 'the task of discovering Eve thus begins with an examination of the material conditions...' (p. 49). So it is not surprising that she located her argument around the techno–materialistic variables such as Israel's pioneer societal status, Palestinian highland agriculture, and the demographic situation during the Iron Age.

Rogerson also points out that Gottwald 'deliberately "demythologises" the chief articles of Israelite faith into socio–economic terms'.[161] If my understanding of Rogerson is correct, he argues that both biblical sociology and biblical theology should go together. He classifies biblical sociology in the category of 'explanation' and biblical theology in the category of 'de-

---

[158] Meyers, p. 13.

[159] For a detailed discussion of these concepts, see G. A. Herion, 'The Impact of Modern and Social Science Assumptions on the Reconstruction of Israelite History', pp. 3–33.

[160] Ibid., p. 14.

[161] Rogerson, 'The Use of Sociology in OT Studies', p. 254. Rogerson adapts Runciman's sociological methodology to evaluate the sociological approach to the Old Testament. There are four theories, namely, reportage, explanation, description, and evaluation. In summary these theories explain respectively, "what happened, why, what it is like, and is it good or bad?" (Rogerson, p. 251), see also J. W. Rogerson, 'Anthropology and the Old Testament', in *The World of Ancient Israel,* pp. 31–35.

scription'.[162] So he advocates a plurality of sociological approaches to the study of the Old Testament.

Similar to Rogerson's approach, Mark G. Brett makes a distinction between 'emic' and 'etic' interpretative interests. He explains: 'emics, is concerned with describing events, meanings, symbols or process from the native's point of view. Etics is concerned with providing scientific accounts of these things, whether the native could accept these accounts or not'.[163] Brett's 'emic' is similar to Rogerson's 'description' and 'etic' to his 'explanation'. Neither Gottwald nor Meyers pays much attention to the 'emic' aspect in their reconstructions of Israelite history. In other words, they never allowed the text to speak in its own terms, clearly from the 'native's' point of view. Rather, we see that like Gottwald, Meyers also explained everything in socio–economic terms (for instance, the eating of the forbidden fruit). For her, moral and religious concerns are secondary to her social egalitarian agenda. Both Gottwald and Meyers think that their sociological explanation is *the* proper and correct explanation for the origin of Israel and also for the reconstruction of the status of women in Israel. This could be regarded as an imperialistic approach.

Meyers' 'circular reasoning' is another flaw. That is, by adopting one of the existing hypotheses (peasant revolt model) concerning the origin of Israel, she read the creation narrative from this perspective and she tried to explain the text in this framework. In order to fit to this mould she even dated the text to the 10th century B. C. and placed it in the highland situation in Canaan. In her treatment the purpose of the text also suited the highland situation, and promoted an egalitarian status of man and woman in pre–monarchic Israel. Her whole argument circled around this theme. As a result she interpreted the creation narrative 'to show that it made sense in terms of these parameters'.[164] Through her social–scientific reading of the text she also claimed that she had established the true meaning of the text. In her treatment of the text she overlooked a number of other possible meanings and other important main themes. So she had to omit a major section of the narrative in her readings and her whole argument revolved around Gen. 3:16.

Throughout her readings she imposes on the biblical text the modern notion of gender equality. In some instances she has attempted to show that woman is in fact superior to man in the creation narrative. Whether this is

---

[162] Ibid., p. 255. 'Explanation attempts to discover the causes of what has been reported. Description is the attempt to expound what it is like for a person or group of persons to be in a particular society or situation'. (p. 250).

[163] Mark G. Brett, *Biblical Criticism in Crisis?* p. 18. See also Brett, 'Four or Five Things to do with Texts: A Taxonomy of Interpretative Interests', pp. 359–365.

[164] See Gunn and Fewell, p. 7. See also p. 8.

fair, or an anachronism, must await a judgement about the validity of her exegetical argument.

EXEGETICAL AND THEOLOGICAL PROBLEMS

Now we will look at more closely how Meyers treats the creation narrative in particular. In line with her broad view as outlined above, she wants to negate the notion of sin in the narrative. To her, the concept of sin and suffering is a later creation. We must now ask, however, whether this view can be substantiated. Can the text be read convincingly without recourse to the ideas of sin and rebellion? We begin by examining Gen.2:16–17.

It seems to me that the introduction of the intensive verb צוה is very significant here. In God's dialogue with man and woman in chapter 3 the commonly used verb אמר (*'amr*) is used. The verb צוה (*swh*) is used to give a command or a charge in most of the occasions in the Old Testament. So from the very use of the verb it is quite clear that it was an injunction, charge, order or a commandment given to the man concerning the way of life in the garden. After the disobedience, the Lord God interrogates the couple repeating the same verb asking 'Have you eaten of the tree which I commanded you not to eat?' (צִוִּיתִיךָ). In the expulsion scene the verb is repeated again in verse 17. By eating the fruit both the man and the woman had disobeyed God. It was not at all an ordinary life statement concerning 'eating' in a highland setting. Here Meyers' explanation of the term 'eating' is only a sociological nuance of the term without considering its meaning in a wider context of the text. The use of the verb תאכל with the permanent prohibition לא ('Thou shall not eat'–KJV) shows the same seriousness as in the case of the decalogue. It is also important to note that the verbs in both verses are given in infinitive absolute forms emphasising the action.

In the serpent's dialogue with the woman, both the serpent and the woman use the non–intensive and ordinary verb אמר (*'amr*) instead of צוה (*zwh*). The verbal emphasis (i. e. infinitive absolute), and the preposition מכל used in 3:1, are also omitted by the woman in 3:2. The יהוה אלהים (*Yhwh 'Elohim*) becomes merely אלהים (*'Elohim*). Wenham points out that the Yahwistic author deliberately used יהוה אלהים (*Yhwh 'elohim*) to declare his conviction that Yahweh is both the humans' covenant partner and also the God of all creation; yet both the woman and the serpent omitted this expression in their dialogue.[165]

The meaning of אף כִּי (*'af ki*) in Gen.3:1 is not clear, though English translations take it as an interrogative form. The BHS proposal to read an interrogative pronoun ה has no textual support. V. P. Hamilton considers it as a feigned expression of surprise and translates it as 'Indeed! To think

---

[165] Wenham, *Genesis 1–15* p. 57. For a discussion of the various details of the conversation between the woman and the serpent see R. W. L. Moberly, 'Did the Serpent get it Right?',*JTS* 39 (1988), pp. 1–27.

that God said you are not to eat of any tree of the garden'![166] Hence he argues that the first words of the serpent are not a question 'but as an expression of shock and surprise. He grossly exaggerates God's prohibition, claiming that God did not allow them access to any of the orchard trees.'[167] In this context it is also interesting to note that the woman too exaggerates and adds to the original injunction and also omits 'every'. Wenham suggests that through these slight alterations to God's remarks, 'the woman has already moved slightly away from God toward the serpent's attitude'.[168] It is important to note here that '[t]he serpent began with a feigned expression of surprise' and later he directed 'a frontal attack on God 's earlier threat (2:17)...'[169]

Richard S. Hess has recently noted the specific aspects of rebellion in Genesis 3.[170] In this context the rebellion involves pride, ignoring or distorting God's word and listening to the serpent. In his view, 'Misusing and perhaps misunderstanding God's word lies at the heart of the first rebellion against God.'[171] He continues to note the whole motivation of eating the forbidden fruit. It was 'to know as God knows, to possess divine wisdom and to seize God's gifts and use them in whatever way the man and the woman wanted'.[172]

In the light of the above discussion Wenham argues that Genesis 2–3 is 'a paradigm of sin, a model of what happens whenever man disobeys God. It is paradigmatic in that it explains through a story what constitutes sin and what sin's consequences are'.[173] Moreover he also thinks that this tradition is found in the covenant theology where disobedience to God's commandments lead to a curse and ultimately death (Deut. 30:15–19). According to Wenham this story is also protohistorical, offering an explanation regarding

---

[166] See Hamilton, *The Book of Genesis Chapters 1–17* , p. 186; see also note 1. Skinner takes it as "a half–interrogative, half–reflexive exclamation', see J. Skinner, *Genesis* (ICC), p. 73. Wenham treats אף כי (*af ki*) as an interrogative expression. See *Genesis 1–15*, pp. 47 and 73. The BDB translates the whole expression 'Has God really said'; other occurrences of this phrase are preceded by an interrogative ה if it introduces a question. See Gen. 18:13 & 23, Amos 2:11. See also Speiser, *Genesis*. He translates it as 'Even though God told you not to eat of any tree in t he Garden...' (p. 21). He also thinks that it is not a question; rather the serpent is distorting a fact (p. 23); Jerome T. Walsh, 'Genesis 2: 4b–3: 24: A Synchronic Approach', *JBL* 92 (1977), p. 164.

[167] Hamilton, pp. 188–89.

[168] Wenham, *Genesis*, p. 73.

[169] Hamilton, p. 189.

[170] Richard S. Hess, 'The Roles of the Woman and the Man in Genesis 3', *Them* 18 (1993), pp. 15–19.

[171] Hess, p. 16.

[172] Ibid., p. 17. Hamilton thinks that woman's sin is a sin of initiative and man's is a sin of acquiescence, *Genesis*, p. 191.

[173] Wenham, p. 90.

man's origins and his sin.[174] We also read from the text that 'The man called his wife's name Eve, because she was the mother of all living' (Gen. 3:20). So the creation narrative has, after all, a prototypical value, not an archetypal value as proposed by Meyers. In other words it is the first account of how sin and rebellion entered this world. As such, it is a fitting beginning to the Old Testament story, in which we see the subsequent effects of sin and how God deals with it. As a matter of fact Meyers contradicts herself in this point. She assumes that Gen. 3 reflects a highland situation: as it was 'God's words to the *first man,* Every man, with respect to the laborious character of his daily life, so also is it the case for the *first woman,* Every woman.'[175] But when she dealt with the question of sin, she found it to have only archetypal value, being an etiological tale. If so, how can it be the story of every woman?

Before I conclude the question of sin, it is appropriate to know the minds of some feminist Old Testament scholars. Alice Ogden Bellis thinks that the 'fall from grace' interpretation can work well in this context because 'it explains how life became so disharmonious. It also makes Gen. 3:16b easy for feminists to handle. Men's domination of women can be explained as a result of sin, rather than God's intention for humanity'.[176] In her analysis of the creation narrative, Phyllis Bird recognises the aspect of sin committed both by man and by woman. She rightly observes that 'the order of their transgressing is unimportant for the question of their guilt; the consequences of their acts (knowledge, shame and pain) are described only when *both* have eaten the forbidden fruit'.[177] She also recognises that both have knowingly disobeyed the divine command, and accepts this disobeying as sin. Hence she writes: 'the serpent is the seducer, and he is made to bear the blame and punishment for the seduction. But the pair who succumbed to his tempting must pay the consequences of their common sin, *the sin of disobeying the divine command*'.[178]

This view is also supported by prominent Old Testament scholars. In his study Rolf Rendtorff shows how the creation in Genesis and the covenant in Exodus (19–34) are endangered by human sin in both cases. He also points out that sin reaches its culmination in chapter 6 where God determined to destroy his own creation.[179] Richard H. Moye thinks 'the story

---

[174] Ibid., pp. 90–91.

[175] Meyers, pp. 93–94; emphasis mine.

[176] A. O. Bellis, *Helpmates, Harlots, Heroes*, p. 63.

[177] Bird, 'Images of Women in the Old Testament', in *The Bible and Liberation*, p. 277; emphasis original.

[178] Ibid., p. 287, note, 90; emphasis mine.

[179] See Rolf Rendtorff, '"Covenant" as a Structuring Concept in Genesis and Exodus', *JBL* 108 (1989), pp. 385–89 [386].

of the Pentateuch as a whole is pre–eminently the story of the fall...'[180] and man's desire for a reunion with God.

Both traditional historical critics and modern literary critics read the narrative as a story of sin. I do not think this can fairly be regarded to be a result of their male bias. In their readings they bring out various aspect of this theme. In his comprehensive analysis of the book of Genesis for instance, Gerhard Von Rad shows how sin reaches its culmination from the sins of Adam and Eve to the Tower of Babel. He sees the spread and progression of sin from Adam and Eve to Cain, Lamech, the angel marriages, the tower of Babel.[181] He also notes the result of sin in every situation. Hence commenting on this situation he writes:

> This succession of narratives, therefore, points out a continually widening chasm between man and God. But God reacts to these outbreaks of human sin with severe judgements. The punishment of Adam and Eve was severe; severer still was Cain's. Then followed the Flood, and the final judgement was the Dispersion, the dissolution of mankind's unity.[182]

In his treatment of the theme of the Pentateuch, Clines also observes the concept of sin in other various details. His analysis of the theme of Gen. 1–11 considers 'sin' to be the main theme in the primeval history.[183] According to him the theme of primeval history seems to be either:

> Mankind tends to destroy what God has made good. Even when God forgives human sin and mitigates the punishment, sin continues to spread, to the point where the world suffers uncreation... Or no matter how drastic man's sin becomes, destroying what God has made good and bringing the world to the brink of uncreation, God's grace never fails to deliver man from the consequences of his sin...[184]

He also links the primeval history with the rest of the Pentateuch through the theme of God's promise.

---

[180] Richard H. Moye, 'In the Beginning: Myth and History in Genesis and Exodus', *JBL* 109 (1990), p. 598.

[181] See Von Rad, *Genesis,* p. 149. See also Von Rad, *Old Testament Theology,* vol. 1., (trans.) D. M. G. Stalker (London: SCM Press, 1975), pp. 154ff.

[182] Ibid. , p. 148.

[183] See David J. A. Clines, *The Theme of the Pentateuch*, pp. 61–79.

[184] Ibid., p. 76. Cf. Derek Kidner, who makes a contrast between 'God's orderly creation and the 'disintegrating work of sin'. *Genesis*, TOTC (London: Tyndale Press, 1967), p. 13.

Alan J. Hauser in his rhetorical reading of the creation narrative finds intimacy and alienation as one of the main themes of Genesis 2–3. He points out that harmony and intimacy existed between the man, the woman and God before the humans' rebellion. This situation was changed as a result of their rebellion by eating the fruit which God had told them not to eat. Then Hauser notes the motif of alienation and strife at various levels between man and woman, man and the ground, man and the animal world, and humanity and God.[185] Contrary to Meyers' claim, Hauser notes that אכל (*'kl*) is the main verb which describes man's rebellion against God (Gen. 3:1, 2, 3, 5, 6, 11, 12, 13) and he also observes that the same verb is used in relation to the consequences that follow their rebellion (Gen. 3: 17–19).[186] Similarly P. D. Miller also relates the term אכל (*'kl*) with sin. 'The word is a command that has to do altogether with eating ([אכל–*'kl*] four times), i.e. what may be eaten and what may not be eaten. The whole issue of responsibility and obedience is tied up with "eating."'[187]

Before we close our discussion it is worth noting the position of an English female scholar. In her treatment of the creation narrative, Mary Hayter clearly finds the aspect of sin in the account. Commenting on Gen.3:16, she writes: 'Man and woman have disrupted their relationship with God. This sin leads to a disruption in their relationship with all creation, including with one another. Woman becomes subservient, man becomes domineering; neither is a healthy position to occupy, neither represents God's original intention for male/female relations'.[188] Along with Phyllis Trible, Hayter also thinks that this situation is descriptive not causative or prescriptive.[189]

When we examine the Old Testament in a wider perspective, there is no difficulty in understanding the concept of sin which emerged in the story of creation in the context of human rebellion. Contrary to Meyers' assumptions that the concept of sin comes from later orphic thought, there are clear parallels in the Old Testament traditions concerning Eden and human rebellion (Ezek. 28:13, 31:9,16,18; 36:35; Isa. 51:3; Joel 2:3). In Ezekiel 28: 12–19 we can find a similar narrative structure and many similar motifs.

---

[185] See Alan Jon Hauser, 'Genesis 2–3: The Theme of Intimacy and Alienation', in *Art and Meaning: Rhetoric in Biblical Literature,* pp. 20–36.

[186] Ibid., p. 32.

[187] P. D. Miller, *Genesis 1–11: Studies in Structure & Theme* (JSOTS 8; Sheffield: JSOT Press, 1978), p. 28.

[188] Mary Hayter, *The New Eve in Christ,* p. 107. A similar theological interpretation is offered by Joy Elasky Fleming, *A Rhetorical Analysis of Genesis 2–3 with Implications for a Theology of Man and Woman.* She treats Gen. 2 as 'God at work' and Gen. 3 as 'sin at work'.

[189] Ibid., p. 114. See also Trible, *God and the Rhetoric,* p. 128. Trible thinks that this situation is because of their shared disobedience.

The context here is the *hubris* of the king of Tyre. In Ezekiel we see the creation themes like Eden, the garden of God, Cherub, iniquity, sin and expulsion. The main difference in Ezekiel is that he places the garden on the mountain of God. My intention here is to point out that within Israel there was a strong tradition concerning the rebellion and fall of humanity. Von Rad notes the apparent relation of this material in Ezekiel with Genesis 3.[190] He finds its origin in common oriental Mesopotamian sources.[191] Westermann also finds very clear parallels between Ezekiel and Genesis 2–3 and points to the Babylonian background of the latter.[192] Wenham underscores the fact that 'whether this is an independent account of the fall or a free poetic application to the Tyrian king is uncertain, but it certainly underlines the compatibility of its theology with prophetic principle'.[193]

At this juncture we also need to consider if there is any tradition in the ANE Texts which might explain the rebellion of humanity. Even though there are many parallel creation stories in ANE texts, my intention here is only to point out traditions similar to the rebellion in the garden. In the Gilgamesh Epic, there is an instance where the wild man Enkidu was seduced by a cult prostitute. As a result his original state was changed. Then the harlot speaks to Enkidu 'Thou art [wi]se, Enkidu, art become like a god!'[194] Westermann shows a series of motifs in this episode similar to the creation narrative. Especially 'the creation of man followed by seduction by a woman which gives rise to a state of existence different from the original, natural state ...The similarity of the words which the woman uses to describe the change is very striking'.[195] So he underlines the fact that the creation narrative of Genesis 2–3 had 'a pre–history both in Israel and in the Ancient Near East'.[196] From the above discussion we can infer that the concept of sin and fall was prevalent both in Israelite and Ancient Near Eastern traditions.

---

[190] Von Rad, *Genesis,* p. 95.

[191] Ibid.

[192] Westermann, *Genesis 1–11*, p. 246.

[193] Wenham, p. 90.

[194] See 'The Epic of Gilgamesh', in *The Ancient Near East: An Anthology of Texts and Pictures*, ANET, (ed.), James B. Pritchard (Oxford: OUP, 1958), Tablet 1, iv, 34, p. 44.

[195] Westermann, p. 247. For a comparison between the Enkidu and the role of the harlot in Gilgamesh with the man and the woman in Genesis 2–3, see John A. Bailey, 'Initiation and the Primal Woman in Gilgamesh and Genesis 2–3', *JBL* 89 (1970), pp. 137–150. Bailey concludes that 'she herself through her disobedience damages the splendid position of equality with the man Yahweh has conferred on her, and assumes the position of inferiority which was hers throughout the ancient Near East. Yet, as a mother, she continues, even after her punishment, to play a central role never achieved by the harlot or any other woman in the Gilgamesh epic'. (p. 150).

[196] Ibid .

Recently, James Barr too has argued that there is no concept of sin in the creation narrative.[197] We have seen that Meyers had a feminist agenda in reading the text in this fashion whereas Barr's concern was with human immortality. So he read this text as a the tale of a lost chance of immortality. In similar vein, political and liberation readers of this narrative find some other aspects as the theme of the story. For instance, James M. Kennedy reads it as a political allegory.[198] To him 'the Eden story of Genesis is not a dispassionate rendering of how the world came to be, but a narrative describing creation in terms conducive to the Israelite elite's preservation of political power and privilege'.[199] In his liberation reading, Wittenberg reads it as a story which criticises the reign of Solomon.[200] These readings, in my view, have failed to do justice to the main theme of the narrative as I have described it. I have mentioned them only to show that our pre–commitment to certain set agendas very much affects and determines our reading. This is true with Meyers' readings too.

We turn now to another of Meyers' themes, namely 'eating'. Meyers argued that eating was the main theme of the narrative, basing her argument mainly on the frequent occurrence of the term אכל (*'kl).* She also treated Gen. 2:15 as the material basis for human life, where man is given the oracle to work and keep the garden. The frequent occurrence of a term is not the only criterion, however, to decide the main theme of any narrative. We need to look at how this term functions in the narrative as a whole. For instance, James Barr has convincingly shown that words have meaning only in their context. Hence he writes: 'the distinctiveness of biblical thought and language has to be settled at the sentence level, that is, by the things the writers say, and not by the words they say them with'.[201] We also need to be aware that אכל (*'kl)* is one of the most frequently occurring verbs in the whole Old Testament. Does this mean that 'eating' is the main theme of the Old Testament?[202]

We must also distinguish the oracle in Gen. 2:15 with Gen. 3:16ff. Even though the man is assigned to work in both texts, in the first, man is as-

[197] James Barr, *The Garden of Eden and the Hope of Immortality* (London: SCM Press, 1992).
[198] James M. Kennedy, 'Peasants in Revolt: Political Allegory in Genesis', *JSOT* 47 (1990), pp. 3–14.
[199] Ibid., p. 4.
[200] See Rogerson, *Genesis*, p. 30.
[201] James Barr, *The Semantics of Biblical Language* (Oxford: OUP, 1961), p. 270. See also Barr, *Comparative Philology and the Text of the Old Testament* (London: SCM Press, 1983), pp. 170ff.
[202] It is estimated that the word אכל occurs 809 times in the Hebrew Bible, see *The Dictionary of Classical Hebrew*, vol. I, (ed.) David J. A. Clines (Sheffield: Sheffield Academic Press, 1993), p. 240.

signed to work inside the garden. There the work seems to be more pleasant due to the favourable situation, whereas in Gen. 3 man is driven outside
the garden where his work is pleasant no more and the working condition is
hostile due to the cursing of the ground. Trible notes that the verb עבד (*'bd*
means 'to serve') which implies respect, reverence and worship.[203] Meyers
failed to distinguish between the condition of work inside the garden and
outside. In this connection Meyers also fails to explain the reasons for the
changed or 'condemned' state of the earth though she recognises that the
ground is accursed.

Now we will move to her specific exegesis of Genesis 3:16. Meyers'
literary interpretation of Gen.3:16a seems to be more convincing than the
traditional translations and interpretations. I have not seen any grammatical
or syntactic problem in translating the verse as 'I will greatly increase your
toil and your pregnancies' as Meyers proposed. In this case, the hendiadys
is not imperative, as she suggested.[204] Moreover, the phrase הרון (*heron)* is
to be translated as 'pregnancy' as she suggested rather than 'childbearing'
in the traditional rendering because הרה *(hrh)*, the verb, usually means 'to
conceive' rather than 'to bear a child'.[205] A typical example is Ruth 4:13
where both aspects are given. We read 'the Lord gave her conception (הריון־
heryon) and she bore a son'. In that case we cannot take conception to be
a result of the curse. James Barr, through his 'argument of actuality'
writes: 'Pregnancy is esteemed as a great blessing by oriental women. Yet
the speech of God to Eve in Gen. 3:16 is, by the usual interpretation, a
statement which represents pregnancy as something punitive or disas-
trous.'[206] This may be the reason for rendering 'childbearing' instead of
'pregnancy' in the translations. Meyers' treatment however of this noun as
plural is unnecessary, however, with its implication that as woman con-

---

[203] Trible, *God and the Rhetoric,* p. 85.

[204] There is no translational problem of treating it as two separate ideas rather than considering it as hendiadys in modern commentaries and translations. KJV translates as
'thy sorrow and thy conception'. Similarly, 'I will increase your labour and groaning'
(NEB); however, interestingly, REB's translation is hendiadic: 'I shall give you great
labour in childbearing'. The LXX, Vulgate and Peshitta also treat the two nouns as
separate concepts. David T. Tsumura, in contrast argues on morphological grounds that
both הרון and עצבון belong to the same nominal pattern, the ‹qatalan› type and so probably do constitute a hendiadys. See 'A Note on הרנך (Gen 3, 16),' *Bib* 75 (1994), pp.
398–400.

[205] See Koehler/Baumgartner, *Lexicon in Veteris Testamenti Libros* (Leiden: E. J. Brill,
1985), pp. 242–43. K–B treats הרון *(heron)* and הריון *(heroyon)* as similar in meaning,
rendering 'pregnancy' or conception as this may be from the same root הרה. See Terry
A. Armstrong *et al., A Reader's Hebrew–English Lexicon of the Old Testament, Four
Volumes in One* (Grand Rapids: Zondervan, 1989), pp. 2 & 575.

[206] James Barr, *Comparative Philology and the Text of the Old Testament,* p. 286.

ceives more, there would be an increase in childbirth; further, the pain factor cannot be eliminated from the text. The thought may be that this ultimately leads to pain and travail. In the Old Testament the Hebrew verb עצב
(*'sb*) has also the meaning of 'physical pain'. Contrary to Meyers' assumption that this verb does not have connotations of physical pain, there are instances where it is used strictly to depict physical pain; for instance, in Ecclesiastes 10:9, where the context is that of the stone worker being hurt by
stones. Here the Niphal form of the verb יעצב (*y'sb*) is used. Though the
usage of this verb is not frequent, the range of meaning which one word
possesses cannot be overlooked.

It is a fact that pain is recorded in the process of childbirth in many
places in the Old Testament. I Chr. 4:9 uses the same noun as in 3:16.[207] It
reads... 'I bore him in pain' (בעצב *be'eseb*). Meyers treats it as an interpretation of the verse in Genesis and so she rejects the validity of the verse as a
separate witness. Nevertheless, other Hebrew words are used in the Old
Testament to convey labour pain in childbirth. In the book of Jeremiah we
come across the phrase 'Pain as of woman in travail' [חיל *hil*] (Jer. 6:24;
22:23; 50:43). Even, in some cases, ילד (*yld*) is used to note the pain of
childbirth. (Will not pangs take hold of you, like those of a woman in labor? (Jer. 13:21– i.e. לדה *ldh*–Qal. inf. constr., see also Gen. 35:16). In
Isaiah 23:4, the concepts of labour and birth occur together. We read 'I
have neither labored [חלתי–*hlty*] nor given birth' [ילדתי–*yldty*]. Also in
Isaiah 66:7–8, 'Before she was in labor [תחיל– *thyl*] she gave birth [ילדה–
yldh]; before her pain [חבל–*hbl*] came upon her she delivered a son' . Here
the word חול (*hul*) is used for labour. Another word which explains the pain
of childbirth is ציר (*sir*). In Isaiah 13:8, 'Pangs (צירים–*sirim*) and agony
(חבלים–*hblim*) will seize them; they will be in anguish like a woman in labor' [יחילון–*yhilun*]. In the above verse the pangs and agony are compared
with the woman who is in labour. The same word ציר (*sir*) is also used in I
Samuel 4:19 to explain the severe pain which the wife of Phinehas had undergone in her labour. In reality women had undergone more severe pain in
their childbearing process than pronounced in Gen. 3:16.[208]

Meyers' translation of 'beget children' for 'bring forth children' or 'give
birth to children' is also vulnerable in the Genesis context. As she argued,
it is true that the verb ילד (*yld*) can be used in both ways, to indicate 'giving birth to children' and also to note in a general sense of 'having chil-

---

[207] Interestingly, Cassuto notes a pun between the noun עצב (pain) and עץ. Hence, he
points out that 'it was with respect to עץ *'es* that the man and woman sinned, and it was
with עצב *'esebh* ['pain'] and עצבון *'issabon* ['toil, suffering'] that they were punished'.
See Cassuto, *Genesis*, p. 165.

[208] Feminist scholars like Phyllis Bird accept the reality of 'acute pain' suffered by
women in Old Testament texts in the process of childbirth. See Bird, 'Images of
Women in the Old Testament', p. 268.

dren'. Since the specific context of Gen. 3:16 is an oracle addressed to the woman as a person, it should probably be translated in the physical sense of bearing or giving birth to children, rather than in a more social sense of begetting children as Meyers proposed. In the last analysis, the context of the passage only can determine which is apt in each case when the same word has a range of meanings. In fact Meyers' argument on this point stands or falls with the interpretation of בעצב (b'esebh) which we have just discussed. If that is pain, then the process of תלדי (tldi) must be on the birth itself.

In the third line it is better to retain 'husband' rather than 'man' as Meyers suggested because the narrator has already told us in the previous chapter the union of man and woman as one flesh (Gen. 2:23–25). They have already attained the status of husband and wife. Moreover, איש ('îš) is always understood in this narrative in a limited sense in relation to the male role.

Meyers' rendering of 'predominate' for the Hebrew verb ימשל (ymsl) is unprecedented and has no support in the Old Testament. משל (msl) is nowhere translated as 'predominate' in the Old Testament. The same verb is used to refer the rule of God over his people and also the rule of human leaders over their people. We also need to remember that the same verb is used to show the rule of rich over poor, slaves over princess, women over men, babes over people, kings over nations and God over people (Prov. 22:7; 19:10; Isa. 3:12; 3:4; 1Kgs. 4:2; Isa. 40:10). In Judg. 8:22–23 the people of Israel ask of Gideon and his son and his grandson to rule over (imperative verb) them. But he replies: 'I will not rule over you [אמשל–'msl]... the Lord will rule over [ימשל–ymsl] you'. Meyers assumes that the husband's rule over his wife is always an absolute, authoritarian rule. If that is the nuance here in Judges, people might not have requested Gideon and his progeny to rule over them. In the light of above intertextual evidences it is better to retain the traditional translation, 'he shall rule over you.' However, it does not follow that the rule of the husband must be an absolute imposition of male will.[209]

---

[209] For a quite different translation and interpretation of משל, see John J. Schmitt, 'Like Eve, Like Adam: msl in Gen.3, 16', Bib72 (1991), pp. 1–22. Through his comprehensive philological, comparative and exegetical study he translates it as 'Yet your desire will be for your husband and he will be like you [having such a desire.]'. He takes the other meaning of the verb 'to represent , be like'. Although we cannot rule out the lexical possibility of translating it as 'he will be like you', the point here is not the identity but the difference and the consequences of disobedience. They were already having this mutual affection in their physical union before the disobedience. So there is no need to reiterate that aspect here; rather here God tells them the changed situation as a result of her part in disobeying God's oracle. It seems to me that, like feminist writers, Schmitt also assumes that the husband's rule over woman is an act of domination. He points out from other parts of Genesis that Eve or Sarah did not seem to be ruled by their husbands. He illustrates Gen. 16 where Abraham asks Sarah to make 'cakes' but she seems

Conclusion

In our reading of Carol Meyers we started with the contributions of social–scientific methods for interpreting the Old Testament. We assessed both the strength and weakness of this methodology. Then we looked into Meyers' methodology in particular. After that Meyers' reading of the creation narrative was presented. In the last section, an evaluation was made of various aspects of her reading. After observing certain strengths of her sociological readings, specific objections and criticisms were raised from different angles. We have noted the following limitations in her work.

First of all, we have pointed out the inadequacy and problems of her methodology. Her sociological tools were inadequate to prove her thesis that women had a balanced gender role during the pre–monarchic period. We have examined her assumptions and statistical data and we have seen that they do not afford clear evidence for her thesis. We have also observed that she was prone to the general weaknesses of sociological method such as 'anachronism' and 'circular reasoning'. In our comparative Indian analogy, we suggested the opposite of what Meyers proposed (i. e. hardship may mean smaller families, not larger). In the light of this, Meyers failed to establish an egalitarian gender role for women either from the Genesis text or from the rest of the Old Testament.

Secondly, we noted that Carol Meyers was pre–occupied with her feminist ideology. Meyers' readings clearly reveal how 'the subtle ways in which scholars' backgrounds and training, heritage, social–class position and even gender influence their views about ancient Israel'.[210] This problem is very evident throughout Meyers' work because she was attempting to demonstrate egalitarian gender roles for both sexes during the pre–monarchic period. She assumed that this situation was changed by the advent of monarchy. In line with this, she dated the Song of Songs to the pre–monarchic period though it is probably to be dated later. This is one of the serious flaws of her readings. This is because Meyers had a feminist case to argue, and she used the sociological tools for the purpose of showing the

---

to ignore his order; instead she listens to the conversation and Abraham sets the table and offers the meal which he prepared. I think Schmitt reads too much into the narrative. The narrative does not say that Sarah did not prepare her meal. What Abraham offered to the guests may not be a substitute, rather probably a part of the meal. We do not know why there is no mention of the meal which Sarah was asked to prepare. This indeed, may be because of the patriarchal culture. She may have prepared it but the narrator only speaks about Abraham. It is also possible that Abraham's meal was served first. Sarah's meal could come after. The narrator does not tell us about the act of eating. In an ancient Near eastern setting women take the place behind the tent especially when the male guests eat their meal (cf. Gen. 19 where Lot prepares a meal for the angels; Lot's wife was present there at the house but it is not mentioned).
[210] Herion, p. 1.

equality of women to men.[211] As a result a comprehensive reading of the text became impossible. So she adapted the evidence which supported her argument and overlooked a considerable part of the narrative that does not; in particular, she ignored theological themes totally.

Thirdly, as with her dating of the Book of Proverbs and Song of Songs, Meyers' pre–monarchic dating of Genesis is arbitrary. The effect of this is to produce a result opposite to that which she derives. Contrary to her assumptions, we have seen that there was no significant change in the status of women during the monarchic period and after. So her conclusions based on these datings cannot be sustained.

Fourthly, we have pointed out that Meyers' treatment of the concept of 'sin' in the creation narrative was very superficial. Our close narratological reading of the text, other texts from the Old Testament and Ancient Near Eastern parallels give clear evidence for human rebellion and sin, even though the specific term 'sin' is not used in the narrative. The above conclusion is supported both by male and female scholars. So on theological grounds her argument should be resisted.

Fifthly, her exegesis and translation of Genesis 3:16 have been challenged. We have ample support from within the Old Testament and from common life situations that naturally childbirth involves pain. Moreover her treatment of the Genesis narrative was selective. As a result she failed to offer a comprehensive analysis of the creation narrative. Instead, she argued that the creation narrative reflects a highland situation with eating, procreation and productivity as the main themes and thereby explaining everything in socio–economic terms.

Sixthly, we need to challenge Meyers' position on hermeneutical grounds. Although Meyers started her work with a recuperative approach, eventually she ended up in a rejectionist stance,[212] thereby rejecting important theological themes within the narrative. In a revisionist strategy one considers that biblical texts are not misogynist *per se* but only the interpretations which are patriarchalised by interpreters.[213] But in her treatment she overlooked the main core of the text. In other words she begins with socio–criticism and ends up in socio–pragmatism.[214] She tried to free 'Eve' from

---

[211] 'The underlying presupposition of feminist interpretation is that women are equal to men. It insists that all texts be interpreted by this principle. Since the biblical texts are historically conditioned and were produced by a patriarchal society, they are patriarchal in character.', Alice Laffey, *Wives, Harlots and Concubines,* p. 2.

[212] In a rejectionist stance, one decides to leave aside biblical traditions in order to be free from sexist patriarchal traditions. Here Meyers undermines and rejects many important theological traditions in her readings.

[213] See Elisabeth Schüssler Fiorenza, *But she said: Feminist Practices of Biblical Interpretation* (Boston: Beacon Press, 1992), pp. 21–24.

[214] For a useful discussion and the distinction between the two, see Thiselton, *New Horizons,* pp. 379ff.

the 'distorting lenses of patriarchal, Judeo–Christian tradition'. In the process, she completely acquitted Eve from any charge of disobedience or sin in the face of the recognition of this theme in a wide range of readings. Because of her feminist commitment she was reluctant to adhere finally to her socio–critical stance. So Meyers' study has lost the prophetic aspect of transformation. The exhortation of another feminist reader Danna Nolan Fewell is relevant. She says: 'our task is not to produce a woman's reading to oppose or to parallel a man's reading; our task is to produce a closer reading, an inclusive reading, a compelling reading that allows for a sexually holistic view of human experience'.[215] This dimension has been lost in Meyers' reading. In this context, it is doubtful whether Meyers could do justice to her general hermeneutical goal that '[a]s a critic of 2,000 years of male bias, I do not want to introduce a 1990s female bias'.[216]

Is she consistent in her hermeneutical method? She began with the assumption that 'the Israelite woman is largely unseen in the pages of the Hebrew Bible'. But her major conclusions concerning the Israelite woman come mainly from textual analysis of Genesis, especially from Gen. 3:16.[217] This is an apparent contradiction. Even though she made use of sociological insights, her major conclusion seems to come from her literary reading of the text. This shows that Meyers' socio–scientific tools were not adequate to bring out an egalitarian status to the ancient Israelite woman. In other words, Meyers' could not fully present 'social reality' without 'textual representation'. This shows that some sort of methodological integration is inevitable if we are to interpret the text totally.

Her treatment of the text is selective and atomistic. Although the term sin is not used in the narrative, the act of disobedience and rebellion is evident from the text. In Genesis 4 when the term sin is introduced in relation to Cain, he could easily understand the implication of the term. If it had been introduced as a new phenomenon the term could not have been under-

---

[215] Danna Nolan Fewell, 'Feminist Reading of the Hebrew Bible: Affirmation, Resistance and Transformation', *JSOT* 39 (1987), p. 85.

[216] See Sasser 'All about Eve', p. 7.

[217] By and large a similar kind of observation has been done by Jobling. However, I would like to point out that we have independently made the similar observation. I have come across his work, only after writing this section. See Jobling, 'Feminism and 'Mode of Production' in Ancient Israel: Search for a Method', in *The Bible and the Politics of Exegesis: Essays in Honor of Norman K. Gottwald on His sixty–Fifth Birthday*, (eds.), Jobling *et al.* (Cleveland, Ohio: Pilgrim Press, 1991), see pp. 243–247. He points out two methodological problems specifically, the first one is Meyers's attempt to ascribe 'a primarily referential function' to the Genesis text in order to support her extratextual arguments. The second one concerns the dating of J in the monarchic period (see p. 246) which we have discussed in detail above.

stood by Cain. From this we can infer that the concept of sin is assumed to be present in chapters 2–3.[218]

When we closely look at the creation narrative there are clear evidences which show that human rebellion is a result of their disobedience. For Meyers, the dialogue of woman with the prudent serpent seems to be a symbol of the intellect of the woman. When we examine the conduct of the woman in the light of God's commandment to the man in Gen. 2 (though woman was not present then, from the narrative we can assume that she was aware of God's commandment concerning the way of life in the garden) there are clear evidences for disobedience and rebellion. Although the specific term 'sin' is absent in the text, the whole context of the text shows disobedience and rebellion. These are understood as sin in a biblical sense. Thiselton rightly says: 'Meaning cannot be restricted simply to the linguistic signs of the text, since it comes into being by interaction between these signs and the process of life in which they are embedded.'[219]

In summary Meyers' readings bring various difficulties on methodological, exegetical, historical, theological and hermeneutical grounds.

OTHER WRITERS

Tikva Frymer–Kensky

Tikva Frymer–Kensky is the Director of Biblical Studies at Reconstructionist Rabbinical College, Philadelphia, Pennsylvania. The readings of Frymer–Kensky are in many respects similar to Carol Meyers. It may not be coincidental that Frymer–Kensky, like Meyers, also hails from an American Jewish background. Frymer–Kensky is an Assyriologist and her interests are in religion, law and literature. She claims also to be a biblicist in the sense of her specialisation in the biblical literature. So she finds 'the Hebrew Bible to be endlessly fascinating in the intensity of its message, the multiplicity of its meaning, the many ramifications of its thinking, and the impact, past and present, of its existence'.[220] Frymer–Kensky has also been influenced by the post–modern idea that no totally objective or true reading of any literature is possible.

Both Meyers and Frymer–Kensky argue for the essential equality of women with men during the biblical period. While Meyers tries to fathom

---

[218] Most of the Commentators consider Genesis 4 as a real sequel to chapters 2–3. See the following discussion.

[219] Anthony C. Thiselton, 'On the Models and Methods: A Conversation with Robert Morgan', in *The Bible in Three Dimensions,* p. 338.

[220] T. S. Frymer–Kensky, *In the Wake of the Goddesses: Women, Culture, and the Biblical Transformation of Pagan Myth* (New York/Toronto: Free Press, 1992), p. ix.

the reality behind the text through archaeological, anthropological and demographic data, Frymer–Kensky focuses on biblical and ancient Near Eastern literature. Frymer–Kensky's starting point is the biblical text itself. She writes: 'Each individual biblical text must be studied and analysed by itself, using all available tools of philological and literary analysis.'[221]

Frymer–Kensky believes the creation–narratives have an ideal of gender equality. She believes that gender–inequality and sexist ideology came to Israel only at the end of the biblical period, in agreement with Meyers. She also agrees with Brenner and Bal when she argues that Eve is 'the Bible's first culture bearer'.[222] Although she treats Adam as 'the first human being', she thinks Adam is 'uncultured' and a simple being. She argues that only the creation of Eve, and especially the eating of the fruit of the knowledge of good and evil resulted in cultural knowledge as expressed by sewing.[223] This is more or less similar to Bal's idea that after the creation of woman, man and Yahweh emerged as characters. She claims, finally, that 'the biblical story of Adam and Eve presents woman and men (sic) as the true suitable companions to each other. The same gender ideology also underlies the other biblical tale of the creation of humanity, Genesis 1'.[224] In other words, she finds an ideal of equality of male and female in both creation accounts. She points out that 'the differences between male and female are only a question of genitalia rather than of character. This view of the essential sameness of men and women is most appropriate to monotheism'.[225]

However, there is a discrepancy between the ideal of the text and the social reality. She notes the actual hierarchical division between men and women as a result of Israel's unquestioning sharing of that social institution with her neighbours.[226] She writes: 'The social system reflected in the Bible did not originate in Israel, nor is it substantially different in the Bible than elsewhere in the ancient Near East. Society was structures (sic) along gender lines.'[227]

This structuring was partly due to the socio–economic realities of life.[228] Against Meyers, she sees the subordination of women to men and male dominance in Gen. 3:16. However, this superior position of the husband is neither justified nor explained by the Bible. It is part of the social order of

---

[221] Ibid., p. 255 note 5.

[222] Ibid., p. 110.

[223] Ibid., p. 109.

[224] Ibid., p. 142.

[225] Ibid.

[226] Ibid., p. 128.

[227] Ibid., p. 120. She does not like to use the term 'patriarchy', to describe gender relationships 'because of its imprecision and its political resonances', p. 120.

[228] Ibid., p.143.

the world. Rather 'women are willing to accept the situation because of the love that they feel for their husbands'.[229]

For Meyers the starting point is not the biblical text since she thinks the text does not reveal the actual situation of women. Meyers is interested in social reality rather than in textual representation. Contrary to Meyers' claims Frymer–Kensky writes: 'we have no way of knowing what women "really" did in ancient Israel'.[230] This is because she thinks that the available written records are not free from the bias of the author and 'they are historiographic documents written with the purpose of interpreting the events of Israel's history and answering the essential concerns of the times in which they were written and rewritten'.[231] Frymer–Kensky's reading thus differs from Meyers' in important ways and she makes the key distinction: 'The Bible has a new religious vision, but it is not a radical *social* document.'[232]

---

[229] Ibid., p. 122–23.
[230] Ibid., p. 118.
[231] Ibid.
[232] Ibid., p. 128.

CHAPTER 5

Feminist Historical–Critical Readings of the Creation Narratives: Phyllis A. Bird

5.0 Preliminary Remarks

The historical–critical approach, in use for more than two centuries, is the traditional method in biblical interpretation. Mainline biblical scholarship considered this as the ideal model for interpreting biblical texts until recent decades. Alternative methods have been developed only during recent decades with the advent of literary, structuralist and post–structuralist models. These modern approaches are still considered *avant–garde* by many biblical scholars, and therefore, the historical–critical method still maintains its hegemony over other methods in biblical interpretation, even though its validity and effectiveness have been constantly challenged from various quarters.

It is not necessary to define and explain historical criticism in the way that we did in the case of the new literary and social–scientific models, as this method is well known among biblical critics. However, we will take on board some of the important advantages and disadvantages of this method in the course of our discussion.[1] Unlike the text–immanent modern methods, the main interest of the historical critics is to establish the original text, and as far as possible, to discover the intention of the author. Then attempts are also made to understand what the original authors meant that text to mean. The main advantage of this method is its attempt to comprehend the text from the original readers' historical, cultural and social milieu. The main criticism levelled against it is concerned with how far one can locate the intention and the mind of the author objectively. Moreover, modern biblical critics believe that texts can have meanings which are unintended and unanticipated by the author. Therefore texts allow polyvalent readings and as a result multiple meanings may be found arising from the same text. As we have already discussed these hermeneutical issues in detail in the

---

[1] For a detailed discussion on various hermeneutical issues see the chapter on 'The Question of Method in Reading the Bible'. However, for a history and development of Old Testament Criticism in the last century, see John Rogerson, *Old Testament Criticism in the Nineteenth Century England and Germany* (London: SPCK, 1984).

preliminary chapter, we will move directly to Phyllis Bird's reading of the creation narrative.

5.1 Phyllis Bird's Reading

5.1.1 Life and work

Phyllis A. Bird, Associate Professor of Old Testament Interpretation at Garrett–Evangelical Theological Seminary, Evanston, Illinois, received her A.B. (B.A.) from the University of California, B.D. from Union Theological Seminary, New York. She did her post–graduate studies at the University of Heidelberg, Germany, and obtained Th.D. from Harvard Divinity School, Massachusetts, USA.

After receiving her doctorate, she worked as the Assistant Professor of Old Testament at Perkins School of Theology (Southern Methodist University), Texas from 1972–1977. From 1977–1985 she served as the Associate Professor of Old Testament in the same institution. Since 1985 she has been serving as the Associate Professor of Old Testament Interpretation in Garret–Evangelical Theological Seminary.

She was a research associate and visiting lecturer in Women's Studies and in Hebrew Bible at Harvard Divinity School, and Visiting Lecturer at the University of Basel. She has also given lectures at many other Theological Seminaries and Universities within the United States and abroad. She has written numerous articles in scholarly journals and contributed articles to many books. Her publications include *The Bible as the Church's Book* (Philadelphia, Westminster, 1982) and *The 1993 J. Thiessen Lectures: Feminism and the Bible: A Critical and Constructive Encounter*[2] (Winnipeg, CMBC Publications, 1994). Some other important books in the area of women and gender issues are in progress.

Bird has served the Church in various capacities. She is an ordained minister of the United Methodist Church, California. She was a member of the National Council of Churches' 'Commission on Faith and Order', and the World Council of Churches' Programme on Theological Education.

5.1.2 Bird's methodology

Bird employs the methodology of literary–historical[3] criticism to read the biblical texts. Although she acknowledges that texts have different mean-

---

[2] Hereafter, *Feminism and the Bible.*

[3] I think it is important to qualify the term 'literary criticism' here since the term has many nuances in biblical criticism. She uses literary criticism here in the traditional sense for 'higher criticism', or source criticism. For a detailed discussion of this, see

ings for all readers, she thinks it is appropriate to read the text in its historical and social contexts. She thinks that it is obligatory to enquire about the
intention of the author (even though we cannot know it fully) since most
biblical materials are rhetorically intended with a particular audience in
mind and they have to persuade. So she considers the reading of the text
historically as an ethical imperative.[4] She writes: 'my concern is precisely
to recover the author's intention, to whatever extent this is possible using
literary–historical methods'.[5] Although she approaches the text with a
'feminist consciousness and commitment', she does not aim to offer a
'feminist reading'.[6] However, she thinks that this will in fact serve feminist
goals. She finds the relevance of her reading in 'a new socio–theological
context, characterised by new questions, perceptions and judgements'.[7] Although Bird mainly employs the historical–critical approach, still she recognises the relevance of other hermeneutical methods, such as rhetorical
and structuralist approaches, to address the topic of Old Testament women
in relation to contemporary concerns.[8]

5.1.3 Hermeneutical assumptions

While many modern OT scholars think that source–criticism is for practical
purposes *passé,* Bird accepts the traditional assumption that Gen. 1–3 comprises two sources, namely 'Priestly' (P) (Gen. 1:1–2:4a) and 'Yahwist' (J)
(Gen. 2: 4b–3:24).[9] She reviews the differences between the two sources
and the intention of each author/editor. She points out that J's account is a

---

Norman Habel, *Literary Criticism of the Old Testament* (Philadelphia: Fortress Press,
1971), pp. 1–17. For the modern use of the term see J. Cheryl Exum & D. J. A. Clines,
The New Literary Criticism and the Hebrew Bible, pp. 11–25. For an excellent survey
of modern literary criticism see, Paul R. House, 'The Rise and Current Status of Literary
Criticism of the Old Testament', in *Beyond Form Criticism: Essays in Old Testament
Literary Criticism,* (ed.), P. R. House (Winona Lake: Eisenbrauns, 1992), pp. 3–22.

[4] Phyllis A. Bird, personal interview at Garret–Evangelical Seminary, Evanston, USA,
November, 1994.

[5] Bird, 'Genesis I–III as a Source for a Contemporary Theology of Sexuality', *Ex Aud*
3 (1987), p. 33, note 9.

[6] See Bird, 'Genesis 3 in der gegenwärtigen biblischen Forschung', *JBTh* 9 (1994; ET)
pp. 1–32. I am grateful to Phyllis Bird for providing me with a copy of her original
English script entitled 'Genesis 3 in Modern Biblical Scholarship'. My references are to
this work, pp. 1–32 [p. 5.].

[7] Bird, 'Male and Female He Created Them', p. 134.

[8] Bird, 'Women, Old Testament', in *ABD* vol. 6, p. 956.

[9] For a review of the source criticism of the Pentateuch see Speiser, *Genesis,* pp. XXII–
XLIII; Wenham, *Genesis 1–15,* pp. XXVI– XXXII; J. Alberto Soggin, *Introduction to
the Old Testament* (London: SCM Press, 1993), pp. 95–106. For criticism of the docu-
mentary hypothesis see Alter, *The Art of Biblical Literature,* pp. 141–147; Joseph Blenkinsopp, *The Pentateuch: An Introduction to the Five Books of the Bible,* pp. 19–25.

circular narrative structure whereas in P the movement is linear. She argues
that the Priestly writer is concerned with the order of nature in the account
of origins, not the culture, whereas in the Yahwist's account the focus is on
'the tension between nature and culture'. Therefore, she makes a distinction between the two accounts at the outset.

Bird thinks the relevance of feminist readings in the whole discussion of
contemporary interpretation is clear. In her own words 'It is feminist theology, or the feminist critique of traditional theology and exegesis, that has
made necessary a new look at the passage... Gen 1:27 has emerged as a text
upon which a corrective anthropology of equality might be built.'[10] She
thinks feminist interpretation originates from the Lord himself. Concerning
the feminist readings, Bird writes:

> [T]he feminist movement is God's work and that (sic) feminist herme-
> neutics is the Lord's planting, a new vine in the Lord's vineyard, or a
> new graft into ancient stock that will enable it to bear much fruit–of
> richer flavor and hardier strain, renewing a spent vine.[11]

According to Bird, feminist hermeneutics can produce more fruit in the
vineyard. However, she understands the inherent tension which could
emerge as a result of the merging of the old and the new.

5.2 Bird's Readings of Gen. 1: 26–28

Feminist interpreters have shown considerable interest in interpreting the
term 'image of God' in Gen. 1:26–28. It is not surprising that virtually
every feminist interpreter led by Phyllis Trible has taken this particular text
to show the equal status of woman with man in creation, mainly because of
the qualifying phrase 'male and female he created them' (Gen. 1:27). On
this basis, the woman is the equal bearer of 'God's image'.

Bird's approach stresses again the virtues of historical–critical exegesis.
Gen. 1:26–27 is one of the most interpreted and reinterpreted passages in
the whole Old Testament.[12] Before offering her own interpretation of the
imago Dei passage, however, Bird criticises atomistic and reductionist interpretations of it, and points out in many interpretations 'attention is fo-

---

[10] Bird, 'Male and Female', p. 133.

[11] Bird, *Feminism and the Bible,* p. 67.

[12] For a comprehensive analysis of the history of interpretation see Gunnlaugur A.
Jónsson, *The Image of God: Genesis 1:26–28 in a Century of Old Testament Research*
(Stockholm: Almqvist & Wiksell, 1988); see also Claus Westerman, *Genesis 1–11,* pp.
147–61; David J. A. Clines, 'The Image of God in Man', *TynB* 19 (1968), pp. 54–61;
Wenham, *Genesis 1–15,* pp. 26–34; J. Barr, 'The Image of God and Natural Theology',
pp. 157– 163.

cused on a single phrase or clause, severing it from its immediate context and from its context within the larger composition'.[13] For instance, Bird notes that Karl Barth's exegesis of *imago Dei* as the *analogia relationis*[14] is a modern concept and foreign to 'the ancient writer's thought and intention'. She asserts that Barth's interpretation of the meaning of sexual distinction in Gen.1:27 is mistaken, though attractive. It was this, in fact, that stimulated Bird's re–examination of the neglected clause ('male and female he created them') in the context of the feminist critique of traditional theology and exegesis.[15]

Bird gives the summary of her argument at the outset. She writes:

> Gen. 1:27 must be understood within the context of vv 26–28, and this complex within the larger structure of the Priestly creation account. V 27 may not be isolated, nor may it be interpreted in relation to v 26 alone; vv 27–28 form an expanded parallel to v 26, in which 27b is a plus, dependent upon and preparatory to the following statement in v 28 and dictated by the juxtaposition in vv 27–28 of the themes of divine likeness and sexual reproduction. The specification of human sexual distinction and its position in the text are determined by the sequence of themes within the account and by the overall structure of announcement and execution report within the chapter.[16]

The above specification of the account, on the one hand aims to detach the concept of sexual distinction from the idea of 'divine image' and from the theme of dominion. And on the other hand, it would associate sexuality

---

[13] Bird, 'Male and Female', p. 130.

[14] For Karl Barth's discussion of *imago Dei* see *CD* 3/1, ET (Edinburgh: T& T Clark, 1958), pp. 183–206. Barth interprets the *imago Dei* not as anything that 'man is or does' but it is the 'I– Thou' relationship within the Deity and the 'I–Thou' relationship between male and female. He writes: 'It is not palpable that we have to do with a clear and simple correspondence, an *analogia relationis,* between this mark of the divine being, namely, that it includes an I and a Thou, and the being of man, male and female. The relationship between the summoning I in God's being and the summoned divine Thou is reflected both in the relationship of God to the man whom He has created, and also in the relationship between the I and the Thou, between male and female, in human existence itself' (p. 196). In fact the 'I–Thou' relationship is a social–philosophical concept first introduced by Martin Buber in his *I and Thou* (trans.) by Ronald Gregor Smith (Edinburgh: T&T Clark, 1937). Especially see the translators introduction, pp. V–XII. Before Karl Barth, Dietrich Bonhoeffer had used this concept in his book, *Schöpfung und Fall* (1937), see *Creation and Fall: A Theological Interpretation of Genesis 1–3*, ET (London: SCM Press, 1959), pp. 33–38.

[15] Bird, 'Male and Female', p. 133.

[16] Ibid., p. 134.

with the theme of fertility in the Priestly creation narrative.[18] In addition, Bird also wants to show the implications of this understanding for contemporary theological anthropology.

5.2.1 Image of God and dominion

Of the various issues that surround the 'image of God' in Genesis 1:26,[19] Bird focuses on the relationship between the term 'image of God' and its relation to the 'male and female' in the passage. The phrase 'image of God' which appears in the early chapters of Genesis in the Priestly source is found only in three passages in the Old Testament (1: 26–27; 5: 1–3 and 9: 5–6). None of these passages explains precisely what the 'image of God' implies. It is not surprising therefore, that there is no scholarly consensus regarding the meaning of 'the image of God' in Gen. 1:26–28. Interpretations have varied from 'spiritual' interpretations to the so called 'physical' interpretation, where man's upright bearing in contrast to animals is interpreted as 'the image of God' in man. The text itself tells us only that that the אדם (humanity) is created in the image and likeness of God, not what either "the image" or the 'likeness of God' means. While צלם (*slm*) may have connotations of a physical image, and דמות (*demut*) suggests a more abstract likeness, the two terms are virtually synonymous in context.[20] Perhaps, significantly, דמות is omitted in Gen. 9: 6. It is context, therefore must govern interpretation. And here two main streams may be discerned, namely the 'functional, and the 'representational'.

Many Old Testament scholars have taken the functional line; that is, they have understood humankind's dominion over the universe either as definitive of the image or as the consequence of their being created in the im-

---

[18] Ibid., cf. Maryanna Cline Horowitz, 'The Image of God—Is Woman Included?', *HTR* 72 (1979), pp. 175–206. Contrary to Bird, she affirms the equality of both sexes in Gen. 1:27 through her historical interpretation. Her historical review of the traditional Jewish and Christian interpretation of this passage, claims that both man and woman are equally created in the image of God.. She also points out that woman was 'not in God's image' was only a rare viewpoint.

[19] Wenham, pp. 27–32.

[20] See Westermann, pp. 145–46; Hamilton, *The Book of Genesis Chapters 1–17*, pp. 135–36; cf. von Rad, *Genesis,* pp. 57–59; Wenham, pp. 29–30.

age of God.[21] This kind of interpretation was supported by the Mesopotamian royal motif, where kings were understood to be the 'image of God' to rule the earth on the god's behalf. Accordingly the 'image of God' is understood in association with the dominion given to humankind to rule over the earth.

Bird, however, follows the 'representational' tradition, accepting that the words צלם and דמות are synonyms with the meaning 'representation' and 'likeness'. She claims that there is no dominion involved in the image. She argues that the adverbial modifier בצלם (*bslm*) which is qualified by כדמות (*kdmt*) in verse 26 explains 'a correspondence of being, a resemblance–not a relationship nor identity, even partial identity.'[22] She argues that the author's 'intention is to describe a resemblance of *adam* to God which distinguishes *adam* from all other creatures—and has consequence[s] for *adam's* relationship to them'.[23] However, Bird argues that the 'resemblance' is not in terms of character or substance but in terms of form only. Bird also denies its connection with ancient Egyptian royal usage where the Pharaoh was depicted as the incarnation of God; — Bird thinks this a concept foreign to Israelite thinking.[24] However, she tries to link the 'image' with the Egyptian wisdom tradition. She writes: 'the language that describes the king as one who stands in a special relationship to the divine world is chosen by the author of Genesis 1 ... to describe humanity as a whole, *adam qua adam,* in its essential nature',[25] thereby democratising the 'image of God' to everyone.

Bird also examines the Akkadian word *salmu*, the cognate of the Hebrew צלם (*slm*) and argues that it is used in a limited range of meaning: i.e. 'likeness or representation,[26] usually of a deity or king, especially as set up in a

---

[21] See von Rad, *Genesis* , pp. 57–60; J. Goldingay, 'The Bible and Sexuality', *SJT* 39 (1986), pp. 175–87; N. H. Snaith, 'The Image of God', *Exp Tim* 91 (1979–80), p. 20; Clines, 'The Image of God in Man', pp. 85–101. For a re–iteration of the functional interpetation see Clines, 'Image of God', in *Dictionary of Paul and His Letters*, pp. 426–427; Ian Hart, 'Genesis 1:1–2:3 as a Prologue to the Book of Genesis', *TynB* 46 (1995), pp. 317–324; P. J. Harland, *The Value of Human Life: A Study of the Story of the Flood (Genesis 6–9* (VTS 64; Leiden: E. J. Brill, 1996), pp. 192–198. By taking the ו before the imperfect verb וירדו as a simple ו to show the purpose of the verb, they translate Gen. 1:26 as 'Let us make man in our image, according to our likeness, *so that* they may have dominion ... the earth'. See Hart, p. 320; Clines, p. 427.
[22] Bird, 'Male and Female', p. 139. Cf. Westermann, pp. 145–46. Here Bird's argument seems to be similar to Westermann's.
[23] Bird, 'Sexual Differentiation and Divine Image', p. 26, note. 7.
[24] 'Male and Female', p. 141.
[25] Ibid ., p. 144.
[26] Bird views the representation not as identity or correspondence. For her 'the image is always a copy, not a double or derivative; it is of different material or kind than the

temple as a visible sign and manifestation of the living god or person'.[27] With this in view, she tries to establish that the אדם is only a representation of God: not the 'image of God' in the sense of *possessing* the divine image but only 'one who is like God in the manner of an image or representation'.[28] Bird does link the notions of 'image' and dominion. She says: 'the notion of the divine image serves here to validate and explain the special status and role of *'ādām* among the creatures'.[29] So Bird interprets כבשה (subdue) as a 'task for the species' and רדו (rule) as 'the position of the species in relation to other orders of creatures'. In doing so, however, she expressly excludes the notion of humanity's dominion over the universe as special representative of God *by virtue* of being created in the 'image of God'. In short, according to Bird, 'image of God' does not contain any qualitative content; nor does it have any link with humanity's dominion of the earth.

5.2.2 Sexual distinction and blessing

Bird thinks that the primary word about the nature of אדם in the *Wortbericht*[30] 'is that this one is like God, created in resemblance to God as an image or representation'. But she rejects the notion of God possessing any form of sexuality because she thinks the P writer guards the distance between God and humanity.[31] She also does not find any special significance, for the 'image' in the clause 'male and female he created them', since the sexual specification is also made in reference to the animals in the creation account and also in the Priestly account of flood story (Gen. 6:19; 7:9).[32]

---

original. The image stands for the original, which it reproduces and shows forth.' See 'Male and Female', p. 142, note 34.

[27] Ibid., p. 142. Bird notes the parallel Egyptian royal ideology such as the concept of the king as 'the image' of the god and also the idea of the Pharaoh as the incarnation of the god on earth. Nevertheless she thinks that the latter concept was foreign to Israelite understanding.

[28] Ibid. p. 138, note 22.

[29] Ibid., p. 138

[30] Bird notes that the Priestly account of creation has a repetitive structure of announcement and execution report (*Wortbericht* and *Tatbericht*). For a discussion of stylistic features of the priestly creation account, see Bernhard W. Anderson, 'A Stylistic Study of the Priestly Creation Story' , in *Canon and Authority: Essays in Old Testament Religion and Theology,* (eds.) G.W. Coats and B. O. Long (Philadelphia: Fortress Press, 1977), pp. 148–162.

[31] Ibid ., p. 148.

[32] Westermann also notes the use of the term זכר and נקבה in reference both to human beings and animals. See, *Genesis 1–11*, p. 160. However, V. H. Hamilton makes a distinction between the sexual differentiation of human beings and the animals. He notes: 'Unlike animals, *man* is not broken down into species (i.e., 'according to their kinds' or 'all kinds of'), but rather is designated by sexuality: *male and female he created them.*

Like Meyers, Bird argues that זכר and נקבה are biological terms rather than sociological terms. Bird supports this line of argument by noting the parallelism of the clause:

בצלם אלהים ברא אתו (in the image of God he created them)

זכר ונקבה ברא אתם (male and female he created them)

She thinks that 'the parallelism of the two cola is progressive, not synonymous. The second statement adds to the first; it does not explicate it'.[33] Moreover it tells us the nature of humanity: '*ādām* is created *like* (i.e., resembling) God, but *as* creature, and hence male and female'.[34]

5.2.3 Fertility and dominion

Another of Bird's concerns is to sever the connection between fertility and dominion. Bird postulates that the *Wortbericht* (verse 26) gives the word about the order (i.e. creation according to divine likeness, and the giving of dominion), the *Tatbericht* (vv. 27–28) while brings the 'sub–theme of sustainability along with the theme of order'.[35] Accordingly, she argues that the introduction of the word of blessing in vv. 27–28 breaks the connection between the image and dominion in v. 26.[36] The result of this argument is that 'fertility and dominion belong to two separate themes or concerns: one, the theme of nature with its sub–theme of sustainability (fertility), the other, the theme of order with its interest in position and function'.[37]

The end result of her thesis provides a non–egalitarian reading of the passage. She writes:

> There is no message of shared dominion here, no word about the distribution of roles, responsibility, and authority between the sexes, no word of sexual equality. What is described is a task for the species (*kibsuhā*) and the position of the species in relation to the other orders of creatures (*redu*).[38]

Bird also points out that the dominant social metaphors to which the key verbs ('subdue' and 'rule') refer are male, 'derived from male experience

---

Sexuality is applied to animal creatures, but not in the Creation story, only later in the Flood narrative (6:19)'. See *The Book of Genesis 1–17*, p. 138.

[33] Ibid., pp. 149–50. Trible takes it as a metaphor explicating the meaning of the 'image of God'. See our discussion on Trible.

[34] Ibid., p. 149; emphasis original.

[35] Ibid., p. 150.

[36] Ibid.

[37] Ibid.

[38] Ibid., p. 151.

and models, the dominant social models of patriarchal society'.[39] She explains that for P like J, the representative and determinant image is male (Gen. 5:1–3, 9:1). Although the P writer talks about the species, he has the male in mind.

5.2.4 The implications of Bird's reading

The implications of the reading of Gen. 1:26–28 for an understanding of P's anthropology are threefold according to Bird.[40] First of all, the notion of P as an equal–rights theologian is eliminated, and this is in line with the rest of the Priestly writings where male names are prominent (genealogies).[41] Moreover, Gen. 1:27 fits well with the general Priestly view of the male's role in society, where the male only functions at the cultic service, excluding women. For instance, circumcision, the essential sign of the covenant people, is only a male practice.

Secondly, Bird's reading also detaches from P 'the equally incongruous notion of a correspondence relationship of the sexes and relationship within the Godhead'.[42] This is mainly because of the transcendent outlook of the Priestly theologian. Finally, this reading suggests that sexual distinction points only to the 'reproductive task and the capacity of the species', and not to social status. In short, 'the Priestly account of creation contains no doctrine of the equality–or inequality–of the sexes, either explicit or implied'.[43]

5.2.5 P and theology of sexuality

Bird thinks that the Priestly account of creation is essential to an Old Testament understanding of the theology of sexuality, both because of its silence and its affirmation. In her opinion, it should be understood alongside that of J, as it appears in juxtaposition within the canonical setting.

Bird considers P's comprehension of 'sexual reproduction as blessing' an important contribution to the theology of sexuality. She explains: 'Sex at its most fundamental, biological level is not to be despised or deprecated.

---

[39] Ibid.

[40] Ibid., see pp. 156ff.

[41] However, Bird does not deny the exegetical soundness of saying that 'woman images the divine as fully as man' since both male and female are human and also in the 'image of God'. Therefore, 'she is consequently as essential as he to an understanding of humanity as God's special sign or representative in the world...' Nonetheless, Bird believes, 'it exceeds what the Priestly writer intended to say or was able to conceive'. ('Male and Female', p. 159).

[42] Ibid., p. 156.

[43] Ibid., p. 157.

It is God's gift and it serves God's purpose in creation by giving to humans the power and the responsibility to participate in the process of continuing creation...'[44] She thinks that since the Priestly account is silent about the social structuring of roles, one has to move, for this topic, to the supplementary account in Genesis 2–3.

5.3 Bird's Reading of Gen. 2–3

Although Bird reads Gen.1 from a strict historical–critical perspective, she does so in combination with a narrative reading of Gen. 2–3. Along with the historical–critical method she also makes use of literary devices by focusing on the theme, structure and plot of the narrative. Accordingly she notes that this narrative varies from the priestly account 'in language, structure, theology and mood'. She considers J's creation narrative as a two–part drama consisting of creation and 'fall' episodes. The main intention of her narrative reading is to show that woman is equal with man in the Yahwistic creation narrative. Since the narrative structure is circular she thinks that 'The first and final acts of creation together describe a single action; the creation of humankind is not complete until the woman stands beside the man, manifesting that essential aspect of humanity hidden or latent in the first exemplar'.[45] Likewise in the account of the 'fall', woman was judged only after the man also ate the fruit. From this she concludes that the 'order of creation' and 'order in the fall' are not considered important by the Yahwist. The resultant implication is that there is no male priority in creation; equally, the woman bears no additional responsibility for disobeying God's commandment first.

5.3.1 The אדם and the woman in the narrative

Bird acknowledges that the narrative is written in androcentric perspective and form. Unlike many other feminists,[46] she considers האדם (*ha–'ādām*) not only as an individual but as a male in Gen. 2. Thus she does not treat 'the human' in the Yahwistic account as an androgynous being.[47] With regard to the creation of the woman Bird emphasises the social and communal aspects of human life and hence the need for a companion and helper for the man. She writes: 'the one alone is not only lonely, but needy/weak; alone he can neither survive nor perpetuate his kind'.[48] However, she

---

[44] Ibid.

[45] Bird, 'Sexual Differentiation', p. 19.

[46] Contra Trible, Meyers, Bal *et al.*

[47] Bird, 'Genesis 3 in Modern Biblical Scholarship', pp. 12–14. Contra Trible and Meyers. See the relevant section in our examination of Trible's and Meyers' work.

[48] Ibid., pp. 12–13, see also 'Genesis I–III as a Source', pp. 37–38.

views the woman as 'one substance with the man'. This is seen in the man's climactic word of recognition that the woman is 'of the same bone and flesh' (Gen. 2:23). She asserts: 'It is only with the woman, however, that the man's need is finally met, for unlike the animals, the woman is not a separate order of creation, but shares fully the nature of *adam*.'[49] By this reading Bird emphasises the identity and equality of the two.

Moreover she does not find any ontological significance in the two–stage creation of man and woman. Bird also assumes a sexual division of labour in the story, namely the male's agricultural labour and the female's reproductive labour.[50] She also holds to the equal responsibility of the man and the woman in the disobedience scene. In her view 'the story clearly means to indict the man and the woman alike. Thus no consequences are reported until both have eaten—and neither the reported reasons (3:6) nor the recorded excuses (3:12–13) affect the judgement that will be passed on both'.[51]

Bird thinks that although the Yahwistic account deals with the relationship between the sexes, unlike the Priestly account, it is concerned with the 'psycho–social' relationships. She finds the 'identity and the equality' of the man and the woman in the social terms אשּׁה (*'iššā*) and אישׁ (*'îš*). She points out that the man's need is only met by the creation of the woman. Although the woman's help is clearly in procreation, 'the account in Genesis 2 subordinates function to passion. The attraction of the sexes is the author's primary interest, the sexual drive whose consummation is conceived as a re–union'.[52] She sees the equality of the sexes in Gen. 2 and does not find any subordination or domination there. Hence Bird's narrative reading of Gen. 2 is in many respects similar to Trible's reading.

5.3.2 *The prohibition and sin*

Bird has made an impressive attempt to deal with the issues of sex and gender in her article 'Genesis 3 in Modern Biblical Scholarship'. She approaches the texts from a feminist perspective because she believes that 'feminist interpretation emerges as a response to the text heard on its own terms, as the product of voices and visions from another world'.[53] Going further than her title, *de facto,* she takes up important issues in both Gen. 2–3. Although Bird thinks that the traditional notion of the 'fall'[54] is foreign

---

[49] Bird, 'Genesis I–III as a Source', p. 38.

[50] Bird, 'Genesis 3 in Modern Biblical Scholarship', p. 13; contra Meyers.

[51] Ibid., p. 15. See also 'Sexual Differentiation', p. 21.

[52] 'Sexual Differentiation', p. 20.

[53] Bird, 'Genesis 3 in Modern Biblical Scholarship', p. 5, note 10.

[54] Along with Bird, other Old Testament scholars, both male and female as we have seen, argued, that Gen. 3 is not a story of 'fall', see Westermann in the section 'Purpose

to the story, she treats Gen. 2:4b–3:24 as a two–act drama which tells about the creation and 'fall' of the first man and woman because she thinks that it is a convenient metaphor to discuss the chapter. Nevertheless she takes the story of the 'fall' as an etiological tale 'describing the fundamental conditions of life as experienced by an ancient Israelite author, life characterised by painful toil, struggle with a hostile environment, estrangement in relationships human and divine, shame in self–consciousness, and death'.[55] Bird argues that the Yahwistic writer was transforming this etiological tale into a crime–and–punishment story, 'in which this condition is construed as a penalty for disobedience of a divine command'.[56] Hence according to Bird the idea of sin may be seen as the Yahwist's addition to the primeval story.

Bird regards the transgression of the divine commandment, in J's view as the first and fundamental sin.[57] However, she thinks that the Yawhist's main concern is with knowledge rather than immortality. This knowledge provides pain and pleasure. 'It is accompanied by estrangement— estrangement from God and estrangement between man and woman. It also brings estrangement from the environmen'.[58]

Bird also deals with another important aspect of Gen. 3 in her discussion of 'sin". She notes that Gen. 3 functions as the interpretative clue to the whole history which follows it. Bird also points out that P became the interpreter of J with regard to the nature of sin.[59] In her view, both the man and woman sinned by their disobedience to the divine command. She explains:

> Both man and woman have heeded another voice over the voice of God, and that is their common sin. The gender–differentiated roles in the drama do not describe gender specific patterns of sin, but they do illus-

---

and Thrust' in *Genesis 1–11*, pp. 275–278; James Barr, *The Garden of Eden and the Hope of Immortality*; Carol Meyers, *Discovering Eve*, and recently C. M. Carmichal, 'The Paradise Myth: Interpreting without Jewish and Christian Spectacles', in *A Walk in the Garden*, pp. 91–104; Ronald A. Simkins, *Creator and Creation: Nature in the World view of Ancient Israel* (Peabody: Hendrickson, 1994), pp. 184 ff.

[55] Bird, 'Genesis 3 in Modern Biblical Scholarship', pp. 6–7. See also 'Bone of My Bone and Flesh of My Flesh', where she gives a comprehensive explanation of sin. Accordingly she writes: 'The story of the primal sin is an etiology of the pain of human existence that draws on traditional myths and motifs to depict a case of disobedience in which human reason challenges divine wisdom and will'. p. 526.

[56] Ibid., p. 30.

[57] Ibid., p. 19.

[58] Ibid., p. 23. Contra Barr who thinks immortality is the main concern of the writer.

[59] Ibid., p. 8, note. 15.

trate differing responses to temptation, one involving active reasoning, the other unreflective acquiescence to another's leading.[60]

The result of Bird's reading seems to be to free the woman from sole responsibility in the matter of humanity's 'fall', and also to show the corporate nature of human disobedience.

5.3.3 The consequence of sin

Bird has argued that the author of Gen. 3 made use of a "crime–and–punishment motif" to describe the basic human conditions of life. She also observes the etiological motif in the punishment (Gen. 3: 14–19). In her opinion, it reveals the burdens and pains of Israelite society.[61] She interprets the announced punishment as judicial sentences which affect the 'source' of their life and work.[62] The man's cultivation of the ground becomes toilsome, and the woman's procreation becomes painful: 'the man from whom she was taken and on whom her work depends will now be her ruler instead of her companion'.[63] She also finds a social dimension to her pain in the woman's dependence on the man, which is absent in the man's. She elaborates the result:

> A hierarchy of order is introduced into the relationship of the primal pair. Mutuality is replaced by rule. Patriarchy is inaugurated—as the sign of life alienated from God. The rule of man over woman, announced in Genesis 3: 16, is the Bible's first statement of hierarchy within the species, and it is presented as the consequence of sin.[64]

---

[60] Ibid., p. 29.

[61] See Bird, 'Image of Women in the Old Testament', in *Religion and Sexism: Images of Woman in the Jewish and Christian Traditions,* (ed.) Rosemary Radford Ruether (New York: Simon and Schuster), 1974, pp. 41–88; reprinted in *The Bible and Liberation: Political and Social Hermeneutics,* (ed.) N.K. Gottwald, pp. 252–88. We will be referring to the reprint. p. 278.

[62] Bird, 'Bone of My Bone', p. 527. For a similar view point see Julie Galumbush, ''*ādām* from '*adāmâ* '*issa* from'*is*: Derivation and Subordination in Genesis 2.4b–3.24', pp. 33–4. For a discussion of hierarchy in the punishment see, Susan Niditch, *Chaos to Comos: Studies in Biblical Patterns of Creation* (Atlanta: Scholars Press, 1985), pp. 30–31.

[63] Ibid. See also 'Images of the Women in the Old Testament', p. 278, where she clearly states that the pangs of childbirth as the common and acute pain suffered by women in the Old Testament. At the same time she also believes that procreation as the woman's primary and essential work in the society. Contra Meyers, who argues that there is no increase of pain in childbirth.

[64] Ibid.

According to Bird, the subordination of the woman to man in Gen. 3 is the consequence of sin. In her estimation: '[t]he Yahwist sees the disobedience of the man and woman to the divine command as the root sin that disturbs the original harmony of creation, and he sees the consequences of that sin in the painful and alienated existence which he knew to be the human lot'.[65] As a result of this, the companion of the Gen. 2 has now become a master, and the subordination of the woman to man has begun.

5.3.4 The woman's subordination as descriptive

Like many other feminist writers Phyllis Bird also believes that the man's ruling over the woman and the resultant subjugation is not a prescriptive state of affairs but merely descriptive. She notes that 'Israel did not use this legend to justify the existing order or to argue for woman's subordination.'[66] She points toward the historical and prophetical books to show that both the Old Testament prophets and historians were looking behind the existing division, alienation, inequality and exploitation to 'an original and intended equality and harmony in creation'.[67]

Bird envisions a future grounded on the prophetic hope of the new creation and new order where there will not be any exploitation and alienation based on species, age, sex, and social status. Moreover, she also finds the knowledge of God in every heart (Jer. 31:31–34), the democratisation of the Spirit (Joel 2:28–29), and most importantly 'the reversal of the prevailing sexual roles: 'a woman protects a man' (Jer. 31:22) as a result of the coming new order.[68] She concludes 'Israel's best statements about woman recognise her as an equal with man, and with him jointly responsible to God

---

[65] Bird, 'Sexual Differentiation', p. 21.

[66] Bird, 'Images of Women in the Old Testament', p. 278. Woman's subordinate status in creation is challenged by Phyllis Trible; Carol Meyers; Mieke Bal; Mary Hayter; *The New Eve in Christ,* p. 114; Alice Ogden Bellis, *Helpmates, Harlots,* p. 63; Fleming , *A Rhetorical Analysis of Gen.2–3 with implications for a Theology of Man and Woman,* p. 272 (My references are from the University Microfiche copy, supplied by The British Library Document Supply Centre); Alice Ogden Bellis, *Helpmates, Harlots,* p. 63.

[67] Ibid ., p. 279.

[68] Ibid. Cf. Trible, she translates it as 'female surrounds man', moreover Trible notes inter–textual aspects between this Jeremian text and Gen. 1:27. Accordingly, she argues that the Genesis text 'provides an external witness to the kind of internal function the noun *neqeba* has here in Jeremiah.' In other words, the noun נקבה (*neqeba*) functions as the object of the verb ברא (*bara*) with God or Yahweh as the subject in both texts, see *God and the Rhetoric,* pp. 47–49, here p. 48. For a similar interpretation see André La-Cocque, *The Feminine Unconventional: Four Subversive Figures in Israel's Tradition* (Minneapolis: Fortress Press, 1990), pp.13–14

and to cohumanity. That Israel rarely lived up to this vision is all too apparent, but the vision should not be denied'.[69]

So like Trible and Meyers, Bird also thinks that woman's subordination is not intended by God.

5.4 Development of Bird's Theology of Sexuality

Phyllis Bird attempts to articulate a theology of sexuality on the basis of her readings of Genesis 1–3. Despite the androcentric perspective and world view of both the Priestly and Yahwistic accounts of creation, Bird takes Gen. 1–3 as a source for a contemporary theology of sexuality.[70] The main difficulty with her argument is her changing viewpoints on the theology of sexuality, especially the relationship and status between man and woman in two accounts of creation. One can find notable changes, even sometimes apparent differences, between her earlier viewpoints and her more recent opinions. We can note mainly three stances concerning her theology of sexuality.

First, she advocates that although there are considerable differences in style and language between the two creation accounts, 'their statements about woman are essentially the same: woman is, together with man, the direct and intentional creation of God and the crown of his creation. Man and woman were made for each other'.[71] Accordingly, in her first article, Bird had a 'functional view' of the 'image of God' in the Priestly creation story. Hence she wrote: 'In contrast to the other creatures, man's primary bond is with God and not with the earth; man's purpose in creation is to rule the earth'.[72] She thought that the clause 'male and female he created them' was an 'expansion and the specification of the first', ('God created mankind (אדם–'ādām) in his own image'.). Her interest seems concerned to show that the woman is not a subsequent creation to the man, rather the genus אדם ('ādām) is bisexual in its created order.[73] She even further went on to suggest that 'The P formulation implies an essential equality of the two sexes'.[74]

She also suggested that the purpose of man's creation is to rule the earth, something she categorically denies in her subsequent essays. She affirmed the clear distinction of the 'human animal' from other creatures by virtue of

---

[69] Ibid.
[70] See Bird, 'Images of Women in the Old Testament', pp. 275–279; 'Male and Female', pp. 155–159; 'Genesis I–III as a Source', pp. 39–44; 'Sexual Differentiation', pp. 21–25.
[71] Ibid., 'Images of Women in the Old Testament', p. 276.
[72] Ibid.
[73] Ibid.
[74] Ibid., p. 287, note 87.

his being created in God's image.[75]   In conclusion, she thought that both creation accounts stated the equal worth of man and woman.

Secondly, she later argued that P's account is not egalitarian although in Genesis 2 'the *equality* of the two [man and woman] is the foundation and prelude to its negation in Genesis 3'.[76] This has been also clearly expressed in her article 'Male and Female He Created Them',which we have already discussed at length. Accordingly she saw 'companionship', 'mutual attraction', 'the sharing of work', and equality between the sexes as a result of this psycho–social relationship in Gen. 2.[77]

Now, thirdly, we will examine her latest thoughts on the theology of sexuality. Her views have been mainly presented in the abbreviated and extended form of her article.[78] This recent article, summarises her earlier one, entitled 'Male and Female He Created them', at the same time, in this article she broadens her hermeneutical outlook by suggesting that 'the meaning of a text cannot finally be limited to the author's (or editor's) understanding or intention'.[79]   Although Bird does not see any basic change in the P writer's intention and assumptions in the text, she now argues that the Priestly text permits an egalitarian reading that is to be understood as 'unintended and unforeseen by the ancient author'.[80] She further posits that this egalitarian reading goes beyond the 'horizon of the ancient author' and it is a result of a 'new context of interpretation'.[81] Therefore Bird argues that the creation accounts allow multivalent and multidimensional readings which move beyond the original terms and intentions because of the new and changing contexts of the interpreter. She thinks this interpretative context should comprise the canon as a whole in the process of interpretation. So she proposes a theology of sexuality in the context of women's experience and feminist critique of patriarchy. The following are her main proposals for a theology of sexuality.[82]

i. The divine image embraces humanity as a whole, so it cannot be limited to any subgroup or individual.

---

[75] Ibid.

[76] Bird, 'Genesis 1–3 as a Source', p. 39; emphasis mine.

[77] See 'Male and Female', p. 158.

[78] 'Sexual Differentiation...,'

[79] Ibid ., p. 24.

[80] Ibid ., p. 29 note 22.

[81] Ibid. Cf. Bird's recent article, 'Genesis 3 in Modern Biblical Scholarship', where she writes: 'feminist interpretation emerges as a response to the text heard on its own terms, as the product of voices and visions from another world. The constructive task of theology (feminist or other) begins in this cross–cultural conversation, as new questions are addressed to the ancient texts from new contexts' (p. 5, note 10).

[82] 'Genesis I–III', pp. 39ff; 'Sexual Differentiation', pp. 21ff.

a. Although the Priestly narrator narrates a male line history,[83] the species אדם is described by a collective/plural and bisexual noun (Gen.1:27 and 5:2), so it does not limit the image to the male of the species.

b. The clear distinction made between the anarthrous noun in Genesis 1 (אדם–'ādām) and the individualised האדם (ha–'ādām) in the Yahwistic account prevents the collapse of the collective into the singular, thereby reducing the image to the male alone, in the manner of the Priestly writer's narrow male line historiography.

ii. Though the notion of ruling is associated with the divine image in the author's cultural milieu, here in Genesis, 'the image' is 'empty' of content and merely describes 'a correspondence conceived in terms of form rather than substance: humankind is God's representation and representative within creation'.[84] So there is no inherent function of rule in the divine image.

iii. As sexuality is shared by all other creatures, human sexuality cannot be distinguished from other orders of creatures.

a. Sexual differentiation in P's statement is merely biological, designed for procreative purposes.

b. The command to 'fill the earth' is not absolute or universal; it was meant for the beginning of life on earth.

iv. The essential equality of the sexes is a central feature of both the narratives. She writes: 'The side–by side appearance of male and female in P's account of simultaneous creation is matched by J's account of face–to–face encounter climaxed by the man's joyful acknowledgement of the woman as his long–sought counterpart'.[85] This implied equality is achieved through P's 'symmetrical construction' and J's 'dramatic action'. Moreover, J's account is intended to complement P's biological factor by providing a psycho–social aspect of sexuality.

In her concluding hermeneutical section Bird suggests that Gen.1 may function as a basic text for a 'feminist egalitarian anthropology' as it does not establish any hierarchy within the species 'either of gender or function'. Nevertheless, she re–affirms that this egalitarian outlook neither makes the P writer a feminist nor denies the writer's patriarchal[86] assumptions. She

---

[83] According to Bird male transition occurs 'when P moves from proto–history (creation) to "history"', 'Sexual Differentiation', p. 29 note 21.

[84] 'Genesis I–III', p. 41.

[85] Bird, 'Sexual Differentiation', p. 23.

[86] Here we have to note that Bird was reluctant to use even the term 'patriarchy' two decades ago due to its indiscriminate use although she believed that ancient Israel was a 'male –centred and male–dominated society'. See 'Images of Women', p. 279, note. 1. I think this was also because the feminist writers then generally thought that the problem mainly lies with the interpretation of the biblical text not with the text *per se*.

concludes 'While the Priestly writer's language is indisputably androcentric and patriarchal, patriarchy is not his message in Genesis 1'.[87]

However, the opinion which she held for about two decades was revised in her more recent article.[88] Now she emphasises the woman's help to the man in procreation as the basic plot of Genesis 2:18–20, against her earlier view about the psycho–social aspect of the man's need for a helper.[89] According to this reading, the woman's role becomes secondary and the man seems to be the pivotal character of the whole narrative. Bird's change of opinion concerning the role of the woman from the psycho–social aspect to merely procreative function is clearly in line with the current trend among feminist readers to show that the biblical texts are irredeemably patriarchal. But this was not the case during the inception of the second wave of feminist readings in the early 1970s. This change of opinion concerning the role of the woman in the creation narrative is a notable feature in the development of Bird's theology of sexuality.

From the above proposal one can infer that Bird articulates a theology of sexuality not from the feminist readings of the text, but only as an implication of her reading for the quest for an egalitarian feminist concern. This is mainly because her historical–critical framework does not address many of the contemporary issues like feminist concerns. So Bird moved out of her old methodological grid to the current reader–response approach. This shows that any interpreter who limits herself/himself to a strict hermeneutical method cannot address all the questions one would like to deal with. However, other feminist interpreters propose a feminist egalitarian interpretation directly from the text itself as an outcome of their committed feminist readings. So Bird's theology of sexuality is implied whereas others are direct. In addition, Bird's readings of creation accounts are not strictly 'feminist' readings of the passage; rather her readings have feminist implications.

5.5 Observation, Discussion and Evaluation

5.5.1 The strength of Bird's reading

In this section I will examine the main strengths and weaknesses of Bird's readings of the creation accounts. One of the main advantages of Bird's

---

[87] 'Sexual Differentiation', p. 25.

[88] Bird, 'Bone of My Bone and Flesh of My Flesh', *TToday* 4 (1994), pp. 521–34.

[89] Ibid., p. 525, see note 13 also. The similar idea that procreation is the only help which the woman could give to the man in the creation narrative is already expressed by D. J. A. Clines. Bird looks to Clines for support in order to establish her view. See Clines, *What Does Eve Do to Help?*, pp. 34–37. See our discussion of Trible on this point.

readings is her attempt to interpret the text in the context of its original so-cio–historical milieu. Bird has also made very clear that she does not want to offer a feminist reading of the text; nonetheless she reads the text with a 'feminist consciousness and commitment'. Through this sort of approach, Bird wants to be more true to the text than those feminist readings where the readers approach the text with a pre–commitment.

We can observe the strength of her readings in her exegetical conclu-sions. Her interpretation of 'male and female he created them', for in-stance, as a biological term indicating sexuality, rather than a social term signifying equality, shows a readiness not to espouse the usual feminist in-terpretations. Again her treatment of האדם (*ha–'ādām*) as a male human be-ing in Gen. 2 and her reading of Gen. 3 as a story of the disobedience of the man are more in line with traditional readings than modern feminist ones. These conclusions speak of a certain detachment in her scholarship.[90] Nev-ertheless, her attempt to articulate a theology of sexuality based on the crea-tion accounts in fact deals with many of the contemporary issues related to gender. Her indications concerning population control and gender–balance are valuable insights. Although she does not want to offer a feminist read-ing, her feminist consciousness makes her reading very relevant to our situation.

5.5.2 The problems of Bird's reading

Having noted the strength of Bird's reading, we must also record some of its limitations. Bird attempted to recover the intention of the author in her reading: she was aiming to do this mainly through interpreting the biblical texts in their ANE context, especially against the background of the Egyp-tian sources. The main problem with this method is the risk of theoretical assumptions involved in this process. For instance, in attempting to assess the influence of the ANE texts how can one decide between Mesopotamian or Egyptian influence? Those who want to emphasise the functional aspect of the 'image of God' can still argue for the Mesopotamian influence, thereby underlining the fact that man is the ruler of the universe by virtue of his being created in the image of God.

Our analysis of feminist readings hitherto reveals that one particular reading is not adequate to deal with the complex nature of the biblical texts. This we have already noted in our evaluation of Trible and Meyers. As with the case of Trible and Meyers we will examine Bird's approach under different headings, namely methodological, exegetical, hermeneutical, theo-logical and practical problems even though there will be a certain degree of overlap between them.

---

[90] Here her reading has more strength than Meyers' reading who totally avoided the as-pect of disobedience and sin.

METHODOLOGICAL DIFFICULTIES

We have seen Phyllis Bird's attempt to reconstruct and locate the original intention of the authors of the creation accounts through her historical–critical approach to the text by drawing insights from the Ancient Near Eastern parallels. She has mainly employed these insights to discuss the meaning of *imago Dei*.

First of all let me address some of the general methodological issues. We have many parallel texts which could throw light on biblical creation so we need to take great care when we interpret the biblical text with the help of Ancient Near Eastern Texts. How may we know which texts influence the biblical text most? In the absence of clear indications, any conclusion which we derive from the parallel remains only a possibility, not something absolute. In some cases, Bird has ascribed more authority to parallel texts rather than the biblical text itself. For instance, in her attempt to dissociate dominion from the divine image, she approached the text diachronically, drawing parallels from Egyptian and Canaanite sources. Arguably this distracted her from the *prima facie* evidence of the text that dominion or rule is a prerogative only of humankind (Gen. 1:26&28).

Again we need to note that the outcome of any historical reading depends on how we choose and interpret our sources, and the questions we ask of the text. In the case of the *imago Dei* interpretation, scholars have used different ANE sources, asked different questions and come to different conclusions. In some cases, different conclusions are drawn from a study of the same source. If we stress one aspect over another, this will considerably affect our conclusion. Therefore, one has to maintain a proper balance in use of the sources. The following examples will illustrate the above argument and will also show that there is a plethora of interpretations and differing viewpoints on the same passage.

James Barr for instance, thinks that the *imago Dei* passage should be interpreted in the context of Deutero–Isaianic religious traditions. He thinks that the P writer is much influenced by Deutero–Isaiah because of similar theological themes like creation, monotheism and the incomparability of God.[91] Here we see Barr interpreting the *imago Dei* mainly against biblical tradition itself rather than focusing on extra–biblical evidences. We will elucidate his arguments in our exegetical section below.

It is quite interesting to note the exegetical conclusions of Helen Schüngel–Straumann, a German feminist scholar, who uses the same his-

---

[91] See Barr, 'The Image of God in the Book of Genesis–A study of Terminology', *BJRL* 51 (1968), pp. 11–26, here see especially pp. 13–14; For a critique of Barr's views see J. Maxwell Miller, 'In the Image and Likeness of God', *JBL* 91 (1972), pp. 297–299. Contra Michael Fishbane who thinks Deutero–Isaiah demythologises P (Gen.1:1–2:4a), see *Biblical Interpretation in Ancient Israel* (Oxford: Clarendon press, 1985), pp. 322–326.

torical–critical methodology of Bird and the same Egyptian royal ideology
to interpret the Priestly creation narrative. Contrary to Bird's conclusion,
she argues that the 'image of God' entails ruling: not 'human rule over
other humans' but 'man and woman rule over the rest of creation'.[92] She
observes the distinction between Egyptian royal ideology and P's viewpoint. In the former, only the King or Queen represented the deity whereas
P considers all 'human beings as God's representatives'. So she regards the
democratisation of the ancient oriental ideology as the contribution of P.[93]
On this point, Schüngel–Straumann's reading has an advantage over
Bird's, perhaps because she has been more alive to the distinctiveness of
the Genesis passage's relation to Egypt, and sought to do justice to the
theme of human ruling there (Gen. 1: 26&28).

In the same vein Jürgen Moltmann argues that in the royal theology, 'the
Pharaoh is the reigning copy of God on earth, his representative, his deputy,
his reflection and his mode of appearance in the world'.[94] Contrary to Bird,
he finds in Pharaoh not the form but the character and substance of god
himself. Hence as far as the interpretation of the 'image of God' is concerned, humanity is not merely to rule but also 'the human being is God's
indirect manifestation on earth'.[95]

The British feminist biblical scholar, Mary Hayter, also provides a balanced view.[96] She concludes for the equal worth of man and woman as
they are created, blessed and commanded to 'fill the earth and subdue it'
together (Gen. 1:28). She writes: '[S]ince man and woman were created
together, with no hint of temporal or ontological superiority, the difference
between the sexes cannot be said to affect their *equal standing*—before
God and one another'.[97] So contrary to Bird, Hayter argues on the basis of
the text that both man and woman are equal in God's creation.[98]

There is no doubt that both man and woman constitute אדם (*'ādām;* see
Gen. 1:26–26, 5: 1–2). Whether this implies 'equality' is a moot point.
Bird may be right that 'male and female he created them', in its immediate

---

[92] See H. Schüngel–Straumann, 'On the Creation of Man and Woman in Genesis 1–3',
pp. 74–75.

[93] Ibid ., p. 74.

[94] See J. Moltmann, *God in Creation: An Ecological Doctrine of Creation* (London:
SCM Press, 1985), p. 219.

[95] Ibid.

[96] See M. Hayter, *The New Eve in Christ,* pp. 85–94.

[97] Ibid.., p. 89; emphasis mine.

[98] Cf. Susan Niditch, who notes that the Priestly writer's view of men and women in the
creation account differs from the 'male centered Priestly writers' of Leviticus. So according to Niditch, '[i]n reading the Hebrew Scriptures as a narrative whole, including
both Gen. 1:27 and Leviticus, one may receive the message that the genders were meant
to be *equal at the beginning*'. See Niditch, 'Genesis', in *The Women's Bible Commentary,* p. 13; emphasis mine.

context, is to do with biological function. That equality cannot be demonstrated as part of an original intention. It is not surprising that feminist authors (like others) part company on a fundamental point like this. The deficiency, however, may lie in historical criticism itself, as a basis for pressing a theological or ideological interpretation.

In practice, Bird seems to acknowledge this difficulty. Her methodological approach seems in fact to be complex. In particular, her readings of the creation narratives conclude for an egalitarian status of the sexes, in tension with her historical–critical investigation. Accordingly she has argued in her first essay that 'the P formulation implies an essential equality of the two sexes'.[99] Similarly, she has also found fundamental equality between the sexes in her narrative reading of the Yahwistic account.[100] However, in her recent writings she thinks that 'help in procreation seems to lie at the base of the plot' of the creation of woman as a "help" for the man (i.e. not 'equality', Gen 2:18 & 20). This seems to be in line with her historical–critical reading of the priestly creation narrative. Although Bird does not find any egalitarian aspects in her analysis of Gen. 1:26–28, interestingly she articulates an egalitarian reading of the text, even though she thinks that those are 'unintended' and 'unforeseen' by the author. Here we see the tension between her historical–critical reading and a kind of reader–response approach which she advocates through this type of reasoning. So, in short, she begins with an egalitarian reading, then she argues against it and finally she ends up again in a kind of feminist egalitarian reading. If she thinks the text allows multivalent readings that, in a way, would weaken her argument for an historical–critical investigation. We need to note that the search for intentionality and a reader–response method are at two extreme poles. Bird's post–modern reader–response reasoning seems similar to that of Trible who also argued that 'new contexts alter texts'. In the end she has not been able to apply strictly the findings of her historical–critical reading for a theology of sexuality that there is no equality between the sexes in the creation order. Rather, she makes possible a kind of feminist egalitarian reading through her reader–response approach.

We can examine some of her presuppositions further. She writes: 'the P writer was not a feminist'. However, the P writer does not need to be a feminist to advocate the equal–standing of man and woman, if that is intended by God for man and woman. The egalitarian outlook cannot be

---

[99] Bird, 'Images of Women in the Old Testament', p. 287, note 87. However, she noted that its implications were not fully understood by the priestly writer. Moreover, she thinks that the prevailing cultural concepts about the roles and activities of men and women failed to reflect this insight and so the male genealogies and male priesthood dominated the rest of his work.

[100] Bird, 'Sexual Differentiation', pp. 19ff; 'Genesis I– III as a Source', pp. 36ff. In fact, Bird combines literary and historical aspects together here.

viewed only as a feminist agenda and the non–egalitarian as a patriarchal ordering.[101] Even though the biblical society was patriarchal, it is not necessary that the biblical writers should always express those perspectives. Although we admit that the biblical writings reflect many of the aspects of patriarchal culture, the biblical writings are not necessarily the mirror of the society in every respect. It can be argued that even in that patriarchal culture, the biblical writer has emphasised the equal worth of man and woman.

EXEGETICAL DIFFICULTIES

The image of god, sexuality and dominion

Although Phyllis Bird's attempt to detach the concept of sexuality from the 'divine image' has advantages,[102] her attempt to dissociate the theme of 'dominion' totally from the 'image of God' is unconvincing since there is *prima facie* evidence in the text itself for humankind's dominion over the universe (Gen. 1:26 &28). Even a cursory reading of the text precisely suggests (1: 26, 28) that fertility and dominion go together. Moreover, this dominion is not merely a male prerogative as God blesses both male and female and commands them to have dominion over the rest of the creation.[103] Secondly, Bird's attempt to detach dominion completely from the 'divine image' may bring humanity down to the level of other creatures over whom God assigns humanity's authority. While it is true that 'the image of God' is not defined in the text, the immediate context and the inter–textual evidence suggest that humanity has been given a certain dominion over the other creation; here we have only to decide whether it is a consequence of being created in the image of God or whether it is a status and function assigned to the human being as a distinct creation of God.[104] We can also have inter–textual support for this case in Psalm 8, where God puts all under the feet of humankind to have dominion over them. We read: 'You have given them dominion over the works of your hands; you have put all things under their feet'(Ps. 8:6 NRSV).

---

[101] Cf. Gottwald. He also thinks that 'biblical writers did not share our perspective on feminism'. See *Tribes of Yahweh*, p. 796–97, note 628.

[102] See Wenham, *Genesis,* p. 33. Even earlier in the fourth century, Gregory of Nyssa (ca. 335–94) offered a similar line of interpretation, who also separated the last phrase of Gen. 1:27 from 'the image of God' and he related this with the animal mode of procreation, see Horowitz, 'the Image of God in Man–Is Woman Included?', pp. 197–98.

[103] Cf. Trible, she rightly argues that the two God–given responsibilities to humankind are procreation and dominion, *God and the Rhetoric*, p. 19; see also Helen Schüngel–Straumann, 'On the Creation of Man and Woman in Genesis 1–3', p. 74.

[104] See von Rad, *Genesis,* pp. 56–58; see also Ronald A. Simkins, *Creator and Creation: Nature in the World view of Ancient Israel,* pp. 199–202. He interprets the text in the wider context of the nature and ecology, still he finds a connection between the 'image of God', human dominion and rule over the earth.

James Barr is one of the recent supporters of Phyllis Bird's exegetical position. Although his aim is to discuss the concept of the image of God in relation to Natural Theology, in the course of discussion he is thoroughly critical of Karl Barth for interpreting 'the image of God' with respect to *analogia relationis*.[105] He looks to Bird for support in his argument against Barth. He agrees with Bird that Barth's argument is fallacious, linguistically, grammatically and culturally.[106] In Barr's view, Barth's interpretation of the phrase 'male and female he created them' as an explanation of the term 'the image of God' is a manifest fallacy. He shows that this particular connection between the phrases is only one among many possibilities, such as the consequence, addition, qualification or modification of the given term 'the image of God'.[107] In this respect Bird and Barr are right.

Barr has taken the point further: Since he assumes that the P writer is influenced by the work of Deutero–Isaiah, he sets the *imago Dei* passage against the sixth century theological context of monotheism, creation, anthropomorphism, condemnation of idolatry. Accordingly, he reads that the primary purpose and function of 'the image of God' is 'to say something about God. Its dynamics develop from the need to clarify speech about *him*. Precisely for that reason one cannot necessarily locate the elements in human existence to which it applies'.[108] So Barr thinks that the concept of the image of God is a 'theologoumenon' which came out of the tensions of Israelite religious traditions. He and Bird have made a strong case for the view that humankind's dominion over the animals is not definitive of the image.

Yet the possibilities are not exhausted with this. Clines' line of argument is also important. With other scholars he has persuasively argued for the uniqueness of the first biblical creation account vis-à-vis others, and sees it as a breakthrough. He argues on the basis of Mesopotamian sources, and writes of the meaning of the image: 'It is that man is in some way and in some degree like God'.[109] However, he argues that 'Man is created not *in* God's image, since God has no image of His own, but *as* God's image, or rather *to be* God's image'.[110] Clines also explains that the image of God

---

[105] See Barr, 'The Image of God and Natural Theology', pp. 156–173.

[106] Ibid., pp. 159–163.

[107] Ibid., p. 160.

[108] Ibid., p. 170; see also Barr, 'The Image of God in the Book of Genesis', pp. 13f.

[109] Clines, 'The Image of God', p. 53.

[110] Ibid., p. 101, see also pp. 74ff. Following *Gesenius' Hebrew Grammar,* Clines takes the proposition ב (*b*) in the noun צלם (*slm*) as *beth essentiae*, meaning 'as' or 'in the capacity of'. For instance, in Exodus 6:3 we read ואֵרָא בְּאֵל שַׁדָּי (I appeared *as* El shaddai). So he takes the *beth* here as *beth* of essence and translates accordingly. See *Gesenius' Hebrew Grammar,* (ed.) & Enlarged by E. Kautzsch, (Sec. ed. 1910), A. E.

lies in the representative function of humankind rather than representation itself. Contrary to Bird's argument, he underlines the functional aspect of the image of God. He says:

> The image is to be understood not so much ontologically as existentially: it comes to expression not in the nature of man so much as in his activity and function. This function is to represent God's lordship to the lower orders of creation. The dominion of man over creation can hardly be excluded from the content of the image itself.[111]

I have already suggested that Bird did not allow sufficiently for the differences and the uniqueness of the biblical account compared with the Egyptian idea of the king as the image of God. She emphasised only the external representational aspects of this image such as form, ignoring the qualitative aspects. Here Wenham rightly notes that the 'image of God' terminology in Egyptian and Mesopotamian thinking, explains 'the king's function and being', and not his 'appearance'.[112] In similar vein Clines writes: 'There were two kinds of images of the gods in Egypt: the plastic form and the living person, the king.'[113] 'The decisive thing in the image of

---

Cowley (Oxford: Clarendon Press, 1985), p. 379. Cf. Ex. 18:4; Pss. 35:2, 146:5; Jb. 23:18.

[111] Clines, p. 101, see also Tryggve N. D. Mettinger, 'Abbild oder Urbild? 'Imago Dei' in traditionsgeschichtlicher Sicht', *ZAW* 86 (1974), p. 411. He reads 'image' as a pattern representing God; cf. Wenham, pp. 31–32. The tendency to avoid this kind of 'functional interpretation' of the image lies behind the present ecological crisis due to humankind's unthoughtful exploitation of nature. As a remedial measure nowadays there is an increasing tendency among scholars to detach the dominion from 'the image of God' as Bird and Barr attempted this refocusing, in a new way, on dominion. Although this concern is extremely valid and reasonable, we are bound to investigate how this was understood in its original setting. Although Clines' treatment of the preposition ב in the צלם as *beth essentiae* is open to question, his functional concept of the humanity being the representative of God on earth appears to be convincing. It is true that God has no image of his own, but the statement that man is created in the image of God, may not be intended to give a one–to–one correspondence between the image of God and humankind, so it is not necessary to take the ב as *beth essentiae*. Wenham also thinks that the above view is untenable because of the interchangeable use of the prepositions ב and כ in the similar passage in Gen. 5: 1, 3. See Wenham, *Genesis*, p. 29, cf. also John F.A. Sawyer, 'The Meaning of בצלם אלהים ('In the Image of God') in Genesis I–XI', *JTS* 25 (1974), pp. 421ff. Sawyer rejects Clines' proposal of *beth essentiae* on stylistic grounds and he does not find any semantic difference between the interchangeable use of the prepositions in the *imago Dei* passages (Gen. 1:26 cf. 5:1); rather he considers it merely as a stylistic variant. Moreover, he thinks that the statement 'in the image of God' does not rule out the possibility that humanity was created in such a way as 'to resemble in some respects both God and angels' (here p. 423).

[112] Wenham, p. 30.

[113] Clines, pp. 80–85.

the god is not the material nor the form, but the divine fluid, which inspires the image in that it takes up its abode in the image.'[114] The Egyptian king himself also has to carry the divine fluid. F. Preisigke writes: 'The visible and tangible body of the king is only the covering for the god or the dwelling of the god. The king's words and acts are expressions of the god dwelling in him'.[115] So Clines argues that the representational quality of the image has only a secondary role, and the possession of the divine fluid is the essential quality in an image.[116] It is unsatisfactory to argue that human beings do not contain any aspect of 'divine image' in them, just because we are not sure about what exactly the content of the image of God is. Bird stresses again and again the similarity between humanity and the rest of creation in terms of sexuality. But she gives too little attention to the dissimilarity and distinctiveness of humankind from other creatures.[117]

Needless to say, humankind in many respects is unique from other creatures. Clines rightly emphasises here the representational aspect of the image of God. He writes:

> The representational image in the Ancient Near East is intended to portray the character of the god whose image it is; thus, for example, a fertility god may be represented by a bull. So in Genesis 1, man is not a mere cipher, chosen at random by God to be His representative, but to some extent also expresses, as the image, the character of God.[118]

In the light of the above discussion it is difficult to sustain Bird's attempt to detach 'the image of God' from the concept of dominion. In her analysis the humanity only has an external similarity with God, so man becomes merely a cipher. Bird has overemphasised one aspect of the 'image of God' at the expense of the other. In her treatment, she did not find any qualitative relations between the 'image of God' and humankind.

---

[114] See K. H. Bernhardt, *Gott and Bild: Ein Beitrag zur Begründung und Deutung des Bilderverbotes im Alten Testament* (Berlin: Evangelische Verlagsanstalt, 1956), pp. 17–68, as cited by Clines, p. 81.

[115] F. Preisigke, *Vom göttlichen Fluidum nach ägyptischer Anschauung* (Heidelberg: Papyrusinstitut, 1920), p. 11, cited in Clines, p. 82.

[116] Clines, p. 82. Cf. Hayter; she thinks the Priestly writer's intention is to say that 'man is in some way like God'.

[117] Hamilton observes that sexuality is applied to animals only in the flood narrative and not in the creation narrative.. He notes: 'Sexuality is not an accident of nature, nor is it simply a biological phenemenon. Instead it is a gift of God'. See Hamilton, p. 138.

[118] Clines, p. 92. Sawyer also finds certain divine resemblance in human beings, see 'The meaning of בצלם אלהים' pp. 423–426. Cf. Sawyer, 'The Image of God, The Wisdom of Serpents and the Knowledge of Good and Evil', in *A Walk in the Garden: Biblical, Iconographical and Literary Images of Garden* (eds.) P. Morris and D. F. A. Sawyer (JSOTS 136; Sheffield: JSOT Press, 1992), pp. 64–73.

From the above analysis, we see that the use of sources does not lead necessarily to particular conclusions. Lohfink has rightly pointed out the complexity of the ANE sources. He says 'an initial idea that of human beings as "image of God" in the ancient Orient, is found to appear in different cultural regions and, in part, within different contexts and with different meanings'.[119] So he looks for 'a context corresponding to the biblical use' of this concept and interestingly finds it in the Mesopotamian rather than in Egyptian ideas. Although he shares many similar ideas with Bird, he draws parallels mainly from the Babylonian literature, for example especially the Atrahasis epic.

J. H. Walton has also shown the difficulty of using ANE sources. He observes:

> The fact that the Israelites viewed man as the centerpiece of creation afforded him a certain dignity, undergirded by the fact that he was created in the image of God. In contrast, Mesopotamians did not see man as created with dignity. Human beings achieved their dignity by the function they served. In Israelite thought, the created world was man–centered. This was not the case in Mesopotamian thinking.[120]

He thus emphasises the contrast between the Mesopotamian sources and Genesis. So various possibilities make our reading difficult. Sources do not automatically 'give' right interpretations. There is still much room for choice and judgement. Bird's reading has perhaps failed to see how complex this process of interpretation is.

The ambiguity of the terms אדם (*'ādām*) and אנוש (*'enosh*)

Bird is very much concerned about the use of male paradigms as representative of the species both in Gen.1 and in Psalm 8.[121] In this context she thinks that what is affirmed in Genesis 1:27b, that is, 'male and female he created them', 'is undermined linguistically and historically by the consistent representation of the species with male images and masculine terms'.[122]

By and large a similar kind of argument is put forward recently by Francis Watson. He points out that the generic אדם (*'ādām*) in Gen. 1: 27 has become the proper name of the first male by Gen. 5: 1–3. As a result 'the concept of the likeness (or image) of God is therefore related far more closely to the male than in the earlier passage'. He also points out that in this text it is *Adam,* the male who is in the likeness of God, instead of the

---

[119] N. Lohfink, *Theology of the Pentateuch: Themes of the Priestly Narrative and Deuteronomy* (trans.) by Linda M. Maloney (Edinburgh: T&T Clark, 1994), p. 4.

[120] See John H. Walton, *Ancient Israelite Literature in its Cultural Context,* p. 29.

[121] See Bird, "'Bone of My Bone and Flesh of my Flesh'", pp. 521– 534.

[122] Ibid., p. 522.

previous inclusive usage. According to Watson, 'The result is a patriarchal chain of transmission: as God makes Adam in his own image and likeness, so Adam passes on his own image and likeness to Seth, even though the original command to "be fruitful and multiply" was addressed to both male and female (1.28).'[123]

Both Bird and Watson agree that the essential duality of humankind as male and female is stressed in the original word about the human species (Gen. 1:27). Both of them similarly think that this has been undermined in the subsequent personification of the term *Adam* as an individual. If there was proper gender–balance in the original creation order (Gen. 1:27 and 5:2) as Bird and Watson think, why then did the priestly writer narrow it down to the male species alone in the subsequent history?

There is some difficulty with both of their assumptions. Contrary to their argument, context and syntax suggest that אדם (*'ādām*) should be translated as a generic noun, 'humankind' or 'humanity' in Gen. 5:2. It is used here in a collective sense because the plural pronouns, as in בראם (*bera'am*–he created them), ויברך אתם (*wybrk 'otham*–he blessed them), and ויקרא את שמם אדם (*wyqra 'et shemam 'ādām* –he called their name humanity) require this translation.[124] Moreover, we also need to bear in mind that here, by most accounts, the Priestly writer is restating what has already been said earlier in Gen. 1:27 where the word is used entirely in a generic sense.

Now we will respond to Watson's argument that 'the image and likeness of God' is restricted only to Adam and his son Seth, even though it was addressed to both male and female in the original command to be 'fruitful and multiply' in Gen. 1:28. First of all we need to note that no change has taken place in the original command. The birth of Seth is a fulfilment of the command to multiply (in a narrative, or even a canonical reading, the juxtaposition of 5: 1–3 with 4: 25–26 (J) where Eve names Seth, may only serve to heighten this point).[125] Adam's emphasis on creating Seth in his own image and likeness could plausibly mean two things. First, this could be a reiteration that even after the fall and the grave sin of murder, human beings are still created in the image of God.[126] Less probably, I think, this may

---

[123] See F. Watson, *Text, Church and the World: Biblical Interpretation in Theological Perspective* (Edinburgh: T&T Clark, 1994), p. 193.

[124] Cf. NRSV which correctly translates אדם here as 'humankind'; my own translation.

[125] Although I acknowledge that this passage belongs to a different source, my argument will be in line with a literary narrative reading of the passage. Ilana Pardes argues that in order to understand the femininity in Gen. 1–3, the analysis of Gen. 4–5 is essential because she finds Eve's role in questioning many of the patriarchal world views by creating and naming children, see Pardes, 'Beyond Genesis 3: The Politics of Maternal Naming', pp. 173–193.

[126] See Sawyer, pp. 421–22; Wenham, p.127.

343335

simply mean that Seth was of similar physical appearance to his father.[127] In either case, this text may not have the patriachalising significance that Watson saw. The priority of the masculine can be seen even in the very text which both Bird and Watson referred to. For instance, the masculine pronoun אתם (*atam* or *otam*) is used even in Gen.1:27 which they claimed to be the 'original word' on sexuality.[128]

Even if we are strict to the sources, then one probably expects Gen. 5 to be understood in the light of Gen. 1, where אדם (*'ādām*) is generic and inclusive of both sexes. The comparison between Gen. 1 and 5 may thus be interpreted in favour of Gen. 5 just as well as against it. Moreover, the changes may be accounted for in terms of the narrative's logic, as the narrator goes on tell of a genealogical development in the primeval history. So the ambiguity built into the term אדם (*'ādām*) is exploited for this purpose. In that case the changes cannot be postulated as a shift in ideology.

The dominance of the male gender is a general feature of the Bible. Instead of talking in inclusive terms the Bible generally talks in male terms. This has been noted even before the feminist movement.[129] Bird thinks that the 'generic masculine' is a 'sign of social and political subordination'.[130] She writes: 'the most serious problem, in my view, concerns the generally unnoted bias of texts that appear to speak in general terms, or may be interpreted inclusively, but are framed in terms of male experience, needs, and perceptions'.[131] So אדם (*'ādām*) could be seen still as an inclusive term within a broadly androcenrtic view of the world. However, Bird has pushed Gen. 5:3 too hard to say that אדם (*'ādām*) has become exclusively male.

In the light of much other Old Testament evidence, it is hard to establish that the generic names אדם (*'ādām*) and אנוש (*'enosh*) became exclusively male images as Bird assumed. Bird thinks that the psalmist's use of אנוש (*'enosh*) and בן–אדם (*ben–'ādām*; Ps. 8:5) are male terms. She also points out that אנוש (*'enosh*) is a masculine noun with no feminine counterpart, and 'the collective *'ādām* is individualised by the use of the 'son" to indicate a member of the class'.[132] First of all, however, we need to remember that אנוש (*'enosh*) is also a generic name with the same meaning as that of אדם (*'ādām*).[133] This noun is probably derived from the verb אנש (*enosh*) mean-

---

[127] Wenham, p. 30.

[128] See Bruce K. Waltke and M. O' Connor (eds.), *An Introduction to Biblical Syntax* (Winona Lake: Eisenbrauns, 1990), p. 108.

[129] See Clarence J. Vos, *Women in Old Testament Worship*, pp. 32–50.

[130] Bird, 'Bone of My Bone', p. 532.

[131] Ibid., pp. 532–33.

[132] Bird, 'Bone of my Bones', p. 522.

[133] See *BDB*, p. 60; cf. *The Hebrew and Aramaic Lexicon of the Old Testament : The New Koehler, Baumgartner in English*, ה–א, vol. I (Leiden: E.J. Brill, 1994), p. 70.

ing 'weak' or 'sick'. In many cases the noun אנוש (*enosh*) is used in the Bible to indicate the feeble and mortal nature of humankind (Ps. 8:5, 90:3; Jb. 25: 4, 6; Is. 51:12). Moreover, the noun בן–אדם (*ben–'ādām*) is used synonymously along with אנוש (*'enosh*) in Hebrew poetry. (Ps. 8:5, 90:3; Jb. 25:6). In some places אדם (*'ādām*) and בן–אנוש (*ben–'enosh*) are used in juxtaposition (see Ps. 144:3).

There is no doubt that humankind was represented in male terms. We should not overlook the ambiguity of the term אדם (*'ādām*) all through the Old Testament usage and also need to remember that the term has been used both as a proper and generic name even after Gen. 5:3. For instance, in Moses' address he refers back to the creation: ('ever since the day that God created human beings [אדם] on the earth', Dt. 4:32).

We note here that אדם (*'ādām*) represents humankind, not merely the male species alone. My point is that though in Gen. 5:3 אדם (*'ādām*) is used as a proper name, it is not appropriate to argue that it excludes the female. It is true that humanity is represented in male terms, but I do not think it is a transition point to an androcentric world view as Bird and Watson argued.[134] Given the absence of inclusive usage, the text may not necessarily be androcentric. Even now in many non–western societies the male represents both sexes. For instance, when somebody says that he/she is the son/daughter of Mr.X, the implication is that he/she is also the son of Mrs.X. In eastern societies people rarely say he/she is the son/daughter of Mr & Mrs. X; rather son/daughter of either Mr. X or Mrs. X. One of the parents is enough to convey the idea. The question is whether it is due to androcentric orientation or due to social and cultural conventions. There is no straightforward answer to this.

Woman protecting man

In some cases Bird seems to push her own exegetical conclusions overlooking other similar possibilities. A typical example could be the way she interprets Jer. 31: 22 ('a woman encompasses a man'– last stich). Any reader of the MT[135] knows that the meaning of the phrase נקבה תסובב גבר ('a female encompasses a man') is enigmatic. The verb סבב (*sbb*) could be either 'encompass' or 'surround'. Following Holladay Bird interpreted it as 'a woman protects a man'. Although this is attractive, we need to note that it is one among several possibilities. It could also be a proverb, or an irony in

---

[134] See also Job. 5: 7, 14:1, 20: 4, 25:6, Is. 45:12. There are quite a number of references to אדם through out the Old Testament which are used in a generic manner.

[135] The LXX rendering does not offer any help as it reads: 'in safety men shall go out', *The Septuagint Version of the Old Testament* (Jeremias XXXVIII: 22) (London: S. Bagster & Sons Ltd/New York: James Pot & Co., n.d).

the sense of something unusual happening in the land.[136] It could also be taken as an image of Israel when she herself would become her own protector rather than being under the protectorship of great powers.[137] Here it seems that Bird, even as historical critic, ignores exegetical possibilities which do not support her case.

HERMENEUTICAL DIFFICULTIES

Feminist mindset

The problem in Bird's interpretation is a hesitation between methods. For instance, her historical–critical investigation leads her to see P as patriarchal and hence not teaching equality. Yet she uses the text in favour of equality and the feminist programme. This seems to be a fundamental hermeneutical problem. In exegesis and analysis of the *imago Dei* passage of Genesis, she does not find any equal status between the man and the woman. Nonetheless, Bird takes the same text as a foundation text for a feminist egalitarian anthropology.[138] At the same time she argues that the equality between the sexes neither makes the priestly writer a feminist nor frees the text from patriarchal assumptions. Here we can observe an apparent tension between her exegesis and hermeneutics.

Bird's treatment of the text is problematic at two levels. That is, first as a historical–critic, she attempts to unearth the intention of the author from the text. However, as a feminist critic, to establish a feminist–egalitarian ideology she finds something 'unintended' and 'unforeseen' by the ancient author in the same text. If a text has many meanings which are unintended by the ancient author, we may ask, what is the relevance of determining authorial intention as Bird does here?

However, Bird's literary reading of the final canonical form of the Yahwistic text still allows an egalitarian reading. This was the case even with her reading of the Priestly narrative of Genesis 1. Although we have noted the methodological difficulty in bringing out an egalitarian reading as advo-

---

[136] For a wide range of opinions see Robert P. Carroll, *Jeremiah*, OTL (London: SCM Press, 1986), pp. 601–602. For a diametrically opposite viewpoint, see C. F. Keil & Delitzsch, *Jeremiah and Lamentations: Commentary on the Old Testament*, Vol. 8 (Grand Rapids: William B. Eerdmans, 1984), pp. 29–30. They provide a sort of chauvinistic reading in contrast to a feminist reading. They advocate that the new thing which God creates involves the woman who is weaker in nature surrounding the man, the stronger one, for help. I do not see anything new about this as far as the man–woman relationship is concerned.

[137] See Douglas Rawlinson Jones, *Jeremiah*, NCBC (Grand Rapids: William B. Eerdmans/London: Marshall Pickering, 1992), p. 396. Cf. also J. A. Thompson, *The Book of Jeremiah*, NICOT (Grand Rapids:Willaim B. Eerdmans, 1980), pp. 575–76.

[138] See Bird, 'Sexual Differentiation and Divine Image', p. 25.

cated by Trible, still there are insights in the Genesis text to be interpreted in a way which would bring a gender–balance.[139]

The problem with Trible and Bird is that both of them have overstated their case. While Trible found equality in everything, Bird in her historical critical reading found exactly the opposite–i.e. no equality at all in P's formulation. I think the truth lies somewhere between these two extreme positions.

Bird versus Trible

I would like to weigh here the similarities and differences between Bird and Trible since both of them have heavily depended on Gen.1:27 to argue their case. Both Bird and Trible rely too much on this phrase: 'male and female he created them'. First of all, regarding the structure of the passage: Trible thinks the phrase 'male and female' explicates the meaning of the 'image of God', as she thinks 'the image of God' and 'male and female' are parallel in structure, whereas Bird argues 'the parallelism of the two cola is progressive, not synonymous. The second statement adds to the first; it does not explicate it'.[140] Bird argues that the phrase here connotes biological function, linking with verse 28 about the procreation, whereas Trible thinks it has a sociological function, and that sexual differentiation entails equality not hierarchy. In short, for Bird, sexual differentiation means procreation, and for Trible equality. Both arguments are partially true, but that is not the full statement of the truth. Sexual differentiation in a broader context entails all these aspects together. Emphasising one aspect over the other is a mistake.

THEOLOGICAL DIFFICULTIES

Phyllis Bird's interpretation of the text in the light of ANE texts brings theological difficulties. Although we may well have insights from the parallel texts, too much reliance on those sources may not yield clear results. Although in a different context, Rogerson notes: 'There is no direct evidence in Genesis 1–11 that these chapters are referring to creation and flood stories known from ancient Mesopotamia, or to Egyptian and Assyrian notions of the king as the image of the god.'[141] So I would argue that the 'ca-

---

[139] See B. S. Childs, *Old Testament Theology in a Canonical Context*, pp. 188–89. Childs' method is somewhat similar to Trible, in focusing on the final form of the text. He notes: 'No differentiation is made between male and female in terms of temporal priority or function. Their creation occurs simultaneously and only together is their creative role described. Surely this is a witness of absolute equality', ibid., p. 189. Cf. Mary Evans, *Woman in the Bible*, pp. 12–17; Mary Hayter, *The New Eve in Christ*, pp. 96ff.

[140] Bird, 'Sexual Differentiation', p. 17.

[141] Rogerson, *Genesis 1–11*, pp. 47–48. Rogerson however, never denies the advantage of understanding Gen. 1–11 in the light of extra–biblical sources. In fact, that is the

nonical' dimension should not be lost from the reading of the biblical texts. In similar vein Rogerson shows the importance of reading the text as 'communication from God to humanity'.[142]

Rogerson suggests certain practical guidelines to determine the authority of any reading. In his view, 'a reading is more likely to be "authoritative" if it eliminates uncertainties'.[143] He illustrates this point by stating that 'the final form of the text exists, whereas the discerning of the sources is theoretical'.[144] In a similar vein he also thinks that 'the motivation of the writers', and the influence on them from other stories from the ancient world seems to be uncertain. So he proposes that 'an interpretation whose aim was to discover the intentionality of the final form of Genesis 1–11 from the inner dynamics of the text was more "authoritative" than readings which resulted from assumptions that were no more than plausible'.[145] This may usefully be brought to bear on Bird's readings. Bird wanted to isolate the sources behind the final form of the text, and determine their influence on it. In some cases, I suggest, she relied too much on extra–biblical sources, and has done too little justice to the evidence within the text itself for a particular case (for instance, the relationship between sexuality and dominion). Another case is the topic of disobedience. This she does not consider original in the text, although it is present now because of the work of the Yahwist. Previously it was an 'etiological tale', 'describing fundamental conditions of life', before the Yahwist writer added the idea of sin.[146] Here too, however, there is unclarity about the status of the pre–canonical text, and thus the real usefulness to her of the historical method she has adopted.[147]

PRACTICAL DIFFICULTIES

Phyllis Bird and the question of authority

The authority of the Bible as God's word and its relevance to Christian faith and practice have been constantly and vigorously challenged in recent years by feminist readers. Bird also has grappled with the issue of authority in

---

point Rogerson is making there. Although context is different, his statement about the relation between Gen. 1–11 and ANE sources remains true.

[142] Rogerson, *Genesis 1–11*, p. 48.

[143] Ibid ., p. 49.

[144] Ibid.

[145] Ibid.

[146] Similar argument was proposed by Westermann, see *Genesis 1–11*, p. 196.

[147] Cf. Childs, he writes: 'There is no canonical warrant for interpreting these chapters as a description of the quality of life constitutive of being human. Rather, the point of the paradisal state is to contest the ontological character of human sinfulness. Mankind was not created in alienation either from God or his fellows.' See *Introduction to the Old Testament as Scripture*, London, SCM, 1979, p. 155.

her recent works.[148]   Because of the prevailing androcentrism in the text
and the culture she asserts that 'Scripture is a human product and instru-
ment, and therefore, culturally conditioned and limited'.[149]   In her view, the
authority of Scripture does not lie with the infallible words of the text or
model behaviour, 'but in the truth of its witness to a creating and redeeming
power, which can and must be known as a present reality'.[150]   Although she
questions traditional views regarding the inspiration, inerrancy, and infalli-
bility of the Scripture, due to its patriarchal nature, she still finds a 'norm
within the tradition and the scriptures'[151] that speaks against the androcentric–patriarchal ordering.   Hence she writes: 'Feminist critique is rooted in
the gospel, or in an ideal of full humanity that is consonant with the gospel,...Christian feminists find resources of judgement and alternative vision
in the gospel transmitted by the church and informed by the Scriptures.'[152]
In short, in Bird's view, the Scripture functions both negatively and positively for feminists, negatively as a weapon of patriarchy and positively as a
critical norm against patriarchy.[153]   How may these two positions be recon-
ciled with each other?

Another implication of Bird's view of biblical authority is that now the
authority does not reside with the text; rather in the 'present reality' which
is seen in its 'redeeming power'. At the same time she finds 'a norm within
the tradition and scriptures'. However, if they do not have any authority
within themselves it is fair to ask how they may function as a norm for
feminists? If the authority resides with feminist experience, then the Bible
has only a secondary authority in feminist hermeneutics. Contrary to Bird's
method of historical–critical investigation, her authority emerges not out of
the text but out of 'present reality'. This is an apparent anomaly.

In the context of diverse materials on the status and position of woman
in the Old Testament, one should have a proper balance in showing both the

---

[148] Bird, 'The Authority of the Bible', in *NIB* vol. 1., pp. 33–64; *Feminism and the Bi-ble.*

[149] Bird, *The Authority of the Bible*, p. 62.

[150] Ibid., p. 63.

[151] This norm is 'interpreting and judging Scripture', ibid., p. 62.

[152] *Feminism and the Bible,* Bird thinks that the heart of the Gospel Message is that 'God has chosen to dwell among us, as one of us, and that we know God because we have seen God in our own likeness'. p. 73. However, Bird seems to be reluctant to use the term Jesus or Christ in her discourse but she only alludes to Jesus' incarnation. In this respect, her theology of incarnation appears to be 'theo–centric'.   Moreover, Bird also tries to find God in the prophet of Montgomery and Memphis, Martin Luther King, and in Mother Theresa; this may be an idea of the incarnation of the deity in other hu-man beings.

[153] Her view concerning authority is some what similar to Mary Ann Tolbert's view. See, Tolbert, 'Defining the Problem: The Bible and Feminist Hermeneutics', *Semeia* 28 (1983), pp. 113–126.

positive and negative about woman in the Old Testament. When we take into consideration the various aspects of life in the ancient orient, probably we may find more positive than negative about woman in the Old Testament.[154] If we can keep a proper balance between these two aspects within the biblical tradition, then we do not have to regard the Bible as irredeemably patriarchal.

Conclusion

We have seen Bird's contribution to biblical hermeneutics in general and her specific contribution to feminist hermeneutics in particular. We will summarise them here.

(i) First of all, Bird has made a contribution to the syntactical question regarding Gen. 1: 26–28. We have noted that James Barr has made use of her conclusions in his discussion of this passage. Moreover, we noted the various syntactical possibilities that he highlighted. This is an important datum for all who would use this text in the feminist argument. This syntactical discussion, therefore, illustrates the complexity of interpretation in this area.

(ii) She also made a contribution to the theological question: Bird's critique of Barth, for his treatment of *imago Dei* as the *analogia relationis* is significant here. Because of the Priestly theology of transcendence, she argued that this sort of correspondence between God and human beings was difficult.

(iii) Another contribution of Bird's is specifically to the feminist question of the 'equality' of sexes. She denied this to P, on the grounds of his patriarchal outlook. Her study reiterates the fact that 'equality' can be argued to be a modern concept read into the text. Accordingly, in her later writings, Bird had to go beyond the horizon of the text to bring out the feminist notion of egalitarianism .

(iv) The challenge Bird has posed to Trible, for all the above reasons, seems to be remarkable. In the same line with Barth, Trible has argued for a 'semantic correspondence' between the 'image of God' and male and female in Gen. 1: 26–28, implying equality between male and female in this creation account. But Bird argued that the passage tells nothing about the sociological function; and the phrase 'male and female' shows only the biological function of procreation. She reminded the contemporary theologian–exegete that 'the Bible is often quite uninterested in, or unable to comprehend, the questions pressed upon the text from modern perspectives and experiences'.[155] If Bird is right, Trible's 'centre' cannot hold.

---

[154] Cf. P. Joyce, 'Feminist Exegesis of the Old Testament', pp. 1–7.

[155] 'Male and Female He Created Them', 1981.

With regard to Bird's methodology, we have noted the problems associated with the selection and use of sources, especially in the case of ancient Near Eastern texts. We have argued that any conclusion based on these texts remains only one among many possibilities. The use of sources, therefore, must be pressed in tandem with proper attention to the text itself, in its canonical form. This aspect has been rightly pointed out by Rogerson.

We have pointed out the complexity of her hermeneutical presuppositions. In fact, we have seen Bird's struggle in advocating a feminist egalitarian reading in the context of modern hermeneutical assumptions, although she found the P source does not allow this reading.

In her first article,[156] she argued for the equality of male and female in both creation accounts. She even went to the extent of suggesting that 'The P formulation implies an essential equality of the two sexes'. This was in line with the revisionary feminist approach during the period. Responding to Barth in her later work, she argued that the P writer was not a feminist, nor was likely to give an egalitarian reading.[157] Nonetheless, she argued that in the 'supplementary' Yahwistic account 'the primary meaning of sexuality is seen in psycho–social' terms which imply that the 'basic tone of the account [is] a tone of mutuality and equality'. Bird's notion of sexuality and equality has not ceased there. In another later work, she has brought out a feminist egalitarian theology of sexuality with the help of a post–modern reader–response approach, arguing there are meanings in the texts which are 'unintended' and 'unforeseen' by the original author, although she still considers the P writer does not bring this out. Her main argument is 'the word once written is released from the author's control to acquire new and unintended, or unenvisioned meanings'.[158] If that is the case, there is no justification for Bird to look for the intention of the author in the text since it has no efficacy due to the emergence of new meanings. At the same time, Bird still maintained her earlier stance on the Yahwistic account, emphasising the equality of the two. However, in her latest work, she has argued in line with Clines that in the Yahwistic account 'procreation seems to lie at the base of the plot' with regard to woman's help to man.[159] In short, Bird began with the equality of sexes in both the creation accounts and ended up now with an opposite conclusion negating this claim. Yet she finds equality in the Priestly writing 'as unintended and unforeseen by the ancient author'. And this egalitarian reading 'belongs to a new context of

---

[156] 'Images of Women in the Old Testament', 1974. See our section on 'the development of Bird's Sexuality'.
[157] '"Male and Female He Created Them"', 1981.
[158] 'Sexual Differentiation and Divine Image', 1991, p. 24.
[159] 'Bone of My Bone and Flesh of My Flesh', 1994, p. 525.

interpretation, in answer to a new question beyond the horizon of the ancient author'.[160]

Therefore, Bird's theology of sexuality derives mainly not out of her historical critical readings, but out of her reading of the text within the framework of 'women's experience and feminist critique of patriarchy'. In the final analysis Bird's reading also promotes a kind of egalitarian status between the male and female although she advocated earlier that the P writer was not an 'equal rights theologian'. Here we find a tension between the findings of her historical critical reading and her articulation of a theology of sexuality. If multiple and changing contexts allow the interpreter to find new meaning, then Bird has no right to critique either Barth or Trible.

Bird's study shows the difficulty involved in analysing and evaluating extra–biblical sources and the question of how much weight should be given to hypothetical previous forms of the canonical text. In any case, it shows the weakness of historical criticism as a tool for proceeding from the text to any kind of synthetic interpretation. This is behind the inconsistency in her work; her hope that historical critical work on the text would lead to results favouring the feminist point of view was not fulfilled. This shows the need always for historical criticism as a method to be supplemented by some other method in the pursuit of a synthetic interpretation.

Other Writers

5.6 Helen Schüngel–Straumann

The German scholar Helen Schüngel–Straumann reads the creation narratives in the traditional source–critical framework.[161] Through this setting, she negates the chronological sequence of Genesis 1 and Gen. 2–3 and hence denies that the latter chapters are an explanation of the former. Like many feminists she believes that anti–woman arguments are not inherent in the text; rather, in her view, they are propagated through the 'history of interpretation'.[162]

In her readings, first Schüngel–Straumann provides the 'reception history of the man–woman theme', then she goes on to give her own reading

---

[160] 'Sexual Differentiation', p. 29, note 22.
[161] Schüngel–Straumann, 'On the creation of Man and Woman in Genesis 1–3: The History and Reception of the Texts Reconsidered', in T. Schneider (ed.), *Mann and Frau: Grundproblem theologischer Anthropologie* (Freiburg: Herder, 1989), pp. 142–66. Reprinted in *A Feminist Companion to Genesis*, pp. 53–76. Although she dates the P source during the exilic period, her dating of the J source is later than tenth century BCE.
[162] Ibid., p. 53.

of the text. We will be examining only her readings of the text, as the former lies beyond the scope of our work.

She takes Gen.2–3 as an aetiological story. Similarly, she thinks that the story of woman is added by the J writer as she thinks that 'the verses on the creation of the woman, the dialogue between the woman and the serpent, and the so called curses do not fit into this context'.[163] Concerning the status of woman, she argues that עזר (*'ezer*) is not a subordinate but rather a 'permanent, equal partner, corresponding to the man as a genuine counterpart' in contrast to the Gilgamesh epic where woman is created only for a short time.[164] She refutes the notion of woman as the 'seductress' and shows that both woman and man eat 'together' from the forbidden tree. She further points out that the author's intention in Genesis 3 is to show that there are set limits for humans. 'To become divine or like Elohim, not to stay human, is the temptation'.[165]

With regard to the curses, she writes that these are not included in the old source. Moreover, she takes J's account of the punishment as aetiological, explaining the situation that prevailed then. She again notes that 'he shall rule over you' is not an 'unconditional command', but rather a miserable situation. Here it is worth quoting her reasoning at length:

> Just as with the other descriptions of given conditions, this sentence explains what happened against God's will at the time when J lives. In other words, a woman steps in the direction intended by God, whenever and wherever she tries to shake off the unjust, oppressive rule of the man. Thus, the feminist movement could be interpreted as a movement towards the original plan of creation which J did not find in his own life time.[166]

In addition she argues that man's rule over the woman is a 'sin', 'breaking away from God', and 'a perversion of the order that God wanted'.[167]

Schüngel–Straumann has an impressive suggestion with regard to the patriarchal nature of the J material. Although she acknowledges 'J's origin in a patriarchal society, she notes that 'J was concerned with the woman as a full human being, wherever he might have gathered his material'.[168] She goes for a balanced status of woman against either the tendency to demon-

---

[163] Ibid., p. 65. Schüngel–Straumann argues this in the light of Ezekiel 28, where woman is not mentioned, and only man is responsible for sin due to his arrogance. She thinks Gen. 2–3 is based on this old myth.

[164] Ibid., pp. 66–67.

[165] Ibid., p. 70. She thinks Elohim refers to the Canaanite gods.

[166] Ibid., p. 71. So Bird.

[167] Ibid., p. 72.

[168] Ibid.

ise 'the woman' or the attempt to 'make an original goddess of her'. She
notes that in contrast to the common belief of J's time, 'this biblical theologian depicts "the woman" as an equal and equally human partner of "the
man"....J wanted to show their *togetherness* ; he does not look at what they
are in her own or his own right'.[169]

She considers that P's theological explanation of creation holds a 'high
degree of authority' by virtue of its position in the Bible, and due to its
theological content, namely 'Man's place in creation, the relationship between God and man, between human beings themselves and with the whole
of creation,...'.[170]

She views Gen. 1:26 (the creation of male and female in God's image)
as a summary of Gen. 2:18 ('It is not good for the man to be alone'). Then
its implication is 'humankind as a whole, in female and male manifestation,
is God's image'.[171] She understands the meaning of 'the image of God' as
ruling (vv 26&28) in the light of ancient oriental Egyptian ideology where
king or queen represents deity. She notes even in Israel only outstanding
individuals perform that role. Contrary to this 'P regards all human beings
as God's representatives.'[172] This democratisation of rule is specially noted
by Schüngel–Straumann. She thinks humankind's rule over other the rest
of creation is a shepherding role: leading and protecting the people. She asserts: 'As God's representative, humankind is responsible for the creatures,
just as God is for the whole of creation.'[173] The outcome of her reading is
twofold. First of all, humankind is permitted to rule over the rest of creation, not other humans. Secondly, both male and female together are qualified for this rule. So she points out that the Genesis statement *'explicitly
excludes'* man's rule over woman.[174] In a way she thinks the P source con-
firms her reading of J (Gen. 2–3) because she thinks if there was any
change concerning this aspect, P would have rectified it. As we have already noted for J, the rule of the man over the woman is the consequence of
sin whereas the P writer who does not deal with 'explicit sin–tale' 'presents, in poetical/rhythmic form, a Creation/Image–of–God statement'.[175]
In summary, she argues that like J, P also does not allow man to rule over
woman. In short in her view 'whenever the man rules over the woman and
she suffers from such rule, this is against the aim of creation, a perversion
of the original plan'.[176]

---

[169] Ibid; emphasis original.
[170] Ibid., p. 73.
[171] Ibid., p. 74.
[172] Ibid.
[173] Ibid.
[174] Ibid., pp. 74–75.
[175] Ibid., p. 74.
[176] Ibid., p. 75.

Schüngel–Straumann believes that both P and J accounts of creation in some respects surpass their ancient Near Eastern counterparts. However, Phyllis Bird places the biblical narratives in parallel with the ancient creation stories. The historical critics (Bird and Schüngel–Straumann) interpret P in the light of J and the literary critics do the reverse (Alter, Trible, Pardes, Bal *et al.*). All these readings show how our approaches shape our conclusions.

5.7 Luise Schottroff

Luise Schottroff, a German feminist scholar, reads the creation narrative (Gen. 1: 1–2: 4a) from a historical perspective.[177] She brings to home the creation narrative by setting it against the Babylonian exile. She thinks this story of creation is addressed to the Jewish people in Babylonian exile. Apart from feminist concerns, she addresses ecological issues, the misuse of God's good creation by humanity through abuse and exploitation. In her view the practical question raised by the creation narrative is whether we live as masters or as image of God.[178]

She argues that in the creation narrative both men and women are images of God 'in the same way'. So she locates anti–feminist attitudes with the interpretations only. For Schottroff, feminist concerns come out of a broader vision. 'It is a vision of justice among peoples. Justice shall reign between black and white, between men and women. All people are created equally in God's likeness. There shall be neither poverty nor wealth. The end of racism and class oppression is also part of the feminist vision'.[179]

Like many feminist writers, Schottroff also thinks that the misery of humanity in Gen. 3:16–19 is not the original intention of the Creator; rather a 'disorder'. She finds that God 'joins man and woman in equality and justice'.[180]

Through her reading Schottroff envisions broader concerns which include both men and women. Her reading crosses the boundaries of feminist concerns. She attempts to make the biblical text relevant to our present struggle against ecological crisis, racism, poverty and class oppression. So her concerns are broader in comparison with many other feminist writers.

---

[177] Schottroff, 'Die Schöpfungsgeschichte Gen. 1, 1–2, 4a', in Luise und Willy Schottroff, *Die Macht der Auferstehung: Sozialgeschichtliche Bibelauslegungen* (Munich: Kaiser Verlag, 1988), pp. 8–26. This has been translated in *A Feminist Companion to Genesis*, 'The Creation Narrative: Genesis 1.1–2.4a', pp. 24–38.

[178] Ibid., p. 35.

[179] Ibid., p. 37.

[180] Ibid. Here she refers to Gen. 2.

5.8 Mary Hayter

The British feminist, Mary Hayter looks at the creation narratives from a literary–historical perspective in her work, *The New Eve in Christ.*[181] She sets apart two chapters[182] to discuss the man–woman relationship in the creation narratives. Her main intention seems to be to refute many of the traditional arguments which place woman in a secondary or a subordinate role both in the Church and in society. So her reading falls under recuperative approach. In that respect her work is similar to Trible. In her exegesis she takes on board many of Trible's exegetical conclusions. However, she seems to avoid Trible's tendency to over–emphasise her points. Hayter's main contribution lies in the fact that she could expose many traditional male interpretations which depict woman as the cause for all evil and thereby assign a subordinate role to woman. She also shares some similarities with Schüngel–Straumann in her argument that both J and P narratives depict woman as an equal partner with man. Like Trible and others she also regards that man's ruling over woman is descriptive not causative or prescriptive.

One of the main problems in her reading is that she unquestioningly accepts some of Trible's arguments, such as that naming involves a set formula. On the whole, however, her reading seems to be a balanced feminist reading of the text.

Conclusion

In this main section of our thesis, we have analysed both sympathetically and critically the feminist readings of Genesis 1–3. We have discussed at length the readings of three major feminist writers, Phyllis Trible, Carol Meyers and Phyllis A. Bird. Although every one approached the text with a revisionary stance to recover the text positive to women, at some points, they were carried beyond their chosen methods by their feminist commitments. So we have pointed out the inadequacies of their arguments in relevant sections. In addition to the above three writers, we have also examined a few other minor feminist writers who have been influenced in one way or another by the above. Our readings show that feminist interpreters read the same text differently, even while using the same methodology.

Despite these differences, almost all the feminist writers are united in exposing the patriarchy and the androcentrism of the biblical text. Each agrees that patriarchy is in the text. However, feminists are deeply divided over the question, how far one could retrieve the text from patriarchal domination and interpretation. Acknowledging the authority of the text,

---

[181] Hayter, *The New Eve in Christ.*
[182] See, pp. 83–117

scholars like Trible and Fleming, Schüngel–Straumann, Schottroff, Korsak, and Meyers, have attempted to depatriarchalise the text by rereading and unearthing feminine imageries. Going one step further, Meyers and Laffey have approached the text with a 'hermeneutics of suspicion' as they have believed that the textual representation is not value–free. Yet, they offered an egalitarian reading of the creation text along with the above revisionary readers. Bird has adapted a different tack; although she has utilised the historical–critical method, at the end she promoted an egalitarian reading against her own conclusions. So those who want to make the text positive to woman, in one way or another underscored the equal status of the woman in the original creation stories. All of them have agreed that the man's rule or domination over the woman is the result of the corporate disobedience of the human couple, irrespective of their background or methodology.

Due to the influence of post–modernism, we have seen that many feminist writers have started reading against the 'grain of the text' to show how patriarchal and androcentric the texts are. So they adopted a 'hermeneutics of resistance' to resist the biblical androcentrism. These do not think that the text can be redeemed from patriarchal bias. Brenner, Rashkow, Fewell, Milne and Bal represent this group. However, Pardes found antithetical female counter–voices in the biblical text itself, challenging patriarchy.

Our study shows that feminist readings are complex both because of the various methodologies and different pre–suppositions employed in reading. It leads to multiple readings and various conclusions concerning the man–woman relationship in Gen. 1–3.

Conclusion

6.1 Is the Old Testament Irredeemably Patriarchal?

Alongside our conclusions to each chapter in relevant sections, we now come to conclusions to our study of feminist readings of Genesis 1–3 as a whole. The main contribution of feminist readings can be seen in the sphere of contemporary debate on androcentrism versus egalitarianism. Interestingly, the creation texts of Gen. 1–3 have been widely used to argue both the case to expose biblical androcentrism and also to establish egalitarianism. One might admit that the feminist biblical critics indeed expose the traditional claim of biblical scholarship to be objective and value–free while it was androcentric and oppressive to women and marginalised them in the Church and academia. Moreover, it also alerts us that there is no value–free, objective biblical criticism as was claimed hitherto. Rather every reader brings to the text his or her own presuppositions. Moreover, feminist readings enabled the traditional scholars to re–examine many of their hermeneutical assumptions in the context of the feminist challenge.

To this extent the feminist socio–critical enterprise has been successful. However, feminist criticism is not a method in biblical studies like Rhetorical Criticism or Structuralist Criticism, but rather a new approach to the reading of the text with gender issues in focus. All feminists use one of the available interpretative methods to read the text feministically. The main difference of their reading from traditional scholarship, therefore, is the difference in presuppositions. Most of the feminist readers read the text mainly through the glasses of gender. Whereas in the traditional readings, there are many hermeneutical foci and gender issues are not a major concern, in feminist scholarship gender concerns are the main focus. As feminist readings address only gender issues, they answer only a few questions among many interpretative questions one could ask to the biblical text. This is the built in limitation in feminist hermeneutics. This illustrates the methodological dilemma of feminism. How far are they adapting existing methods, and operating within mainline scholarship; and how far are they doing something radically different?

The main scholars whom we have examined, Trible, Meyers, Bird, have made use of traditional hermeneutical methods, namely, Rhetorical Criticism, Social–scientific Criticism and Historical–Criticism. Trible has arguably been successful in bringing a 'feminist reading' out of her method. But neither Meyers nor Bird was able to offer a fully feminist reading within the framework of her own methodology. Therefore, they moved beyond their initial methods to a literary reading in Meyers' case and a kind of reader–response in Bird in order to fulfil their feminist goals. Nevertheless, each had a single focus, namely, to argue for 'egalitarianism' in the text.

With regard to their hermeneutical strategies, feminist interpreters have used various hermeneutical approaches in reading the creation texts. In the first phase, in the 1970's, the main approach was the *hermeneutics of recuperation.* Accordingly, feminist scholars like, P. Trible and P. Bird offered a revisionary reading, and thereby attempted to free biblical interpretation from the patriarchal domination and through their reading, they tried to reclaim the biblical texts in a way that was positive to women. At this stage, for Trible and Bird, the problem was not with the text *per se* but only with the misogynist interpretations. However, many feminists after them, thought that the problem of patriarchy was deeper and very much embedded within the text itself. So they opted for a *hermeneutic of suspicion* to read the text. Using a sociological method, Carol Meyers argued that the textual representation of women in the Bible is biased due to its patriarchal orientation, so she applied a hermeneutic of suspicion to try to unearth the social reality which lies behind the text.

In the present postmodern phase, feminist readers employ a strategy of *hermeneutics of resistance.* Accordingly, many feminists argue that the biblical text cannot be redeemed and their main goal is to show the patriarchal domination inherent in the text. So they read 'against the grain of the text' to expose its androcentric world–view. Since every reading is equally valid in postmodern understanding, these readings are mainly geared to serve their feminist goals and agendas. So the texts are treated apart from their ancient historical, religious and faith contexts. Many of them have used the text as a 'springboard' to serve their interests. In these readings, no distinction is made between the character of God and human characters. So God is also under serious scrutiny and criticism as any other character in the narrative. Moreover, one of the main aims of postmodern readings is to resist the concept of the 'original meaning' and the objective truth. This approach validates every reading as legitimate. Pardes, Rashkow, Brenner, Bal and Fewell in some degree represent this phase. Even the moderate revisionary readers like Trible and Bird showed postmodern tendencies in their later writings.

These phases illustrate the central question, namely is the Old Testament irredeemably patriarchal? We have seen that feminists approach the text with various hermeneutical presuppositions and theological stances to tackle this question. Our study reveals that despite decades of feminist research, feminists themselves are increasingly divided over their findings. On the one hand, underscoring the religious authority of the text, Trible, Fleming, Korsak, Schüngel–Straumann, Schottroff, Hayter and Rashkow (earlier stage) have argued that although patriarchy is in the text and its interpretations, that is not the 'ideal' biblical world view. It can be overcome through interpretations and reinterpretations. So in hermeneutical terms, this approach comes under socio–criticism, challenging and exposing oppressive structures (in our case patriarchy). Further, in this approach, generally there is room for the fusion of "two horizons' (Gadamer and Thiselton), that is the horizon of the text and the horizon of the interpreter.

On the other hand, Rashkow (later stage), Fewell, Brenner, and Milne argued that the text is irredeemably patriarchal and tried to establish their own self–contained 'feminist academy'. In this approach, there is no room for external critique as they outrightly reject meaning <u>in</u> the text and there is no desire to make sense of the text. Hence, it falls into socio–pragmatism. It does not have 'fusion of horizons' as interpretative process solely at the disposal of the reader.

Some writers are hard to classify. Pardes finds female counter–voices or counter–traditions operating within the Scripture, challenging the dominant male voices. Brenner's recent approach in gendering the text and thereby finding the women's voices is similar to this. Although Meyers and Laffey questioned the authority of the text due to its patriarchy, interestingly, both of them have advocated an egalitarian reading. Although Bal has approached the text with an apathetic attitude, still she found equality in the text. In short, although the above writers do not subscribe to biblical authority completely due to the Bible's patriarchal nature, still they find some things favourable to woman in the text.

The question posed above (is the OT irredeemably patriarchal or not?) reveals the basic hermeneutical issue for feminist scholarship. It conceals within it the question of the 'meaning of the text'. We discussed earlier the issue of 'original meaning' and 'authorial intention' (ch. 1) and found that these concepts are still useful in the modern hermeneutical debate. It is interesting that feminist scholars recognise this, albeit in different ways. 'Egalitarian' readings do so rather positively (also, I think, Watson in his own ways). Others do negatively, e.g. Bal– who says there may be such a thing, but she is not interested in it. Those who see the text as 'irretrievably patriarchal' also agree that there is meaning somehow in the text; the text in its own terms is irreducible.

6.2 The Communicative Intention of the Text

The belief that the text implies meanings in its own terms that are at some level unavoidable has been one of the contentions of this thesis. This has been a basis for evaluation of the theories encountered. The issue then is how far 'meanings' or 'intentions' at the biblical horizon may correspond to or fuse with modern questions and concerns.

Contrary to many feminist writers and indeed others, through this study I have argued that the biblical texts are neither irredeemably patriarchal nor

thoroughly chauvinist as Milne, Jobling, and Clines have argued, nor ide-
ally egalitarian in every respect as Trible and others have advocated.
Rather I argue that the question of equality or inequality falls outside the
concern of the creation account. At the same time, however, the creation
account seems to be generally positive to woman. Clines shows:

> Woman, though by no means man's equal, nevertheless enjoyed a higher
> dignity in Israel than elsewhere in the ancient world; perhaps the most
> striking expression of her status is found in the phrase "a helper, a coun-
> terpart to man" in Genesis 2:18.[1]

At the same time, I admit that there are both positive and negative texts
concerning women in the Old Testament and indeed that the text is shaped
in a patriarchal cultural setting, and reflects an androcentric world view.
However, this does not necessitate that the biblical writers should subscribe
whole–heartedly to their given culture. On the contrary, the creation accounts are understood to be a polemic against the existing cultural norms.
Those who argue for the irretrievably patriarchal nature of the text are
prone to this wrong assumption. Moreover, we are also forced to believe
that the 'communicative intention' of the creation text is to perpetuate patriarchy if the above position is right. On the other hand, those who find ideal
equality in the text may merely be reading modern egalitarian notions into
it. So one needs to be careful in dealing with the diverse material concerning the place of woman in the Old Testament. Danna Nolan Fewell rightly
says: 'we cannot naively accept positive feminist texts as unmediated words
of liberation, neither can we reject negative patriarchal texts as unredeem-
able words of subjugation'.[2] Hitherto, most of the feminists overemphasised
one or the other aspect only.

It seems to me that the real issue is not whether the text is egalitarian or
sexist; it is rather whether the text is positive towards women or anti–
women. As we have already discussed in relevant sections, imposing egalitarianism upon the ancient texts seems to be anachronistic. Feminist readings have highlighted that there are both 'positive' and 'negative' elements
in the biblical texts concerning woman. How do we deal with both positive
and negative? Can we 'maximise the positive' as Paul Joyce suggests or do
we go for a 'theological hermeneutic' as Watson suggests? Accordingly,
Watson suggests that 'the oppression of women does not have the first
word, it is necessary to show that in the nexus of creation and fall there occurs a transition from an egalitarian intention to patriarchal reality. Patriarchy is not grounded in the ultimate order of things; it contravenes the crea-

---

[1] Clines, 'The Image of God in Man', p. 94.
[2] D. N. Fewell, 'Feminist Reading of the Hebrew Bible: Affirmation, Resistance and
Transformation', *JSOT* 39 (1987), p. 82.

tor's intention'.[3] Furthermore, he thinks the existing 'tension between divine purpose and human reality' is not a permanent one. Moreover, he points to the exodus paradigm of liberation from oppression as a model for the elimination of this tension. For him, this exodus paradigm could function as a positive factor towards the deliverance of women from the patriarchal ordering. So Both P. Joyce and F. Watson try to make the biblical tradition meaningful to women despite its patriarchy. In other words, it is arguable that biblical patriarchy is not seen as prescriptive, but only descriptive.

The advantage of this line of argument is that patriarchy can be seen as one among many oppressive structures like anti–semitism, slavery, racism, apartheid, colonial dehumanisation and other similar kinds of oppression. In this context we need to remember the fact that even the womanist (black feminist) writers like Renita J. Weems and others think that they are marginalised and oppressed by white feminists. How far should the mainline feminist scholars try to mend their relationship with black womanists before they mend their relationship with male world?[4] This division between feminists and womanists itself shows that the mainline feminist scholars have failed to address many issues which fall outside the category of gender. These can be overcome to a certain extent and humanity can strive for a changed order of things where everyone is treated with equal worth. If we could mend some of the above oppressive structures in the Church and society in the past, surely we can rectify the problem of patriarchy too. Therefore, in that sense too, the biblical texts can be redeemed from their patriarchal colouring. So we argue that the Bible can function still as both positive and meaningful to women if we recognise the patriarchal domination as a result of the 'fallen' state of affairs.

This line of argument takes for granted that one may look to the text itself for its meaning. It shows too, however, that this is not to advocate a naive view of meaning that sees it as locked within the text. Rather the search for the meaning of the text is only a part of the hermeneutical process which involves both text and reader. Moreover, as we have argued in the methodological chapter, the primary purpose of the biblical text is for a 'communicative function' between God and humanity. In that respect, the text is 'speech acts' of God, given in a particular 'communicative context', and are 'intended to function in a particular manner'. Therefore, hermeneutics in-

---

[3] F. Watson, *Text, Church and World,* p. 191.

[4] There is also apparent tension between Jewish and Christian feminists. A. Brenner writes: 'While feminists are ostensibly committed to fight discrimination on any grounds, anti–Jewish (anti–Israeli) sentiments have been expressed within feminist theory and exegesis'. See *A Feminist Companion to the Hebrew Bible in the New Testament,* p. 26. This final volume of the Feminist Companion to the Bible (first series) addresses this issue at various levels.

volves this dimension of the setting of the text in a theological tradition–
ultimately a theological hermeneutic. So a theological hermeneutic of the
text is vital in dealing with the biblical patriarchy. This theological hermeneutic as we have argued elsewhere assumes that the primary intention of
the biblical text is religious rather than aesthetic.

Those who do not subscribe to the above world–view, still continue to
treat the text as irredeemably patriarchal (e.g. Bal). One of the important
aspects we have noted in our study is that one's presupposition determines
the outcome of any reading, whether it is feminist or sexist. For instance,
many feminists consider that patriarchy is embedded in the text by men as a
device to subordinate women. Many male scholars also share this viewpoint
(Jobling, Clines *et al.*). However, many feminist scholars like Trible and
Fleming who want to remain in the Christian tradition through their recuperative hermeneutics view patriarchal ordering as a result of the 'fall' only.
In fact, Fleming approaches the text with mixed presuppositions (i. e. feminist and theologically conservative). For instance, at one point she has attempted to bring the concept of *protoevangelium* out of the text.

In general feminist readings raise the fundamental hermeneutical question. That is, how far one can read an interpretation *into* a text, instead of
deriving an interpretation *from* a text. The postmodern feminist Bal rightly
recognises this difficulty. She writes:

> There can be no doubt that my interpretations are thoroughly anachronis-
> tic if one wishes to find the 'original meaning' of the stories. I hope it
> has been clear enough that such was not my purpose. Quite the contrary.
> My readings present an alternative to other readings, not a 'correct,' let
> alone the 'only possible' interpretation of what the texts 'really say.'
> Texts trigger readings; that is what they are: the occasion of a reaction.[5]

From the above, one can infer that Bal recognises the fact that finding
the 'original meaning' is also a legitimate purpose in reading. This remains
the case, whether one is trying to find the original meaning of a text or providing an alternative reading in opposition to the original meaning. Moreover, Bal admits that '[if] one can easily disagree with my readings, if only
because one does not share my interests...'.[6] This statement in a way invites
the criticism that feminist readings only have validity among those who
subscribe to their 'interests'. In other words, in modern hermeneutical
terms, feminists or those who are sympathetic to feminist concerns form a
self–contained 'academic community'. What then about the ecclesiastical
academic community who believe that the text primarily has religious sig-

---

[5] Bal, *Lethal Love*, p. 132.
[6] Ibid.

nificance and who therefore have an interest in 'original meaning'? If that
is the case, the scope of feminist readings is limited in comparison with
those readers who are committed to find the "original meaning". Another
problem which Bal's reading raises is the question of the nature of the text.
Is the Bible merely a mythological literary document as she presupposed?
Does the negation of the religious nature of the text in itself limit the outcome of her reading? Is Bal's iconoclastic tendency towards religious readings and her alternative reading project some kind of 'dominance' in the
reading method itself? Is she not using the text as a 'springboard' to say
what she wanted to say?

In many cases feminists lacked a methodological integration so that they
could not achieve what they aimed for. For instance, Meyers' social–
scientific methodology was not adequate to prove her egalitarian case, so
she offered a literary reading along with her sociological method. Here lies
the paradox, the main reason for opting for a social–scientific method, was
due to the inadequacy of the textual representation; but finally, her main
thesis came out of her literary reading of the Genesis chapters. Similarly,
Bird began with exploring the intention of the original author and finally
she looked for something which moved beyond the horizon of the original
author. This shows the inadequacy of any single method to deal with the
multiple hermeneutical issues inherent in a text.

6.3 Further Implications

Feminist readings cannot claim universal significance as the outlook and
value of each culture is different from others. For instance, we have seen
that Indian women's involvement in production tasks cannot guarantee
them high status as in a Western setting. Let me cite another example closer
to home. As a whole the Indian cultural and social situation provides only a
subordinate role to women. The preference of boys over girls in India, is
deeply embedded in certain naïve cultural norms and other superstitious beliefs. For instance, in Indian psyche, a male is inevitable to perpetuate the
family line. According to the Hindu religious rite, an eldest son has got the
prerogative to light the funeral pyre after his father's death. Again, our
family ties and traditions demand that sons should take care of their parents
when they get old. Above all, the economic constraints in getting a daughter married cannot be overlooked due to the Indian dowry system. Therefore, female foetuses are terminated after sex determination through the ul-
tra–scan and other similar technical devices, because girls are considered to
be a burden and boys an asset to the parents in the dominant Hindu Indian
culture. The growing disparity in gender ratio underscores the discrimination against the female.

Postnatal murder is another way to do away with female children. It is
reported from all parts of our country how mercilessly little girls are being

killed soon after their birth. For instance, if an infant is found to be a girl, an ear of grain is put in her throat by her own mother or other in-laws to choke the child to death. In many cases no motherly attention is paid to the newborn, leaving the girl to die unattended. Even if a girl is let to live, gender discrimination and bias continue against her throughout life. Discrimination is evident in the areas of nutrition, education, employment, inheritance, divorce and all other fields. Dowry death, bride burning, child marriage, *Sati* and similar atrocities against women are still common in modern India. In that cultural context, the value and the honour which the Bible attributes to woman is arguably far greater than any other religion could offer to Indian women. Contrary to Western feminist thinking, the Bible, even in the context of traditional interpretation of it, is not enslaving for Indian women; rather it is a source of liberation for them. So modern feminists could offer very little liberation to Indian women through their feminist reading of these texts. In this context, Glenn Yocum rightly notes that for many Euro–American feminists'

> categories of analysis are not always universalisable and that therefore not all of their political objectives can readily be exported across major cultural divides such as those between an urban–dwelling bourgeois intelligentsia and many women in India, most of whom live in villages and significant numbers of whom are illiterate (but definitely not therefore unintelligent, inarticulate, or lacking in worldly sense).[7]

However, having been influenced by Western feminist egalitarian thinking, some Indian liberation theologians have attempted an egalitarian Indian feminist theology. Drawing from Hindu religious symbols, especially from the concept of *'Arthaneeswara'*, Indian feminist theologian Padma Gallup attempted an egalitarian reading of Gen 1:26–27, as we have seen in our discussion. Sugirtharajah, another male Asian theologian, supported her reading. But they have overlooked the vital fact that Hindu religious tradition itself is the main cause for the lower position of women in India. We cannot overlook the fact that *Sati*[8] (self–immolation of widows in husband's funeral pyre), the Devadasi system (temple prostitution of young girls) and many other similar social customs are deeply rooted in the Hindu religion and way of life. Moreover, this kind of liberationism is theologically problematic as it leads to syncretism. Needless to say, to a great extent, the Hindu way of life and value system has resulted in the low status of women

---

[7] G. Yocum, 'Burning "widows", Sacred "Prostitutes", and "Perfect Wives": Recent Studies of Hindu Women', *RelSRev* 20 (1994), pp. 277–285 [p. 284].

[8] Although *Sati* was declared illegal by British Governor–General William Bentinck in 1829, due to the recent Hindu religious awakening, an eighteen–year–old girl immolated herself on her husband's funeral pyre in 1987, in the State of Rajasthan.

and their oppression and exploitation in India. The tendency to go back to the Hindu tradition could be devastating.[9]

Furthermore, the feminist readings we have studied do not address the issues which the Church confronts now such as the marriage bond, family solidarity, single–parenthood, separation and divorce, homosexuality, co-habitation etc. In the row over the Church of England's report on "couples living together without marrying', Mary Kenny wrote: 'One of the reasons why Christianity always attracted women was that it elevated monogamy and regarded marriage as a serious and dignified state in which women had an equal value with men. Christianity preached that women should not be traded for dowries or bride–prices, or sold into marriage against their will' (see Mary Kenny, 'They' re looking at the family in the wrong way', in *The Daily Telegraph,* June 7, 1995, p. 23).

If the feminists fail to address these contemporary issues, their re–reading will not be able to secure their egalitarian position. Despite many hermeneutical problems, Genesis 1–3 still can be used as a source text for the articulation of the theology of sexuality as Bird has shown.

A further point concerns 'inclusive language'. When we make judge-ments we need to bear in mind that inclusive language is a modern notion. So in the ancient context it was appropriate to use male gender in an inclu-sive manner. Therefore, in spite of assumptions to the contrary, the absence of the female gender in biblical usage should not be taken as an indication of androcentrism. Not only in the Scriptures but in all other ancient writ-ings, it was customary to use the male gender in an inclusive sense. A more important question is how people understood gender and patriarchy in his-torical times. No doubt, like all the ancient societies, Israelite society was also patriarchal. But the question to be asked is how Israelite women thought about their status, and how far they enjoyed status and freedom within that patriarchal structure.

It is debatable how far masculine language expresses anything about the status of women in the Old Testament in general. Comparative studies throw some light on this aspect. George Tavard examines the relationship between male language and the social status of women and he argues that male language is not an ideology which determines the social status of women. For instance, in his study he reveals that in the Turkish language

---

[9] Sugirtharajah advocates a pluralistic approach to the text, thereby seeing the Bible as one among many other religious traditions. He writes: 'In an earlier, combative mis-sionary era , the Bible was used as a yardstick to evaluate other scriptural texts. But in a changed theological climate, where other religions tend to exert a great influence and no one text can claim exclusive possession of the truth, the task is not to be combative but to complement each other's textual resources'. Sugirtharajah's proposal shows how syncretistic and misleading his suggestions are! See R. S. Sugirtharajah, 'The Bible and its Asian Readers', p. 58.

there is no distinction corresponding to 'he', 'she', or 'it'. Only one gender is used for everything and everybody. However, when we study the status of women in traditional Turkish society, it is apparent that the Turkish way of life was not very encouraging to women.[10] Tavard persuasively argues that grammatical gender does not signify sex. In his view, the fact that 'gender is simply a taxonomic denomination that is unrelated to sex appears clearly from the fact that Swahili distinguishes among six different genders none of which corresponds to male or female'.[11] From this comparative study, I suggest conversely that inclusive language does not necessarily mean a high status for women. One thing is evident as we have seen earlier, despite the patriarchal social structure of the Bible, the status and position of women in Israel was far better than in the neighbouring societies, even though we cannot find ideal equality between the sexes in the biblical texts.

Clines notes: 'the image of God does not subsist in the male but in mankind, within which woman also belongs. Thus the most basic statement about man, according to Genesis 1, that he is the image of God, does not find its full meaning in man alone, but in man and woman'.[12] Most of the revisionary feminist readers argued that the 'original intention' of the creation text was equality between sexes and the subsequent male domination was a result of the changed state of affairs. For instance, Meyers recently argued that although gender inequalities prevailed in ancient Israelite society, 'there is a concomitant absence of categorical discrimination or official subordination' in the Hebrew Bible.[13] In other words, Meyers finds no 'prescriptive gender hierarchies' in the text. This line of explanation seems to be attractive and reasonable to tackle the question of biblical patriarchy and androcentrism. Many male scholars also have supported this interpretation (e.g. Watson, G. Wenham). But still I doubt whether the present debate on equality of the sexes was really a concern for an ancient Near Eastern culture. It seems to me that the issue there is not equality nor subordination but harmony between the sexes. Moreover, the sociological question of equality was not addressed in the text as no tension existed between man and woman at that point in the narrative. So addressing the question of equality to this text itself seems to be inappropriate.

---

[10] George H. Tavard, 'Sexist Language in Theology', *TS* 36 (1975), pp. 705–706.

[11] Ibid., p. 706. He also points out that 'Bantu' language has sixteen genders and in no way it suggests that it has sixteen sexes. For further discussion on this issue see Donald D. Hook and Alvin F. Kimel, 'The Pronouns of Deity: A Theolinguistic Critique of Feminist Proposals', *SJT* 46 (1993), pp. 299–305.

[12] Clines, 'The Image of God in Man', p. 95. Before the arrival of the feminist movement in 1970s, it was quite normal to use 'mankind' in the sense of humankind. No doubt, Clines would have meant corporately when he used "man" for both sexes. Concerning the status of the woman, Clines notes that the Israelite woman had higher dignity than elsewhere in the ancient world.

[13] Meyers, 'The Creation of Patriarchy in the West', p. 9.

6.4 Are Feminist Readings Open to Critique?

In my view, one of the most serious hermeneutical difficulties which feminist interpreters bring into the text is their 'pre–understanding' of text as oppressive and always against woman. Susan Heine notes:

> One of the greatest problems of feminism and feminist theology seems to me to lie in the fact that women form a negative theory out of their hurt and their negative experience and claim universal validity for it. It is then the "nature" of the male to be destructive, the "nature" of the Christian tradition to damage people, to eliminate women from history, to demonise the feminine. This absolutising of negative experience, even though–it must be acknowledged–it is largely dominant, creates prejudice and weakens ethical claims.[14]

Feminist criticism is a typical example of an ideological criticism. Yet feminist critics are reticent about the inherent 'ideology' involved in feminist readings. As R. M. Schwartz and others have rightly shown, 'the ideological character of ideological reading is as necessary to expose and guard against as any other reading'.[15] Again they point out that '[i]t is incumbent on ideological critics to subject their approaches to critical self–appraisal to expose their own agendas, knowing all the while that it is impossible to expose everything completely'.[16] Most of the feminist interpreters are reluctant to expose their work to scrutiny; rather, in line with postmodern thinking, they develop a self–defence and claim that every reading is equally valid, whatever their readings are.

However, in the ultimate analysis, Trible, Meyers, Bird, Bal, Laffey, Fleming, and Rashkow and others have concluded that the creation accounts in Genesis say that male and female are equal, irrespective of their reading methods and hermeneutical presuppositions. It does reveal that whatever their differences are, almost all the feminists wanted to convey the message that women are equal to man in the creation order. For instance, Trible advocated an egalitarian theology out of the phrase 'male and female he created them', whereas Bird brought out an egalitarian theology, neither from the reading of this text (what lies in front of the text) nor from the intention of the author (what lies behind the text) but as something unintended by the author (out of readers response–here Bird's response to the text as a result of her reading). However, using Gottwald's egalitarian ide-

---

[14] S. Heine, *Women and Early Christianity: Are the Feminist Scholars Right?* (London: SCM Press, 1987), pp. 3–4

[15] See R. M. Schwartz *et al,. The Postmodern Bible: The Bible and Culture Collective,* p. 302.

[16] Ibid., p. 280.

als Meyers attempted to unearth the social world behind the text to show that women had an equal footing with men in the premonarchic highland in Canaan. This unequivocal egalitarianism is one of the prominent inherent ideologies which feminists find in the text. Moreover, although feminists critique the Bible, feminism is not allowed to be critiqued by the Bible. This is a contradiction. In Trible's original proposal, there was room for the Bible and feminism critiquing each other; however, in practice, this dimension has been lost.

Quite recently, the egalitarian reading of the creation accounts has been defended by Francis Watson, based on creation texts, who argues that an 'egalitarian reading [is] exegetically possible as well as theologically necessary'.[17] In the same vein, Reuven Kimelman argues that the creation text 'points in the direction of an egalitarian reading'.[18] One of the fundamental hermeneutical questions to be addressed in this regard is, whether this reading is in line either with the original meaning of the text in its historical context or a contextual reading for our own situation. In my judgement, some feminist readings combine both these aspects together (e.g. Bird, Meyers cf. Watson), however others seem to be a committed reading either of an egalitarian model or an androcentric one (Trible, Laffey, Pardes, Milne etc.). Therefore, there is a strong commitment in every feminist reading to bring out their own concerns either positively or negatively. This is exactly the hermeneutical problem we need to tackle in the text as the biblical texts reflect both positive and negative aspects concerning woman. Overemphasising one aspect while suppressing the other remains a difficulty in feminist hermeneutics. A proper comprehension of these two is vital in articulating a balanced reading. Moreover, as Paul Joyce has rightly pointed out, one needs to be aware that reading Scripture is mainly a 'theological endeavour'. He notes: 'Such a recognition will compel us to reflect self–critically upon this task and upon the difficult question of how we can appropriately express the authority of the Bible within such a process.'[19] Ignoring these aspects and focusing on one's own particular interest will ultimately lead to socio–pragmatic reading. Trible and others have started with socio–critical hermeneutics and they have made many useful constructive criticisms of the androcentric outlook of the text in general; however,

---

[17] F. Watson, *Text, Church, and World*, p. 320, note 9. However, in an earlier article, he argued for the subordinate status of women in the context of Paul's interpretation of Genesis 1–3. See Watson, 'Strategies of Recovery and Resistance: Hermeneutical Reflections on Genesis 1–3 and its Pauline Reception', *JSNT* 45 (1992), pp. 79–103.

[18] See Reuven Kimelman, 'The Seduction of Eve and the Exegetical Politics of Gender', *BibInt* 4 (1996), pp. 1–39.

[19] Paul Joyce, 'Feminist Exegesis of the Old Testament: Some Critical Reflections', p. 6.

eventually their readings also begin to reflect unduly their fundamental concern, thereby falling prey to socio–pragmatism.

We have been discussing some of the problems arising in the attempt to fuse the 'two horizons', that is how to make the text conform to the declared programme, while remaining open to being led by the text itself? We summarise our argument here. Feminist scholars have well attempted to bring about an engagement between the struggles reflected in the text and modern struggles. Yet they have not wholly succeeded. The introduction of 'inclusive language' is an example. In our analysis we have seen that it is not actually a guarantee of inclusiveness, or liberation. Again we saw that feminist readings are not universal, even within a 'feminist' framework such as the situation of Indian women, or a 'black womanists' critique of feminism and the failure of feminism to interact with contemporary issues (Mary Kenney).

Our examples show that the hermeneutical issues are more complicated than many feminists have seen. The situations we have illustrated are not only many, but also complex. The danger of feminism is that it forces text/interpretation on to set tracks, e.g. the concept of 'equality' can be a distraction from real issues. The overriding issue in modern hermeneutics, for feminists as for others, is to bring about an engagement between the struggles reflected in the text and modern struggles. This can be achieved with an honest respect for the text itself.

Bibliography

Abrams, M. H., *The Mirror and the Lamp: Romantic Theory and the Critical Tradition*, New York: OUP, 1953.

– *A Glossary of Literary Terms* (4th ed.), New York: Holt, Rinehart & Winston, 1981.

Achtemeier, E., 'The Impossible Possibility: Evaluating the Feminist Approach to Bible and Theology', *Int* 42 (1988), 45–57.

Ahlström, G. W., *Who were the Israelites?*, Winona Lake: Eisenbrauns, 1986.

– *The History of Ancient Palestine from the Paleolithic Period to Alexander's Conquest* (JSOTS 146), Sheffield: JSOT Press, 1993.

Alter, Robert, *The Art of Biblical Narrative*, London/Sydney: George Allen and Unwin, 1981.

– *The World of Biblical Literature*, London: SPCK, 1992.

Alter, R. & F. Kermode (eds.), *The Literary Guide to the Bible*, London: Collins, 1987.

Anderson, B. W., 'A Stylistic Study of the Priestly Creation Story', in *Canon and Authority: Essays in Old Testament Religion and Theology*, G.W. Coats & B. O. Long (eds.), Philadelphia: Fortress Press, 1977, 148–162.

Armstrong, T. A. *et al.*, *A Reader's Hebrew–English Lexicon of the Old Testament, Four Volumes in One*, Grand Rapids, Michigan, Zondervan, 1989.

Atkinson, D., *The Message of Genesis 1–11: The Dawn of Creation* (BST), Leicester: IVP/Illinois: Downers Grove, 1990.

Austin, J. L., *How to do Things with Words*, Oxford: OUP, 1973.

Bagster & Sons, *The Septuagint Version of the Old Testament with an English Translation*, London: S. Bagster & Sons Ltd/ New York: James Pott & Co, n. d.

Bailey, J. A., 'Initiation and the Primal Woman in Gilgamesh and in Genesis 2–3', *JBL* (1970), 137–150.

Bal, Mieke, *Lethal Love: Feminist Literary Readings of Biblical Love Stories*, Bloomington, Indianapolis: Indiana University Press, 1987.

– 'Sexuality, Sin and Sorrow: The Emergence of Female Character: A Reading of Genesis 1–3', in *The Female Body in Western Culture*, S. R. Suleiman (ed.), Cambridge, Massachusetts/London: HUP, 1986, 317–338.

– (ed.) *Anti–Covenant: Counter–Reading Women's Lives in the Hebrew Bible* (JSOTS 81; BALS 22), Sheffield: The Almond Press, 1989.

Bar–Efrat, S., *Narrative Art in the Bible* (JSOTS 70), Sheffield: Almond Press, 1989.

Barth, K., *Church Dogmatics 3/1*, Edinburgh: T&T Clark, 1958.

Barr, James, *The Semantics of Biblical Language*, Oxford: OUP, 1961.

– 'The Image of God in the Book of Genesis–A Study of Terminology', *BJRL* 51(1968), 11–26.

– *Comparative Philology and the Text of the Old Testament*, Oxford: OUP, 1968/London: SCM, 1983.

– *Biblical Faith and Natural Theology: The Gifford Lectures for 1991 Delivered in the University of Edinburgh*, Oxford: Clarendon Press, 1993.

– *The Garden of Eden and the Hope of Immortality*, London: SCM Press, 1992.

Barton, J., 'Classifying Biblical Criticism', *JSOT* 29 (1984), 19–35.

– *What is the Bible?*, London: SPCK, 1991.

– *Reading the Old Testament: Method in Biblical Study*, London: Darton Longman and Todd, 1984.

– 'Reading the Bible as Literature: Two Questions for Biblical Critics', *JLT* 1 (1987), 135–153.

– 'Biblical Criticism and Interpretation 1: Old Testament', in *Modern Christian Thought,* Alister McGrath (ed.), Oxford: Blackwell, 1993, 35–41.

– 'Historical Criticism and Literary Interpretation: Is there any Common Ground?', in *Crossing the Boundaries: Essays in Honour of Michael D. Goulder* (BIS 8), S. E. Porter *et al.* (eds.), Leiden/New York/Köln: E. J. Brill, 1994, 3–15.

Barton, S. C., 'Social–scientific Approaches to Paul', in *Dictionary of Paul and His Letters* , G. F. Hawthorne *et al.* (eds), Leicester: IVP, 1993, 892–900.

Bass, D. C., 'Women's Studies and Biblical Studies: An Historical Perspective', *JSOT* 22 (1982), 6–12.

Bauckham, R., *The Bible in Politics: How to Read the Bible Politically,* London: SPCK, 1989.

Beattie, D. R. G., 'What is Genesis 2–3 About?', *Exp Tim* 92 (1980), 8–10.

Beauvoir, S. de, *The Second Sex*, trans. by H. M. Parshley, London: Jonathan Cape, 1953.

Bechtel, L. M., 'Rethinking the Interpretation of Genesis 2.4b–3.24', in *A Feminist Companion to Genesis*, 77–117.

– 'Genesis 2. 4b–3. 24: A Myth about Human Maturation', *JSOT* 67 (1995), 3–26.

Bellis, A. O., *Helpmates, Harlots, Heroes: Women's Stories in the Bible,* Louisville: W/JKP, 1994.

Berlin, Adele, *Poetics and Interpretation of Biblical Narrative,* Winona Lake: Eisenbrauns, 1994 (Almond Press, 1983, BALS 9)

Bernhardt, K. H., *Gott und Bild: Ein Beitrag zur Begründung und Deutung des Bilderverbotes im Alten Testament,* Berlin: Evangelische Verlagsanstalt, 1956.

Beyerle, Stefan, 'Feministische Theologie und alttestamentliche Exegese', *BN* 59 (1991), 7–11.

Bimson, J. J., 'The Origins of Israel in Canaan: An Examination of Recent Theories', *Them* 15 (1989), 4–15.

Bird, Phyllis, 'Images of Women in the Old Testament', in *The Bible and Liberation: Political and Social Hermeneutics*, N. K. Gottwald (ed.), New York: Orbis, 1983, 252–306.

– 'Male and Female He created Them: Gen 1:27b in the Context of the Priestly Account of Creation', *HTR* 74 (1981), 129–59.

– 'Genesis 1–3 as a Source for a Contemporary Theology of Sexuality', *Ex Aud* 3 (1987), 31–44.

– 'To Play the Harlot: An Enquiry into an Old Testament Metaphor', in *Gender and Difference in Ancient Israel,* P. L. Day (ed.), Minneapolis: Fortress Press, 1989, 75–94.

– 'The Place of Women in the Israelite Cultus' in *Ancient Israelite Religion,* Miller P. D. Jr., *et al.* (ed), Philadelphia: Fortress Press, 1987, 397–419.

– 'Israelite Religion and the Faith of Israel's Daughters: Reflections on Gender and Religious Definition', in *The Bible and the Politics of Exegesis: Essays in Honor of N. K. Gottwald on his Sixty–Fifth Birthday* David Jobling *et al.* (ed.), Cleveland Ohio: Pilgrim Press, 1991, 97– 108.

– 'Sexual Differentiation and Divine Image in the Genesis Creation Texts', in *Image of God and Gender Models in Judeo–Christian Tradition,* K. Børresen (ed.), Oslo: Solum Forlag, 1991.

– 'Women, Old Testament', in *ABD,* Vol. 6. NewYork/London/Toronto/Sydney/ Auckland: Doubleday 1993, 951–957.

– '"Bone of My Bone and Flesh of my Flesh"', *TToday* 4 (1994), 521–34.

– *Feminism and the Bible: A Critical and Constructive Encounter,* (J. J. Thiessen Lectures), Winnipeg, Manitoba: CMBC, 1994.

– 'The Authority of the Bible', in *The New Interpreters Bible,* vol. 1, Nashville: Abingdon Press, 1994, 33–64.

– 'Genesis 3 in der gegenwärtigen biblischen Forschung', *JBTh* 9 (1994), 1–32 [ET].

Blackburn, S., Logocentrism', in *Oxford Dictionary of Philosophy*, Oxford/New York: OUP, 1996, 224.

Bleicher, Josef, *Contemporary Hermeneutics: Hermeneutics as Method, Philosophy and Critique,* London: Routledge & Keegan Paul, 1980.

Blenkinsopp, J., *The Pentateuch: An Introduction to the First Five Books of the Bible,* New York/London/Toronto/Sydney/Auckland: Doubleday, 1992.

Bonhoeffer, D., *Creation and Fall: A Theological Interpretation of Genesis 1–3* (original *Schöfung und Fall,* 1937), London: SCM, 1959.

Boomershine, T. E.,'The Structure of Narrative Rhetoric in Gen. 2–3', *Semeia* 18 (1980), 113–29.

Bray, Gerald, *Biblical Interpretation: Past and Present,* Leicester: Apollos, 1996.

Brenner, A., *The Israelite Woman: Social Role and Literary Type in Biblical Narrative,* Sheffield: JSOT Press, 1985.

– *The Song of Songs* (OTG), Sheffield: JSOT Press, 1989.

– 'Who's Afraid of Feminist Criticism? Who's Afraid of Biblical Humour? The Case of the Obtuse Foreign Ruler in the Hebrew Bible', *JSOT* 63 (1994), 38–55.

Brenner & F. Van Dijk–Hemmes, *On Gendering Texts: Female and Male Voices in the Hebrew Bible,* (BIS 1), Leiden/New York/Köln: E. J. Brill, 1993.

Brenner, A., (ed.), *A Feminist Companion to the Song of Songs* (FCB 1), Sheffield: Sheffield Academic Press, 1993.

– *A Feminist Companion to Genesis* (FCB 2), 1993.

– *A Feminist Companion to Ruth* (FCB 3), 1993.

– *A Feminist Companion to Judges* (FCB 4), 1993.

– *A Feminist Companion to Samuel and Kings* (FCB 5), 1994.

– *A Feminist Companion to Exodus to Deuteronomy* (FCB 6),1994.

– *A Feminist Companion to Esther, Judith, and Susanna* (FCB 7), 1995.

– *A Feminist Companion to the Latter Prophets* (FCB 8), 1995.

– *A Feminist Companion to Wisdom Literature* (FCB 9), 1995.
– *A Feminist Companion to the Hebrew Bible in the New Testament* (FCB 10), 1996.
– *A Feminist Companion to Reading the Bible: Approaches, Methods, and Strategies,*
    1997.
Brett, M. G., *Biblical Criticism in Crisis?: The Impact of the Canonical Approach on
    Old Testament Studies,* Cambridge: CUP, 1991.
– 'The Future of Reader Criticisms?', in *The Open Text: New Directions for Biblical
    Studies?,* F. Watson (ed.), London: SCM, 1993, 13–31.
– 'Motives and Intentions in Genesis', *JTS* 42 (1991), 1–16.
– 'Four or Five Things to do with Texts: A Taxonomy of Interpretative Interests', in
    *The Bible in Three Dimensions: Essays in Celebration of Forty Years of Biblical
    Studies in the University of Sheffield* (JSOTS 87), D.J. A. Clines *et al.*(eds.), Shef-
    field: JSOT Press, 1990, 357–377.
Brown, F., S. R. Driver, & C. A. Briggs, *The New Brown–Driver–Briggs–Gesenius He-
    brew and English Lexicon,* Peabody, Massachusetts: Hendrickson, 1979 (Oxford,
    1907).
Brueggemann, W., 'Of the Same Flesh and Bone, (Gen, 2: 23a)', *CBQ* 32 (1970), 532–
    542.
Buber, M., *I and Thou,* trans. by R. G. Smith, Edinburgh: T & T Clark, 1937.
Bushnell, K. C., *God's Word to Women: One Hundred Bible Studies on Woman's Place
    in the Divine Economy,* (original 1923, n.p & n. d).
Caird, G. B., *The Language and Imagery of the Bible* , London: Duckworth, 1980.
Camp, C. V., *Wisdom and the Feminine in the Book of Proverbs* (BALS 11), Sheffield:
    Almond Press, 1985.
Carmichael, C. M., 'The Paradise Myth: Interpreting without Jewish and Christian Spec-
    tacles', in *A Walk in the Garden: Biblical Iconographical and Literary Images of
    Eden* (JSOTS 136), P. Morris & D. Sawyer (eds.), Sheffield: JSOT Press, 91–104.
Carroll, R. P., *Jeremiah* (OTL), London: SCM Press, 1986.
Cassuto, U., *A Commentary on the Book of Genesis: From Adam to Noah:A Commen-
    tary on Genesis I—VI 8,* trans. by I. Abrahams, Jerusalem: The Magnes Press, 1989
    (1961).
Chaney, M. L., 'Ancient Palestinian Peasant Movements and the Formation of Pre–
    monarchic Israel', in *Palestine in Transition: The Emergence of Ancient Israel*
    (SWBA 2), D. N. Freedman &D. F. Graf (eds.), Sheffield: Almond Press, 1983, 39–
    90.
Childs, B. S., *Old Testament Theology in a Canonical Context,* London: SCM Press,
    1985.
– *Introduction to the Old Testament as Scripture,* London: SCM Press, 1979.
Clements, R.E. (ed.), *The World of Ancient Israel: Sociological, Anthropological and
    Political Perspectives,* Cambridge/New York/New Rochelle/Melbourne/Sydney:
    CUP, 1989.
Clifford, R. J. & R. E. Murphy, 'Genesis', in *NJBC*, London: Geoffrey Chapman, 1989,
    8–43.
Clines, D. J. A., 'The Image of God in Man', *TynB* 19 (1968), 53–103.

- *The Theme of the Pentateuch* (JSOTS 10), Sheffield: JSOT Press, 1986 (1978).
- *What Does Eve Do to Help? and Other Readerly Questions to the Old Testament* (JSOTS 94), Sheffield: JSOT Press, 1990.
- 'Possibilities and Priorities of Biblical Interpretation in an International Perspective', *BibInt* 1 (1993), 67–87.
- (ed.), *The Dictionary of Classical Hebrew* vol. 1, Sheffield: Sheffield Academic Press, 1993.
- 'A World Established on Water (Psalm 24): Reader–Response, Deconstruction and Bespoke Interpretation', in *The New Literary Criticism and the Hebrew Bible:* (JSOTS 143), Sheffield: JSOT Press, 1993, 79–90.
- 'The Image of God in Man', in *Dictionary of Paul and His Letters,* G. F.Hawthorne *et al.* (eds), Leicester: IVP, 1993, 426–427.
- *Interested Parties: The Ideology of Writers and Readers of the Hebrew Bible,* (JSOTS 205), Sheffield: Sheffield Academic Press, 1995.

Coats, G. W., *Genesis with an Introduction to Narrative Literature,* Grand Rapids, Michigan: William B. Eerdmans Publishing, 1983.

Collins, A. Y. (ed.), *Feminist Perspectives on Biblical Scholarship*, Chico, California: Scholars Press, 1985.

- 'The Historical–Critical and Feminist Readings of Genesis 1: 26–28', in *Hebrew Bible or Old Testament?: Studying the Bible in Judaism and Christianity,* R. Brooks *et al.* (eds.), Notre Dame: Notre Dame University Press, 1990, 197–199.

Collins, R., *Three Sociological Traditions,* Oxford: OUP, 1985.

Coote, R. B., *Early Israel: A New Horizon,* Minneapolis: Fortress Press, 1990.

Coote, R. B. & K. W. Whitelam, *The Emergence of Early Israel in Historical Perspective,* (SWBA 5), Sheffield: Almond Press, 1987.

Coote, R. B. & D. R. Ord, *The Bible's First History* , Philadelphia: Fortress Press, 1989.

Cotterell, P. & M. Turner, *Linguistics & Biblical Interpretation*, London: SPCK, 1989.

Culler, Jonathan, *On Deconstruction: Theory and Critics after Structuralism*, London/Melbourne/Henley: Routledge & Kegan Paul, 1983.

Culley, R. C., *Themes and Variations: A Study of Action in Biblical Narrative,* Atlanta: Scholars Press, 1992.

Das, Veena, 'Indian Women: Work, Power and Status', in *Indian Women: From Purdah to Modernity,* B.R. Nanda (ed.), New Delhi: Vikas Publishing House, 1976, 129–145.

Davies, P. R., *Whose Bible is it Anyway?* (JSOTS 204), Sheffield: Sheffield Academic Press, 1995.

Davis, Margaret, 'Literary Criticism', in *A Dictionary of Biblical Interpretation,* R. J. Coggins and J. L. Houlden (ed.), London: SCM Press, 1990, 402–405.

Delitzsch, Franz, *A New Commentary on Genesis* vol. 1, trans. by S. Taylor, Edinburgh: T& T Clark, 1888.

Dennis, Trevor, *Sarah Laughed: Women's Voices in the Old Testament,* London: SPCK, 1994.

Derrida, J., *Of Grammatology,* trans. Gayatri Chakravorty Spivak, Baltimore: Johns Hopkins University Press, 1974.

Detweiler, R., & V. K. Robbins, 'From New Criticism to Poststructuralism: Twentieth Century Hermeneutics', in *Reading the Text: Biblical Criticism and Literary Theory*, S. Prickett (ed.), Cambridge, USA/Oxford: Blackwell, 1991, 225– 280.

Dozeman, T. B., 'O. T. Rhetorical Criticism', *ABD* vol. 5, New York/London/Toronto/ Sydney/Auckland: Doubleday, 1992, 712–715.

Dragga, Sam, 'Genesis 2–3: A Story of Liberation', *JSOT* 55 (1992), 3–13.

Driver, S. R., *The Book of Genesis* (10th ed.), London: Methuen & Co. Ltd., 1916.

Edelman, D., *Discovering Eve: Ancient Israelite Women in Context* (book review), in *BA* 53 (1990), 43–45.

Emerton, J. A., 'Wisdom', in *Tradition and Interpretation: Essays by Members of the Society for Old Testament Study*, G. W. Anderson (ed.), Oxford: Clarendon Press, 1979, 214–237.

Emmerson, G. I.,'Women in Ancient Israel', in *The World of Ancient Israel: Sociological, Anthropological and Political Perspectives,* 371–394.

– Book Review of *Discovering Eve* , *Theology* 93 (1990), 66–67.

Eskenazi, T. C., 'Out from the Shadows: Biblical Women in the Post–Exilic Era', *JSOT* 54 (1992), 25–43.

Evans , Mary, *Women in the Bible* , Exeter: Paternoster Press, 1983.

Exum, J. C., 'You Shall Let Every Daughter Live: A Study of Exodus 1: 8–2:10', *Semeia* 28 (1983), 63–82.

– 'Mother in Israel: A Familiar Story Reconsidered', in *Feminist Interpretation of the Bible* , L. M. Russel (ed.), Oxford/New York: Basil Blackwell, 1985, 73–85.

– 'The Mothers of Israel: The Patriarchal Narratives from a Feminist Perspective', *BibRev* 2 (1986), 60–67.

– 'Murder They Wrote: Ideology and the Manipulation of Female Presence in Biblical Narrative', *USQR* 43 (1989), 19–39.

– *Fragmented Women: Feminist(Sub)versions of Biblical Narrative* (JSOTS 163), Sheffield: JSOT Press, 1993.

Exum J. C. & Clines (eds), *The New Literary Criticism and the Hebrew Bible* (JSOTS 143), Sheffield: JSOT Press, 1993.

Farmer, K. A., *Who Knows What is Good?: A Commentary on the Book of Proverbs & Ecclesiastes* (ITC), Grand Rapids: Wm. B. Eerdmans/Edinburgh: Handsel Press, 1991.

Fee, Gordon D. & D. Stuart, *How to Read the Bible for all its Worth: A Guide to Understanding the Bible*, Grand Rapids, Michigan: Zondervan, 1982/ London: Scripture Union, 1983.

Fetterly, J., *The Resisting Reader: A Feminist Approach to American Fiction*, Bloomington: Indiana University Press, 1978.

Fewell, D. N., 'Feminist Criticism of the Hebrew Bible: Affirmation, Resistance, and Transformation', *JSOT* 39 (1987), 39–65.

– 'Reading the Bible Ideologically: Feminist Criticism' in *To Each Its Own Meaning: An Introduction to BiblicalInterpretations and their Applications*, S. L. McKenzie & S. R. Haynes (eds.), Louisville, Ky: Westminster/John Knox, 1993, 237–251.

Fewell, D. N. & D. M. Gunn, *Gender, Power, and Promise: The Subject of the Bible's First Story*, Nashville: Abingdon, 1993.

– 'Genesis 2–3: Women, Men and God', in *Narrative in the Hebrew Bible,* Oxford: OUP, 1993, 194–205.

– 'Controlling Perspectives: Women, Men, and the Authority of Violence in Judges 4 and 5', *JAAR* 56 (1990), 389–411.

– 'Tipping the Balance: Sternberg's Reader and the Rape of Dinah', *JBL* 110 (1991), 193–211.

Finkelstein, I., *The Archaeology of the Israelite Settlement*, Jerusalem: Israel Exploration Society, 1988.

Fish, Stanley, *Is there a Text in this Class?: The Authority of Interpretive Communities,* Cambridge, Massachusetts: HUP, 1980.

Fishbane, M., *Biblical Interpretation in Ancient Israel*, Oxford: Clarendon Press, 1985.

Fleming, J. E., *A Rhetorical Analysis of Genesis 2–3 with Implications for a Theology of Man and Woman*, unpublished thesis submitted to the University of Strasbourg, France, 1987.

Fleming, J. E. & J. R. Maxson, *Man and Woman in Biblical Unity: Theology from Genesis 2–3,* Minnesota: Saint Paul, 1993.

Foh, Susan, 'What is the Woman's desire?', *WTJ* 37 (1975), 376– 383.

Fowler, R. M., 'Who is "the Reader" in Reader–Response Criticism?', *Semeia* 31 (1985), 5–23.

Freedman, D. N. & D. F. Graf, *Palestine in Transition: The Emergence of Ancient Israel* (SWBA 2), Sheffield: The Almond Press, 1983.

Freedman, D. R., 'Woman, a Power Equal to Man', *BARev* 9 (1983), 56–58.

Fretheim, T. E., 'The Book of Genesis: Introduction, Commentary, and Reflections', in *NIB*, Nashville: Abingdon Press, 1994 vol.1, 319ff.

Frick, F. S., *The Formation of the State in Israel: A Survey of Models and Theories,* (SWBA 2), Sheffield: Almond Press, 1985.

Fritz, V., 'Conquest or Settlement?: The Early Iron Age in Palestine', *BA* (1987), 84–100.

Frymer–Kensky, T., *In the Wake of Goddess: Women, Culture, and the Biblical Transformation of Pagan Myth,* New York/Toronto: Free Press (Macmillan), 1992.

Fulkerson, M. M., 'Contesting Feminist Canons: Discourse and the Problems of Sexist Texts', *JFSR* 7 (1991), 53–73.

Gadamer, H. G., *Truth and Method,* London: Sheed and Ward, 1981.

Galambush, J., '*'ādām* from *'ādāmâ, 'iššā* from *'îš*',: Derivation and Subordination in Genesis2.4b–3.24', in *History and Interpretation: Essays in Honour of John H. Hayes,* (JSOTS 173), M. P. Graham *et al.* (eds.), Sheffield: JSOT Press, 1993, 33–46.

Gallup, P., 'Doing Theology–An Asian Feminist Perspective', in *Commission on Theological Concerns Bulletin* (Christian Conference in Asia, 4, 1983).

Gardner, Anne, 'Genesis 2: 4b–3: A Mythological Paradigm of Sexual Equality or of the Religious History of Pre–exilic Israel?', *SJT* 43 (1990), 1–18.

Gifford, C. S., 'American Women and the Bible: The Nature of Woman as a Hermeneutical Issue', in *Feminist Perspectives on Biblical Scholarship,* A. Y. Collins (ed.), Chico, California: Scholars Press, 1985, p. 11– 33.

Gitay. Y., 'Rhetorical Criticism', in *To Each its Own Meaning* , 135–149.

Goldingay, J., 'The Bible and Sexuality', *SJT* 39 (1986), 175–188.

– 'How far Do Readers Make Sense?: Interpreting Biblical Narrative', *Them* 18 (1993), 5–10.

– *Models for Scripture* , Grand Rapids, Michigan: William B. Eerdmans/Carlisle: Paternoster Press, 1994.

– *Models for Interpretation of Scripture*, Grand Rapids, Michigan: William B. Eerdmans/ Carlisle: Paternoster Press, 1995.

Good, E. M., *Irony in the Old Testament,* Sheffield: Almond Press, 1981.

Gottwald, N. K.,'Domain Assumptions and Societal Models in the Study of Pre–monarchic Israel', in *Congress Volume, Edinburgh, 1974* (VTS 27) Leiden: E. J. Brill, 1975, 89–100.

– *The Tribes of Yahweh: A Sociology of the Religion of Liberated Israel, 1250–1050 B. C. E.,* London: SCM, 1980.

– *The Hebrew Bible: A Socio–Literary Introduction,* Philadelphia: Fortress Press, 1985.

– 'Sociological Method in the Study of Ancient Israel', in *The Bible and Liberation: Political and Social Hermeneutics,* (rev. ed.), N. K. Gottwald & R. A. Horsley (eds), New York: Orbis/London: SPCK, 1993, 142–45.

– 'Sociology of Ancient Israel', in *ABD* vol. 6, Nashville: Doubleday, 1992, 79–89.

– *The Hebrew Bible in its Social World and in Ours,* Atlanta: Scholars Press, 1993.

Goulder, M. D., *The Song of Fourteen Songs,* (JSOTS 36), Sheffield: JSOT Press, 1986.

Greenwood, D. C., *Structuralism and the Biblical Text*, Berlin/New York/Amsterdam: Mouton Publishers, 1985.

Habel, N. C., 'The Future of Social Justice Research in the Hebrew Scriptures: Questions of Authority and Relevance', in *Old Testament Interpretation: Past, Present, and Future* (G. M.Tucker Festschrift), J. L. Mays *et al.* (eds.), Edinburgh: T& T Clark, 1995, 277–291.

– *Literary Criticism of the Old Testament* , Philadelphia: Fortress Press, 1971.

Hackett, Jo Ann, 'Women's Studies and the Hebrew Bible' in *The Future of Biblical Studies: The Hebrew Scriptures* , R. E. Friedman & H. G. M. Williamson (eds.), Atlanta: Scholars Press, 1987, 141–164.

Hamilton, V., *The Book of Genesis, Chapters 1–17* (NICOT), Grand Rapids, Michigan: William B. Eerdmans, 1990.

Hanson, P. D., 'Masculine Metaphors for God and Sex Determination in the Old Testament', *EcR* 27 (1975), 316–24.

Harland, P. J., *The Value of Human Life: A Study of the Story of the Flood(Gen 6–9)* , VTS 64, Leiden/New York/Köln: E. J. Brill,1996.

Hart, I., 'Genesis 1: 1–2: 3 as a Prologue to the Book of Genesis', *TynB* 46 (1995), 317–324.

Hauser, A. J., 'Genesis 2–3: The Theme of Intimacy and Alienation', in *Art and Meaning: Rhetoric in Biblical Literature*, (JSOTS 19), Sheffield: JSOT Press, D. J. A. Clines *et al.* (eds.), 1982, 20–36.

– 'Israel's Conquest of Palestine: A Peasants' Rebellion?', *JSOT* 7 (1978), pp. 2–19.

Hayter, M., *The New Eve in Christ: The Use and Abuse of the Bible in the Debate about Women in the Church*, London: SPCK, 1987.

Heidegger, M., *Being and Time,* trans. by J. Macquarrie & E.Robinson, London: SCM, 1962.

Heine, Susan, *Woman and Early Christianity: Are the Feminist Scholars Right?*, London: SCM, 1987.

– *Christianity and the Goddesses: Can Christianity Cope with Sexuality?*, London: SCM, 1988.

Herion, G. A., 'The Impact of Modern and Social Science Assumptions on the Reconstruction of Israelite History', *JSOT* 34 (1986), 3–33.

Hess, Richard S., 'The Roles of Woman and the Man in Genesis 3', *Them* 18 (1993), 15–19.

– 'Splitting the Adam: the Usage of *'Adām* in Genesis I–V', in *Studies in the Pentateuch,* (VTS 41), J. A. Emerton (ed.), Leiden/New York/København/Köln: E. J. Brill, 1990, 1–15.

Higgins, Jean M., ' The Myth of Eve: The Temptress', *JAAR* 44 (1976), 639– 647.

– 'Anastasius Sinaita and the Superiority of the Woman', *JBL* 97 (1978), 253–56.

Holladay, C. R., 'Contemporary Methods of Reading the Bible', in *NIB* vol. 1, Nashville: Abingdon Press, 1994, 125–149.

Hopkins, D. C., *The Highlands of Canaan: Agricultural Life in the Early Iron Age* (SWBA 3), Sheffield: Almond Press, 1985.

– 'Life on the Land: The Subsistence Struggles of Early Israel', *BA* 50 (1987), 178–191.

Horowitz, M. C., 'The Image of God—Is Woman Included?', *HTR* 72 (1979), 175–206.

House, P. R., 'The Rise and Current Status of Literary Criticism of the Old Testament', in *Beyond Form Criticism: Essays in Old Testament Literary Criticism*, P. R. House (ed), Indiana, Winona Lake: Eisenbrauns, 1992, 3–22.

Howard, D. M., 'Rhetorical Criticism in Old Testament Studies', *BBR* 4 (1994), 87–104.

Jacobson, R., 'The Structuralist and the Bible', *Int* xxviii (1974), 146–164.

Jackson, J. J. & M. Kessler,*Rhetorical Criticism: Essays in Honor of James Muilenburg,* Pittsburgh: Pickwick, 1974.

Jeanrond, W. G., *Theological Hermeneutics: Development and Significance*, Basingstoke/London: Macmillan, 1991.

– *Text and Interpretation as Categories of Theological Thinking,* Dublin: Gill & Macmillan, 1988.

– 'After Hermeneutics: The Relationship between Theology and Biblical Studies', in *The Open Text: New Directions for Biblical Studies?*, F. Watson (ed.), London: SCM, 1993, 85–102.

Jobling, David, *The Sense of Biblical Narrative: Structural Analyses in the Hebrew Bible*, (JSOTS 39), Sheffield: Sheffield Academic Press, 1987.

– 'Feminism and "Mode of Production" in Ancient Israel: Search for a Method', in *The Bible and Politics of Exegesis: Essays in Honor of Norman K .Gottwald on His Sixty–Fifth Birthday,* D. Jobling *et al.* (eds.), Cleveland, Ohio: Pilgrim Press, 1991, 239–251.

Jónsson, G. A., *The Image of God: Genesis 1:26–28 in a Century of Old Testament Research,* Stockholm: Almqvist & Wiksell, 1988.

Jones, D. R., *Jeremiah* (NCBC), Grand Rapids, Michigan: William B. Eerdmans/London: Marshall Pickering, 1992.

Josipovici, G., *The Book of God: A Response to the Bible,* New Haven, Conn./London: Yale Univ. Press, 1988.

Joyce, Paul, 'First Among Equals?: The Historical–Critical Approach in the Marketplace of Methods', in *Crossing the Boundaries: Essays in Honour of Michael D. Goulder* (BIS 8), S. E. Porter *et al.* (eds.), Leiden/New York/Köln: E. J. Brill, 1994, 17–27.

– 'Feminist Exegesis of the Old Testament: Some Critical Reflections', in *After Eve: Women, Theology and the Christian Tradition,* J. M. Soskice (ed.), London: Collins, Marshall Pickering, 1990, 1–9.

Kaiser, Walter. C.,*Toward an Old Testament Ethics,* Grand Rapids, Michigan: Zondervan Publishing House, 1983.

Kautzsch, E. (ed.),*Gesenius' Hebrew Grammar,* rev. by A. E. Cowley, Oxford: Clarendon Press, 1985 (1910).

Keegan, T. J., 'Biblical Criticism and the Challenge of Postmodernism', *BibInt* 3 (1995), 1–14.

Keil, C. F. & F. Delitzsch, *Jeremiah and Lamentations: Commentary on the Old Testament,* vol. 8, Grand Rapids, Michigan: William B. Eerdmans Publishing Co., 1984.

Kenny, Mary, 'They're Looking at the Family in the Wrong Way', in *The Daily Telegraph,* June 7 (1995), p. 23.

Kennedy, G. A., *New Testament Interpretation through Rhetorical Criticism,* North Carolina: University of North Carolina Press, 1984.

Kennedy, J. M., 'Peasants in Revolt: Political Allegory in Genesis', *JSOT* 47 (1990), 3–14.

Kessler, M., 'A Methodological Setting for Rhetorical Criticism', in *Art and Meaning: Rhetoric in Biblical Literature* (JSOTS 19), Sheffield: JSOT Press, D. J. A. Clines *et al.* (eds.), 1982, 1–19.

Kidner, D., *Genesis* (TOTC), London: Tyndale Press, 1967.

Kikawada, I. M., 'The Shape of Genesis 11: 1–9', in *Rhetorical Criticism: Essays in Honor of James Muilenburg,* J. J. Jackson & M. Kessler (eds.), Pittsburgh: Pennsylvania, 1974, 18–32.

– 'Two Notes on Eve', *JBL* 91 (1972), 33–37.

Kimel, A. F., 'The Pronouns of Deity: A Theolinguistic Critique of Feminist Proposals', *SJT* 46 (1993), 297–323.

Kimelman, R., 'The Seduction of Eve and the Exegetical Politics of Gender', *BibInt* 4 (1996), 1–39.

Koehler, L. & W. Baumgartner, *Lexicon in Veteris Testamenti Libros,* Leiden: E. J. Brill, 1985.

Köhler, Hanne, '1 Mose 2, 4b–3, 24: Erdkreatur', in *Feministisch Gelesen,* Eva Renate Schmidt (ed.), Vol. 1, pp. 17–24. Stuttgart: Kreuz, 1988.

– *The Hebrew and Aramaic Lexicon of the Old Testament : The New Koehler – Baumgartner in English,* ∏ vol. 1, Leiden/New York/ Köln: E. J. Brill, 1994.

Korsak, M. P., *At the Start...Genesis Made New: A Translation of the Hebrew Text,* Kessel–Lo: Van der Poorten Press, 1992.

– 'Genesis: A New Look', in *A Feminist Companion to Genesis,* 39–52.

Kreitzer, L. J., *The Old Testament in Fiction and Film: On Reversing the Hermeneutical Flow* , Sheffield: Sheffield Academic Press, 1994.

LaCocque, A., *The Feminine Unconventional: Four Subversive Figures in Israel's Tradition,* Minneapolis: Fortress Press, 1990.

Laffey, Alice L., *Wives, Harlots and Concubines: The Old Testament in Feminist Perspective,* London : SPCK, 1990 (Fortress Press, 1988).

Lan, K. P., 'Discovering the Bible in the Non–biblical World', in *The Bible and Liberation: Political and Social Hermeneutics,* revised, N. K. Gottwald *et al.* (eds.), New York: Orbis/London: SPCK, 1993, 17–30.

Lanser, S. S., '(Feminist) Criticism in the Garden: Inferring Genesis 2–3' *Semeia* 41 (1988), 67–84.

Lebra J. *et al.* (eds.), *Women and Work in India: Continuity and Change,* New Delhi: Promila & Co., 1984.

Lemche, N. P., *Early Israel: Anthropological and Historical Studies on the Israelite Society Before the Monarchy,* (VTS 37), Leiden: E. J. Brill, 1985.

– *Ancient Israel: A New History of Israelite Society,* Sheffield: JSOT Press, 1988.

Lévi–Strauss, C., *Anthropology and Myth: Lectures 1957–1982,* New York: Basil Blackwell, 1987.

Lohfink, N., *Theology of the Pentateuch: Themes of the Priestly Narrative and Deuteronomy,* trans. by L. M. Maloney, Edinburgh: T & T Clark, 1994.

Lundin, R. *et al.* (eds.), *The Responsibility of Hermeneutics,* Grand Rapids: William B. Eerdmans/ Exeter: Paternoster Press, 1985.

Maddox, R. L., 'Contemporary Hermeneutic Philosophy and Theological Studies', *RelS* 21 (1985), 517–529.

Maly, E. H., 'Genesis', in *JBC,* R. E. Brown *et al.* (eds.) London/Dublin/Melbourne: Geoffrey Chapman, 1968, 1–46.

Mary, Corona, 'Woman in Creation Story', *Jeev* (1991), 95–106.

Martin, Francis, *The Feminist Question: Feminist Theology in the Light of Christian Tradition,* Grand Rapids, Michigan: William B. Eerdmans, 1994.

Mayes, A. D. H., 'Sociology and the Old Testament', in *The World of Ancient Israel:* Cambridge/New York/New Rochelle/Melbourne/Sydney: CUP, 1989, 39–63.

– *The Old Testament in Sociological Perspective,* London: Marshall Pickering, 1989.

McKane, W., *Proverbs* (OTL), London: SCM Press, 1970.

McKenzie, J. L., 'The Literary Characteristics of Genesis 2–3' *TS* 15 (1954), 541–572.

McKnight, E. V., *The Bible and the Reader: An Introduction to Literary Criticism,* Philadelphia: Fortress Press, 1985.

– 'A Biblical Criticism for American Biblical Scholarship', in *Society of Biblical Literature Seminar,* P. Achtemeir (ed.), Chico: Scholars Press, 1980, 123–134.

– *Post–Modern Use of the Bible: The Emergence of Reader–Oriented Criticism,* Nashville: Abingdon Press, 1988.

Mendenhall, G. E., 'The Hebrew Conquest of Palestine', *BA* 25 (1962), 66–87.

– *The Tenth Generation: The Origins of the Biblical Tradition,* Baltimore: Johns Hopkins University Press, 1973.

– 'The Shady Side of Wisdom: The Date and Purpose of Genesis 3', in *A Light unto My Path: Old Testament Studies in Honor of Jacob M. Meyers* (GTS IV), H. N. Bream *et al.* (eds.), Philadelphia: Temple Univ. Press, 1974, 319–334.

– 'Ancient Israel's Hyphenated History', in *Palestine in Transition: The Emergence of Ancient Israel* (SWBA 2), D. N. Freedman &D. F. Graf (eds.), Sheffield: Almond Press, 1983, 91–103.

Mettinger, T. N. D., *In Search of God: The Meaning and Message of the Everlasting Names,* Philadelphia: Fortress Press, 1988.

– 'Abbild oder Urbild? "Imago Dei" in traditionsgeschichtlicher Sicht', *ZAW* 86 (1974), 403–24.

Meyers, C., 'The Roots of Restriction: Women in Early Israel', *BA* 41 (1978), 91–103.

– 'Procreation, Production and Protection: Male–female Balance in Early Israel', *JAAR* 51 (1983), 569–93.

– 'Gender Roles and Genesis 3:16 Revisited', in *The Word of the Lord shall Go forth',* M. O' Connor, & Meyers (eds.), Indiana: Winona Lake, 1983, 337–54.

– 'Gender Imagery in the Song of Songs', *HAR* 10 (1986), 209–223.

– *Discovering Eve: Ancient Israelite Women in Context,* Oxford: OUP, 1988.

– 'Women and the Domestic Economy of Early Israel', in *Women's Earliest Records: From Ancient Egypt and Western Asia* (BJS 166), B. S. Lesko (ed.), Atlanta: Scholars Press, 1989, 265–281.

– '"To Her Mother's House": Considering a Counterpart to the Israelite *Bêt 'ab'*, in *The Bible and the Politics of Exegesis* (Gottwald Festschrift), D. Jobling *et al.* (eds.), Cleveland, Ohio: Pilgrim, 1991, 39–51.

– 'Of Drums and Damsels: Women's Performance in Ancient Israel', *BA* 54 (1991), 16–27.

– 'Everyday Life: Women in the Period of the Hebrew Bible', in *The Women's Bible Commentary,* C. A. Newsom *et al.* (eds.), Westminster: John Knox/London: SPCK, 1992, 244–251.

– 'Returning Home: Ruth 1: 8 and the Gendering of the Book of Ruth', in *A Feminist Companion to Ruth,* 85–114.

– 'The Hannah Narrative in Feminist Perspective', in *A Feminist Companion to Samuel and Kings* , 93–104.

–   'The Creation of Patriarchy in the West: A Consideration of Judeo–Christian Tradition', in *Foundations of Gender Inequality*, A. Zagarell (ed.), Kalamazoo: New Issues Press, 1994, 1–36.

Miller, John M., 'Depatriarchalizing God in Biblical Interpretation: A Critique', *CBQ* 48 (1986), 609–616.

Miller, M., 'In the Image and Likeness of God', *JBL* 91 (1972), 289–304.

Miller, P. D., *Genesis 1–11: Studies in Structure and Theme,* (JSOTS 8), Sheffield: JSOT Press, 1978.

Millet, Kate, *Sexual Politics,* London: Virago, 1977 (1969).

Milne, Pamela J., 'Eve and Adam: Is a Feminist Reading Possible', *BibRev* IV (1988), 12–21, 39.

–   'The Patriarchal Stamp of Scripture : The Implications of Structural Analyses for Feminist Hermeneutics', *JFSR* 5 (1989), 17–34.

Moltmann, J., *God in Creation: An Ecological Doctrine of Creation,* London: SCM Press, 1985.

Morgan, R. & J. Barton, *Biblical Interpretation* (OBS), Oxford: OUP, 1989.

Moye, R. H., 'In the Beginning: Myth and History in Genesis and Exodus', *JBL* 109 (1990), 577–598.

Murphy, C., 'Women and the Bible', *AM* (Aug. 1993), 39–64.

Murphy, R. E., 'Song of Songs Book of', in *ABD* vol. 6., Nashville: Doubleday, 1992, 150–55.

Muilenburg, J., 'Form Criticism and Beyond', *JBL* 88 (1969), pp. 1–18.

Naidoff, B. D., 'A Man to Work the Soil: A New Interpretation of Genesis 2–3', *JSOT* 5 (1978), 2–14.

Neuer, Werner, *Man and Woman in Christian Perspective,* trans. by G. Wenham, London/Sydney/Auckland/Toronto: Hodder and Stoughton, 1990.

Neusner, J. (trans),*Genesis Rabbah: The Judaic Commentary to the Book of Genesis, A New American Translation, Parashiyyot One through Thirty–Three on Genesis 1; 1to 8;14,* vol.1, (BJS 104), Atlanta: Scholars Press, 1985.

Newsom, C. A. *et al.* (eds), *The Women's Bible Commentary,*Westminster: John Knox/London: SPCK, 1992.

Niditch, Susan, 'Genesis', in *The Women's Bible Commentary*, C. Newsom *et al.* (eds.), 10–25.

–   *Chaos to Cosmos: Studies in Biblical Patterns of Creation,* Atlanta, Georgia: Scholars Press, 1985.

Noble, P. R., 'Hermeneutics and Post–Modernism: Can We have a Radical Reader–Response Theory? Part I', *RelS* 30 (1994), 419–36.

–   'Hermeneutics and Post–Modernism: Can We have a Radical Reader–Response Theory? Part II', *RelS* 31 (1995), 1–22.

Nowell, Irene, 'Roles of Women in the Old Testament', *BibToday* 28 (1990), 364–68.

O' Connor, K., 'The Invitation of Wisdom Woman: A Feminine Image of God', *BibToday* 29 (1991) 87–93.

Osborne, G. R., *Hermeneutical Spiral: A Comprehensive Introduction to Biblical Interpretation* , Downers Grove, Illinois: IVP, 1991.

Osiek, Carolyn, 'The Feminist and the Bible: Hermeneutical Alternatives', in *Feminist Perspectives on Biblical Scholarship*: A. Y. Collins (ed.), Chico, California: Scholars Press, 1985, 94–105.

Pardes, Ilana, *Countertraditions in the Bible: A Feminist Approach*, Cambridge, Massachusetts/London: HUP, 1992.

–   'Beyond Genesis 3: The Politics of Maternal Naming', in *A Feminist Companion to Genesis,* pp. 173–193.

Pannenberg, W., 'Feminine Language of God', *ATJ* 48 (1993), 27–29.

Park, S., 'Understanding the Bible from Women's Perspective', *Voices from the Third World* X (June 1987), 66–75.

Patrick, D. & A. Scult, *Rhetoric and Biblical Interpretation*, (JSOTS 82; BALS 26) Sheffield: Almond Press, 1990.

Patte, Daniel, *What is Structural Exegesis?*, Philadelphia: Fortress Press, 1976.

Petersen, D. L., *The Roles of Israel's Prophets* (JSOTS 17), Sheffield: JSOT Press, 1981.

Pinnock, C. H. 'The Work of the Holy Spirit in Hermeneutics', *JPT* 2 (1993), 3–23.

Pope, M. H., *Song of Songs: A New Translation with Introduction and Commentary* (AB), New York: Doubleday, 1977.

Powell, M. A. (compiled) *The Bible and Modern Literary Criticism: A Critical Assessment and Annotated Bibliograpy,* New York/ Westport/ Connecticut/ London: Greenwood Press, 1992.

–   *What is Narrative Criticism?: A New Approach to the Bible*, London: SPCK, 1993.

Preisigke, F., *Vom göttlichen Fluidum nach ägyptischer Anschauung*, Heidelberg: Berlin/Leipzig: Papyrusinstitut, 1920.

Pritchard, J. B. (ed.), *The Ancient Near East: The Anthology of Texts and Pictures,* Oxford: OUP, 1958.

Ramsey, G. W., 'Is Name–giving an Act of Domination in Genesis 2: 23 and Elsewhere?', *CBQ* 50 (1988), 24–35.

Rashkow, I. N., *Upon the Dark Places: Anti–Semitism and Sexism in English Renaissance Biblical Translation*, (BALS 28), Sheffield: Almond Press, 1990.

–   *The Phallacy of Genesis: A Feminist–Psychoanalytic Approach,* Louisville, Kentucky, W/JKP, 1993.

Rendtorff, R., 'The Paradigm is Changing: Hopes and Fears', *BibInt* 1 (1993), 34–53.

–   *Canon and Theology: Overtures to an Old Testament Theology*, trans. & (ed.) by M. Kohl, Edinburgh: T &T Clark, 1993.

–   '"Covenant" as a Structuring Concept in Genesis and Exodus', *JBL* 108 (1989), 385–389.

–   *The Old Testament: An Introduction,* London: SCM Press, 1985.

Ricoeur, Paul, 'Biblical Hermeneutics', *Semeia* 4 (1975), 27–148.

–   *Essays on Biblical Interpretation*, L. S. Mudge (ed.), Philadelphia: Fortress Press/London: SPCK, 1981.

–   *Hermeneutics and the Human Sciences,* Cambridge/New York: CUP, 1981.

–   *Interpretation Theory: Discourse and the Surplus of Meaning*, Fort Worth, Texas: Christian University Press, 1976.

Richards, I. A., *The Philosophy of Rhetoric*, Oxford: OUP, 1936.

Rogerson, J. W., 'The Use of Sociology in Old Testament Studies', in *Congress Volume, Salamanca, 1983,* (VTS 36), J. A. Emerton (ed.), Leiden: E. J. Brill, 1985, 245–256.

– *Old Testament Criticism in the Nineteenth Century: England and Germany*, London: SPCK, 1984.

– 'Was Early Israel a Segmentary Society?', *JSOT* 36 (1986), 17–26.

– Genesis 1–11 (OTG), Sheffield: Sheffield Academic Press, 1991.

– 'What Does it Mean to be Human? The Central Question of Old Testament Theology', in *The Bible in Three Dimensions: Essays in Celebration of Forty Years of Biblical Studies in the University of Sheffield* (JSOTS 87), D. J. A. Clines *et al.* (eds.), Sheffield: JSOT Press, 1990, 285–298.

– 'Anthropology and the Old Testament', in *The World of Ancient Israel: Sociological, Anthropological and Political Perspectives,* R. E. Clements (ed.), Cambridge/New York/New Rochelle/Melbourne/Sydney: CUP, 1989. 17–37.

Rosenberg, D. & H. Bloom, *The Book of J,* London: Faber & Faber, 1991.

Rossi, Alice S., 'Preface: Feminist Lives and Works', in *The Feminist Papers: From Adam to de Beauvoir,* A. S. Rossi (ed.), New York/London: Columbia University Press, 1973, ix–xix.

Ruether, R. R., 'Feminism and Patriarchal Religion: Principles of Ideological Critique of the Bible', *JSOT* 22 (1982), 54–66.

– *Sexism and God Talk,* London: SCM, 1983.

– 'Feminist Interpretation: A Method of Correlation', in *Feminist Interpretation of the Bible,* L. M. Russell (ed.), Oxford/New York: Basil Blackwell, 1985, 111–124.

Russell, L. M., 'Authority and the Challenge of Feminist Interpretation', in *Feminist Interpretation of the Bible,* L. M. Russell (ed.), Oxford/New York: Basil Blackwell, 1985, 55–64.

Sakenfeld, K. D., 'The Bible and Woman: Bane or Blessing?' *TToday* 32 (1975), 222–233.

– 'Feminist Uses of Biblical Materials', in *Feminist Interpretation of the Bible,* L. M. Russell (ed.), Oxford/New York: Basil Blackwell, 1985, 55–64.

– 'Old Testament Perspectives: Methodological Issues', *JSOT* 22 (1982), 13–20.

– 'Feminist Biblical Interpretation', *TToday* 46 (1989), 154–168.

– 'In the Wilderness, Awaiting the Land: The Daughters of Zelophehad and Feminist Interpretation', *PSB* 19 (1988), 179–196.

Sasson, J. M., 'On Choosing Models for Recreating Israelite Pre–Monarchic History', *JSOT* 21 (1981), 3–24.

Sampson, Philip, 'The Rise of Postmodernity', in *Faith and Modernity,* P. Sampson *et al.* (eds.), Oxford: Regnum Press, 1994, 29–57.

Sasser, W., 'All About Eve', *DM* (1994), 2–7.

Saussure, F. de, *Course in General Linguistics,* (rev. ed.), trans. by W. Baskin, London: Peter Owen, 1974.

Sawyer, D. F. A.,'Resurrecting Eve? Feminist Critique of the Garden of Eden', in *A Walk in the Garden: Biblical Iconographical and Literary Images of Eden,* (JSOTS 136), P. Morris & D. Sawyer (eds.), Sheffield: JSOT Press, 1992, 273–288.

Sawyer, J. F. A., 'The Image of God, the Wisdom of Serpents and the Knowledge of Good and Evil', in *A Walk in the Garden,* P. Morris & D. Sawyer (eds.), Sheffield: JSOT Press, 1992 64–73.

–   'The Meaning of בצלם אלהים ("In the Image of God") in Genesis I–XI', *JTS* 25 (1974), 418–26.

Schmidt, E. R., 'Mögliche Kriterien für eine feministische Bibelauslegung', in *Feministisch gelesen,* E. R. Schmidt *et al.* (eds.), Stuttgart: Kreuz, 1988, 12–16.

Schmitt. J. J., 'Like Eve, Like Adam: *msl* in Gen 3,16', *Bib* 72 (1991), 1–22.

Schneiders, S. M.,'Feminist Hermeneutics', in *Hearing the New Testament: Strategies for Interpretation,* J. B. Green (ed.), Grand Rapids, Michigan: Wm. B. Eerdmans/ Carlisle: Paternoster Press, 1995, 349–369.

Schottroff, Luise, 'Die Schöpfungsgeschichte Gen. 1, 1– 2, 4a', in Luise and Willy Schottroff, *Die Macht der Auferstehung: Sozialgeschichtliche Bibelauslegungen,* Munich: Kaiser Verlag , 1988, 8–26.

–   'The Creation Narrative: Genesis 1. 1–2.4a', in *A Feminist Companion to Genesis ,* 24–38.

Schüngel–Straumann, H., 'On the Creation of Man and Woman in Genesis 1–3: The History and Reception of the Texts Reconsidered', in *A Feminist Companion to Genesis,* 53–76.

Schüssler Fiorenza, E., *But She said: Feminist Practices of Biblical Interpretation,* Boston: Beacon Press, 1992.

–   *Bread Not Stone: The Challenge of Feminist Biblical Interpretation,* Boston: Beacon Press, 1984.

–   *In Memory of Her: A Feminist Theological Reconstruction of Christian Origins,* New York: Cross Road Publishing, 1985.

–   'The Ethics of Biblical Interpretation: De–Centering Biblical Scholarship', *JBL* (1988), 3–17.

–   (ed.), *Searching the Scriptures: A Feminist Introduction,* vol.1, New York: Crossroad Publishing Company/London: SCM, 1994.

–   *Discipleship of Equals: A Critical Feminist Ekklesia–logy of Liberation,* London, SCM, 1993.

Schwartz, R. M. *et al.,The Postmodern Bible: The Bible and Culture Collective,* New Haven & London: Yale University Press, 1995.

Sharma, U., *Women, Work, and Property in North–West India,* London/New York: Tavistock Publications, 1980.

Silva, M., 'Contemporary Theories of Biblical Interpretation', in *NIB* vol. 1, Nashville: Abingdon Press, 1994, 107–124.

Simkins, R. A., *Creator and Creation: Nature in the World view of Ancient Israel,* Peabody, Massachusetts: Hendrickson, 1994.

Skinner, J., *Genesis* (ICC), 2nd ed., Edinburgh: T & T Clark, 1956.

Snaith, J. G., *Song of Songs,* (NCBC), Grand Rapids, Michigan: William B. Eerdmans, 1993.

Snaith, N. H., 'The Image of God', *Exp Tim* 91 (1979–80), 20.

Soggin, J. A., *Introduction to the Old Testament,* London: SCM Press, 1993 (1976).

Soskice, J. M., *Metaphor and Religious Language,* Oxford: Clarenden Press, 1985.

SPCK (Publisher), *The Family in Contemporary Society,* London: SPCK, 1958.

Speiser, E. A., *Genesis: A New Translation with Introduction and Commentary,* (AB), New York: Doubleday, 1964.

Spivey, Robert. A., 'Structuralism and Biblical Studies: The Uninvited Guest', *Int* 28 (1974), 133–145.

Sproul, B. C., *Principal Myths: Creating the World,* San Francisco: Harper and Row, 1979.

Stanton, E. C., *The Woman's Bible* Part I & II, (original 1895 and 1898) rept., Salem, New Hampshire: Ayer Company, Publishers Inc, 1988.

Sternberg, M., *The Poetics of Biblical Narrative: Ideological Literature and the Drama of Reading,* Bloomington: Indiana University Press, 1985.

Stratton, B. J., *Out of Eden: Reading, Rhetoric, and Ideology in Genesis 2–3* (JSOTS 208), Sheffield: Sheffield Academic Press, 1995.

Sugirtharajah, R. S., 'The Bible and its Asian Readers', *BibInt* 1(1993), 54–66.

Tavard, G. H., 'Sexist Language in Theology', *TS* 36 (1975), 700–724.

Terrien, Samuel, *Till the Heart Sings: A Biblical Theology of Manhood and Womanhood,* Philadelphia: Fortress Press, 1985.

Thiselton, A. C., *The Two Horizons: New Testament Hermeneutics and Philosophical Description with Special Reference to Heidegger, Bultmann, Gadamer and Wittgenstein,* Grand Rapids, Michigan: Eerdmans/Exeter: Paternoster, 1980.

– *New Horizons in Hermeneutics: The Theory and Practice of Transforming Biblical Reading,* London: Harper Collins, 1992.

– 'On Models and Methods, A Conversation with Robert Morgan', in *The Bible in Three Dimensions: Essays in Celebration of Biblical Studies in the University of Sheffield* (JSOTS 87), Sheffield: JSOT Press, 1990, 337–356.

– 'Structuralism and Biblical Studies: Method or Ideology?', *Exp Tim* 89 (1978), 329–335.

Thompson, J. A., *The Book of Jeremiah* (NICOT), Grand Rapids, Michigan: William B. Eerdmans, 1980.

Tolbert, M. A., 'Defining the Problem: The Bible and Feminist Hermeneutics', *Semeia* 28 (1983), 113–126.

– 'Protestant Feminists and the Bible: On the Horns of a Dilemma', in *The Pleasure of Her Text: Feminist Readings of Biblical and Historical Texts,* A. Bach (ed.), Philadelphia: Trinity Press, 1990, 5–23.

Tompkins, J. P., *Reader Response Criticism: From Formalism to Post–Structuralism,* Baltimore/London: Johns Hopkins University Press, 1980.

Trible, P., (Guest ed.), 'The Effects of Women's Studies on Biblical Studies: An Introduction', *JSOT* 22 (1982), 3–5.

- 'Feminist Hermeneutics and Biblical Studies', *The Christian Century* (3–10 Feb. 1982), 116–118.
- 'Depatriarchalizing in Biblical Interpretation', *JAAR* 41 (1973), 30–48.
- 'God, Nature of, in the OT', in *IDBS*, Nashville: Abingdon, 1976, 368–369.
- 'Post Script: Jottings on the Journey', in *Feminist Interpretation of the Bible,* 147–149.
- *God and the Rhetoric of Sexuality,* London: SCM, 1992 (Fortress Press, 1978).
- *Texts of Terror: Literary Feminist Readings of Biblical Narratives,* London: SCM, 1992. (Fortress Press, 1984).
- 'Bringing Miriam out of the Shadows', *BibRev* 5 (1989), 14–25, 34.
- 'Five Loaves and Two Fishes: Feminist Hermeneutics and Biblical Theology', *TS* 50 (1989), 279–95.
- 'Feminist Hermeneutics and Biblical Theology', in *The Flowering of Old Testament Theology,* B. C. Ollenburger *et al.* (eds.), Winona Lake: Eisenbrauns, 1992, 448–464.
- 'Treasures Old and New: Biblical Theology and the Challenge of Feminism', in *The Open Text: New Directions for Biblical Studies,* F. Watson (ed.), London: SCM, 1993, 32–56.
- *Rhetorical Criticism: Context, Method, and the Book of Jonah* Minneapolis: Fortress Press, 1994.

Tsumura, D. T., 'A Note on הרנך (Gen 3,16)' *Bib* 75 (1994), 398–400.

Vawter, B., *On Genesis: A New Reading* , New York: Doubleday & Co, Inc, 1977.

Van Seters, J., *Abraham in History and Tradition,* New Haven/London: Yale Univ. Press, 1975.

Vogels, W., 'It is not Good that the "Mensch" Should be Alone; I will Make him/her a Helper fit for him/her', *Eg T* 9 (1978), 9–35.

Von Rad, G., *Genesis,* (OTL), London: SCM, 1961.
- *Old Testament Theology: The Theology of Israel's Historical Traditions,* vol.1, trans. by D. M. G. Stalker, London: SCM, 1975.

Vos, Clarence J., *Woman in Old Testament Worship,* Amsterdem: N.V. Verenigde Drukkerijen Judels & Brinkman– Delft, 1968.

Yocum, G., 'Burning "Widows," Sacred "Prostitutes," and "Perfect Wives": Recent Studies of Hindu Women', *RelSRev* 20 (1994), 277–285.

Wallace, H. N., *The Eden Narrative,* Atlanta: Scholars Press, 1985.

Wallis, L., *Sociological Study of the Bible,* Chicago, 1912.

Walhout, C., 'Texts and Actions', in *The Responsibility of Hermeneutics*: Grand Rapids: William B. Eerdmans/Exeter: Paternoster Press, 1985, 34–42.

Walsh, J. T., 'Genesis 2: 4b–3: 24: A Synchronic Approach', *JBL* 96 (1977), 161–177.

Walton, J. H., *Ancient Israelite Literature in its Cultural Context: A Survey of Parallels between Biblical and Ancient Near Eastern Texts,* Grand Rapids, Michigan: Zondervan, 1989.

Waltke, B. K. & M. O' Connor (eds.), *An Introduction to Biblical Syntax,* Winona Lake, Indiana: Eisenbrauns, 1990.

Warner, M. (ed.), *The Bible as Rhetoric: Studies in Biblical Persuasion and Credibility,* London/New York: Routledge, 1990.

Watson, D. F. & A. J. Hauser, *Rhetorical Criticism of the Bible: A Comprehensive Bibliography with Notes on History and Method* (BIS 4), Leiden/New York/Köln: E. J. Brill, 1994.

Watson, F., *Text, Church and the World: Biblical Interpretation in Theological Perspective,* Edinburgh: T & T Clark, 1994.

– 'Strategies of Recovery and Resistance: Hermeneutical Reflections on Genesis 1–3 and its Pauline Reception', *JSNT* 45 (1992), 79–103.

Weber, M., *Ancient Judaism,* New York: Charles Scribener's Sons, 1952.

Weems, R. J., *Just a Sister Away: A Womanist Vision of Women's Relationships in the Bible,* San Diego, California: Luramedia, 1988.

– 'Reading Her Way through the Struggle: African American Women and the Bible' in *The Bible and Liberation: Political and Social Hermeneutics,* (rev. ed.), N. K. Gottwald & R. A. Horsley (eds), New York: Orbis/London: SPCK, 1993, 31–50.

Weippert, M., *The Settlement of the Israelite Tribes in Palestine,* London: SCM Press, 1971.

Wenham, G. J., *Genesis 1–15* (WBC 1), Milton Keynes: Word U. K. 1991 (original Dallas: Word Publishing, 1987).

Westermann, C., *Genesis 1–11, A Commentary,* trans. by J. J. Scullion, London: SPCK/ Minneapolis: Augsburg, 1984.

– *Creation,* Philadelphia: Fortress Press/London: SPCK, 1974.

Wevers, J. W., *Notes on the Greek Text of Genesis,* Atlanta: Scholars Press, 1993.

White, H. C., *Narration and Discourse in the Book of Genesis*, Cambridge: CUP, 1991.

– 'Introduction: Speech Act Theory and Literary Criticism', *Semeia* 41 (1988), 1–24.

– 'The Value of Speech Act Theory for Old Testament Hermeneutics', *Semeia* 41 (1988), 41–63.

Whitelam, K. W., 'Recreating the History of Israel', *JSOT* 35 (1986), 45–70.

Whiston, W. (trans.), *The Works of Josephus,: Complete and Unabridged,* Peabody: Hendrickson, 1992.

Wilfong, M. M., 'Genesis 2: 18–24' (Expository Article), *Int* 42 (1988), 58–63.

Wilson, R. R., *Prophecy and Society in Ancient Israel,* Philadelphia: Fortress Press, 1980.

– *Sociological Approaches to the Old Testament,* Philadelphia: Fortress Press, 1984.

Williams, A. J., 'The Relationship of Genesis 3: 20 to the Serpent', *ZAW* 89 (1979), 357–74.

Williams, J. G., *Women Recounted: Narrative thinking and the God of Israel,* (BALS 6), Sheffield: Almond Press, 1982.

Wolde, E., van, *A Semiotic Analysis of Genesis 2–3: A Semiotic Theory and Method of Analysis Applied to the Story of the Garden of Eden* (SSN 25), Assen: Van Gorum, 1989.

– *Words Become Worlds: Semantic Studies of Genesis 1–11* (BIS 6), Leiden/New York/Köln: E. J. Brill, 1994.

Wyatt, N., 'Interpreting the Creation and Fall Story in Genesis 2–3', *ZAW* 93 (1981), 10–21.

Subject Index

Adam, 30, 54, 60, 62, 63, 65, 72,
77, 79, 83, 86, 101, 104, 122, 126,
127, 128, 129, 134, 137, 153, 176,
182, 187, 216, 217, 250, 255, 259,
261, 262
Androcentric, X, 27, 38, 52, 67,
95, 96, 102, 110, 119, 120, 163,
171, 199, 204, 207, 219, 223,
231, 233, 234, 236, 244

communicative function, 19, 20,
100, 237
corresponding companion, 59, 83
creation narrative, XI, 30, 32, 33,
45, 56, 61, 68, 69, 71, 76, 78,
89, 91, 97, 100, 101, 104, 109,
112, 119, 120, 121, 126, 129,
132, 134, 137, 150, 151, 152,
162, 168, 172, 173, 175, 177,
178, 179, 183, 184, 186, 190,
194, 199, 207, 210, 215, 226,
229

Deconstruction, 15, 39, 93, 133
Determinate meaning, 13, 15, 21,
23

Earth creature, 57, 58, 62, 63, 76,
77, 80, 85, 110, 134, 135, 136
Earthling, 58, 152
Eros, 56, 57, 64, 65, 66, 91, 111
Eve, 3, 12, 13, 31, 38, 41, 58, 61,
63, 66, 71, 72, 73, 81, 84, 85,
86, 90, 91, 95, 101, 104, 106,
107, 110, 114, 115, 122, 123,
124, 125, 126, 127, 128, 129,
132, 134, 135, 137, 145, 146,
147, 148, 150, 151, 153, 156,
157, 158, 161, 162, 164, 165,
171, 175, 176, 177, 180, 182,
184, 185, 187, 201, 203, 207,
210, 217, 221, 230, 244, 251,

252, 255, 256, 257, 258, 259,
261, 262

Feminine Imagery, 105
Feminist approach, 31, 91, 105,
225
Feminist ideology, 97, 183
Feminist methods, 92
Feminist Old Testament theology,
53

Gender roles, 150, 162, 169, 183

Hermeneutical clue, 54, 55
Hermeneutics of recuperation, 36,
38, 234
Hermeneutics of resistance, 39,
231, 234
Hermeneutics of suspicion, 5, 18,
38, 97, 144, 230
Hermeneutics of understanding, 4

Image of God, 54, 68, 70, 71, 72,
74, 96, 111, 192, 194, 195, 196,
197, 198, 204, 208, 209, 210,
212, 213, 214, 215, 216, 217,
221, 224, 228, 229, 242
Indeterminate meaning, 13
Interpretative community, 17, 24,
108

Linguistic theories, 4, 7, 13, 15
Literary reading, 8, 18, 45, 51, 64,
81, 89, 99, 101, 114, 121, 185,
220, 234, 239
Literary theories, 7, 26

Man's rule, 89, 90, 113, 114, 120,
227, 228, 231
Methodological Clue, 54

Narrative Reading, 10, 18, 199,
200, 211, 217

Patriarchal, XII, 7, 27, 34, 35, 36,
37, 38, 39, 52, 53, 56, 57, 70,
74, 91, 94, 96, 97, 99, 101, 102,
104, 105, 106, 107, 108, 109,
110, 111, 114, 115, 121, 122,
123, 126, 130, 132, 133, 136,
137, 144, 146, 162, 167, 183,
184, 185, 198, 206, 207, 212,
217, 220, 223, 224, 227, 230,
231, 234, 235, 236, 237, 238,
241, 242
Philosophical theories, 7
Pluralism, 21
Post-modern, 11
Psycho–Analytic Reading, 126,
133

Reader response, 128, 162

Rhetorical criticism, 9, 16, 46, 47,
48, 49, 50, 54, 55, 80, 109
Rhetorical reading, 49, 63, 177

Socio–critical hermeneutics, 6, 7,
17, 28, 70, 244
Socio–Literary Reading, 129
Sociology and Old Testament, 139
Socio–pragmatic, 17, 23, 28, 96,
98, 111, 244
Speech Act Theory, 16, 19, 78, 85,
88, 99
Structuralist Reading, 104
Subordination of woman, 66, 89

Topical Clue, 54, 55, 70, 97, 109

Wisdom tale, 155, 168
Woman's Bible, 32, 33, 38, 86,
263
Woman's desire, 57, 253
Womanist, 41, 237
Womanist writers, 41

Author Index

Abrams, 7, 8, 9, 10, 15, 16, 26, 47, 247
Achtemeier, 12, 79, 247
Ahlström, 147, 163, 247
Alter, 10, 19, 26, 49, 50, 72, 73, 74, 191, 247
Anderson, 169, 196, 247, 252
Armstrong, 180, 247
Atkinson, 59, 76, 247
Austin, 13, 16, 78, 99, 100, 247

Bailey, 178, 247
Bal, 18, 27, 39, 41, 58, 61, 65, 77, 78, 87, 88, 98, 129, 131, 133, 134, 135, 136, 155, 187, 199, 203, 231, 234, 235, 238, 243, 247
Bar–Efrat, 9, 10, 74, 87, 247
Barr, 71, 118, 179, 180, 192, 201, 209, 212, 213, 214, 224, 247
Barth, 71, 193, 224, 225, 226, 247
Barton, 7, 11, 21, 22, 105, 107, 143, 144, 248, 259
Bass, 32, 248
Bauckham, 97, 248
Beattie, 150, 248
Beauvoir, 29, 34, 70, 248, 261
Bechtel, 82, 137, 150, 152, 248
Bellis, 61, 99, 175, 203, 248
Berlin, 10, 14, 248, 254, 260
Bernhardt, 248
Beyerle, 25, 248
Bimson, 165, 248
Bird, 18, 27, 36, 37, 45, 71, 72, 73, 74, 75, 79, 80, 81, 98, 102, 106, 126, 153, 175, 181, 189, 190, 191, 192, 193, 194, 195, 196, 197, 198, 199, 200, 201, 202, 203, 204, 205, 206, 207, 208, 209, 210, 211, 212, 213, 214, 215, 216, 217, 218, 219, 220, 221, 222, 223, 224, 225, 226,
227, 229, 230, 233, 234, 239, 241, 243, 244, 248
Blackburn, 10, 249
Bleicher, 5, 249
Blenkinsopp, 168, 191, 249
Bonhoeffer, 193, 249
Boomershine, 85, 249
Bray, 19, 249
Brenner, 18, 39, 40, 74, 106, 121, 129, 130, 169, 187, 231, 234, 235, 237, 249
Brett, 20, 21, 22, 25, 26, 72, 172, 250
Brown, 250
Brueggemann, 89, 250
Buber, 193, 250
Bushnell, 61, 250

Caird, 95, 250
Camp, 170, 250
Carmichael, 250
Carroll, 220, 250
Cassuto, 60, 62, 120, 122, 126, 158, 181, 250
Chaney, 147, 250
Childs, 27, 76, 80, 83, 221, 222, 250
Clements, 41, 250, 261
Clifford, 69, 250
Clines, 3, 12, 13, 21, 23, 24, 46, 47, 61, 72, 73, 75, 81, 82, 83, 84, 85, 101, 104, 105, 106, 107, 117, 125, 127, 139, 176, 179, 191, 192, 195, 207, 213, 214, 215, 225, 236, 238, 242, 250, 252, 255, 256, 261
Coats, 76, 196, 247, 251
Collins, 4, 10, 31, 72, 106, 132, 141, 247, 251, 254, 256, 260, 263
Connor, 146, 218, 258, 259, 264
Coote, 90, 142, 251
Cotterell, 25, 54, 71, 117, 251

Crook, 33, 34
Culler, 15, 36, 39, 251
Culley, 18, 19, 51, 76, 251

Das, 89, 167, 251
Davies, 14, 131, 251
Delitzsch, 82, 83, 220, 251, 256
Dennis, 61, 125, 251
Derrida, 13, 15, 251
Detweiler, 9, 10, 13, 46, 252
Dozeman, 48, 252
Dragga, 252
Driver, 60, 123, 158, 159, 250, 252

Edelman, 165, 166, 252
Emerton, 77, 139, 169, 252, 255,
    261
Emmerson, 36, 41, 61, 62, 91, 126,
    162, 170, 252
Eskenazi, 170, 252
Evans, 36, 41, 61, 63, 91, 221, 252
Exum, 12, 21, 37, 39, 46, 191, 252

Farmer, 97, 252
Fee, 9, 252
Fetterly, 39, 252
Fewell, 9, 18, 27, 39, 40, 59, 81,
    91, 92, 101, 118, 130, 131, 132,
    133, 143, 172, 185, 231, 234,
    235, 236, 252, 253
Finkelstein, 142, 147, 164, 253
Fish, 11, 12, 13, 17, 18, 253
Fishbane, 209, 253
Fleming, 36, 61, 86, 112, 113, 114,
    177, 203, 231, 234, 238, 243,
    253
Foh, 66, 159, 253
Fowler, 9, 11, 253
Freedman, 62, 141, 250, 253, 258
Fretheim, 124, 125, 253
Frick, 141, 253
Fritz, 142, 253
Frymer, 186, 187, 188, 253
Fulkerson, 12, 253

Gadamer, 5, 6, 100, 235, 253, 263

Galambush, 79, 88, 89, 253
Gallup, 59, 240, 253
Gardner, 74, 77, 79, 253
Gifford, 31, 32, 33, 34, 71, 247,
    254
Gitay, 46, 47, 48, 99, 254
Goldingay, 21, 22, 23, 94, 103,
    195, 254
Good, 132, 215, 252, 254
Gottwald, 37, 38, 42, 46, 140, 141,
    142, 145, 146, 147, 148, 163,
    168, 171, 172, 185, 202, 212,
    243, 248, 249, 254, 256, 257,
    258, 265
Goulder, 22, 169, 248, 254, 256
Greenwood, 4, 14, 254, 260
Grimké, 30, 31

Habel, 168, 191, 254
Hackett, 73, 254
Hamilton, 76, 169, 173, 174, 194,
    196, 215, 254
Hanson, 95, 254
Harland, 195, 254
Hart, 195, 254
Hauser, 47, 48, 80, 163, 177, 255,
    265
Hayter, 31, 36, 41, 58, 61, 63, 71,
    91, 95, 177, 203, 210, 215, 221,
    230, 234, 255
Heidegger, 4, 6, 255, 263
Heine, 94, 105, 243, 255
Herion, 143, 144, 171, 183, 255
Hess, 77, 78, 79, 87, 174, 255
Higgins, 60, 86, 255
Holladay, 22, 219, 255

Jackson, 49, 112, 255, 256
Jacobson, 13, 14, 255
Jeanrond, 3, 4, 5, 6, 17, 19, 21, 25,
    26, 27, 255
Jobling, 11, 38, 64, 80, 101, 103,
    104, 105, 137, 185, 236, 238,
    249, 256, 258
Jones, 220, 256
Jónsson, 192, 256

Josipovici, 256
Joyce, 22, 106, 132, 167, 224, 236, 244, 256

Kaiser, 61, 62, 159, 229, 256, 262
Kautzsch, 213, 256
Keegan, 5, 11, 18, 249, 256
Keil, 220, 256
Kennedy, 48, 179, 256
Kenny, 241, 256
Kessler, 47, 49, 112, 256
Kidner, 176, 256
Kikawada, 112, 125, 256
Kimel, 242, 256
Kimelman, 244, 257
Koehler, 180, 218, 257
Köhler, 58, 257
Korsak, 36, 84, 119, 120, 231, 234, 257
Kreitzer, 74, 257

Laffey, 38, 41, 91, 114, 115, 184, 231, 235, 243, 244, 257
Lan, 59, 257
Lanser, 74, 78, 79, 85, 88, 89, 93, 104, 257
Lebra, 167, 257
Lemche, 141, 163, 257
Lévi–Strauss, 13, 257
Lohfink, 216, 257
Lundin, 15, 257

Maddox, 5, 257
Maly, 69, 257
Martin, 4, 47, 50, 54, 68, 147, 193, 223, 257
Mary, 12, 31, 36, 41, 58, 61, 84, 91, 102, 105, 107, 119, 203, 210, 221, 223, 230, 241, 245, 252, 256, 257
Mayes, 141, 142, 257
McKane, 169, 257
McKnight, 12, 258
Mendenhall, 141, 146, 147, 163, 168, 258
Mettinger, 95, 214, 258

Meyers, 18, 38, 45, 46, 58, 61, 66, 72, 90, 91, 113, 139, 144, 145, 146, 147, 148, 149, 150, 151, 152, 153, 154, 155, 156, 157, 158, 159, 160, 161, 162, 163, 164, 165, 166, 167, 168, 169, 170, 171, 172, 173, 175, 177, 179, 180, 181, 182, 183, 184, 185, 186, 187, 188, 197, 199, 200, 202, 204, 208, 230, 233, 234, 235, 239, 242, 243, 244, 258
Miller, 37, 68, 177, 209, 249, 259
Millet, 34, 70, 259
Milne, 39, 101, 104, 105, 137, 231, 235, 236, 244, 259
Moltmann, 210, 259
Morgan, 4, 11, 21, 22, 186, 259, 263
Moye, 175, 176, 259
Muilenburg, 48, 49, 55, 112, 255, 256, 259
Murphy, 69, 169, 250, 259
Murray, 29, 30

Naidoff, 259
Neuer, 75, 89, 259
Neusner, 90, 259
Newsom, 41, 258, 259
Niditch, 65, 202, 210, 259
Noble, 17, 18, 259
Nowell, 259

Osborne, 22, 25, 99, 259
Osiek, 36, 260

Pannenberg, 95, 260
Pardes, 39, 79, 94, 97, 98, 104, 105, 121, 122, 123, 124, 125, 126, 131, 132, 217, 229, 231, 234, 235, 244, 260
Park, 59, 260
Patrick, 37, 50, 63, 79, 260
Patte, 14, 18, 260
Petersen, 140, 260
Pinnock, 19, 260

Pope, 169, 260
Powell, 4, 7, 8, 9, 12, 26, 47, 49,
    50, 260
Preisigke, 215, 260
Pritchard, 178, 260

Radford Ruether, 31, 102, 112,
    202
Ramsey, 85, 124, 260
Rashkow, 27, 39, 40, 54, 57, 61,
    62, 65, 66, 126, 127, 128, 129,
    231, 234, 235, 243, 260
Rendtorff, 22, 68, 169, 175, 260
Richards, 54, 70, 71, 261
Ricoeur, 5, 6, 100, 260
Rogerson, 6, 7, 19, 22, 25, 72, 80,
    108, 139, 142, 163, 165, 171,
    172, 179, 189, 221, 225, 261
Rosenberg, 154, 261
Rossi, 29, 261
Russell, 107, 108, 261

Sakenfeld, 35, 61, 63, 86, 92, 99,
    170, 261
Sampson, 10, 261
Sarah, 30, 31, 61, 125, 182, 251
Sasser, 38, 185, 261
Sasson, 140, 141, 261
Saussure, 13, 261
Sawyer, 74, 107, 214, 215, 217,
    250, 262
Schmidt, 35, 58, 257, 262
Schmitt, 182, 262
Schneiders, 96, 262
Schottroff, 36, 229, 231, 234, 262
Schüngel, 36, 169, 209, 212, 226,
    227, 228, 230, 234, 262
Schüssler Fiorenza, 32, 36, 38, 98,
    102, 184, 262
Schwartz, 11, 243, 262
Sharma, 167, 262
Silva, 22, 262
Simkins, 201, 212, 262
Skinner, 60, 158, 159, 174, 262
Snaith, 169, 195, 263
Soggin, 191, 263

Soskice, 54, 71, 106, 132, 256, 263
Speiser, 58, 60, 76, 158, 168, 174,
    191, 263
Spivey, 14, 263
Sproul, 151, 263
Stanton, 32, 33, 42, 86, 121, 153,
    263
Sternberg, 10, 40, 49, 99, 253, 263
Stratton, 89, 92, 263
Stuart, 9, 252
Sugirtharajah, 59, 240, 241, 263

Tavard, 241, 242, 263
Terrien, 61, 117, 127, 263
Thiselton, 4, 5, 6, 7, 10, 12, 14, 17,
    19, 20, 21, 22, 23, 25, 70, 93,
    96, 98, 103, 104, 110, 111, 135,
    184, 186, 235, 263
Thompson, 100, 220, 263
Tolbert, 37, 102, 105, 106, 132,
    223, 263
Tompkins, 12, 263
Trible, 18, 20, 27, 30, 31, 35, 36,
    37, 41, 42, 45, 46, 48, 49, 51,
    52, 53, 54, 55, 56, 57, 58, 59,
    60, 61, 62, 63, 64, 65, 66, 67,
    68, 69, 70, 71, 72, 73, 74, 75,
    76, 77, 78, 79, 80, 81, 83, 84,
    85, 86, 87, 88, 91, 92, 93, 94,
    96, 97, 98, 99, 100, 101, 102,
    103, 104, 105, 108, 109, 110,
    111, 112, 113, 114, 115, 119,
    121, 124, 127, 128, 129, 133,
    134, 135, 136, 137, 152, 153,
    155, 177, 180, 192, 197, 199,
    200, 203, 207, 208, 211, 212,
    221, 224, 226, 229, 230, 233,
    234, 236, 238, 243, 244, 263
Tsumura, 180, 264

Van Seters, 169, 264
Vawter, 76, 264
Vogels, 82, 116, 117, 137, 264
Von Rad, 63, 68, 69, 75, 76, 87,
    125, 168, 176, 178, 264
Vos, 81, 82, 218, 264

Paternoster Biblical Monographs
(All titles uniform with this volume)
Dates in bold are of projected publication

Joseph Abraham
Eve: Accused or Acquitted?
A Reconsideration of Feminist Readings of the Creation Narrative Texts in Genesis 1–3
Two contrary views dominate contemporary feminist biblical scholarship. One finds in the Bible an unequivocal equality between the sexes from the very creation of humanity, whilst the other sees the biblical text as irredeemably patriarchal and androcentric. Dr Abraham enters into dialogue with both camps as well as introducing his own method of approach. An invaluable tool for any one who is interested in this contemporary debate.
2002 / 0-85364-971-5 / xxiv + 272pp

Octavian D. Baban
Mimesis and Luke's on the Road Encounters in Luke-Acts
Luke's Theology of the Way and its Literary Representation
The book argues on theological and literary (mimetic) grounds that Luke's on-the-road encounters, especially those belonging to the post-Easter period, are part of his complex theology of the Way. Jesus' teaching and that of the apostles is presented by Luke as a challenging answer to the Hellenistic reader's thirst for adventure, good literature, and existential paradigms.
2005 */ 1-84227-253-5 / approx. 374pp*

Paul Barker
The Triumph of Grace in Deuteronomy
This book is a textual and theological analysis of the interaction between the sin and faithlessness of Israel and the grace of Yahweh in response, looking especially at Deuteronomy chapters 1–3, 8–10 and 29–30. The author argues that the grace of Yahweh is determinative for the ongoing relationship between Yahweh and Israel and that Deuteronomy anticipates and fully expects Israel to be faithless.
2004 / 1-84227-226-8 / xxii + 270pp

Jonathan F. Bayes
The Weakness of the Law
God's Law and the Christian in New Testament Perspective
A study of the four New Testament books which refer to the law as weak (Acts, Romans, Galatians, Hebrews) leads to a defence of the third use in the Reformed debate about the law in the life of the believer.
2000 / 0-85364-957-X / xii + 244pp

Mark Bonnington
The Antioch Episode of Galatians 2:11-14 in Historical and Cultural Context
The Galatians 2 'incident' in Antioch over table-fellowship suggests significant disagreement between the leading apostles. This book analyses the background to the disagreement by locating the incident within the dynamics of social interaction between Jews and Gentiles. It proposes a new way of understanding the relationship between the individuals and issues involved.
2005 / 1-84227-050-8 / approx. 350pp

David Bostock
A Portrayal of Trust
The Theme of Faith in the Hezekiah Narratives
This study provides detailed and sensitive readings of the Hezekiah narratives (2 Kings 18–20 and Isaiah 36–39) from a theological perspective. It concentrates on the theme of faith, using narrative criticism as its methodology. Attention is paid especially to setting, plot, point of view and characterization within the narratives. A largely positive portrayal of Hezekiah emerges that underlines the importance and relevance of scripture.
2005 / 1-84227-314-0 / approx. 300pp

Mark Bredin
Jesus, Revolutionary of Peace
A Non-violent Christology in the Book of Revelation
This book aims to demonstrate that the figure of Jesus in the Book of Revelation can best be understood as an active non-violent revolutionary.
2003 / 1-84227-153-9 / xviii + 262pp

Robinson Butarbutar
Paul and Conflict Resolution
An Exegetical Study of Paul's Apostolic Paradigm in 1 Corinthians 9
The author sees the apostolic paradigm in 1 Corinthians 9 as part of Paul's unified arguments in 1 Corinthians 8–10 in which he seeks to mediate in the dispute over the issue of food offered to idols. The book also sees its relevance for dispute-resolution today, taking the conflict within the author's church as an example.
2006 / 1-84227-315-9 / approx. 280pp

Daniel J-S Chae
Paul as Apostle to the Gentiles
His Apostolic Self-awareness and its Influence on the Soteriological Argument in Romans
Opposing 'the post-Holocaust interpretation of Romans', Daniel Chae competently demonstrates that Paul argues for the equality of Jew and Gentile in Romans. Chae's fresh exegetical interpretation is academically outstanding and spiritually encouraging.
1997 / 0-85364-829-8 / xiv + 378pp

Luke L. Cheung
The Genre, Composition and Hermeneutics of the Epistle of James
The present work examines the employment of the wisdom genre with a certain compositional structure and the interpretation of the law through the Jesus tradition of the double love command by the author of the Epistle of James to serve his purpose in promoting perfection and warning against doubleness among the eschatologically renewed people of God in the Diaspora.
2003 / 1-84227-062-1 / xvi + 372pp

Youngmo Cho
Spirit and Kingdom in the Writings of Luke and Paul
The relationship between Spirit and Kingdom is a relatively unexplored area in Lukan and Pauline studies. This book offers a fresh perspective of two biblical writers on the subject. It explores the difference between Luke's and Paul's understanding of the Spirit by examining the specific question of the relationship of the concept of the Spirit to the concept of the Kingdom of God in each writer.
2005 / 1-84227-316-7 / approx. 270pp

Andrew C. Clark
Parallel Lives
The Relation of Paul to the Apostles in the Lucan Perspective
This study of the Peter-Paul parallels in Acts argues that their purpose was to emphasize the themes of continuity in salvation history and the unity of the Jewish and Gentile missions. New light is shed on Luke's literary techniques, partly through a comparison with Plutarch.
2001 / 1-84227-035-4 / xviii + 386pp

Andrew D. Clarke
Secular and Christian Leadership in Corinth
A Socio-Historical and Exegetical Study of 1 Corinthians 1–6
This volume is an investigation into the leadership structures and dynamics of first-century Roman Corinth. These are compared with the practice of leadership in the Corinthian Christian community which are reflected in 1 Corinthians 1–6, and contrasted with Paul's own principles of Christian leadership.
2005 / 1-84227-229-2 / 200pp

Stephen Finamore
God, Order and Chaos
René Girard and the Apocalypse
Readers are often disturbed by the images of destruction in the book of Revelation and unsure why they are unleashed after the exaltation of Jesus. This book examines past approaches to these texts and uses René Girard's theories to revive some old ideas and propose some new ones.
2005 / 1-84227-197-0 / approx. 344pp

David G. Firth
Surrendering Retribution in the Psalms
Responses to Violence in the Individual Complaints
In *Surrendering Retribution in the Psalms*, David Firth examines the ways in which the book of Psalms inculcates a model response to violence through the repetition of standard patterns of prayer. Rather than seeking justification for retributive violence, Psalms encourages not only a surrender of the right of retribution to Yahweh, but also sets limits on the retribution that can be sought in imprecations. Arising initially from the author's experience in South Africa, the possibilities of this model to a particular context of violence is then briefly explored.
2005 / 1-84227-337-X / xviii + 154pp

Scott J. Hafemann
Suffering and Ministry in the Spirit
Paul's Defence of His Ministry in II Corinthians 2:14–3:3
Shedding new light on the way Paul defended his apostleship, the author offers a careful, detailed study of 2 Corinthians 2:14–3:3 linked with other key passages throughout 1 and 2 Corinthians. Demonstrating the unity and coherence of Paul's argument in this passage, the author shows that Paul's suffering served as the vehicle for revealing God's power and glory through the Spirit.
2000 / 0-85364-967-7 / xiv + 262pp

Scott J. Hafemann
Paul, Moses and the History of Israel
The Letter/Spirit Contrast and the Argument from Scripture in 2 Corinthians 3
An exegetical study of the call of Moses, the second giving of the Law (Exodus
32–34), the new covenant, and the prophetic understanding of the history of
Israel in 2 Corinthians 3. Hafemann's work demonstrates Paul's contextual use
of the Old Testament and the essential unity between the Law and the Gospel
within the context of the distinctive ministries of Moses and Paul.
2005 / 1-84227-317-5 / xii + 498pp

Douglas S. McComiskey
Lukan Theology in the Light of the Gospel's Literary Structure
Luke's Gospel was purposefully written with theology embedded in its patterned
literary structure. A critical analysis of this cyclical structure provides new
windows into Luke's interpretation of the individual pericopes comprising the
Gospel and illuminates several of his theological interests.
2004 / 1-84227-148-2 / xviii + 388pp

Stephen Motyer
Your Father the Devil?
A New Approach to John and 'The Jews'
Who are 'the Jews' in John's Gospel? Defending John against the charge of
antisemitism, Motyer argues that, far from demonising the Jews, the Gospel
seeks to present Jesus as 'Good News for Jews' in a late first century setting.
1997 / 0-85364-832-8 / xiv + 260pp

Esther Ng
Reconstructing Christian Origins?
The Feminist Theology of Elizabeth Schüssler Fiorenza: An Evaluation
In a detailed evaluation, the author challenges Elizabeth Schüssler Fiorenza's
reconstruction of early Christian origins and her underlying presuppositions. The
author also presents her own views on women's roles both then and now.
2002 / 1-84227-055-9 / xxiv + 468pp

Robin Parry
Old Testament Story and Christian Ethics
The Rape of Dinah as a Case Study
What is the role of story in ethics and, more particularly, what is the role of Old Testament story in Christian ethics? This book, drawing on the work of contemporary philosophers, argues that narrative is crucial in the ethical shaping of people and, drawing on the work of contemporary Old Testament scholars, that story plays a key role in Old Testament ethics. Parry then argues that when situated in canonical context Old Testament stories can be reappropriated by Christian readers in their own ethical formation. The shocking story of the rape of Dinah and the massacre of the Shechemites provides a fascinating case study for exploring the parameters within which Christian ethical appropriations of Old Testament stories can live.

2004 / 1-84227-210-1 / xx + 350pp

Ian Paul
Power to See the World Anew
The Value of Paul Ricoeur's Hermeneutic of Metaphor in Interpreting the Symbolism of Revelation 12 and 13
This book is a study of the hermeneutics of metaphor of Paul Ricoeur, one of the most important writers on hermeneutics and metaphor of the last century. It sets out the key points of his theory, important criticisms of his work, and how his approach, modified in the light of these criticisms, offers a methodological framework for reading apocalyptic texts.

2006 / 1-84227-056-7 / approx. 350pp

Robert L. Plummer
Paul's Understanding of the Church's Mission
Did the Apostle Paul Expect the Early Christian Communities to Evangelize?
This book engages in a careful study of Paul's letters to determine if the apostle expected the communities to which he wrote to engage in missionary activity. It helpfully summarizes the discussion on this debated issue, judiciously handling contested texts, and provides a way forward in addressing this critical question. While admitting that Paul rarely explicitly commands the communities he founded to evangelize, Plummer amasses significant incidental data to provide a convincing case that Paul did indeed expect his churches to engage in mission activity. Throughout the study, Plummer progressively builds a theological basis for the church's mission that is both distinctively Pauline and compelling.

2006 / 1-84227-333-7 / approx. 324pp

David Powys
'Hell': A Hard Look at a Hard Question
The Fate of the Unrighteous in New Testament Thought
This comprehensive treatment seeks to unlock the original meaning of terms and
phrases long thought to support the traditional doctrine of hell. It concludes that
there is an alternative—one which is more biblical, and which can positively
revive the rationale for Christian mission.
1997 / 0-85364-831-X / xxii + 478pp

Sorin Sabou
Between Horror and Hope
Paul's Metaphorical Language of Death in Romans 6.1-11
This book argues that Paul's metaphorical language of death in Romans 6.1-11
conveys two aspects: horror and hope. The 'horror' aspect is conveyed by the
'crucifixion' language, and the 'hope' aspect by 'burial' language. The life of
the Christian believer is understood, as relationship with sin is concerned ('death
to sin'), between these two realities: horror and hope.
2005 / 1-84227-322-1 / approx. 224pp

Rosalind Selby
The Comical Doctrine
The Epistemology of New Testament Hermeneutics
This book argues that the gospel breaks through postmodernity's critique of
truth and the referential possibilities of textuality with its gift of grace. With a
rigorous, philosophical challenge to modernist and postmodernist assumptions,
Selby offers an alternative epistemology to all who would still read with faith
and with academic credibility.
2005 / 1-84227-212-8 / approx. 350pp

Kiwoong Son
Zion Symbolism in Hebrews
Hebrews 12.18-24 as a Hermeneutical Key to the Epistle
This book challenges the general tendency of understanding the Epistle to the
Hebrews against a Hellenistic background and suggests that the Epistle should
be understood in the light of the Jewish apocalyptic tradition. The author
especially argues for the importance of the theological symbolism of Sinai and
Zion (Heb. 12:18-24) as it provides the Epistle's theological background as well
as the rhetorical basis of the superiority motif of Jesus throughout the Epistle.
2005 / 1-84227-368-X / approx. 280pp

Kevin Walton
Thou Traveller Unknown
The Presence and Absence of God in the Jacob Narrative
The author offers a fresh reading of the story of Jacob in the book of Genesis through the paradox of divine presence and absence. The work also seeks to make a contribution to Pentateuchal studies by bringing together a close reading of the final text with historical critical insights, doing justice to the text's historical depth, final form and canonical status.
2003 / 1-84227-059-1 / xvi + 238pp

George M. Wieland
The Significance of Salvation
A Study of Salvation Language in the Pastoral Epistles
The language and ideas of salvation pervade the three Pastoral Epistles. This study offers a close examination of their soteriological statements. In all three letters the idea of salvation is found to play a vital paraenetic role, but each also exhibits distinctive soteriological emphases. The results challenge common assumptions about the Pastoral Epistles as a corpus.
2005 / 1-84227-257-8 / approx. 324pp

Alistair Wilson
When Will These Things Happen?
A Study of Jesus as Judge in Matthew 21–25
This study seeks to allow Matthew's carefully constructed presentation of Jesus to be given full weight in the modern evaluation of Jesus' eschatology. Careful analysis of the text of Matthew 21–25 reveals Jesus to be standing firmly in the Jewish prophetic and wisdom traditions as he proclaims and enacts imminent judgement on the Jewish authorities then boldly claims the central role in the final and universal judgement.
2004 / 1-84227-146-6 / xxii + 272pp

Lindsay Wilson
Joseph Wise and Otherwise
The Intersection of Covenant and Wisdom in Genesis 37–50
This book offers a careful literary reading of Genesis 37–50 that argues that the Joseph story contains both strong covenant themes and many wisdom-like elements. The connections between the two helps to explore how covenant and wisdom might intersect in an integrated biblical theology.
2004 / 1-84227-140-7 / xvi + 340pp

Stephen I. Wright
The Voice of Jesus
Studies in the Interpretation of Six Gospel Parables
This literary study considers how the 'voice' of Jesus has been heard in different periods of parable interpretation, and how the categories of figure and trope may help us towards a sensitive reading of the parables today.
2000 / 0-85364-975-8 / xiv + 280pp

Paternoster:
thinking faith

Paternoster
9 Holdom Avenue,
Bletchley,
Milton Keynes MK1 1QR,
United Kingdom
Web: www.authenticmedia.co.uk/paternoster

Paternoster Theological Monographs

(All titles uniform with this volume)
Dates in bold are of projected publication

Emil Bartos
Deification in Eastern Orthodox Theology
An Evaluation and Critique of the Theology of Dumitru Staniloae
Bartos studies a fundamental yet neglected aspect of Orthodox theology: deification. By examining the doctrines of anthropology, christology, soteriology and ecclesiology as they relate to deification, he provides an important contribution to contemporary dialogue between Eastern and Western theologians.
1999 / 0-85364-956-1 / xii + 370pp

Graham Buxton
The Trinity, Creation and Pastoral Ministry
Imaging the Perichoretic God
In this book the author proposes a three-way conversation between theology, science and pastoral ministry. His approach draws on a Trinitarian understanding of God as a relational being of love, whose life 'spills over' into all created reality, human and non-human. By locating human meaning and purpose within God's 'creation-community' this book offers the possibility of a transforming engagement between those in pastoral ministry and the scientific community.
2005 / 1-84227-369-8 / approx. 380 pp

Iain D. Campbell
Fixing the Indemnity
The Life and Work of George Adam Smith
When Old Testament scholar George Adam Smith (1856–1942) delivered the Lyman Beecher lectures at Yale University in 1899, he confidently declared that 'modern criticism has won its war against traditional theories. It only remains to fix the amount of the indemnity.' In this biography, Iain D. Campbell assesses Smith's critical approach to the Old Testament and evaluates its consequences, showing that Smith's life and work still raises questions about the relationship between biblical scholarship and evangelical faith.
2004 / 1-84227-228-4 / xx + 256pp

Tim Chester
Mission and the Coming of God
Eschatology, the Trinity and Mission in the Theology of Jürgen Moltmann
This book explores the theology and missiology of the influential contemporary
theologian, Jürgen Moltmann. It highlights the important contribution Moltmann
has made while offering a critique of his thought from an evangelical
perspective. In so doing, it touches on pertinent issues for evangelical
missiology. The conclusion takes Calvin as a starting point, proposing 'an
eschatology of the cross' which offers a critique of the over-realised
eschatologies in liberation theology and certain forms of evangelicalism.
2006 / 1-84227-320-5 / approx. 224pp

Sylvia Wilkey Collinson
Making Disciples
The Significance of Jesus' Educational Strategy for Today's Church
This study examines the biblical practice of discipling, formulates a definition,
and makes comparisons with modern models of education. A recommendation is
made for greater attention to its practice today.
2004 / 1-84227-116-4 / xiv + 278pp

Darrell Cosden
A Theology of Work
Work and the New Creation
Through dialogue with Moltmann, Pope John Paul II and others, this book
develops a genitive 'theology of work', presenting a theological definition of
work and a model for a theological ethics of work that shows work's nature,
value and meaning now and eschatologically. Work is shown to be a
transformative activity consisting of three dynamically inter-related dimensions:
the instrumental, relational and ontological.
2005 / 1-84227-332-9 / xvi + 208pp

Stephen M. Dunning
The Crisis and the Quest
A Kierkegaardian Reading of Charles Williams
Employing Kierkegaardian categories and analysis, this study investigates both
the central crisis in Charles Williams's authorship between hermetism and
Christianity (Kierkegaard's Religions A and B), and the quest to resolve this
crisis, a quest that ultimately presses the bounds of orthodoxy.
2000 / 0-85364-985-5 / xxiv + 254pp

Keith Ferdinando
The Triumph of Christ in African Perspective
A Study of Demonology and Redemption in the African Context
The book explores the implications of the gospel for traditional African fears of occult aggression. It analyses such traditional approaches to suffering and biblical responses to fears of demonic evil, concluding with an evaluation of African beliefs from the perspective of the gospel.
1999 / 0-85364-830-1 / xviii + 450pp

Andrew Goddard
Living the Word, Resisting the World
The Life and Thought of Jacques Ellul
This work offers a definitive study of both the life and thought of the French Reformed thinker Jacques Ellul (1912-1994). It will prove an indispensable resource for those interested in this influential theologian and sociologist and for Christian ethics and political thought generally.
2002 / 1-84227-053-2 / xxiv + 378pp

David Hilborn
The Words of our Lips
Language-Use in Free Church Worship
Studies of liturgical language have tended to focus on the written canons of Roman Catholic and Anglican communities. By contrast, David Hilborn analyses the more extemporary approach of English Nonconformity. Drawing on recent developments in linguistic pragmatics, he explores similarities and differences between 'fixed' and 'free' worship, and argues for the interdependence of each.
2006 */ 0-85364-977-4 / approx. 350pp*

Roger Hitching
The Church and Deaf People
A Study of Identity, Communication and Relationships with Special Reference to the Ecclesiology of Jürgen Moltmann
In *The Church and Deaf People* Roger Hitching sensitively examines the history and present experience of deaf people and finds similarities between aspects of sign language and Moltmann's theological method that 'open up' new ways of understanding theological concepts.
2003 / 1-84227-222-5 / xxii + 236pp

John G. Kelly
One God, One People
The Differentiated Unity of the People of God in the Theology of
Jürgen Moltmann
The author expounds and critiques Moltmann's doctrine of God and highlights
the systematic connections between it and Moltmann's influential discussion of
Israel. He then proposes a fresh approach to Jewish–Christian relations building
on Moltmann's work using insights from Habermas and Rawls.
2005 / 0-85346-969-3 / approx. 350pp

Mark F.W. Lovatt
Confronting the Will-to-Power
A Reconsideration of the Theology of Reinhold Niebuhr
Confronting the Will-to-Power is an analysis of the theology of Reinhold
Niebuhr, arguing that his work is an attempt to identify, and provide a practical
theological answer to, the existence and nature of human evil.
2001 / 1-84227-054-0 / xviii + 216pp

Neil B. MacDonald
Karl Barth and the Strange New World within the Bible
Barth, Wittgenstein, and the Metadilemmas of the Enlightenment
Barth's discovery of the strange new world within the Bible is examined in the
context of Kant, Hume, Overbeck, and, most importantly, Wittgenstein.
MacDonald covers some fundamental issues in theology today: epistemology,
the final form of the text and biblical truth-claims.
2000 / 0-85364-970-7 / xxvi + 374pp

Keith A. Mascord
Alvin Plantinga and Christian Apologetics
This book draws together the contributions of the philosopher Alvin Plantinga to
the major contemporary challenges to Christian belief, highlighting in particular
his ground-breaking work in epistemology and the problem of evil. Plantinga's
theory that both theistic and Christian belief is warrantedly basic is explored and
critiqued, and an assessment offered as to the significance of his work for
apologetic theory and practice.
2005 / 1-84227-256-X / approx. 304pp

Gillian McCulloch
The Deconstruction of Dualism in Theology
With Reference to Ecofeminist Theology and New Age Spirituality
This book challenges eco-theological anti-dualism in Christian theology, arguing that dualism has a twofold function in Christian religious discourse. Firstly, it enables us to express the discontinuities and divisions that are part of the process of reality. Secondly, dualistic language allows us to express the mysteries of divine transcendence/immanence and the survival of the soul without collapsing into monism and materialism, both of which are problematic for Christian epistemology.
2002 / 1-84227-044-3 / xii + 282pp

Leslie McCurdy
Attributes and Atonement
The Holy Love of God in the Theology of P.T. Forsyth
Attributes and Atonement is an intriguing full-length study of P.T. Forsyth's doctrine of the cross as it relates particularly to God's holy love. It includes an unparalleled bibliography of both primary and secondary material relating to Forsyth.
1999 / 0-85364-833-6 / xiv + 328pp

Nozomu Miyahira
Towards a Theology of the Concord of God
A Japanese Perspective on the Trinity
This book introduces a new Japanese theology and a unique Trinitarian formula based on the Japanese intellectual climate: three betweennesses and one concord. It also presents a new interpretation of the Trinity, a co-subordinationism, which is in line with orthodox Trinitarianism; each single person of the Trinity is eternally and equally subordinate (or serviceable) to the other persons, so that they retain the mutual dynamic equality.
2000 / 0-85364-863-8 / xiv + 256pp

Eddy José Muskus
The Origins and Early Development of Liberation Theology in Latin America
With Particular Reference to Gustavo Gutiérrez
This work challenges the fundamental premise of Liberation Theology, 'opting for the poor', and its claim that Christ is found in them. It also argues that Liberation Theology emerged as a direct result of the failure of the Roman Catholic Church in Latin America.
2002 / 0-85364-974-X / xiv + 296pp

Jim Purves
The Triune God and the Charismatic Movement
A Critical Appraisal from a Scottish Perspective
All emotion and no theology? Or a fundamental challenge to reappraise and realign our trinitarian theology in the light of Christian experience? This study of charismatic renewal as it found expression within Scotland at the end of the twentieth century evaluates the use of Patristic, Reformed and contemporary models of the Trinity in explaining the workings of the Holy Spirit.
2004 / 1-84227-321-3 / xxiv + 246pp

Anna Robbins
Methods in the Madness
Diversity in Twentieth-Century Christian Social Ethics
The author compares the ethical methods of Walter Rauschenbusch, Reinhold Niebuhr and others. She argues that unless Christians are clear about the ways that theology and philosophy are expressed practically they may lose the ability to discuss social ethics across contexts, let alone reach effective agreements.
2004 / 1-84227-211-X / xx + 294pp

Ed Rybarczyk
Beyond Salvation
Eastern Orthodoxy and Classical Pentecostalism on Becoming Like Christ
At first glance eastern Orthodoxy and classical Pentecostalism seem quite distinct. This ground-breaking study shows they share much in common, especially as it concerns the experiential elements of following Christ. Both traditions assert that authentic Christianity transcends the wooden categories of modernism.
2004 / 1-84227-144-X / xii + 356pp

Signe Sandsmark
Is World View Neutral Education Possible and Desirable?
A Christian Response to Liberal Arguments
(Published jointly with The Stapleford Centre)
This book discusses reasons for belief in world view neutrality, and argues that 'neutral' education will have a hidden, but strong world view influence. It discusses the place for Christian education in the common school.
2000 / 0-85364-973-1 / xiv + 182pp

Hazel Sherman
Reading Zechariah
The Allegorical Tradition of Biblical Interpretation through the Commentary of
Didymus the Blind and Theodore of Mopsuestia
A close reading of the commentary on Zechariah by Didymus the Blind
alongside that of Theodore of Mopsuestia suggests that popular categorising of
Antiochene and Alexandrian biblical exegesis as 'historical' or 'allegorical' is
inadequate and misleading.
2005 / 1-84227-213-6 / approx. 280pp

Andrew Sloane
On Being a Christian in the Academy
Nicholas Wolterstorff and the Practice of Christian Scholarship
An exposition and critical appraisal of Nicholas Wolterstorff's epistemology in
the light of the philosophy of science, and an application of his thought to the
practice of Christian scholarship.
2003 / 1-84227-058-3 / xvi + 274pp

Damon W.K. So
Jesus' Revelation of His Father
A Narrative-Conceptual Study of the Trinity with Special Reference to
Karl Barth
This book explores the trinitarian dynamics in the context of Jesus' revelation of
his Father in his earthly ministry with references to key passages in Matthew's
Gospel. It develops from the exegeses of these passages a non-linear concept of
revelation which links Jesus' communion with his Father to his revelatory words
and actions through a nuanced understanding of the Holy Spirit, with references
to K. Barth, G.W.H. Lampe, J.D.G. Dunn and E. Irving.
2005 / 1-84227-323-X / approx. 380pp

Daniel Strange
The Possibility of Salvation Among the Unevangelised
An Analysis of Inclusivism in Recent Evangelical Theology
For evangelical theologians the 'fate of the unevangelised' impinges upon
fundamental tenets of evangelical identity. The position known as 'inclusivism',
defined by the belief that the unevangelised can be ontologically saved by Christ
whilst being epistemologically unaware of him, has been defended most
vigorously by the Canadian evangelical Clark H. Pinnock. Through a detailed
analysis and critique of Pinnock's work, this book examines a cluster of issues
surrounding the unevangelised and its implications for christology, soteriology
and the doctrine of revelation.
2002 / 1-84227-047-8 / xviii + 362pp

Scott Swain
God According to the Gospel
Biblical Narrative and the Identity of God in the Theology of Robert W. Jenson
Robert W. Jenson is one of the leading voices in contemporary Trinitarian theology. His boldest contribution in this area concerns his use of biblical narrative both to ground and explicate the Christian doctrine of God. *God According to the Gospel* critically examines Jenson's proposal and suggests an alternative way of reading the biblical portrayal of the triune God.
2006 / 1-84227-258-6 / approx. 180pp

Justyn Terry
The Justifying Judgement of God
A Reassessment of the Place of Judgement in the Saving Work of Christ
The argument of this book is that judgement, understood as the whole process of bringing justice, is the primary metaphor of atonement, with others, such as victory, redemption and sacrifice, subordinate to it. Judgement also provides the proper context for understanding penal substitution and the call to repentance, baptism, eucharist and holiness.
2005 / 1-84227-370-1 / approx. 274 pp

Graham Tomlin
The Power of the Cross
Theology and the Death of Christ in Paul, Luther and Pascal
This book explores the theology of the cross in St Paul, Luther and Pascal. It offers new perspectives on the theology of each, and some implications for the nature of power, apologetics, theology and church life in a postmodern context.
1999 / 0-85364-984-7 / xiv + 344pp

Adonis Vidu
Postliberal Theological Method
A Critical Study
The postliberal theology of Hans Frei, George Lindbeck, Ronald Thiemann, John Milbank and others is one of the more influential contemporary options. This book focuses on several aspects pertaining to its theological method, specifically its understanding of background, hermeneutics, epistemic justification, ontology, the nature of doctrine and, finally, Christological method.
2005 / 1-84227-395-7 / approx. 324pp

Graham J. Watts
Revelation and the Spirit
*A Comparative Study of the Relationship between the Doctrine of Revelation
and Pneumatology in the Theology of Eberhard Jüngel and of
Wolfhart Pannenberg*
The relationship between revelation and pneumatology is relatively unexplored.
This approach offers a fresh angle on two important twentieth century
theologians and raises pneumatological questions which are theologically crucial
and relevant to mission in a postmodern culture.
2005 / 1-84227-104-0 / xxii + 232pp

Nigel G. Wright
Disavowing Constantine
*Mission, Church and the Social Order in the Theologies of John Howard Yoder
and Jürgen Moltmann*
This book is a timely restatement of a radical theology of church and state in the
Anabaptist and Baptist tradition. Dr Wright constructs his argument in dialogue
and debate with Yoder and Moltmann, major contributors to a free church
perspective.
2000 / 0-85364-978-2 / xvi + 252pp

Paternoster
9 Holdom Avenue,
Bletchley,
Milton Keynes MK1 1QR,
United Kingdom
Web: www.authenticmedia.co.uk/paternoster

July 2005